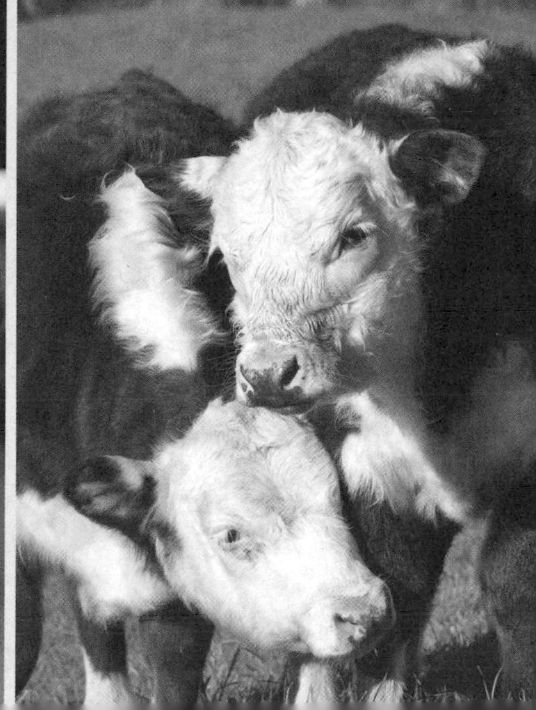

DISCOVER

Maine, Vermont & New Hampshire

Imagine yourself in New England: walking a dirt road lined with brilliant maple leaves, watching a rocky shoreline from a slender lighthouse, or beside a white-steepled church on a village green.

All lined up along the international border, Maine, Vermont, and New Hampshire claim a lion's share of the region's most iconic scenes. And while there are vibrant cities to explore here—especially the thrumming coastal hub of Portland—the spirit of the three states lies in their small towns, mountains, and the seemingly endless coastline.

Drive the shore of New Hampshire and Maine to see lobster traps piled high, as locals line up at summertime seafood shacks. Vermont's back roads lead to maple sugar shacks and dairy farms, and rivers in all three states invite swimming on warm afternoons.

Winter storms blanket the high mountains in deep drifts of snow, so travelers willing to brave the cold are rewarded with great skiing and riding, or can bundle up for a trip through the hills by horse-drawn sleigh.

And while all of New England lights up in the fall, the varied terrain in the northern states means even more dramatic contrasts and gorgeous foliage. Whether you're looking for outdoor adventures, farm-to-table dining, or the perfect autumn drive, Maine, Vermont, and New Hampshire offer a lifetime of escapes.

Clockwise from top left: autumn at Strawbery Banke; lupine blossoms; spirits from Mad River Distillers; Killington Peak; tugboats in Portsmouth; Ogunquit's Marginal Way.

6 TOP EXPERIENCES

1 **Acadia National Park:** Catch America's first sunrise from Cadillac Mountain, then find a million tide pools in this historic national park (page 204).

2 **Fall Foliage:** The changing colors spread from north to south; chase them from Vermont's extravagant maple forests to the fiery hues of New Hampshire's White Mountains (page 16).

3 **Hiking New Hampshire's White Mountains:** Hike through a rocky landscape of summits, valleys, and plants found nowhere else (page 119).

4 Maine Lobster Feasts: Whether you're dining on reinvented lobster rolls or sitting down to a traditional feast, these crustaceans are quintessential New England (page 180).

<<<

5 Skiing and Snowboarding in Vermont's Green Mountains: Choose your mountain—Vermont's peaks offer some of the finest skiing and riding in the region (page 46).

>>>

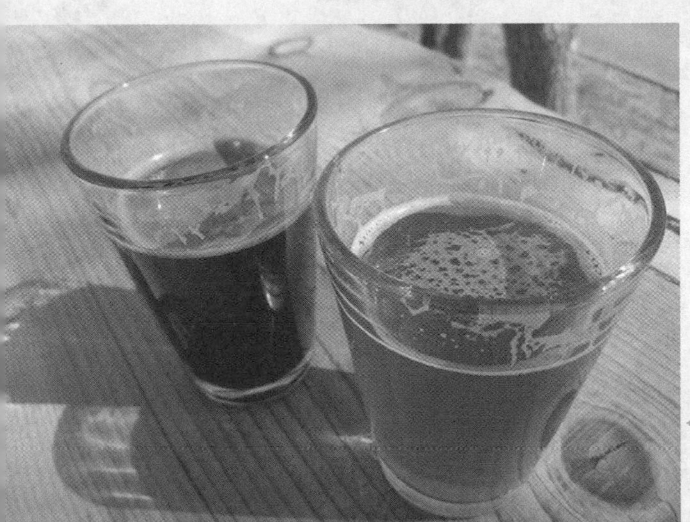

6 Burlington's Breweries: Vermont has more breweries per capita than any other state, and many of its award-winning craft beers (and ciders!) are only available locally (page 70).

<<<

Planning Your Trip

Where to Go

Vermont

Rolling hills rise into the peaks of the **Green Mountains,** a forested landscape that enfolds **apple orchards,** sugar maples, and dairy farms. Life in Vermont is defined by the seasons: Sugarmakers boil sap into **maple syrup** in the early spring, **fall foliage** ignites the trees, and winter brings skiers for New England's finest **skiing and riding.** Not that it's all maple syrup and cheddar—the offbeat state has a culture all its own, from its insistently liberal values to circus schools, cutting-edge craft beer, and endless opportunities for **outdoor adventures.**

New Hampshire Seacoast and Lakes Region

Despite a fierce culture of independence, the Granite State's not entirely insulated from the outside world—New Hampshire extends a slender arm of land to the ocean that shouldn't be overlooked. Easily **walkable** and fun to explore, Portsmouth is among the finest destinations in New England for an immersion in **colonial and maritime history,** while **Hampton Beach** is a whirlwind of tanning oil, fried dough, and cruising crowds. Just inland, the forested landscape is webbed with a vast network of lakes, from the hyped-up vacation towns on **Lake Winnepesaukee** to quiet **Squam Lakes,** where silent mornings are broken only by the sound of calling loons.

The White Mountains

Bare rocky peaks emerge from the forest in the rugged heart of the state, where the **Presidential Range** sets the stage for **Mount Washington,**

fall foliage and the Stowe Community Church in Stowe, Vermont

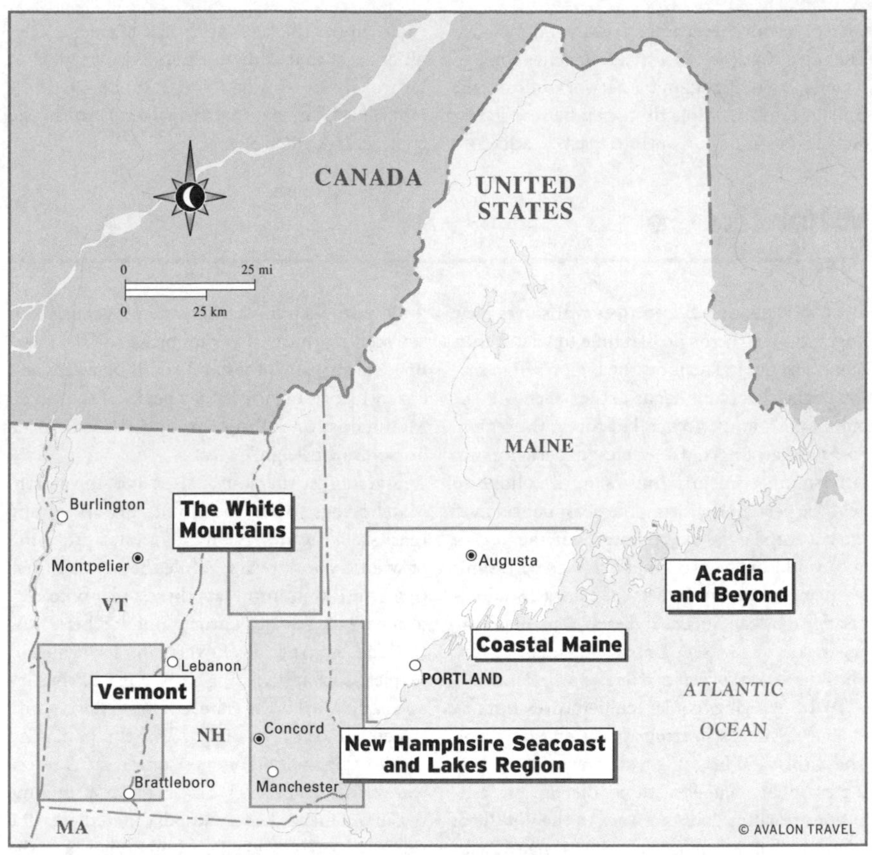

the tallest mountain in New England. The fierce alpine zone is home to tiny **flowers** found nowhere else on earth, but it's surprisingly easy to reach: by car, wood-powered railway, or on foot, following one of the steep tracks that wind through the Whites. It's not all sweaty adventures, though, since historic hotels, swimming holes, and one of the region's most **scenic drives** offer a relaxing alternative to a weekend of peak-bagging.

Coastal Maine

From the seaside chic of **downtown Portland** to a fractured map of bays, peninsulas, and harbors, coastal Maine invites long days of exploring. Catch sunrise at a whitewashed lighthouse, or survey the very best **lobster rolls** from Kittery to Camden. Hop a schooner for a downwind run, then find your own perfect beach for an afternoon in the sand (or rocks). This is one of New England's most popular tourist destinations, but the scale of the coast gives everyone some breathing room: Once you get beyond the vacation towns that line Route 1, an untouched version of Maine beckons down long, narrow roads that all seem to lead to the sea.

Acadia and Beyond

Sprawling from **Mount Desert Island** to the facing mainland, Acadia National Park is unlike any other. Bare **pink granite peaks** dip into alpine lakes, all with views across the Atlantic coast. The top of **Cadillac Mountain** catches some of America's first light, and a network of carriage trails means the whole thing can be reached by bicycle, or on foot. Continue past Acadia and you're in the thick of Downeast Maine: a long, quiet coast that ends in the fishing outpost of Lubec, whose candy-striped **West Quoddy Head Light** is the **easternmost point** in the continental United States.

When to Go

Dramatic seasonal changes transform New England—but there's no bad time to visit. When schools let out in late June, the region's high season begins. Everyone heads to the beach—or the mountains—and prices spike around the region. Some of New England's sweetest experiences are pure summertime: finding swimming holes to beat the heat, and visiting the seasonal seafood shacks at the edge of the water. For the best of both worlds, plan a trip that overlaps with summer temperatures but bucks the crowds. Students disappear by late August and early September, the ocean is as warm as it's gonna get, and prices dip until the arrival of leaf peepers.

Autumn brings cooler temperatures and one of New England's starring attractions: fall color. The displays of bright leaves start to pick up at the end of September, with northernmost destinations reaching "peak foliage" in the middle of October. This season is a favorite for many, with warm, sunny days that alternate with crisp nights, and fall brings a host of fleeting pleasures: picking apples at local orchards, evenings cool enough for a crackling campfire, and outings fueled by cinnamon-scented cider donuts.

Winter weather begins in earnest at the end of December. The region can enter a deep freeze for weeks at a time—there's usually one or two weeks in northern New England when the mercury shivers in the single digits (or below). But for lovers of skiing, skating, and gorgeously frozen scenery, those winter months are a bonanza. Bring plenty of clothes and you'll be warm and cozy while riding the snowy peaks of the Green Mountains, or rolling through the hills on a horse-drawn sleigh.

Starting in the south, then moving north, March brings **spring** in fits and starts. Blooming lilacs scent the air, and in the forest, a profusion of wildflowers appears. While the weather stays fitful until well into May, there's plenty to recommend the season. Throughout northern New England, but especially in Vermont, spring means maple syrup, and visiting between late February and early April is the chance to taste the region's sweetest harvest straight from the pan. And maple syrup's not the only seasonal treat: A recent wave of interest in foraged foods mean springtime restaurant menus feature woodsy ingredients like ramps, a kind of wild onion, and fiddleheads, the bright green tendrils of ostrich ferns.

The easiest place to fly into for launching a trip in New England is **Boston,** though **Portland, Maine,** is another major hub for the area. International visitors will need valid **passports** or **visas** to fly into the United States. If you are renting a car in any city, plan to pick it up after spending time there, as **paid parking** and **crowded streets** makes it easier to explore by public transport.

The Best of Maine, Vermont & New Hampshire

Blending history, culture, and New England's most gorgeous scenery, this two-week trip is a whirlwind introduction to the best of the region, from the lighthouses of Penobscot Bay to Green Mountain valleys. Starting in the maritime city of Portland means an instant immersion in Maine culture before diving into the charms of the Mid-Coast, then rising into the Appalachian Mountain Range. You'll need a car to squeeze the hits into eight days.

Day 1

Plan to arrive in **Portland** in time for a sunset sail across **Casco Bay,** hopping one of the city's historic schooners, then wrap up the evening with a steaming bowl of clam chowder on the waterfront. If you're itching to hit the town, visit a few of Portland's great craft breweries, or dress up for drinks at the **Portland Hunt & Alpine Club.**

Day 2

Take a morning walk through the **Old Port,** and if you're up for more time on the water, take the mail boat route to the **Casco Bay Islands** for a glimpse of offshore life within sight of the city skyline. A seafood lunch at Eventide Oyster Co. is a must, followed by an afternoon of browsing the wonderful Portland Museum of Art.

Day 3

Wake up early for a sweet breakfast from the **Holy Donut,** then plot a course along the shore—make your first destination the **Maine Maritime Museum,** in the shipbuilding city of Bath. When you've got your fill of salty history, duck down onto **Georgetown Island** for a classic lobster roll at **Five Islands Lobster Co.** From there, continue to the picturesque harbor town of Camden, stopping to stretch your legs on the short walk to **Owl's Head Light.**

the schooner *Lewis R. French* by Owl's Head

Fabulous Foliage

As the first cold days arrive in the beginning of **autumn,** the weather frosts the tips of trees with a wash of pale yellow and orange. It's an early sign of the changing season. Weeks later, the forests will be alight in brilliant hues, a display that can be shocking in its vividness.

Experiencing the changing colors is truly a highlight of exploring New England, but what's really happening in the trees? Leaves get their verdant hue from a healthy dose of chlorophyll, a key ingredient in plants' transformation of sunlight into sugars. As the season changes, chlorophyll dwindles, draining off the green color as it goes.

The yellow and gold that begins to appear are from **carotenoids,** plant pigments that have been in the leaves all along, but masked by the lush greens of midsummer. But what about the brilliant reds? Those are due to anthocyanins, the same brilliant pigments that lend cranberries, red apples, and cherries their **vibrant hues.** Anthocyanins are mostly produced in the autumn, and depending on conditions, trees might have just a little—or enough for a gaudy leaf show.

It's hard to plan for the perfect fall trip, as varied weather conditions mean the leaves change at different times each year. Colors begin to change in mid-September, continuing through mid-October. The first color appears at northern latitudes and high altitudes, working south and toward sea level as the season progresses.

- **Kancamagus Highway, New Hampshire:** The twists and turns of this 34-mile road through the White Mountains passes through gorgeous forests that are brilliant in autumn.

fall colors in New Hampshire

- **Mad River Valley, Vermont:** A broad valley flanked with peaks on each side, this gorgeous spot offers wide-open views and easy access to higher-elevation terrain.
- **Acadia National Park, Maine:** Offset by the island's many evergreen trees, fall colors are especially dramatic here, with kettle ponds and harbors to reflect the leaves.

Days 4-5

Make a beeline for **Mount Desert Island,** where Acadia National Park encompasses some of the finest coastal scenery in Maine. On day one, choose a hike: Walk across the gentle sandbar to Bar Island, hop across the boulders on the **Ship Harbor Trail,** or try the vertiginous route up the Beehive, a mound of bare rock with views across the Penobscot Bay.

Ambitious travelers can rise early to catch sunrise from the summit of Mount Desert Island, which catches mainland America's first rays for much of the year. Bring a bike or rent some wheels for a day on the carriage trails, then pause for a Mount Desert Island tradition: fresh **popovers** with sweet strawberry jam. If you're hankering for a lobster dinner, there's no better place than **Thurston's Lobster Pound,**

hiking the White Mountains

downtown Woodstock

where you choose your bug from a tank of crawling critters, then eat with the waves beneath your feet.

Day 6

Get a taste of backwoods Maine as you drive across the state to New Hampshire's **White Mountains,** heading from the seaside all the way to the top of **Mount Washington**—by car, cog railway, or on foot. Whatever option you choose, make your way to the historic Omni Mount Washington Resort for sunset drinks on the broad balcony, with views back toward the mountains.

Day 7

Dust off your hiking boots for another day in the White Mountains: There are all-day epics like the Presidential Traverse, or you can meander the gentle trail to **Diana's Baths,** a series of pools that are perfect for cooling off. For a more easygoing tour through the mountains, book a ticket on the **Conway Scenic Railway,** whose **Notch Trail** catches some of the region's most dramatic scenery.

Day 8

Duck into the southern **Green Mountains,** where you'll trade rocky summits for lush valleys. Adorable **Woodstock** is the perfect village home for a night, with bright **covered bridges,** art galleries for browsing, and even an old-fashioned town crier message board. After getting your bearings, head to the nearby **Calvin Coolidge State Historic Site** to visit the presidential family home and cheese factory, then pause for beers at **Long Trail Brewing Company,** a local craft beer pioneer.

WITH MORE TIME

If you have time before heading home, stay in Vermont and explore more of the countryside. Go **apple picking** at the **Scott Farm Orchard** or head to the hills outside **Montpelier** for a tour of a **maple sugarhouse.**

Wild Places: Shores and Summits

Make a swooping descent through the finest of the region's scenery, stopping to spy on moose, wander endless beaches, and trace perfect back roads on two wheels. There's a lifetime of exploring to do in these wild places, but this trip includes the undisputed highlights.

Days 1-2

Start where the **Appalachian Trail** ends—in the mountain landscape of **Baxter State Park. Mount Katahdin** isn't New England's highest mountain, but it's certainly the toughest, especially if you take on the iconic **Knife Edge,** a vertiginous trail that teeters along a narrow ridge of boulders.

Days 3-4

Rest your mountain legs on the drive to **Mount Desert Island,** where the hiking is a tad less punishing. You could push for a sunrise trek to the peak of **Cadillac Mountain,** or just take it easy on the shore, poking around the tide pools and beaches in **Acadia National Park.**

Choose your sport for day two: There's stunning rock climbing that rises straight from the waves at **Otter Cliffs,** and on-island guiding companies can get you fully kitted out. Otherwise, take to the seas for a kayak trip along the edge of Mount Desert Island, watching for whales and seals along the way.

Days 5-6

It's back to wild peaks and footpaths when you head to the **White Mountains,** where the **Presidential Range** rises above all comers. The fittest travelers could take on the whole series of mountains—an enormous hike often

hiking Mount Katahdin's Knife Edge

Winter Wonderland

EXPLORING FROZEN NEW ENGLAND ON SKIS, SLEIGHS, AND SKATES

Bundle up for some time in the snow, and you'll be amply rewarded—New England sparkles through the winter, and hours out of doors just make it sweeter to pass a long winter night by the fire.

- **O'er the hills you go:** Head to Vermont's **Shelburne Farms** for an old-fashioned sleigh ride, complete with Percheron draft horses and jingling bells (page 76).
- **Get some turns in the Green Mountains:** Vermont's rolling terrain offers some of the best skiing and riding around, from the mammoth slopes of **Killington Resort** (page 43) to the old school charms of the skier-only **Mad River Valley** (page 49). And if you prefer to earn your turns, there's endless cross country in the state, starting with the **Stowe Mountain Resort** (page 60), still owned by the Austrian singers of *Sound of Music* fame.
- **Ski New Hampshire:** The White Mountains of New Hampshire are excellent for skiing. **Bretton Woods Mountain Resort** (page 120) offers stunning views from 97 trails, ranging from beginner to expert. **Cannon Mountain** (page 128) boasts the longest vertical drop in the state.
- **Have the run of Acadia:** There's not always enough snow on Mount Desert Island for cross-country skiing, but when the temperatures drop, you'll have miles of carriage roads—and can lay tracks all the way to the top of **Cadillac Mountain** (page 207).

skiing the Green Mountains

called the **"Death March"**—but there are trails for all abilities, and plenty of rivers for post-walk soaks. Watch for moose as you hop from rock to rock, or join one of the **moose-spotting tours** that stalk the enormous animals in their favorite hangouts.

Days 7-8

From there, take a few hours to drive to Vermont's **Green Mountains.** In the winter, visitors can **ski** and **snowboard** in the hills of the **Mad River Valley** at **Sugarbush** and **Mad River Glen.**

Vermont

Vermont's back roads and byways lead to picturesque villages, winding rivers, and orchards hung with heirloom fruit.

Among the most rural of the United States, Vermont can seem unchanged by passing time. More than half of Vermont's roads remain unpaved, simple dirt tracks that lead to dairy farms, villages, and leafy forests. The small state is divided by the spine of the Green Mountains, whose rocky peaks barely break above the tree line. And more than elsewhere in New England, it's a place defined by the seasons, from brilliant fall colors to snowy winters and springtime maple syrup.

But Vermont's true charm lies in a blend of traditional ways and innovation. In the Northeast Kingdom, generations-old dairy families partner with young cheese makers. Maple syrup producers collect sap on horse-drawn sleds, gathering it into state-of-the-art sugarhouses powered by the sun. Fiercely independent since the American Revolution, Vermonters have a politics all their own, with yearly town hall meetings and a legislature that was America's first to legalize gay marriage.

For a very Vermont blend of old and new, follow country roads to art-filled towns, craft breweries, and farm-to-table restaurants. Drive into the Green Mountains to summit rocky peaks and find the perfect line down a ski slope, or spend a weekend lingering in one of Vermont's many swimming holes. To experience the state's cultural capital, head to the lakeshore city of Burlington, where a colorful blend of students, old hippies, Yankees, and recent immigrants add a jolt of progressive energy to Vermont's country charm.

PLANNING YOUR TIME

You could breeze through Vermont in a couple of days, but travelers who slow down to the pace of this area will discover much to explore. Choose a home base in the south or the north—those regions are small enough to see on day trips from a single location. The southern mountains are gentler and a bit more touristy, while the north holds Vermont's highest peaks and most vibrant city, the cultural capital of Burlington.

Previous: skiing at Mad River Glen; grazing sheep. **Above:** sugar house and pails in Stowe.

Look for ★ to find recommended sights, activities, dining, and lodging.

Highlights

★ **Apple Picking at Scott Farm Orchard:** Fill up on heirloom fruit and literary history at this stunning property, where Rudyard Kipling's Vermont home presides over rolling lanes of apple trees (page 24).

★ **President Calvin Coolidge State Historic Site:** See the childhood home of the former president, who was sworn in by his father in the family parlor (page 38).

★ **Skiing the Mad River Valley:** Find some of Vermont's best lines in this northern valley, where Sugarbush and Mad River Glen offer two entirely different takes on Green Mountain riding (page 49).

★ **Morse Farm Maple Sugarworks:** See how the sweet stuff is made on a tour of a sugarhouse in the hills outside of Montpelier (page 56).

★ **Burlington Bike Path:** This lakeside bike path winds past art installations and perfect picnic spots, then extends into the middle of Lake Champlain on a three-mile-long raised causeway (page 72).

★ **Shelburne Farms:** Catch a springtime batch of baby lambs, eat ultra-local fare at a historic inn, then explore the sprawling farms on a network of walking trails (page 76).

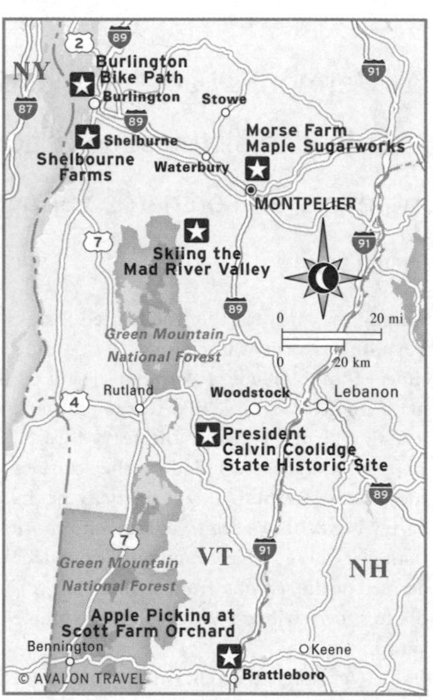

Vermont

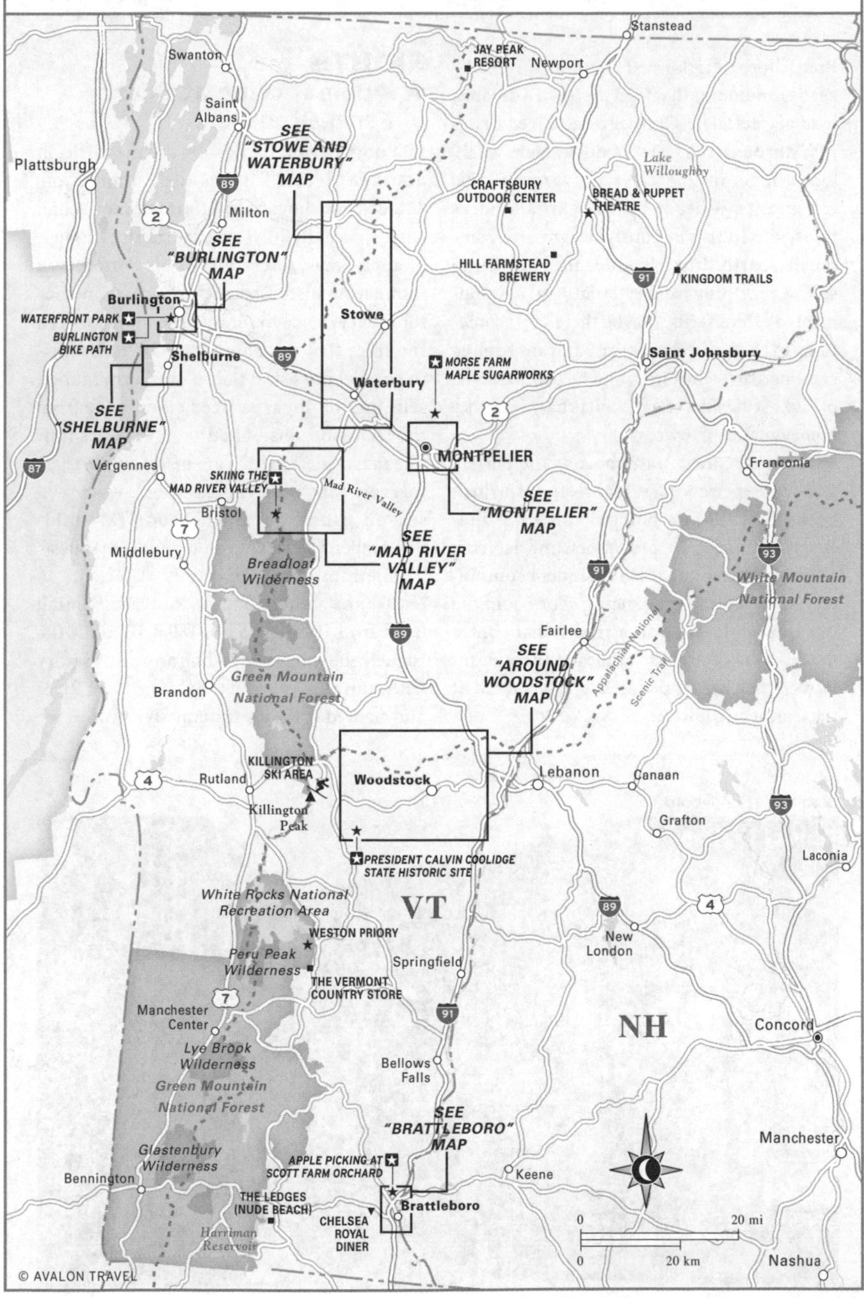
Stanstead
Swanton
JAY PEAK RESORT
Newport
Saint Albans
SEE "STOWE AND WATERBURY" MAP
Plattsburgh
Lake Willoughby
89
CRAFTSBURY OUTDOOR CENTER
BREAD & PUPPET THEATRE
2
Milton
SEE "BURLINGTON" MAP
HILL FARMSTEAD BREWERY
91
KINGDOM TRAILS
Burlington
WATERFRONT PARK
Stowe
BURLINGTON BIKE PATH
Shelburne
89
MORSE FARM MAPLE SUGARWORKS
Saint Johnsbury
Waterbury
2
SEE "SHELBURNE" MAP
MONTPELIER
87
Vergennes
Franconia
SKIING THE MAD RIVER VALLEY
Mad River Valley
Bristol
SEE "MONTPELIER" MAP
7
SEE "MAD RIVER VALLEY" MAP
Middlebury
93
Breadloaf Wilderness
91
White Mountain National Forest
89
Fairlee
Appalachian National Scenic Trail
SEE "AROUND WOODSTOCK" MAP
Green Mountain National Forest
Brandon
KILLINGTON SKI AREA
Lebanon
Canaan
4
Rutland
Woodstock
Killington Peak
93
Grafton
PRESIDENT CALVIN COOLIDGE STATE HISTORIC SITE
Laconia
White Rocks National Recreation Area
VT
89
4
WESTON PRIORY
New London
Peru Peak Wilderness
Springfield
THE VERMONT COUNTRY STORE
7
91
Manchester Center
NH
Concord
Lye Brook Wilderness
Bellows Falls
Green Mountain National Forest
SEE "BRATTLEBORO" MAP
Manchester
Glastenbury Wilderness
APPLE PICKING AT SCOTT FARM ORCHARD
Bennington
Keene
THE LEDGES (NUDE BEACH)
Brattleboro
CHELSEA ROYAL DINER
0
20 mi
Harriman Reservoir
0
20 km
Nashua

Brattleboro

Brattleboro's brick-lined center is framed by gentle mountains that lend the town a dreamy, insular feel. The Connecticut River drifts right through the heart of downtown, where locals linger in cozy cafés and farm-to-table restaurants. A heady blend of art and ideas infuse life in this famously progressive community, partly driven by students that come to study everything from international development to circus skills. Maybe there's just something in the air, because even Rudyard Kipling came here to be inspired, and he penned some of his best-loved work at Naulakha, his quirky home outside of town.

For the visitor, Brattleboro is the perfect place to experience Vermont's free-spirited, intellectual side by rubbing elbows with unreconstructed hippies, professors, and aspiring clowns at one of the town's frequent community events. Strap on dancing shoes, join the lineup and do-si-do in a traditional contra dance, browse organic apples at the vibrant farmers market, or paddle a pretty stretch of the Connecticut River.

SIGHTS

★ Apple Picking at Scott Farm Orchard

Just north of Brattleboro is the magnificent **Scott Farm** (707 Kipling Rd., Dummerston, 802/254-6868, www.scottfarmvermont.com, 8am-5pm daily July-Nov.), a rolling expanse of apple trees, forest, and fields dotted with fascinating historic structures. It's a memorable experience to pick your own fruit from the trees that march up and down the hills in parallel lines, and the on-site Farm Market sells jugs of unpasteurized cider made from the farm's dozens of heirloom varieties (unlike most ciders, which are made from easier-to-grow Macintosh apples). Pick-your-own season usually extends Labor Day-mid-September, but call ahead for apple updates.

The rambling property is also home to **Naulakha,** where author Rudyard Kipling lived from 1893 through 1896. He built the vaguely ship-shaped building on a promontory with stunning views of the Connecticut River and named it for an Indian adventure story

downtown Brattleboro

Brattleboro

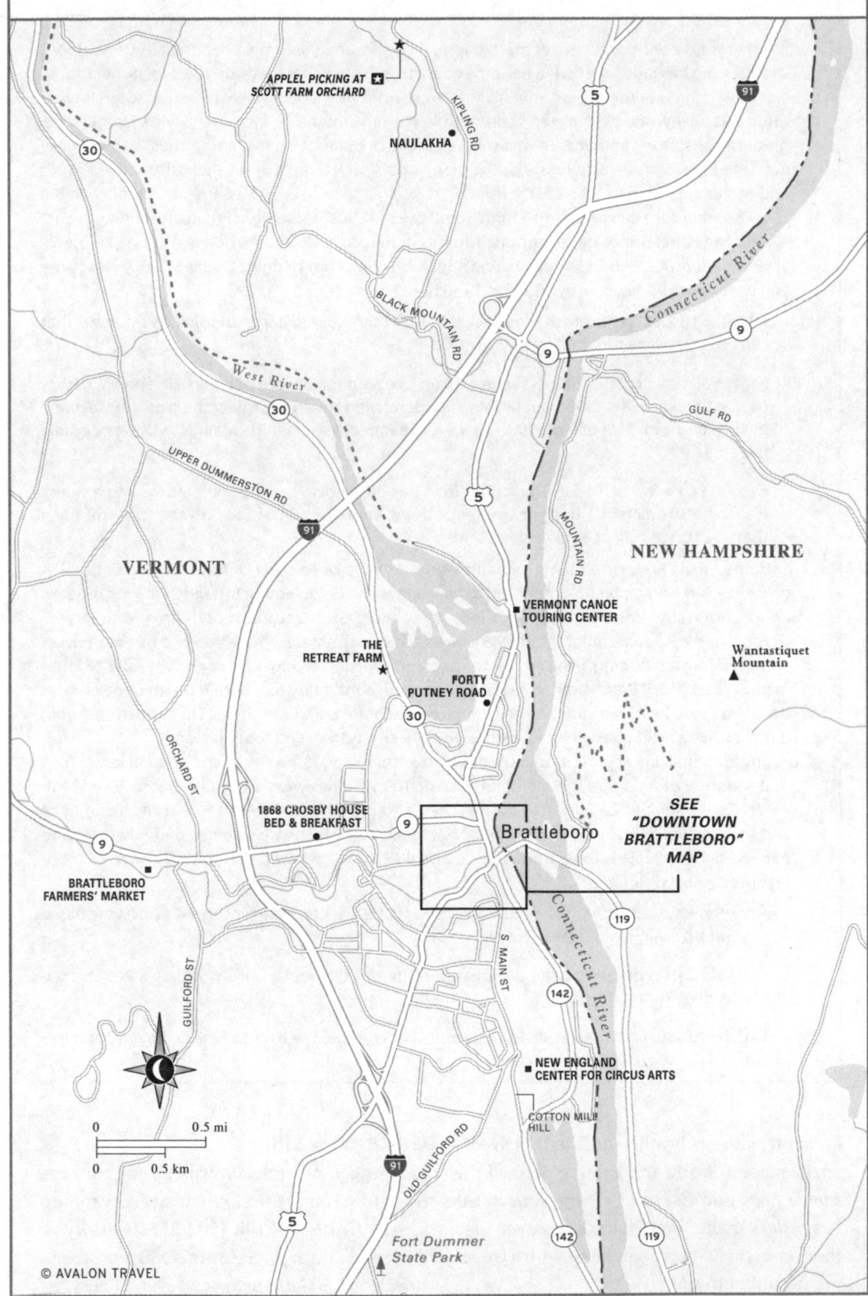
APPLEL PICKING AT
SCOTT FARM ORCHARD
KIPLING RD
NAULAKHA
5
91
30
BLACK MOUNTAIN RD
Connecticut River
9
West River
GULF RD
UPPER DUMMERSTON RD
MOUNTAIN RD
NEW HAMPSHIRE
VERMONT
VERMONT CANOE
TOURING CENTER
THE
RETREAT FARM
Wantastiquet
Mountain
FORTY
PUTNEY ROAD
ORCHARD ST
1868 CROSBY HOUSE
BED & BREAKFAST
Brattleboro
SEE
"DOWNTOWN
BRATTLEBORO"
MAP
BRATTLEBORO
FARMERS' MARKET
119
S MAIN ST
GUILFORD ST
142
NEW ENGLAND
CENTER FOR CIRCUS ARTS
COTTON MILL
HILL
0
0.5 mi
0
0.5 km
OLD GUILFORD RD
Fort Dummer
State Park
© AVALON TRAVEL

On Heritage and Heirlooms

Hang around a Vermont farmers market long enough, and you'll start hearing about heirloom varieties and heritage breeds. Is a heritage cow a tough old heifer that's survived for generations? Not quite. Heritage breeds are animals that were bred over time to be well suited to their environments. Many, however, weren't compatible with the intensive, industrial style of large-scale modern agriculture, and until recently were on the brink of being lost altogether. Farmers raise heritage breeds for diverse reasons, but many chefs seek them out for their distinctive flavors and menu appeal. **Burlington's Farmhouse Tap & Grill** (160 Bank St., 802/859-0888, www.farmhousetg.com, 11:30am-11pm Mon.-Thurs., 11:30am-midnight Fri., 10am-midnight Sat., 10am-11pm Sun.) brings heritage pork into its kitchen, as does **Hen of the Wood** (55 Cherry St., Burlington, 802/540-0534, www.henofthewood.com, 4pm-midnight daily, $22-30). Next time you pass a pasture, keep an eye out for these heritage critters:

- **Highland Cattle:** Scottish breed of cows with long, curved horns and shaggy red coats that can grow to over a foot during the winter.
- **Mangalitsa Pig:** Hungarian swine with an extraordinary fleece of curly hair. The breed was near extinction in the 1990s, but farming cooperatives formed to protect the pigs, whose name means "hog with a lot of lard" in Hungarian. (That might explain the Mangalitsa's wonderfully juicy meat.)
- **Cochin Chicken:** This eye-catching fowl has outlandish bundles of feathers and a sweet disposition. Their fabulous plumage keeps them warm throughout the winter, so Vermonters that keep them collect eggs all year long.

Heirloom also refers to plants: old cultivars that have been passed down by generations of growers. Like heritage breeds, they tend to be fruits and vegetables that just didn't fit with modern agriculture's requirement that produce look shiny and fresh after three months in cold storage.

You'll find heirloom tomatoes at every farm stand in the state, where you can fill your basket with heirloom everything, from apples to zucchini. Root aficionados can attend the **Gilfeather Turnip Festival** (Wardsboro, www.friendsofwardsborolibrary.org, late Oct.), which celebrates the town's own heirloom variety with turnip recipe contests and weigh-ins. The Gilfeather Turnip is technically a rutabaga, with white skin, white flesh, and a sweet, rooty flavor.

But for heirloom apples, it doesn't get better than **Scott Farm,** a shrine to eclectic fruit that's worthy of a pilgrimage. They grow over 100 varieties with intriguing names like Lamb Abbey Pearmain and Zabergau Reinette. They also grow other off-beat tree fruits like quince and medlar (which make a memorable appearance in Shakespeare's *Romeo and Juliet*). During harvest season, Scott Farm's produce is available in stores around Vermont. Don't miss these favorite heirloom varieties:

- **Ananas Reinette:** A small, yellow apple that dates back to 16th-century France. As the name suggests, it really does taste like a pineapple.
- **Esopus Spitzenberg:** An oblong apple with red skin and a full flavor that was a favorite of President Thomas Jefferson.
- **Hubbardston Nonsuch:** A dessert apple that's red-gold, with crisp flesh and plenty of sugar.

he wrote with his brother-in-law. It proved a fertile place to work, and Kipling penned the *Jungle Book* and *Captains Courageous* at his heavy desk in the "bow." The only way to visit the home is as an overnight guest with a three-night minimum stay.

Gallery Walk

Snow, sleet, or shine, crowds throng the center of town on the first Friday of every month for the **Gallery Walk** (802/257-2616, www.gallerywalk.org, 5:30pm-8:30pm, free), Brattleboro's signature social event. Everyone

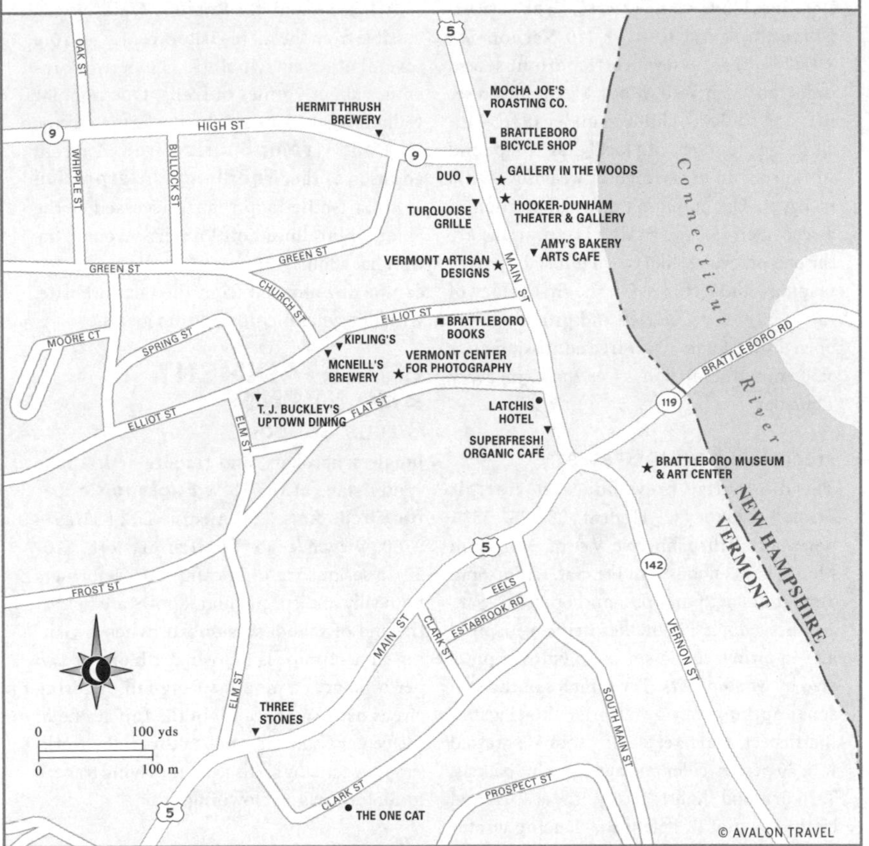

in town comes out for it, and no other experience will give you a better feel for Brattleboro's unique spirit. The streets take on a festival atmosphere as neighbors catch up on news and pore over their friends' latest creations while juggling snacks and wine. A free map and guide (available online) will help you plot a course through the 50-some venues, which are mostly concentrated on Elliot and Main Streets.

Don't miss the exquisite **Gallery in the Woods** (145 Main St., 802/257-4777, www.galleryinthewoods.com, 11am-5:30pm Mon.-Sat., noon-5pm Sun.), whose focus on the "Visionary, Surreal, Fantastic and Sacred" results in surprisingly grounded and relatable exhibits that range from folk traditions to fine art. Another gem is the **Vermont Center for Photography** (49 Flat St., 802/251-6051, www.vcphoto.org, noon-5pm Fri.-Sun.), which hosts work by some of the region's most skilled and creative photographers. There's a broad range of mediums on display at **Vermont Artisan Designs** (106 Main St., 802/257-7044, www.vtart.com, 10am-5pm Sun.-Thurs., 10am-6pm Fri.-Sat.), and it's an ideal place to browse for unique handmade gifts.

Brattleboro Museum & Art Center

Recent exhibits at the eclectic **Brattleboro Museum & Art Center** (10 Vernon St., 802/257-0124, www.brattleboromuseum.org, 11am-5pm Wed.-Mon., $8 adults, $6 seniors, $4 students, children under 18 free) included photographs of a local drag troupe and work from an experimental weaving studio in Egypt. The museum's unusual location in a renovated railway station is a draw, as are the one-off events, like yo-yo tutorials, poetry readings, and lectures. On the first Friday of the month, the galleries and gift shop stay open until 8:30pm, with free admission after 5:30pm, and admission is free 2pm-5pm every Thursday.

Hermit Thrush Brewery

The diminutive brew house at **Hermit Thrush Brewery** (29 High St., 802/257-2337, www.hermitthrushbrewery.com, 3pm-8pm Mon.-Thurs., noon-9pm Fri.-Sat., 11am-6pm Sun., tours at 2pm, 4pm, and 6pm Fri.-Sat., 2-ounce samples $2) makes Belgian-inspired ales in a tiny, rustic space downtown powered by wood pellets. Try samples of the seasonal options, but don't miss the flagship Brattlebeer, a tart, refreshing sour ale brewed with 20 percent cider and aged in wine barrels. Tart, dry, and slightly fruity, it was "inspired by the town of Brattleboro." During winter months, the brewery closes one hour earlier.

The Retreat Farm

On the outskirts of town, the **Retreat Farm** (350 Linden St., 802/490-2270, www.retreatfarm.org, 10am-4pm Wed.-Sat., noon-4pm Sun. early June-Oct., $7 adults, $5 children 2-18) has a family-friendly "petting farm" with dozens of animals that range from familiar to exotic. The 475-acre property is still a working farm owned by the Windham Foundation, a private organization dedicated to preserving Vermont's rural traditions. In the spirit of being a "gateway farm," the Retreat offers plenty of ways to interact with the resident critters, so you can scratch a pig's belly, go eye-to-eye with a one-ton ox, and snag a selfie with an impossibly adorable dwarf goat.

All year round, the **Retreat Trails** are accessible from the main visitors center or from several other entry points. The network includes about 9 miles of trails. One popular walk travels 1.15 miles from the farm to scenic **Ice Pond** via **Morningside Trail.** A recent addition is the **Woodlands Interpretive Trail,** a 1-mile loop that is accessed at the Solar Hill trailhead off Western Avenue; the trail has a folksy, 30-minute audio guide that can be downloaded from the farm website, with idiosyncratic stories from locals.

ENTERTAINMENT AND EVENTS

Circus School

Jugglers, acrobats, and trapeze artists take center stage at the **New England Center for Circus Arts** (209 Austine Dr., 802/254-9780, www.necenterforcircusarts.org, $10-20), a serious training camp for performers both silly and spectacular. Shows are held at the end of school sessions, or when a visiting circus troupe is in town, with one or two performances a month spring-fall. Aspiring circus performers can join the fun at one of the center's shorter, one- to three-day workshops, practicing skills from the flying trapeze to contortion and clowning.

Nightlife

With in-house craft brews on tap and a prime riverside location, **Whetstone Station** (36 Bridge St., 802/490-2354, www.whetstonestation.com, 11:30am-10pm Sun.-Thurs., 11:30am-11pm Fri.-Sat.) is a year-round favorite. Take advantage of sunny weather on the rooftop deck or the beer garden: The main restaurant serves a slightly dressed up menu of pub fare, while the beer garden serves a slightly dressed down menu of pub fare.

There are bars named for Rudyard Kipling in places from Michigan to Mumbai, but **Kipling's** (78 Elliot St., 802/257-4848, 11:30am-8pm Mon.-Tues., 11:30am-2am Wed.-Fri., 3pm-2am Sat.) has a distinctively

Scenic Byways

DRIVING VERMONT'S ROUTE 100

Easily one of the prettiest roads in all of New England, **Route 100** winds north-south through quiet valleys, farmland, and historic villages. It sticks to the eastern side of the Green Mountains, and it's spectacular in foliage season, when bright colors illuminate the surrounding hills. Route 100 is ideal for a long weekend of exploration, as some of Vermont's most interesting destinations are right at the edge of the road. Starting at Route 9—the scenic byway that links Brattleboro and Bennington—here are some favorite stops from south to north.

Route 9 to Route 4

Route 100 bisects Route 9 just a few miles west of Hogback Mountain, a gentle peak that commands 100-mile views of the rolling hills to the south. Head north through a series of river valleys to the picture-perfect town of **Weston,** where the **Vermont Country Store** (657 Main St., Weston, www.vermontcountrystore.com, 802/824-3184) tends old-fashioned displays of everything from flannel nightgowns to penny candy. Time your visit to the morning, afternoon, or evening prayers at the Benedictine **Weston Priory** (58 Priory Hill Rd., Weston, 802/824-5409, www.westonpriory.org) to join the monks for a traditional sung service that's sometimes held outside during the summer months.

Continue north through the woods of Okemo State Forest, then duck onto the 100A cutoff that passes through Plymouth Notch and **President Calvin Coolidge State Historic Site** (3780 Rte. 100A, 802/672-3773, www.historicsites.vermont.gov/directory/Coolidge), where the president was raised and sworn into office. Pause to graze the samples at the Coolidge family's nearby cheese factory, **Plymouth Artisan Cheese** (106 Messer Hill Rd., 802/672-3650, www.plymouthartisancheese.com), then continue up Route 100A to the **Long Trail Brewing Company** (5520 Rte. 4, Bridgewater Corners, 802/672-5011, www.longtrail.com), a pioneer of Vermont craft brewing.

Route 4 to I-89

Get back on Route 100 where it rolls right to the base of **Killington Peak,** then continue north along the White River, passing through the pretty country towns of Stockbridge and Rochester, then entering the **Mad River Valley.** Duck off the road onto Warren's tiny Main Street, where you'll find a few artists' galleries, a covered bridge, and the **Warren Store** (248 Main St., Warren, 802/496-3864, www.warrenstore.com), an old-fashioned country store that's a community hub. In hot weather, don't miss the chance to cool off in one of Warren's spectacular **swimming holes,** then continue to the valley town of **Waitsfield** to taste locally made apple brandy at **Mad River Distillers** (114 Rte. 100, Waitsfield, 802/496-6973, www.madriverdistillers.com), or **rent an inner tube** for a float down the Mad River.

North of I-89

The mountains get bigger from here, so stop to fortify yourself with a scoop from the **Ben & Jerry's ice cream factory** (1281 Rte. 100, Waterbury, 802/882-2034, www.benjerry.com), or a freshly made **cider donut** from **Cold Hollow Cider Mill** (3600 Rte. 100, Waterbury Center, 800/327-7537, www.coldhollow.com), where you can watch apples turn into juice before your eyes. You'll cruise right through the resort town of **Stowe** as you head north—if you're traveling in the snow-free months, take a detour from Route 100 to drive Route 108 through **Smugglers' Notch,** a steeply winding and gorgeous stretch of road rimmed by granite boulders (watch out for rock climbers!).

When you get back onto Route 100 for the final stretch, you'll be in the Northeast Kingdom, where there are far more cows, mountains, and moose than people. Route 100 ends a bit unceremoniously by intersecting Route 105, but then you're just a hop away from the classic Kingdom town of Newport, where you can sample ice cider, artisan cheese, and other northern delights at the **Northeast Kingdom Tasting Center** (150 Main St., Newport, 802/334-1790, www.nektastingcenter.com).

Brattleboro feel, with a mashup of Irish bar, fish-and-chips joint, local hangout, and literary mecca (try the James Joyce burger). This is the sort of bar where regulars bang out tunes on the piano, and it's a good place to mingle with the locals.

The Arts

The landmark art deco building that houses the **Latchis Theatre** (50 Main St., 802/254-6300, http://theater.latchis.com, $9 adults, $7 children and seniors, $7 matinees) is as much a part of the show as anything on the screen. Its 750-seat main theater has an iridescent mural of the zodiac on the ceiling and frolicking Greeks along the walls. Three movie theaters show a mix of first-run and independent films. The 1938 building is also a hotel.

On the other end of the spectrum, patrons of the **Hooker-Dunham Theater & Gallery** (139 Main St., 802/254-9276, www.hooker-dunham.org, events $5-20, gallery admission free) enjoy its funky subterranean feel. This venue showcases art-house films, folk and chamber music, and avant-garde theater.

Festivals and Events

Follow step-by-step instructions from the caller, and you'll be twirling and swinging along with a crowd at **The Brattleboro Dance** (118 Elliot St., www.brattcontra.org, 7pm-10pm, $10-12 adults, $8 students), a bi-monthly traditional contra dance with live music and a welcoming set of regulars. Beginners can show up at 6:45pm for a bit of practice, and dancers should bring a pair of clean, soft-soled shoes to change into (though you'll likely spot some bare feet in the crowd).

Each June the cows take over for the **Strolling of the Heifers** (www.strollingoftheheifers.org, early June), a parade that celebrates the area's agrarian history and draws attention to the challenges faced by local farmers. In an opening parade, the pride of the pastures saunter down the street, followed by cow floats and kids in cow costumes. During the day, a Dairy Fest features free ice cream, cheese tastings, and a "celebrity" milking contest. Events recently added to the celebration include a Green Expo showcasing environmentally sustainable products and lifestyles, and a fiercely competitive Grilled Cheese Cook-Off, pitting professional and amateur chefs against each other for the coveted Golden Spatula. For a true taste of country living—and some enthusiastic swings and twirls—don't miss the evening community contra dance.

SPORTS AND RECREATION

Biking

With easygoing traffic and loads of scenic country roads, Brattleboro is the perfect place to ditch four wheels for two. If you've got your own bike, the Windham Regional Commission creates useful pdf bicycle suitability maps (www.windhamregional.org/bikemap), and 21-speed hybrid bikes are available to rent at **Brattleboro Bicycle Shop** (165 Main St., 802/254-8644, www.bratbike.com, $25 per day). The friendly staff is happy to suggest rides in the area, which are either flat out-and-backs in the Connecticut River Valley, or hilly climbs into the Green Mountains. As is the case throughout Vermont, some of the finest riding is on unpaved dirt roads, which outnumber the nearby asphalt options three to one, and are an ideal way to escape into quiet country hollows.

Boating

Canoes, kayaks, and tubes can be rented from the **Vermont Canoe Touring Center** (451 Putney Rd., 802/257-5008, www.vermontcanoetouringcenter.com, kayaks from $20, canoes from $25, tubes $20 per day, reservations required) at the intersection of the Connecticut and West Rivers. The stretch of the Connecticut above Vernon Dam is wide and pleasant, with some small islands along the way for paddlers to get out and explore; the West River is smaller but similarly peaceful, though it can also offer some great Class II and III whitewater in the early spring when the snow melts, or on one of a few release dates from the upstream dam each year.

Hiking

Three short, gentle nature trails leave from the Fort Dummer State Park Campground; the 1-mile **Sunrise Trail** and the 0.5-mile **Sunset Trail** loop through the forest, and the 0.5-mile **Broad Brook Trail** leads from the southern edge of the campground loop to a river swimming hole that's a pleasantly shady haven on a hot summer day.

Brattleboro's rolling skyline is dominated by **Wantastiquet Mountain,** but the trail to the top of the 1,368-foot peak starts in New Hampshire, just across the Connecticut River. To reach the trailhead, take Route 119 across the river from downtown Brattleboro and turn left onto Mountain Road just after the second bridge. The trailhead is 0.9 mile from downtown Brattleboro at a small parking area on the right side of the road. The 1.5 miles of switchbacks earn you sweeping views of the Connecticut valley from the summit, where an exposed granite slab makes an excellent picnic spot.

Swimming

The Connecticut River looks temptingly cool as it burbles past town, but there are cleaner, more peaceful options a short drive outside of the city limits. Though the river is generally too shallow for swimming, just flopping into a pool at **Stickney Brook Falls** is a delightful way to spend a hot afternoon. The series of gentle falls is on the left-hand side of Stickney Brook Road; from downtown Brattleboro, drive north on Route 30 and continue 3.7 miles past the I-91 underpass. Turn left on Stickney Brook Road and watch for cars parked along the road.

Stickney Brook is a tributary of the **West River,** which runs parallel to Route 30 north of Brattleboro. There are excellent swimming holes all along the waterway, notably just under the West Dummerston covered bridge (7.3 miles north of Brattleboro, with a sometimes strong current).

Half an hour west of Brattleboro, the sinuous **Harrington Reservoir** is pocked with pleasant spots to slip into the water. To reach the reservoir, drive west on Route 9 to the intersection with Route 100 in Wilmington. Access points and swimming beaches are located on the right side of Route 100, several with picnic areas and grills. The reservoir's most famous swim spot is **The Ledges,** a pristine, clothing-optional crook in the shoreline that's back in the buff after losing its nudist privileges in a hotly contested town vote. Thanks to support from groups like AANR—that's the American Association for Nude Recreation—the vote was eventually overturned.

SHOPPING

Downtown Brattleboro has an eclectic mix of shops that invites leisurely browsing, like **Boomerang** (12 Elliot St., 802/257-6911, www.boomerangvermont.com, 10am-6pm daily), which stocks new, used, and vintage clothing for men and women and many picks with flair.

Books tower from floor to ceiling at **Brattleboro Books** (36 Elliot St., 802/257-7777, www.brattleborobooks.com, 10am-6pm Mon.-Sat., 11am-5pm Sun.), an independent store with the best selection in town, including many used and out-of-print copies.

You can find one-of-a-kind gifts at **Vermont Artisan Designs** (106 Main St., 802/257-7044, www.vtart.com, 10am-6pm Mon.-Thurs. and Sat., 10am-8pm Fri., 10am-5pm Sun.), which features pottery, furniture, and other crafts made by artisans from across the state.

FOOD

The contrast between the thoughtful menus and the offbeat setting—a 1925 Worcester diner car—only heighten the experience at ★ **T. J. Buckley's Uptown Dining** (132 Elliot St., 802/257-4922, www.tjbuckleysuptowndining.com, 5:30pm-9:30pm Thurs.-Sun., open some Wed. summer, $40), a long-standing Brattleboro favorite. There are just eight tables, so chef-owner Michael Fuller gives personal attention to each dish and offers a handful of options nightly. All of them feature bold flavor combinations, such as venison with eggplant caponata, truffle oil, and fresh currants, or the quail with duck leg confit and root vegetables.

Exposed brick and an open kitchen make dining at ★ **duo** (136 Main St., 802/251-4141, www.duorestaurants.com, 5pm-9pm Mon.-Thurs., 5pm-10pm Fri., 9am-2pm and 5pm-10pm Sat., 9am-2pm and 5pm-9pm $18-24) a convivial and cozy experience. The fresh, farm-to-table menus bring diverse influences to bear on seasonal ingredients. Recent starters included fried pickled radishes and potted hot pastrami served with remoulade, sauerkraut, and rye. The pork chop is perfectly prepared and arrives alongside cornbread, bacon, and rhubarb chow chow.

With a brightly lit industrial-chic space right in the center of town, **Turquoise Grille** (128 Main St., 802/254-2327, www.turquoisegrille.com, 11am-3pm and 5pm-9pm Mon.-Sat., 9:30am-3pm Sun., $7-18) beckons on gray afternoons. The menu has global versions of meat on bread, with Turkish flair: kofte and kebabs alongside pulled pork, bratwurst, and burgers.

The unexpectedness of ★ **Three Stones Restaurant** (105 Canal St., 802/246-1035, www.3stonesrestaurant.com, 5pm-9pm Wed.-Sun., $12-16) is enchanting. A ramshackle exterior gives way to a warm and vivid interior with a decidedly casual feel. This family-run joint prepares classic foods of the Yucatán Peninsula in southern Mexico, like *panuchos*, a stuffed, refried tortilla; *salbutes*, fried maize cakes piled high with meat and vegetables; and *cochinita adobado*, slow-cooked pork that melts in your mouth. Don't miss the *onzicil*, a sauce made from toasted pepitas and tomatoes.

For those who love classic diner fare, but want their ingredients sustainably sourced, the **Chelsea Royal Diner** (487 Marlboro Rd., 802/254-8399, www.chelsearoyaldiner.com, 5:30am-9pm daily, $5-11) offers the best of both worlds, complete with blue plate specials.

Tucked into a cozy basement nook, **Mocha Joe's Roasting Co.** (82 Main St., 802/257-7794, www.mochajoes.com, 7am-8pm Mon.-Thurs., 7am-9pm Fri., 7:30am-9pm Sat., 7:30am-8pm Sun.) roasts coffee sourced from around the world, with direct trade programs in Cameroon and Nicaragua. The café serves pastries and snacks, but the brews are the real focus, and the friendly space may tempt you to while away the morning.

Vegetable lovers who've tired of Vermont's typically meat-heavy menus should head to ★ **Superfresh! Organic Café** (30 Main St., 802/579-1751, www.superfreshcafe.com, 10am-4pm Mon.-Wed., 10am-9pm Thurs., 10am-10pm Fri.-Sat., 10am-9pm Sun., $7-14), which fills plates with vibrant salads, filling sandwiches and wraps, and ample gluten-free options. You'll find plenty of smoothies, vegan "mylks," and elixirs for what ails you. The laid-back, artsy style is right at home in downtown Brattleboro, attracting a colorful crowd of locals.

Markets

The **Brattleboro Farmers' Market** (www.brattleborofarmersmarket.com, 9am-2pm Sat. May-Oct., 10am-2pm Tues. June-Oct.) is the best in southern Vermont, with piles of local produce, cheese, and meat from local farms, crafters, and producers. Snap up artisanal kimchi, gelato, and pasta, among many other things. The Saturday market is on Route 9 near the covered bridge; the Tuesday market is at Whetstone pathway, on lower Main Street.

ACCOMMODATIONS AND CAMPING

$100-150

Diminutive and homey, **The One Cat** (34 Clark St., 802/579-1905, www.theonecatvermont.com, $95-165) is as funky as Brattleboro itself. The two guest rooms—New England and Brighton—are named for the Anglo-American couple's homes, with respective decorative flourishes, as well as televisions,

DVD players, and coffeemakers. The tiny library is full of intriguing books and calls out for intimate wintertime reading. A full English breakfast is served, and a 20 percent discount is available for guests who arrive without cars.

$150-250

Despite the confusing name—which has led some guests to look for the wrong street address—**Forty Putney Road** (192 Putney Rd., 800/941-2413, www.fortyputneyroad.com, $100-240) is at 192 Putney Road, and the meticulous bed-and-breakfast couldn't be cuter. The pristine white house is surrounded by specimen trees and meticulous gardens outside, and filled with serenely decorated rooms evocative of the Provençal and English countryside. A full gourmet breakfast is included.

The lobby at the **Latchis Hotel** (50 Main St., 802/254-6300, www.latchis.com, $115-190) retains art deco flourishes from its heyday in the 1930s, and for some, it doesn't get any better than a room at a downtown movie theater. Period details like terrazzo floors and chrome fixtures maintain historical cool; ongoing renovations are sprucing up the down-at-the-heels rooms; and suites with small sitting rooms are available.

Sweet old-fashioned rooms have romantic appeal at the **1868 Crosby House Bed & Breakfast** (175 Western Ave., 802/257-7145, www.crosbyhouse.com, $160-199). Three individual rooms have queen-size beds and fireplaces; the largest has a double-whirlpool bath. Fans of dress-up will love the special afternoon tea at which the innkeepers lay out a selection of gloves and hats for guests, along with feathers and other accessories for decorating. The nearby Retreat Trails are perfect for morning walks.

Over $250

Slow down for a few days on the property that surrounds **Scott Farm Orchard** (707 Kipling Rd., Dummerston, 802/254-6868, www.scottfarmvermont.com), and you'll be rewarded with a sublimely peaceful retreat into scattered apple orchards and shady forests. The **Landmark Trust USA** (www.landmarktrustusa.org) maintains five historic buildings that are destinations worth planning a trip around, especially the exquisite **Naulakha** (sleeps 8, 3-night minimum stay, $390-450), Rudyard Kipling's scrupulously maintained home. The property favors historical preservation over modern-day comforts, but the grounds offer sweeping views of the Wantastiquet Range, where Kipling loved to watch Mount Monadnack break the clouds "like a giant thumb-nail pointing heavenwards." The other on-site rentals include the Kiplings' charming **Carriage House** (sleeps 4, 3-night minimum stay, $275), a renovated sugarhouse, and two historical farmhouses. All properties must be booked in advance, and have minimum stay requirements.

Camping

A 1908 dam on the Connecticut River flooded Fort Dummer—Vermont's first permanent European settlement—but the area around it has been preserved as **Fort Dummer State Park** (517 Old Guilford Rd., 802/254-2610, www.vtstateparks.com/htm/fortdummer.htm, mid-May-Labor Day, campsites and lean-tos $18-27). The 217-acre forest is just south of downtown, with a pleasant mix of oak, beech, and birch trees that shelter wild turkeys and ruffed grouse. The campground's 50 wooded tent sites are comfortable, if not particularly private, or you can spend the night in one of 10 more-secluded lean-tos. Hot showers and a dump station are available, but no hookups.

INFORMATION AND SERVICES

The **Brattleboro Area Chamber of Commerce** (180 Main St., 802/254-4565, www.brattleborochamber.org, 9am-5pm Mon.-Fri.) runs a visitors center downtown.

The area's premier hospital is **Brattleboro Memorial Hospital** (17 Belmont Ave., 802/257-0341, www.bmhvt.org). For pharmacy needs, there's **Rite Aid Pharmacy** (499 Canal St., 802/257-4204 and **Walgreens**

(476 Canal St., 802/254-5633). For nonmedical emergencies, contact the **Brattleboro Police** (230 Main St., 802/257-7946).

Banks are found all over the downtown area, particularly on Main Street. ATMs are plentiful around retail stores, in and around hotels, and in convenience stores. Most cafés have **wireless Internet.** Computers are available for public use at **Brooks Memorial Library** (224 Main St., 10am-9pm Wed., 10am-6pm Thurs.-Fri., 10am-5pm Sat.).

GETTING THERE AND AROUND

Just off the north-south I-91, Brattleboro is the eastern edge of Vermont's east-west Route 9, a scenic, two-lane highway that's known as the **Molly Stark Byway,** named for the wife of a Revolutionary-era general. Brattleboro is also on both of Vermont's Amtrak lines, the Ethan Allen Express from **New York City**, and The Vermonter, which travels from **Washington DC** (800/872-7245, www.amtrak.com, from NYC 5.5 hrs., from $65; from DC 8.75 hrs., from $135), and which now allow bicycles. **Greyhound Bus** (800/231-2222, www.greyhound.com) links Brattleboro with cities around the region, and taxi service is available from **Brattleboro Taxi** (802/254-6446, www.brattleborotaxi.com).

Metered parking is available all over downtown Brattleboro, and the town's small downtown is compact and easy to navigate. Three city bus lines connect at the Flat Street Transportation Center in downtown; rides within town are $1, buses operate Monday-Saturday, and a service map is available at www.crtransit.org.

Woodstock and Vicinity

With a bit of starch and a lot of history, this picture-book village is among the prettiest in New England. Rolling hills and farms are the perfect backdrop for Woodstock's covered bridges, elegant homes, and tiny town center. That "country gentleman" feel is no accident—this part of Vermont was a rural escape for some of the 19th century's most affluent U.S. families, and names like Rockefeller, Billings, and Marsh continue to define today's landscape of historic inns, parks, and farms.

In part due to its carefully maintained past, Woodstock attracts transplants from urban areas around the East. This blend of new and old lends an unusual vitality to the small town, where upscale restaurants, art galleries, and boutiques cheerfully coexist with farm stores and a quirky "town crier," a community blackboard listing contra dances and church suppers.

Just outside of Woodstock are a pair of appealing villages that are ideal for afternoon excursions. To the east, little Quechee has a renowned glassblowing studio and a deep, glacier-carved gorge. Southwest of Woodstock is the idyllic valley of Plymouth Notch, where the future President Coolidge was raised on the family farm—the creamery his father founded in 1890 makes award-winning cheese to this day.

SIGHTS

Woodstock

BILLINGS FARM & MUSEUM

One of Woodstock's most successful native sons was Frederick Billings, who made his money as a San Francisco lawyer in the heat of the gold rush. In the 1870s, he returned to Woodstock and bought the old Charles Marsh Farm, which he transformed into a model dairy farm complete with imported Jersey cows. Today visitors to the grounds of the **Billings Farm & Museum** (53 Elm St., 802/457-2355, www.billingsfarm.org, 10am-5pm daily Apr.-Oct., 10am-4pm Sat.-Sun. Nov.-Feb., $15 adults, $14 seniors, $8 children 5-15, $4 children 3-4, children under 3 free) can tour the property in wagons drawn by Percheron draft horses, meet the well-groomed herd of milking cows, and churn fresh cream into butter. The farm produces two varieties of cheddar from a herd of all Jersey cows: full-flavored and creamy sweet cheddar and butter cheddar, which is slightly salty with a rich, melting texture.

Next door, **Marsh-Billings-Rockefeller National Historical Park** (54 Elm St., 802/457-3368, www.nps.gov/mabi, 10am-5pm daily Memorial Day-Oct., $8 adults, $4 seniors, children 15 and under free) frames the mansion built by natural philosopher Charles Marsh 1805-1807 and bought by Billings in 1861. The mansion, open for tours by advance reservation, has a Tiffany stained-glass window and an extensive collection of American landscape paintings. In 1934, Billings's granddaughter married Laurance Rockefeller, and they donated the land to the National Park Service in 1992. The main visitors center is the former Carriage Barn, which houses a permanent exhibit about conservation history, a reading library, and a bookstore. **Combination tickets** ($20 adults, $15 seniors) include two-day admission to both Billings Farm and Marsh-Billings-Rockefeller National Historical Park.

SUGARBUSH FARM

Cows and other farm animals can be found at **Sugarbush Farm** (591 Sugarbush Farm Rd., 802/457-1757, www.sugarbushfarm.com, 8am-5pm Mon.-Fri., 9am-5pm Sat.-Sun. and holidays), which produces excellent cheddar cheese and keeps its maple sugar shack open all year (though syrup is generally made between February and April). To get here, take a right across the covered bridge at the small village of Taftsville and follow the signs to the farm. Call ahead for road conditions in winter and early spring.

DANA HOUSE MUSEUM

For a glimpse into Woodstock's nonagricultural past, visit the **Dana–Thomas House Museum** (26 Elm St., 802/457-1822, www.woodstockhistorical.org, 1pm-5pm Wed.-Sat., 11am-4pm Sun. June-mid-Oct., free), a federal-style home once owned by a prosperous local dry goods merchant. Now a museum run by the Woodstock Historical Society, it contains period rooms full of fine china, antique furniture, kitchen instruments, and children's toys.

Woodstock countryside

Woodstock

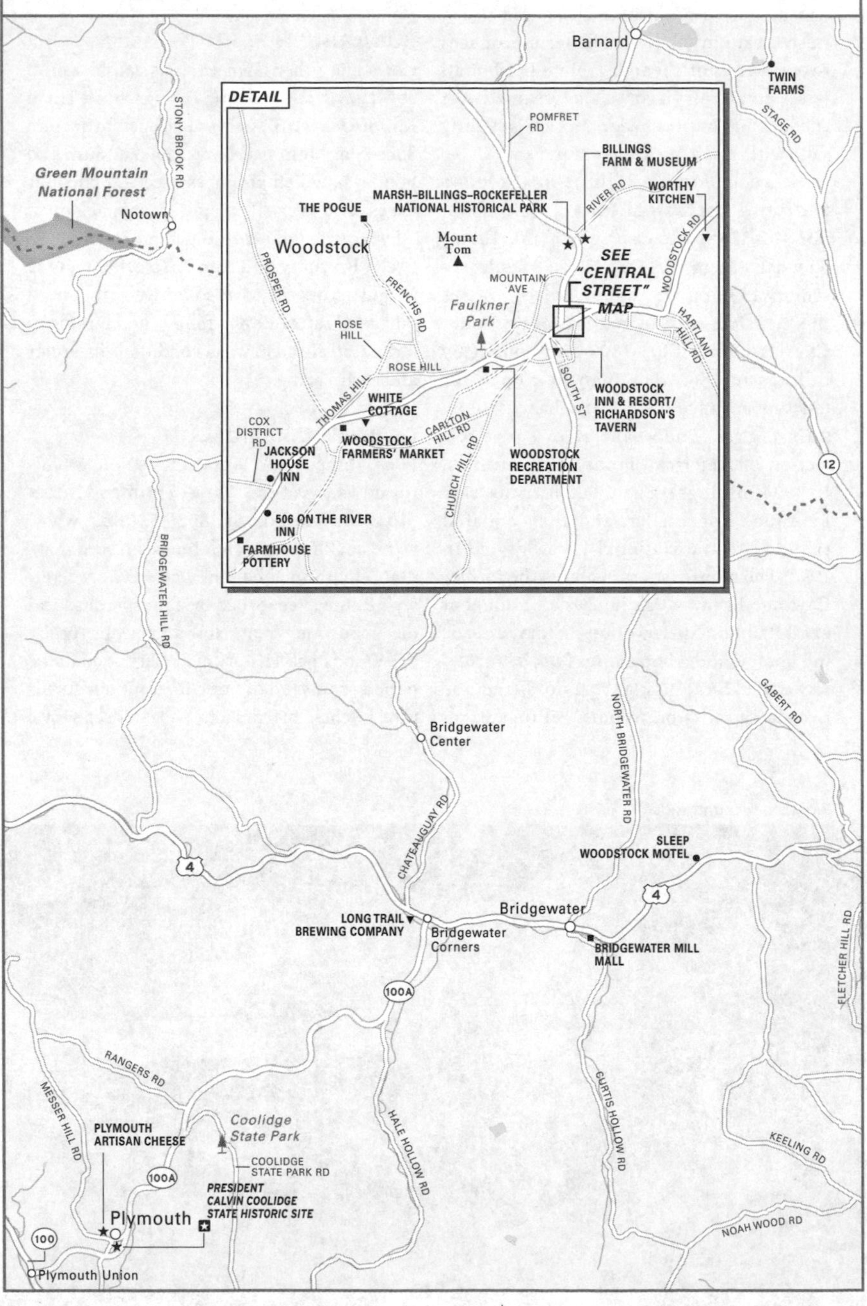
Barnard
TWIN FARMS
STAGE RD
DETAIL
POMFRET RD
BILLINGS FARM & MUSEUM
STONY BROOK RD
Green Mountain National Forest
Notown
MARSH–BILLINGS–ROCKEFELLER NATIONAL HISTORICAL PARK
RIVER RD
WORTHY KITCHEN
THE POGUE
Mount Tom
Woodstock
WOODSTOCK RD
SEE "CENTRAL STREET" MAP
PROSPER RD
FRENCHS RD
MOUNTAIN AVE
Faulkner Park
HARTLAND HILL RD
ROSE HILL
ROSE HILL
SOUTH ST
WHITE COTTAGE
THOMAS HILL
WOODSTOCK INN & RESORT/ RICHARDSON'S TAVERN
COX DISTRICT RD
CARLTON HILL RD
WOODSTOCK FARMERS' MARKET
JACKSON HOUSE INN
CHURCH HILL RD
WOODSTOCK RECREATION DEPARTMENT
12
506 ON THE RIVER INN
FARMHOUSE POTTERY
BRIDGEWATER HILL RD
GABERT RD
Bridgewater Center
NORTH BRIDGEWATER RD
CHATEAUGUAY RD
SLEEP WOODSTOCK MOTEL
4
4
LONG TRAIL BREWING COMPANY
Bridgewater
Bridgewater Corners
BRIDGEWATER MILL MALL
FLETCHER HILL RD
100A
RANGERS RD
MESSER HILL RD
CURTIS HOLLOW RD
Coolidge State Park
PLYMOUTH ARTISAN CHEESE
HALE HOLLOW RD
KEELING RD
COOLIDGE STATE PARK RD
100A
PRESIDENT CALVIN COOLIDGE STATE HISTORIC SITE
Plymouth
NOAH WOOD RD
100
Plymouth Union

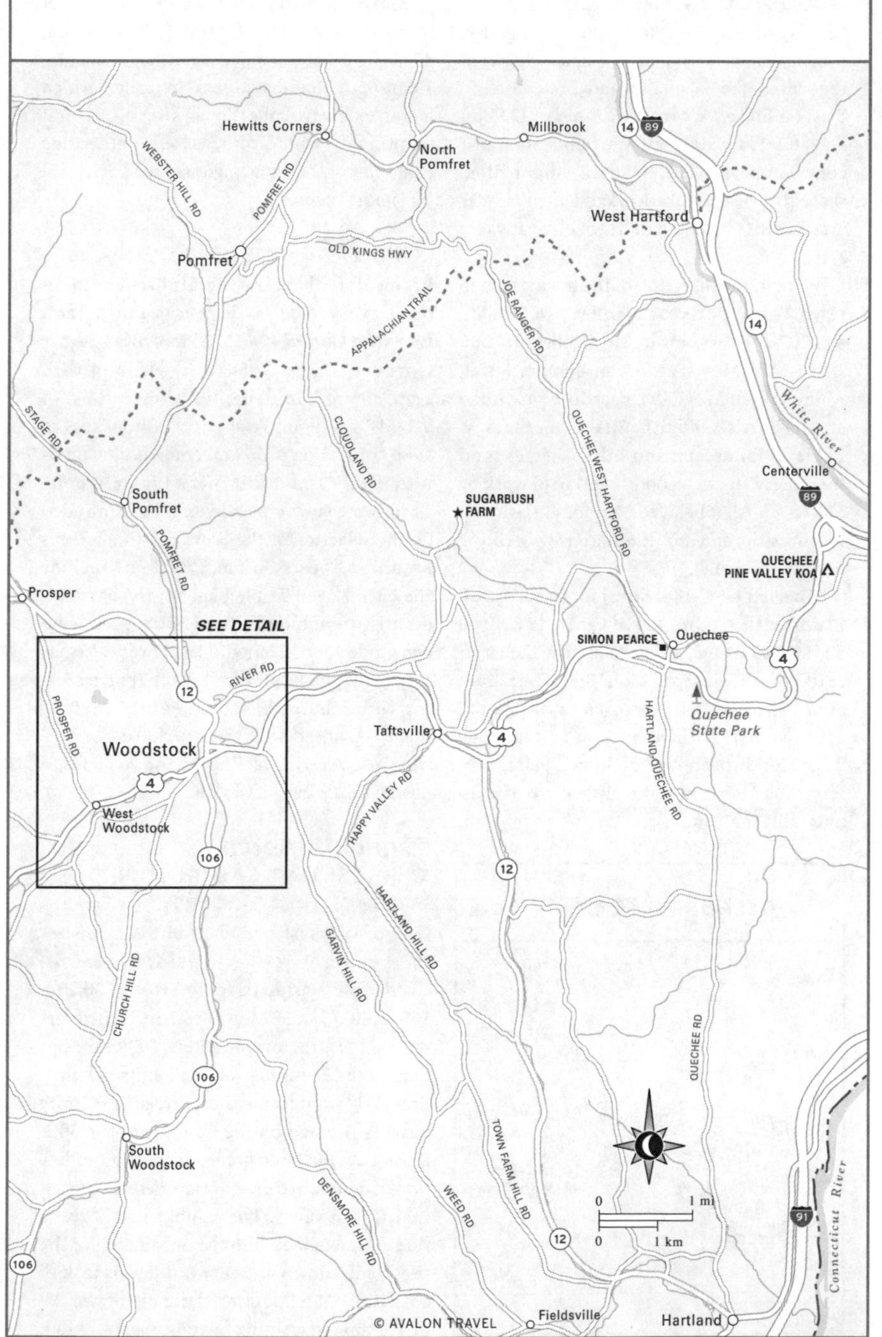
Hewitts Corners
Millbrook
North Pomfret
West Hartford
Pomfret
WEBSTER HILL RD
POMFRET RD
OLD KINGS HWY
APPALACHIAN TRAIL
JOE RANGER RD
CLOUDLAND RD
QUECHEE WEST HARTFORD RD
STAGE RD
White River
Centerville
South Pomfret
SUGARBUSH FARM
QUECHEE/ PINE VALLEY KOA
Prosper
SEE DETAIL
SIMON PEARCE
Quechee
RIVER RD
Quechee State Park
PROSPER RD
Woodstock
Taftsville
HARTLAND-QUECHEE RD
West Woodstock
HAPPY VALLEY RD
HARTLAND HILL RD
GARVIN HILL RD
CHURCH HILL RD
QUECHEE RD
South Woodstock
DENSMORE HILL RD
WEED RD
TOWN FARM HILL RD
0
1 mi
0
1 km
Connecticut River
© AVALON TRAVEL
Fieldsville
Hartland

WOODSTOCK'S ART GALLERIES

It's easy to visit the town's vibrant art galleries on foot, as they're in a compact cluster at the center of town, on Elm and Center Streets. Start on Elm at **Artemis Global Art** (23 Elm St., 802/234-8900, www.artemisglobalart.com, 11am-5pm daily), an airy, light-filled space that displays the work of Dutch painter **Ton Schulten** and a handful of other abstract artists.

Walk in the direction of the town green to reach **The Woodstock Gallery** (6 Elm St., 802/457-2012, www.woodstockgalleryvt.com, 10am-5pm Mon.-Sat., noon-4:30pm Sun.), where the imagery is closer to home. Fine and folk artists offer their takes on the New England landscape and other themes, and the gallery stocks a good selection of work by **Sabra Field,** a beloved Vermont artist who captures the spirit of the state with striking woodblock prints.

Turn left on Center Street for a short stroll to **Collective—the Art of Craft** (46 Central St., 802/457-1298, www.collective-theartofcraft.com, 10am-5pm Mon.-Sat., 11am-4pm Sun.), where a small group of local artists and artisans display their work in an old stone mill. Handwoven fabrics, blown glass, pottery, woodwork, and metalwork are of a remarkably high quality.

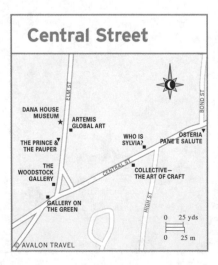

Central Street

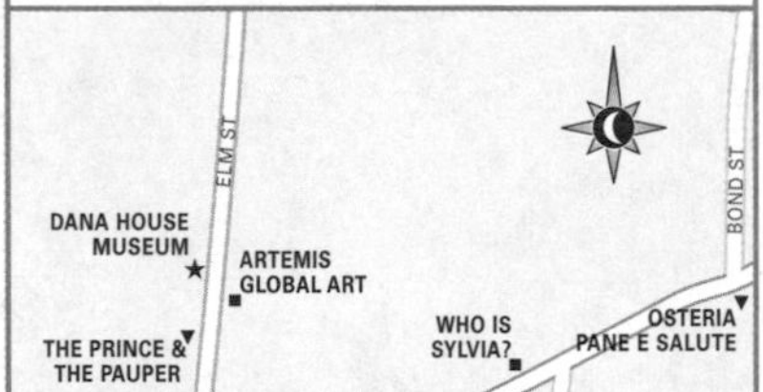

ELM ST
BOND ST
DANA HOUSE MUSEUM
ARTEMIS GLOBAL ART
THE PRINCE & THE PAUPER
WHO IS SYLVIA?
OSTERIA PANE E SALUTE
THE WOODSTOCK GALLERY
CENTRAL ST
COLLECTIVE–THE ART OF CRAFT
GALLERY ON THE GREEN
HIGH ST
0 25 yds
0 25 m
© AVALON TRAVEL

Make a U-turn and head back up the street to **Gallery on the Green** (1 The Green, 802/457-4956, www.galleryonthegreen.com, 10am-6pm Mon.-Sat., 10am-4pm Sun.), which has an extensive collection of sweetly pastoral paintings by Chip Evans, as well as other fine examples of the New England "red barns and Holsteins" genre.

LONG TRAIL BREWING COMPANY

Back before there was a craft brewery in almost every village, there was **Long Trail Brewing Company** (5520 Rte. 4, Bridgewater Corners, 802/672-5011, www.longtrail.com, 10am-7pm daily), 15 minutes west of Woodstock. Long Trail started filling kegs in 1989, and its flagship amber ale is now ubiquitous in Vermont. If that's the only Long Trail brew you've tried, you'll be astounded by the selection at the brewery, which keeps around 13 beers on tap. Standouts include the barrel-aged Triple Bag, but the bartenders are through-and-through beer geeks who can guide your selection. The brewery also has a menu of pub food served 11am-7pm, featuring wings, burgers, and other beer-friendly meals. A raised walkway overlooks the bottling and brewing facility, giving you a fascinating bird's-eye view of the action.

Plymouth Notch

★ PRESIDENT CALVIN COOLIDGE STATE HISTORIC SITE

One of the best presidential historic sites in the country, the **President Calvin Coolidge State Historic Site** (3780 Rte. 100A, 802/672-3773, www.historicsites.vermont.gov/directory/coolidge, 9:30am-5pm daily late May-mid-Oct., $9 adults, $2 children 6-14, children under 6 free, $25 family pass) is situated on the grounds of the 30th president's boyhood home, a sprawling collection of houses, barns, and factories in a mountain-ringed valley. The exhibits inside give a rare intimate look into the upbringing of the president known as Silent Cal for his lack of emotion, but who restored the dignity of the office during a time of widespread scandal.

The family parlor preserves the spot where Coolidge was sworn into office—by his father, a notary public. Even in 1924, when Coolidge ran for reelection, the homestead swearing-in must have seemed like a scene from a simple, earlier time—one radio campaign ad described it in heavily nostalgic terms, pitching Cal as a rustic counterpoint to Washington DC's modernity and urban sophistication.

PLYMOUTH ARTISAN CHEESE

Nearby **Plymouth Artisan Cheese** (106 Messer Hill Rd., 802/672-3650, www.plymouthartisancheese.com, 10am-5pm daily) was founded in 1890 by John Coolidge, Calvin Coolidge's father. Its granular curd cheeses were once relatively common in the United States, but are now rare. Learn about the cheese-making process at the on-site museum, then sample everything from squeaky-fresh cheese curds to granular aged cheeses that have been hand-dipped in wax.

Quechee

The mission of the **Vermont Institute of Natural Science** (VINS, Rte. 4 just west of Quechee Gorge, 802/359-5000, www.vinsweb.org, 10am-5pm daily mid-Apr.-Oct., 10am-4pm daily Nov.-mid-Apr., $15 adults, $14 seniors, $13 children 4-17, children 3 and under free) is to rescue and rehabilitate birds of prey, including hawks, owls, and eagles, and display them for the education of visitors. Watching the raptors watch you is an unforgettable experience; the birds are released when fully healed, but a recent visit included a great horned owl, merlin falcons, and other fiercely captivating creatures.

Try to time your visit with one of the raptor educational programs, held at 11am, or their feeding time at 2:45pm. VINS puts on other educational programs throughout the day, and also has an hour-long interpretive nature trail that winds through the forested property.

Even if you're not in the market for the high-end glassware, **Simon Pearce** (1760 Main St., the Mill at Quechee, 802/295-2711, www.simonpearce.com, 10am-9pm daily) is a fascinating stop that's seven miles east of Woodstock in the village of Quechee. Located in an old mill building run entirely by hydroelectric power, the studio is open to the public, who can watch glassblowers blow bubbles into glowing orange balls of 2,400-degree silica. It's an extraordinary sight, especially the way multiple craftspeople coordinate individual components of a delicate wineglass, with precise timing and handiwork. If they slip up, of course, that's one more glass for the shelf of perfect-seeming "seconds" that are available for purchase at somewhat lower prices.

ENTERTAINMENT AND EVENTS

Each year toward the end of sugaring season (late Mar.-early Apr.), many of Vermont's sugarhouses open their doors for the **Maple Open House Weekend** (www.vermontmaple.org/events), which is an excellent chance to rub shoulders with sugarmakers and sample the state's sweetest treats, like sugar on snow (often served with a pickle, which is better than it sounds).

Billings Farm & Museum sponsors many special events throughout the summer, including **Cow Appreciation Day** every July, which includes a judging of the Jerseys, ice cream and butter making, and (always gripping) dairy trivia, as well as a **Harvest** celebration in October with husking competitions and cider pressing. In late July, Woodstock gets wordy during **Bookstock** (www.bookstockvt.org), a festival that attracts an intriguing lineup of writers. While the town maintains an events page, the best resource is kept up by the helpful owner of **Sleep Woodstock Motel** (www.sleepwoodstock.com/upcoming-events).

SHOPPING

Downtown Woodstock

Handmade pottery with a gorgeously modern aesthetic is the main draw at **Farmhouse Pottery** (1837 Rte. 4, 802/774-8373, www.farmhousepottery.com, 10am-5pm Mon.-Sat., 10am-4pm Sun.), where you can watch the artisans at work. The store also stocks maple rolling pins, candles, and a seemingly endless array of beautiful things. Not your average vintage store, **Who Is Sylvia?** (26 Central St., 802/457-1110, 11am-5pm Sun.-Mon. and Thurs., 11am-6pm Fri.-Sat.) stocks flapper dresses, pillbox hats, brocade jackets, and other hard-to-find items dating back more than a century.

Bridgewater Mill Mall

Six miles west of Woodstock on Route 4, **Bridgewater Mill Mall** is filled with studio space for artisans and craftspeople. A highlight is **Shackleton Thomas** (102 Mill Rd., Bridgewater, 802/672-5175, www.shackletonthomas.com, 10am-5pm Tues.-Sat., 11am-4pm Sun.), where Charles Shackleton—a distant relation of Antarctic explorer Ernest Shackleton—crafts simple but elegant Shaker and modern-style furniture. It's fascinating to watch the woodcarvers, who train for years, and the display room is also stocked with eclectic gifts with unusual charm.

SPORTS AND RECREATION

Hiking

In addition to the exhibits at **Marsh-Billings-Rockefeller National Historical Park** (54 Elm St., 802/457-3368, www.nps.gov/mabi, 10am-5pm daily Memorial Day-Oct., $8 adults, $4 seniors, children 15 and under free), the preserve has 20 miles of walking trails, which are accessible from the park entrance on Route 12 and a parking lot on Prosper Road. The roads circle around the slopes of Mount Tom, which is forested with old-growth hemlock, beech, and sugar maples. Popular hikes include the 0.7-mile loop around the mountain pond called **The Pogue** and the gentle, 1-mile climb up to the **South Summit** of Mount Tom, which lords over Woodstock and the river below. No mountain bikes are allowed on the trails; in the winter, they are groomed for cross-country skiing.

It's also possible to walk 2.75 miles round-trip to the summit of **Mount Tom,** starting at the centrally located **Middle Covered Bridge** on Mountain Avenue. Cross the bridge and follow Mountain Avenue as it curves around to the left along a rock wall. An opening in the rock wall leads to the **Faulkner Trail** at Faulkner Park, where it begins to switchback up the gentle south flank of the peak. The last 300 feet of the trail get a bit steeper, giving wide views of the Green Mountains. Allow an hour for the hike.

Seven miles east of Woodstock, **Quechee State Park** (5800 Woodstock Rd., Hartford, 802/295-2990, www.vtstateparks.com/htm/quechee.htm, May 20-Oct. 16, free) has a pleasant 2.2-mile round-trip trail into Vermont's deepest gorge, which was carved by retreating glaciers. While the park's self-nomination as "Vermont's Little Grand Canyon" might set visitors up for a disappointment, the walk is lovely. The **Quechee Gorge Trail** hike takes about an hour and starts from the visitors center.

Swimming

There's an actual swimming pool inside the **Woodstock Recreation Department** (54 River St., 802/457-1502, www.woodstockrec.com, 6am-8pm Mon.-Fri., 8am-2pm Sat., 9am-1pm Sun.), but the real treat is a dip in the **Ottauquechee River.** There's a short path that leaves from right behind the Rec Department, descending to a gentle swimming area that's suitable for families. On the very hottest days, the finest place to swim is in the **Quechee Gorge,** where the water seems to stay cool through the heat of the summer. To reach the best swimming area, take the trail from the visitors center, turn left (downstream) as the Quechee Gorge Trail turns upstream, then follow the river for roughly 0.5 mile to a broad swimming hole.

FOOD

Dining on mostly fried, salty fare at a "snack bar" is a quintessential summer experience in Vermont, and **White Cottage** (863 Woodstock Rd., 802/457-3455, 11am-10pm daily May-Oct., $3-22, cash only) is a fine place to get your fix. Golden mounds of fried clams come with tartar sauce and lemon, maple creemees are piled high on sugar cones, and hamburgers are simple and to-the-point. Snack bar food doesn't vary much from place to place, but White Cottage's outdoor tables, riverside location, and friendly staff make it a favorite—and you can wade in the river while you wait for your order.

Pick up supplies at the confusingly named **Woodstock Farmers' Market** (979 W. Woodstock Rd., 802/457-3658, www.woodstockfarmersmarket.com, 7:30am-7pm Tues.-Sat., 8am-6pm Sun.), which turns out to be a specialty food shop that stocks plenty of locally made treats, cheese, beer, wine, and everything else you might need for a showstopping picnic on the road.

Along with excellent espresso, **Mon Vert Cafe** (28 Central St., 802/457-7143, www.monvertcafe.com, 7:30am-4pm Mon.-Sat., 8am-4pm Sun., $8-11) has fresh breakfast and lunch in a sunny and stylish spot. Breakfast burritos and baked goods give way to a lunch menu of sandwiches and panini. The café also prepares food to go, which makes for great road tripping supplies.

Sedate and sophisticated, **The Prince & The Pauper** (24 Elm St., 802/457-1818, www.princeandpauper.com, 5:30pm-8:30pm Sun.-Thurs., 5:30pm-9pm Fri.-Sat., $18-25) serves fine dining classics—don't miss the restaurant's signature *carré d'agneau royale*, a tender dish of lamb, spinach, and mushrooms wrapped in puff pastry—in a candlelit country setting. Think high-backed wooden booths, exposed beams, and local art for sale on the wall. It's an ideal date setting, though families and groups are also welcome.

If you've had enough of Woodstock's white tablecloth scene, you may be ready for a meal at the relaxed and convivial ★ **Worthy Kitchen** (442 E. Woodstock Rd., 802/457-7281, www.worthyvermont.com, 4pm-9pm Mon.-Thurs., 4pm-10pm Fri., 11:30am-10pm Sat., 11:30am-9pm Sun., $8-15), a "farm diner" that has a hearty selection of pub food with flair, from fried chicken to poutine. Burritos, nachos, and burgers are other favorites, and there's an excellent beer selection.

ACCOMMODATIONS AND CAMPING

Woodstock has some of the most appealing accommodations in the state. Prices tend to be higher than elsewhere and rise dramatically during peak foliage season, while off-season prices may be significantly lower than those listed.

$100-150

There's nothing fancy about **Sleep Woodstock Motel** (4324 W. Woodstock Rd., 802/332-6336, www.sleepwoodstock.com, $88-178, 2-bedroom suite $250-450), but a 2017 renovation has revitalized the property. The roadside motel was built in 1959, and rooms retain a retro feel, but bathrooms are new and everything feels fresh and sunny. The motel is a short drive west of the center.

$150-250

Elegant, well-appointed rooms at the ★ **Jackson House Inn** (43 Senior Ln., 802/457-2065, www.jacksonhouse.com, $189-339) manage to avoid fussiness. Quarters in the main house are somewhat more in keeping with the old-fashioned style of the place, but new additions come with perks like massage tubs. Each one is different, so peek into a few before making your choice. The crackling fire is an appealing place to thaw, but in summer months the broad porch entices. The congenial owners, Rick and Kathy, are devoted to local food, and Rick prepares sumptuous breakfasts with ingredients from area farms.

The **506 on the River Inn** (1653 Rte. 4, 802/457-5000, www.ontheriverwoodstock.com, $139-379) was renovated in 2014 and has an appealingly chic take on Woodstock's genteel country style. Throw pillows are emblazoned with folksy Vermont expressions, antiques are used with restraint, and welcome extras include a game room, library, and toddler playroom. Breakfast is well prepared and lavish, served in a dining room and bar that open to the public at night. The inn's bistro menu covers classed-up pub food and child-friendly diner standbys like mac and cheese.

Over $250

You can't miss the grand ★ **Woodstock Inn & Resort** (14 The Green, 802/457-1100 or 800/448-7900, www.woodstockinn.com, $235-820), which dominates the green in the heart of the village. The rooms and facilities are some of the prettiest in Vermont, full of thoughtful touches and design. This location has been a tourist destination since a tavern with accommodations was established in 1793, but Laurance Rockefeller built the current structure in the 1970s. There are seemingly endless facilities: spa, fitness center, cruiser bikes for exploring the town, organic gardens, and a celebrated 18-hole golf course. You can come take courses on farming and falconry, or just watch the weather from the glassed-in conservatory.

The exquisite and extravagant **Twin Farms** (452 Royalton Turnpike, Barnard, 800/894-6327, www.twinfarms.com, $1,450-2,800) is the former home of journalist Dorothy Thompson and Nobel laureate Sinclair Lewis, who was known for his stirring critiques of capitalism and materialism. Even he might be tempted by this alluring and romantic resort, where the rooms are kitted out with four-poster beds, fireplaces, whirlpool tubs, rare woods, and museum art, with views over a breathtaking property. Twin Farms is all-inclusive and offers an impressive suite of activities, along with remarkable food and drink.

Camping

Quechee State Park (5800 Woodstock Rd., Hartford, 802/295-2990, www.vtstateparks.com/htm/quechee.htm, mid-May-mid-Oct.) has some excellent spots for river **swimming** near a bustling, friendly **campground,** with lean-tos and 45 RV and tent sites along a forested loop (tents $18-24, lean-tos $25-29). There is a dump station, but no hookups; fully powered sites in this area are limited, and the closest option is 2.6 miles farther east, at the **Quechee/Pine Valley KOA** (3700 E. Woodstock Rd., White River Junction, May 1-Oct. 15, tents $28-36, RVs $45-70).

INFORMATION AND SERVICES

The **Woodstock Area Chamber of Commerce** (888/469-6378, www.woodstockvt.com) runs a **welcome center** (3 Mechanic St., 802/432-1100, 9am-5pm daily) and an information booth (on the green). The well-stocked, independent **Woodstock Pharmacy** (19 Central St., 802/457-1306) is conveniently located in the center of town, as are the ATM machines at **People's United Bank** (2 The Green, 802/457-2660) and **Citizens Bank** (431 Woodstock Rd., 802/457-3666,). In an emergency, contact the **Woodstock Police** (454 Rte. 4, 802/457-1420).

GETTING THERE AND AROUND

Route 4 runs straight through the heart of Woodstock, which is easily walkable once you arrive. There's **Amtrak** service to **White River Junction,** 15 miles to the east of Woodstock (800/872-7245, www.amtrak.com), and it's possible to continue to Woodstock on **Vermont Translines** (844/888-7267, www.vttranslines.com), which has daily service from White River Junction to Woodstock, Killington, and Rutland.

Parking in the village is metered 10am-4pm Monday-Saturday, but it's often possible to find free parking on the west side of town. Woodstock also has an unusual parking validation policy—if you get a ticket in a metered spot, you can bring it to any merchant or restaurant, who can validate it (cancel it) for free.

Killington

Following the Ottauquechee River through the southern Green Mountains, Route 4 rolls right to the foot of the imposing Killington Peak. It's been a ski resort since 1958, and was ambitious from the first chair—Killington strung lift after lift on the neighboring peaks and became one of the first mountains to install snowmaking equipment. (It's still known as the first resort to open and last to close each year, though springtime skiing may require dodging patches of grass.)

The mountain's very size and popularity led to some unattractive development on its flank—and the long, twisting Killington Road is now a very un-Vermont stretch of hotels, restaurants, and nightclubs extending up to the summit. Locals may roll their eyes, but for some it's a welcome bit of civilization and fun in the middle of the woods.

The mountain can get crowded on big winter weekends, though Killington's scale offers notable advantages: varied terrain, 3,000 feet of vertical drop, and its unique "good snow guarantee." If you don't like the conditions, you can return your lift ticket. In recent years, Killington has added a popular downhill mountain biking area, with lift service and Vermont's most challenging terrain.

SIGHTS

Skiing and Riding

The mountain that gives Killington its name is only one of six peaks that make up **Killington Resort** (4763 Killington Rd., 800/621-6867, www.killington.com, $105 adults, $89 seniors, $81 youth 7-18, children under 7 and seniors over 80 ski free), a massive ski resort that boasts more than 200 trails. But the main event is still Killington Peak, where most of the toughest trails start their descent. The peak is accessible from the express gondola from the K-1 Lodge at the top of Killington Road.

Ten minutes west of Killington, the co-owned **Pico Mountain** (Rte. 4, 2 miles west of Killington Rd., 866/667-7426, www.picomountain.com, $76 adults, $59 seniors, $65 youth 7-18, children under 7 and seniors over 80 ski free) is a quieter and less crowded mountain, with 50-some trails and

Killington Resort

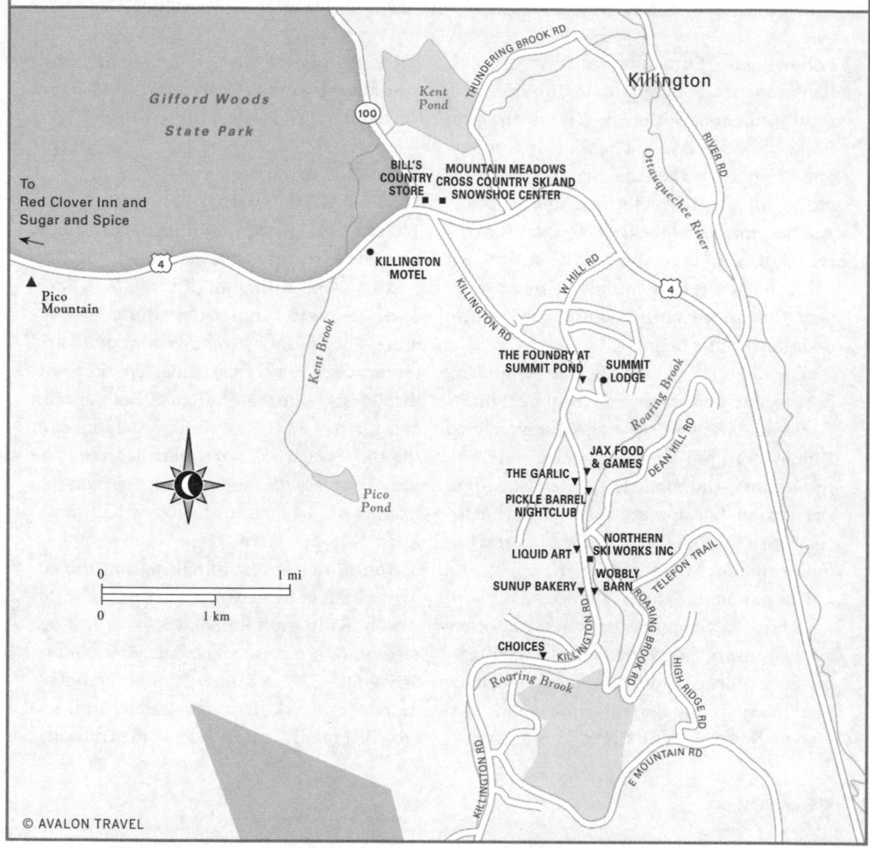

a family-friendly reputation. Pico is closed Tuesday-Wednesday outside of peak skiing weeks.

As might be expected, skiing is not the only way to hit the hill. **Killington Snowmobile Tours** (802/422-2121, www.snowmobilevermont.com) offers one-hour gentle rides along groomed ski trails ($99 single/$139 double), as well as a more challenging 25-mile, two-hour backcountry ride through Calvin Coolidge State Forest ($154/$199).

Both skate and classic skiers will love the gentle terrain at **Mountain Meadows Cross Country Ski and Snowshoe Center** (Rte. 4 at Rte. 100, 802/775-7077, www.xcskiing.net, $19 adults, $16 seniors, $8 youth, children under 6 free), where you can rent skis and snowshoes.

In the summer months, Killington has **mountain biking** on trails served by the K-1 Express Gondola and the Snowshed Express Quad, which ranges from relatively approachable beginner trails to serious and challenging downhilling. A full day of lift and trail access is $55 for adults, or you can sweat your way up the hill and ride the trails for $20. The resort also rents protective gear and full-suspension bikes.

ENTERTAINMENT AND EVENTS

Nightlife

For 50 years, the classic Killington spot has been the **Wobbly Barn** (2229 Killington Rd., 802/422-6171, www.wobblybarn.com, 8pm-2am daily Nov.-Apr., $20 cover for events), where there's a consistently boisterous crowd watching live music and dancing.

Toward the bottom of the access road, **JAX Food & Games** (1667 Killington Rd., 802/422-5334, www.supportinglocalmusic.com, 3pm-2am daily) is a fun venue with plenty of live music and a game room containing air hockey, arcade games, and pool. The **Pickle Barrel Night Club** (1741 Killington Rd., 802/422-3035, www.picklebarrelnightclub.com, 8pm-2am Thurs.-Sun. Oct.-Apr., $20 cover for events) has three levels of dancing space, each with its own bar and loud music that tends to attract a young party crowd.

Festivals and Events

Most months feature at least one or two festivals at Killington, so check the resort's **Events Calendar** (www.killington.com). Every summer, the **Killington Music Festival** (802/773-4003, www.killingtonmusicfestival.org) stages a series of classical music events called Music in the Mountains, with musicians from around the country. The weekend before Labor Day, a thousand motorcyclists invade town for the **Killington Classic Motorcycle Rally** (518/798-7888, www.killingtonclassic.com). Events include a cycle rodeo and bike judging.

The **Killington Foliage Weekend** and **Brewfest Weekend** (802/422-6237, www.killington.com) overlap in the town center and on the local slopes every year, getting under way in late September and early October. Family activities, from hayrides to gondola tours, are a highlight, as are the handcrafted beers served.

SPORTS AND RECREATION

Hiking

In addition to the hiking trails at Killington, a popular short trek is the one up to the scenic overlook on Deer Leap Mountain, located in **Gifford Woods State Park** (34 Gifford Woods Rd., 802/775-5354, www.vtstateparks.com). The trail starts behind the Inn at Long Trail on Route 4 and is two miles round-trip to fantastic views of Pico Peak and Killington Mountain.

To summit the main attraction, trek the **Bucklin Trail** to the top of Killington Peak. The 7.2-mile out-and-back starts from the Bucklin Trailhead (20 Wheelerville Rd., Mendon) and follows a west-facing ridgeline for 3.3 miles before intersecting with the Long Trail. A 0.2-mile spur from the Long Trail leads to the rocky, exposed peak, where you can see all the way to Mount Mansfield on a clear day.

Swimming and Fishing

The Appalachian Trail runs right past **Kent Pond** (access on Thundering Brook Rd., off Rte. 4), but you don't have to be a "thru-hiker" to enjoy the scenic swimming spot. The pond is ringed by low mountains and stocked with both brook and rainbow trout.

SHOPPING

Each of the resorts have ski shops with everything you need for a day in the snow, but one of the best off-mountain stores is **Northern Ski Works** (2089 Killington Rd., next to the Wobbly Barn, 802/422-9675, www.northernski.com, 8am-8pm Mon.-Thurs., 8am-11pm Fri., 7:30am-9pm Sat., 7:30am-8pm Sun. Oct.-Apr.). It's where to head for all manner of equipment, from snowshoes and helmets to boards and, of course, skis.

FOOD

For classic American fare done with flair, **The Foundry at Summit Pond** (63 Summit Path, 802/422-5335, www.foundrykillington.com,

TOP EXPERIENCE

Skiing and Snowboarding in the Green Mountains

Killington might be the most accessible mountain resort from southern New England, but skiers and riders will find great places to play in the snow up and down the spine of the Green Mountains. Each resort has its own personality, from Killington's "Beast of the East" bravado to the far-flung slopes of Jay Peak. Here are some favorite places to get in some turns:

Tucked into the hills of the Mad River Valley, **Sugarbush** and **Mad River Glen** offer two entirely different takes on the resort experience. **Sugarbush** (1840 Sugarbush Access Rd., Warren, 802/583-6300 or 800/537-8427, www.sugarbush.com, $84-91 adults, $65-71 seniors and youth 7-18, children under 7 free) has more than 100 trails descending from two main peaks, with high-speed chairs, extensive grooming, and terrain for everybody. **Mad River Glen** (Rte. 17, 5 miles west of Waitsfield, 802/496-3551, www.madriverglen.com, $60-75 adults, $55-59 seniors and youth 6-18) is the crusty old-timer of the Vermont world—keep your eyes out for leather telemark boots on the trails, where no snowboards are allowed. The cooperatively owned Mad River Glen calls itself a place where "skiing is still a sport, not an industry," which means limited grooming or snowmaking.

The mountains get bigger and more dramatic as you head north, and **Stowe** (7416 Mountain Rd., Stowe, 800/253-3000, www.stowe.com, $92-124 adults, $82-114 seniors, $72-104 children) towers above them all, climbing the slopes of Mount Mansfield, the highest peak in Vermont. Fancy base lodges and resort amenities make this Vermont skiing at its most elegant, but the mountain itself is the real draw: There are 40 miles of riding, a superfast gondola, and extensive snowmaking that smooths over the pesky Eastern thaws. Just on the other side of the mountains, **Smugglers' Notch** (4323 Rte. 108, Jeffersonville, 800/370-3186, www.smuggs.com, $72 adults, $54 youth 6-18 and seniors) has positioned itself as the family-friendly mountain, with lots of kids classes and a money-back "fun guarantee."

As far north as you can go, **Jay Peak Resort** (4850 Rte. 242, Jay, 802/988-2611, www.jaypeakresort.com, $72 adults, $47 seniors, $57 youth 6-18, $16 children 5 and under) gets a massive amount of snow on 50 miles of trails, with legendary glades and lots of backcountry terrain just beyond the patrolled boundaries.

And the skiing doesn't stop with the downhill resorts—many resorts have cross-country areas, and there are purpose-built destinations for cross-country skiers around the state. Two great options are the 60 miles of trails at **Trapp Family Lodge** (700 Trapp Hill Rd., Stowe, 802/253-8511 or 800/826-7000, www.trappfamily.com, $25 adults, $20 seniors, $15 youth 12-18, $10 children 6-11, children under 6 free), or the Northeast Kingdom's **Craftsbury Outdoor Center** (535 Lost Nation Rd., Craftsbury Common, 802/586-7767, www.craftsbury.com, $10 adults, $5 students and seniors, children 6 and under free), whose massive network of trails is popular with both skate and classic skiers.

3pm-10pm Mon.-Thurs., 11:30am-11pm Fri.-Sat., 11am-10pm Sun., $18-50) is a popular spot. Its steaks are superlative, there's an appealing raw bar, and the apple pie is a delight. The Tavern bar menu includes a more relaxed selection of sandwiches. Don't miss the ice-skating pond, just beside the restaurant.

You won't miss **Liquid Art** (37 Miller Brook Rd., 802/422-2787, www.liquidartvt.com, mid Nov.-May 8am-9pm Mon.-Tue., 8am-10pm Wed.-Fri., 7am-10pm Sat., 7am-9pm Sun.; hours vary in off-season, $4-10) in an eye-catching blue building beside Killington Road. It always opens an hour before the lifts and has a hearty breakfast menu and locally roasted coffee. The menu is available all day, and the sandwiches and light fare include the most plentiful vegetarian options in town.

With a cozy feel and a popular bar, **The Garlic** (1724 Killington Rd., 802/422-5055, www.thegarlicvermont.net, 5pm-10pm Mon.-Fri., 4pm-10pm Sat.-Sun., $10-30) serves Italian classics like osso buco and pasta puttanesca that are perfect for a post-ski meal. It's cozy, dim, and the closest that Killington's eateries get to subdued.

The cheerful early birds at **Sunup Bakery** (2250 Killington Rd., 802/422-3865, www.sunupbakery.com, 7am-5pm Mon.-Fri., 6:30am-5pm Sat.-Sun. Nov.-Apr., 7am-3pm Fri.-Sun. May-June, 7am-3pm Thurs.-Mon. July-Oct., $3-8) will get you adventure-ready with a carb-loaded lineup of pastries (seriously, try the espresso bread pudding muffin), soups, and sandwiches of every stripe. The café uses plenty of local ingredients and is housed in a perky chalet on the main road.

ACCOMMODATIONS AND CAMPING

$100-150

The rooms at the **Killington Motel** (1946 Rte. 4, 800/366-0493, www.killingtonmotel.com, $119-240) are clean and comfortable, and the owners, Robin and Steve, are friendly enough to inspire a loyal following who return year after year. The place has an unselfconsciously retro vibe, and is one of the best places for value in the area. Steve roasts coffee beans on-site, and wintertime rates include an appealing breakfast.

Several generations of Saint Bernards have greeted guests at the **Summit Lodge** (200 Summit Rd., off Killington Rd., 800/635-6343, www.summitlodgevermont.com, $99-219), which is as famous for its canine companions as it is for its congenial staff. Even though the lodge is only a few minutes away from Killington Resort, its position at the top of a steep hill makes it feel secluded. Rooms are nothing fancy but are quiet and clean, with friendly service. A pool and reading room offer extra relaxation.

$150-250

Twenty minutes away from the ski lifts, the **Red Clover Inn** (7 Woodward Rd., Mendon, 802/775-2290, www.redcloverinn.com, $199-340) feels a world away from Killington's bustling scene. Set on a rambling property that once housed a goat farm, the guest rooms retain a country charm and quiet that's enhanced by the lack of in-room televisions. The inn's restaurant and diminutive bar are enough to keep you in for the evening, with local beers, cocktails, and a well-crafted menu that makes the dining room a destination.

Over $250

If you book a slope-side room at the **Killington Grand Resort Hotel** (228 E. Mountain Rd., 802/422-5001, www.killington.com, $350 and up), you can spend your evening watching the grooming machines crawl up and down the mountain like glowworms. The comfortable rooms include access to the excellent health club, and there's a spa and restaurant on-site.

Camping

Gifford Woods State Park (34 Gifford Woods Rd., 802/775-5354, www.vtstateparks.com) has 4 cabins, 22 tent sites, and 20 lean-tos for overnights (campsites $18-29, cabins $48-50). The northern tent loop is much more secluded than the southern one. Several "prime" lean-tos are especially secluded in one of Vermont's only old-growth hardwood forests, made up of giant sugar maple, white ash, and beech trees.

INFORMATION AND SERVICES

The **Killington Chamber of Commerce** (2026 Rte. 4, 802/773-4181, 9am-5pm Mon.-Fri., 10am-5pm Sat.-Sun. June-Nov., 9am-5pm Mon.-Fri., 10am-2pm Sat.-Sun. Dec.-May, www.killingtonchamber.com) operates a visitors information center at the intersection of Route 4 and Killington Road. Near the same intersection is a branch of **Lake Sunapee Bank** (1995 Rte. 4, 802/773-2581). Additional ATM machines are available at **Merchants Bank** (286 Rte. 7 S., Rutland, 802/747-5000, 9am-5pm Mon.-Thurs., 9am-6pm Fri.) as well as at Killington Resort's base lodge. For condos and hotel reservations, you can also try the helpful **Killington Resort's Central Reservations** (800/621-6867), which is especially useful for large groups.

GETTING THERE AND AROUND

Killington is the high point of Route 4, and towers over the intersection with Route 100. For such a popular destination, public transport options are limited. It's possible to schedule pickup service with **Killington Transportation** (802/770-3977) from Rutland or White River Junction. Within Killington, the resort offers shuttle bus service between the various base lodges and nearby lodging. Ski buses depart for Killington from **Boston** (508/340-1034, www.newenglandsnowbus.com, $50-89) and **New York City** (www.ovrride.com, from $129), which can be a great deal as a transport/lift tickets/lodging package.

Mad River Valley

The peaks that flank the Mad River Valley seem to protect it from passing time. A blend of pastoral beauty and culture have made it a haven for artists, farmers, and eccentrics, while the valley's two ski resorts have grown into serious skiing destinations.

It's a compact place—just 30 minutes from one end to the other—and nowhere else in Vermont can you find such iconic, varied scenery and activities so close together. Incredible skiing, vibrant agriculture, forested hikes to waterfalls, and impeccable food and drink make this spirited region a perfect distillation of the state.

WARREN

Not a shingle is out of place in Warren's achingly cute center, whose general store, artists' studios, and single elegant inn look more like a movie set than a real town. But this rural community is also home to Sugarbush resort, a sprawling cluster of six peaks with 53 miles of trails, not to mention an additional 2,000 acres of wild backcountry.

And while Warren might seem a bit prim at first glance, there's serious verve behind the colonial facade. Immerse yourself in it during Warren's justifiably famous Fourth of July parade, an unrestrained celebration that is among the most independent of Vermont's Independence Day events. Locals spend the year constructing complicated floats with themes that range from politics to all-purpose Vermont pride, and accompany them through town in sundry dress (and undress).

There are no banks or ATMs in the tiny Warren center. The closest one is at the gas station two miles north of town: Mac's Market (114 Route 100, Warren, 802/496-3366, 9am-6pm daily).

Sights

Warren has its own covered bridge, the 55-foot-long **Warren Bridge,** which sports an unusual asymmetrical design. (The angles on the eastern and western sides are slightly different.) The bridge is off Route 100, just below downtown.

Events

Warren's Fourth of July parade is an unorthodox event that always seems more about the independence of small-town Vermont than the United States. Eye-catching floats and costumes often have a political theme that set this parade apart from simple flag waving, but it's also a welcoming and thoroughly entertaining glimpse of life in the Mad River Valley. The parade starts at 10am on Main Street, and festivities wrap up by 8:30pm. Fireworks are held at Sugarbush resort in the evening. The parade is free to attend, but a $1 donation is requested at the entrance to the town; in return, you'll receive a numbered "buddy badge." There's

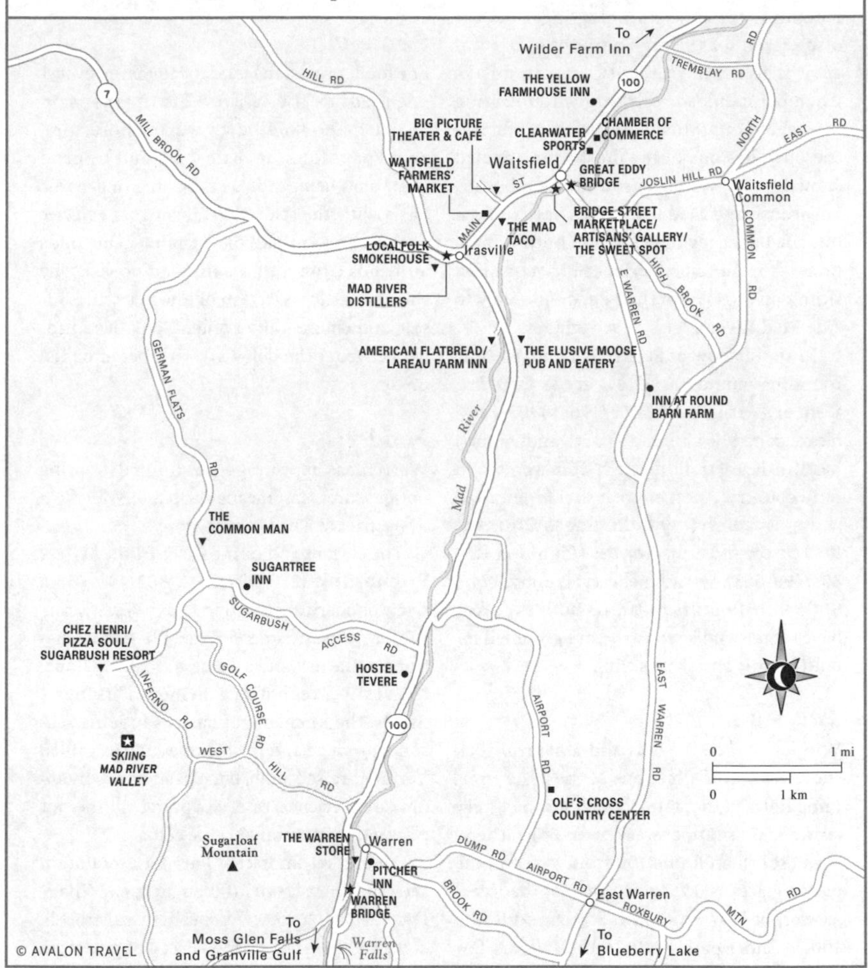

two of every number, and the badges are given out randomly. If you find your matching pair, the two of you can head to the village gazebo to collect a prize. Parking can be a challenge, but a free shuttle bus is available (www.madrivervalley.com/4th).

Sports and Recreation

★ SKIING

Once known as Mascara Mountain for its tendency to draw the jet-setting crowd, **Sugarbush** (1840 Sugarbush Access Rd., 802/583-6300 or 800/537-8427, www.sugarbush.com, $84-91 adults, $65-71 seniors and youth 7-18, children under 7 free) has come a long way to rightly earn its place as Vermont's "Second Slope," often favorably described as a more welcoming "alternative" to Killington. It's second to Killington in the number and difficulty of the slopes it offers. Sugarbush boasts 111 trails descending from two summits, Lincoln Peak and

Mount Ellen. But it may have the most difficult trail in the East: the rock-and-glade ride known as the Rumble. Sugarbush is also prized for the high amount of natural snow it gets each year, as storms from Lake Champlain unload their cargo after passing over the mountains. Not that it needs it—the Bush has one of the most sophisticated snowmaking systems around. As a bonus, Sugarbush and Mad River Glen have worked out lift packages that include both mountains—so you can experience big-mountain skiing on Sugarbush then head up-valley to ride Mad River Glen's gnarly glades.

In the shadow of Sugarbush and the surrounding mountains, **Ole's Cross Country Center** (Airport Rd., 802/496-3430, www.olesxc.com, $18 adults, $15 youth and seniors) has 30 miles of trails through deep woods and farm country. Another great spot for forested skiing is **Blueberry Lake Cross Country and Snowshoeing Center** (Plunkton Rd., 802/496-6687, www.blueberrylakeskivt.com, $14), with 19 miles of trails. Both ski areas have rentals and lessons and are groomed for both Nordic and skate skiing.

SWIMMING

With crystal clear pools and a natural rock slide, **Warren Falls** is one of the best swimming holes in the state, though it can be very crowded on summer weekends. To get there, travel south on Route 100 from Warren; the parking area is 0.75 mile south of the intersection of Warren's Main Street and Route 100. A short path leads to the falls. A few miles farther south in Granville (population 309), **Moss Glen Falls** is another scenic spot (without swimming, however). A multipitched cataract that drops 125 feet through a narrow gorge, the waterfall is just as beautiful frozen in winter as it is gushing in summer. A viewing platform is accessible from the highway. The falls themselves are part of the **Granville Gulf State Reservation,** a seven-mile stretch of pathless wilderness that is among the most scenic drives in the Green Mountains. Keep an eye out for the moose that frequent the area's streams and beaver ponds.

Shopping

For food, provisions, and local gossip, everyone heads to **The Warren Store** (284 Main St., 802/496-3864, www.warrenstore.com, 8am-7pm Mon.-Sat., 8am-6pm Sun.). Spend a few days here, and you'll be on a first-name basis with the friendly staff at this eclectic provisions shop, full of Vermont-made odds and ends (from pillows to salad bowls). The shop has a nice selection of unusual wines for sale and churns out excellent, creative sandwiches from the deli—all with bread baked on-site.

Food

Warren has appealing—but limited—dining options. Breakfast means a trip into Waitsfield or pastries at The Warren Store.

The elegant and refined **275 Main at The Pitcher Inn** (275 Main St., 802/496-6350, www.pitcherinn.com, 6pm-9pm Wed.-Mon., $26-36) boasts a superlative and hefty international wine list, and a menu to match. Global in its influences but local in most of its ingredients, the kitchen emphasizes organic seasonal produce and fresh game such as grilled Vermont-raised lamb. For a particularly memorable experience, reserve a private dinner for two in the restaurant's wine cellar.

An unlikely morsel of Paris in a mountain setting, **Chez Henri** (80 Sugarbush Village Dr., 802/583-2600, www.chezhenrisugarbush.com, 11:30am-11pm Mon.-Fri., 4:30pm-11pm Sat.-Sun., $19-43) makes dining a transporting experience. Classic bistro meals like *canard aux fruits* and onion soup *gratinée* are served in an intimate setting warmed by an open fire.

Snag thin-crust pizzas with all the fixings at **Pizza Soul** (Sugarbush Village, 802/496-6202, www.pizzasoul.com, 11:30am-8:30pm Sun. and Tues., 11:30am-4pm Wed., 11:30am-8:30pm, Thu., 11:30am-11pm Fri.-Sat., pizzas $14-23), a quirky joint right at the base of the mountain.

Accommodations

UNDER $100

If the valley's ubiquitous antiques and romance aren't for you, try the stylish ★ **Hostel Tevere** (203 Powderhound Rd., 802/496-9222, www.hosteltevere.com, dorm beds $38 summer, $40 winter). It's a convivial place to land after a day on the slopes or floating the Mad River, and the hostel's bar keeps some of the best local brews on tap. There's also a winter dart league on Thursday nights that's open to visitors, and the bar regularly hosts live music on Friday (early-to-bed types should request a dormitory that's farther from the stage). All dorms are mixed gender, with 5-7 beds; linens are provided, and towels are available for rent ($2).

$150-250

Right at the base of the Sugarbush access road, **The Warren Lodge** (731 Rte. 100, 802/496-3084, www.thewarrenlodge.com, $99-175) was entirely renovated in 2016 with a blend of rustic design and modern comfort. Motel-style standard rooms have refrigerators and flat-screen televisions, and there are a range of suites, a cottage, and an efficiency that are a good deal for groups.

OVER $250

Exquisitely decorated, the Relais & Chateaux-designated **Pitcher Inn** (275 Main St., 802/496-6350, www.pitcherinn.com, $425-800) houses 11 rooms and suites—each individually decorated in a Vermont theme and with Wi-Fi, CD players, TVs, whirlpool tubs, and radiant floor heating; a few have wood-burning fireplaces. There's also a stand-alone spa on the property, offering everything from hair care and pedicures to facials.

WAITSFIELD

Of this village's original settlers, 11 of 13 were veterans of the Battle of Lexington, the kickoff to the Revolutionary War. Bits of the original colonial architecture remain sprinkled throughout the town, which is the cultural center of the valley. Beyond the picture-perfect historical facades are start-up technology companies, artisans, and artists. It's a sophisticated community that enjoys an extraordinary quality of life.

Waitsfield's restaurants and accommodations make it a logical base for exploring the valley, and even if you're just passing through, it's a compelling place to pass an afternoon visiting little shops and enjoying the sunny beach by the town's covered bridge.

Sights

MAD RIVER GLEN

In an era of ski-resort consolidation, rising lift-ticket prices, and runaway base-lodge development, **Mad River Glen** (MRG, Rte. 17, 5 miles west of Waitsfield, 802/496-3551, www.madriverglen.com, $60-75 adults, $55-59 seniors and youth 6-18) has its own agenda. MRG is the only cooperatively owned ski resort in the United States, and the only one on the National Register of Historic Places. The 1,800 skier-owners still staunchly ban snowboards and limit grooming to about half the trails, mostly novice and intermediate pistes.

It's an unfashionable outlook that has earned passionate supporters, including a devoted set of lift-served telemark skiers, whom you can spot dropping their knees all over the hill. Mad River Glen's motto is "Ski it if you can," and the mountain's steep, narrow, and notoriously hairy advanced trails (about half the runs) are truly challenging. Experts should take a run at Paradise, a precipitous tumble down exposed ledges, rocky moguls, and a frozen waterfall to get to the bottom. In practice, though, the resort is a friendly, community-oriented place where families and skiers of all abilities are welcomed. Just don't try to sneak in a snowboard.

MAD RIVER DISTILLERS

Sample maple rum, bourbon whiskey, and other spirits at the Waitsfield tasting room of **Mad River Distillers** (Rte. 100 and Rte. 17, 802/496-3330, www.madriverdistillers.com, noon-6pm Wed. Sun.). This Warren-based distillery sources many of its ingredients from within the state, and the bottles have been racking up awards. Don't miss the Malvados, a Calvados-inspired apple brandy made with fruit from Shoreham's Champlain Orchards.

COVERED BRIDGE

Waitsfield's historical downtown is anchored by the 1833 **Great Eddy Bridge,** the second-oldest operating covered bridge in the state, which crosses the Mad River at the intersection of Route 100 and Bridge Street. (Only the Pulp Mill Bridge in Middlebury is older.) During the flooding following Hurricane Irene in 2011, the water line came up all the way to the base of the bridge, but the span stood, a testament to the nearly 200-year-old construction. There's also a little beach and swimming hole right under the bridge.

Entertainment and Events

The sophisticated, artsy vibe at **Big Picture Theater and Cafe** (48 Carroll Rd., off Rte. 100, 802/496-8994, www.bigpicturetheater.info, 8am-9pm daily) makes for one-stop evening fun—cutting-edge movies, film series, even an on-site restaurant where you can dine before the show ($9-18, reservations recommended).

During August, the whole valley comes alive for the month-long **Festival of the Arts** (802/496-6682, www.vermontartfest.com), in which the area's many artisans hold art shows and classes, and local restaurants and lodgings offer special rates and events.

Sports and Recreation

The Mad River Valley abounds with recreational activities. In addition to the suggestions below, the Mad River Glen ski area runs the **Mad River Glen Naturalist Program** (802/496-3551, www.madriverglen.com/naturalist), with guided tours that range from moonlit snowshoeing expeditions to wildlife-tracking trips to rock climbing.

HIKING AND BIKING

With a bit of a drive there's great hiking based out of Waitsfield, and three out of five of the peaks in Vermont above 4,000 feet rise from the Mad River Valley. While not the highest mountain in Vermont, the distinctly shaped **Camel's Hump** is one of the best loved. Originally named "Camel's Rump," its shape is identifiable for miles around, and its summit is a great chance to see the unique (and uniquely fragile) eastern alpine ecosystem.

The most popular ascent is up the seven-mile **Monroe Trail,** a rock-hopping ascent

skiing at Mad River Glen

from a birch-and-beech forest up to the unique alpine vegetation zone of its undeveloped summit. The parking area for the trail is at the end of Camel's Hump Road in Duxbury. There is a trail map available on the website for **Camel's Hump State Park** (www.vtstateparks.com/camelshump.html). The state park itself doesn't have a visitors center or services, but ample information on access is available on the website.

Two more peaks, **Mount Ellen** and **Mount Abraham,** can be hiked singly or together, following the Long Trail along the 4,000-foot ridge between them. For information on all of these hikes, contact the **Green Mountain Club** (802/244-7037, www.greenmountainclub.org), or pick up a copy of the club's indispensable *Long Trail Guide,* available at most bookstores and outdoors stores in Vermont.

This is an idyllic area for cycling, and you can take your pick of the Mad River Valley's beautiful back roads. If you're feeling ambitious, you can tackle the "gaps," the steep mountain passes that lead to the neighboring Champlain Valley. Lincoln Gap and Appalachian Gap, two of the steepest in the state, can be connected in a leg-punishing loop that does a staggering amount of climbing in 35 miles.

If the mountains seem too daunting, the **Mad River Path Association** (802/496-7284, www.madriverpath.com) manages several walking and biking trails that weave in and out of the villages of the valley, taking in farms, woodlands, and bridges along the way. Bicycles can be rented from **Clearwater Sports** (4147 Main St., Rte. 100, Waitsfield, 802/496-2708, www.clearwatersports.com, bike rental from $25/day).

BOATING AND TUBING

With a steady flow and the occasional patch of white water, the Mad River is ideal for anything that floats. **Clearwater Sports** (4147 Main St., Rte. 100, Waitsfield, 802/496-2708, www.clearwatersports.com) leads affordable all-day tours on the Mad and Winooski Rivers ($80 per person), as well as moonlight paddles. It also offers canoe and kayak rentals ($40-90) and inner tubes ($18), with an optional shuttle service. Book ahead when possible. For a quick dip, there's also swimming beneath the **Great Eddy Bridge** in downtown Waitsfield.

ICE-SKATING

Waitsfield's outdoor skating rink, the **Skatium** (Village Sq., 802/496-8909) is a community gathering place in winter. The rink has skate rentals during public skating hours, generally all day on Saturday and Sunday from early December to as long as the ice lasts, as well as other hours during the week that vary by season. During the winter, call the rink directly for a full schedule.

HORSEBACK RIDING

Ride in Viking style on an Icelandic horse. In addition to the usual walk, trot, canter, and gallop, they've got a fifth gait, the tölt, a fluid, running walk. The **Vermont Icelandic Horse Farm** (3061 N. Fayston Rd., 802/496-7141, www.icelandichorses.com, rides $60-200) breeds well-mannered purebreds for rides that last an hour or all day.

Shopping

Step into the **Artisans' Gallery** (20 Bridge St., 802/496-6256, www.vtartisansgallery.com, 11am-6pm daily), in the Old Village area of Waitsfield, and prepare to feel bewildered by the enormous selection. Upward of 175 local craftspeople sell their goods here, which means you'll have no problem finding jewelry, woodblock prints, hand-painted wooden bowls, and stoneware.

The most respected outdoors outfitter in the area, **Clearwater Sports** (4147 Main St., 802/496-2708, www.clearwatersports.com, 10am-6pm Mon.-Fri., 9am-6pm Sat., 10am-5pm Sun.) offers scads of gear and all the equipment rentals and guided tours you need to put it to proper use.

As in many of Vermont's small towns, the **Waitsfield Farmers' Market** (Mad River Green, 802/472-8027, www.

waitsfieldfarmersmarket.com, 9am-1pm Sat. May-Oct.) is one of the week's most important social events, where residents come down from the hills and stock up on community (and gossip) along with fresh produce and prepared foods. There is perhaps no better way to clue into the spirit of the valley than the boisterous event full of craft booths, organic produce from local farms, and stages full of folk, Latin, and Celtic musical performers.

Food

★ **American Flatbread** (48 Lareau Rd., 802/496-8856, www.americanflatbread.com, 5pm-9:30pm Thurs.-Sun., $7-16) has a devoted following, and deservedly so. Thursday-Sunday nights, the unassuming farmhouse setting turns into a party, swarmed by lovers of the organic menu of wholesome and gourmet pies, salads, and desserts made entirely from sustainable, farm-fresh Vermont ingredients. Reservations aren't accepted, but do as the locals do and show up at 5pm to put your name on the wait list. You can request a specific time to come back, or just wait by the bonfire with a pint until your name is called.

There's usually a crowd at **Localfolk Smokehouse** (Rte. 17 and Rte. 100, 802/496-5623, www.localfolkvt.com, 4pm-close Tues.-Sat., $6-17), a ramshackle-looking barbecue joint in an old Waitsfield barn. The menu has barbecue classics, tacos, and pub snacks, but regulars head straight for the meats: pulled pork, ribs, and chicken, smoked on-site and served with Southern-style sides. There's often music on weekends, and the late night local scene can be boisterous.

Tucked into an unpromising-looking cluster of shops on Route 100, ★ **The Mad Taco** (5101 Main St., 802/496-3832, www.themadtaco.com, 11am-9pm daily, $9-11) serves Mexican favorites with rebellious flair. Snag a burrito or taco loaded up with carnitas or yams, and head straight for the assortment of house-made salsas and hot sauces. They come in squeeze bottles marked with a heat rating of 1-10—the spicy stuff is no joke. The Mad Taco also has a bar stocked with favorite local brews on draft and a few Mexican options in bottles.

In an adorable riverside shop, **The Sweet Spot** (40 Bridge St., 802/496-9199, 8am-4pm Mon.-Thurs., 8am-6pm Fri.-Sat., 8am-2pm Sun., $2-8) is exactly that. Creative homemade tarts and cookies and quality espresso drinks, as well as a dreamy assortment of house-made ice creams make this a perfect place to fortify yourself for an afternoon's adventures. If you're looking for something a bit more bracing to go with your brownie, The Sweet Spot also serves a nicely chosen list of cocktails, including some classic ice cream drinks.

Accommodations

$100-150

Under the same ownership—and on the same property—as the lovably bohemian American Flatbread, **Lareau Farm Inn** (48 Lareau Rd., 802/496-4949, www.lareaufarminn.com, shared bath $100, private bath $125-145) names its rooms after principles its management holds dear—love, patience, and respect among them. The inn has the rambling feel of a family farmhouse and is enjoyably relaxed. With delicious breakfasts and free wireless Internet included—not to mention the attention of a genuinely warm staff—Lareau couldn't offer better value.

Bright, creative touches make the vibrant rooms at the ★ **Wilder Farm Inn** (1460 Rte. 100, 800/496-8878, www.wilderfarminn.com, $152-192) as appealing as the homey common areas and rambling grounds. The owners, Linda and Luke, have decorated each one in a different style—from shabby chic to contemporary—so check out the options before choosing where to lay your head. The inn lends guests snowshoes for winter outings and inner tubes for trips down the Mad River, just across the street.

On a quiet property just outside of town, the **Yellow Farmhouse Inn** (550 Old Country Rd., 802/496-4623, https://yellowfarmhouseinn.com, $149-159) is as comfortable as it is lovely: With woodstoves in the guest rooms, it is especially cozy in the winter. Home-baked cookies, lavish breakfasts, and friendly hosts make this a spot that many travelers come to year after year.

OVER $250

The ultraromantic ★ **Inn at the Round Barn Farm** (1661 E. Warren Rd., 802/496-2276, www.theroundbarn.com, $205-330) is a harmonious blend of old-fashioned style and thoughtful modern luxuries. Most rooms in the 19th-century farmhouse have skylights, king-size beds, whirlpool tubs, gas fireplaces, and jaw-dropping mountain views. Executive chef Charlie Menard prepares a multicourse breakfast that is both generous and refined, a memorable experience.

GETTING THERE AND AROUND

Waitsfield and Warren are both on Route 100, which is easily accessed from I-89. The **Mad Bus** (802/496-7433, www.madrivervalley.com) shuttle stops at various locations in Waitsfield and Warren, with connections to Sugarbush, Mad River Glen, and Montpelier.

INFORMATION AND SERVICES

The **Mad River Valley Chamber of Commerce** (4061 Rte. 100/Main St., 800/828-4748, www.madrivervalley.com) runs a small visitors information center with maps, brochures, and sporadic staffing. An ATM is located at **Chittenden Bank** (Mad River Shopping Center, 802/496-2585).

Montpelier

Wrapped by forested hills and bisected by the Winooski River, America's tiniest capital city has a small-town soul. Everyone seems to know each other in the downtown cafés, the natural food co-op, and at the traditional contra dances held at the Capital City Grange.

It's an easy place to explore on foot, and federal-style brick buildings and Victorian mansions lend a bit of pomp to the capital's diminutive downtown. At the center of it all is the gold-capped capitol, dramatic against a leafy backdrop that changes with the seasons. Just as America's founders intended, most of Vermont's representatives undertake political life as a kind of community-serving side hustle, so if the politicians look more like farmers, professors, and retirees than the average DC politico, that's because they are.

SIGHTS

State House

Montpelier's impressive **State House** (115 State St., 802/828 2228, www.legislature.vermont.gov, 7:45am-4:15pm Mon.-Fri., 11am-3pm Sat. July-Oct., guided tours every half hour 10am-3:30pm Mon.-Fri. late June-Oct.) dominates State Street with a 57-foot golden dome above a columned Renaissance Revival building that was built in 1859.

Fittingly for the state, the dome is topped by a wooden statue of Ceres, the goddess of agriculture. Look for a **statue of Ethan Allen,** the Revolutionary War figure, in the Greek Revival front portico, and a **cannon** that was seized at the Battle of Bennington (having completed Revolutionary service, it's now permanently trained on the Department of Motor Vehicles across the street). Tours of the building's interior take in statues and paintings of Vermont politicians who figured in state and national history, including Presidents Coolidge and Chester A. Arthur. You can also explore on your own, by accessing a cell phone **audio guide** (802/526-3221, vermontstatehouse.toursphere.com) that corresponds to numbered locations within the State House.

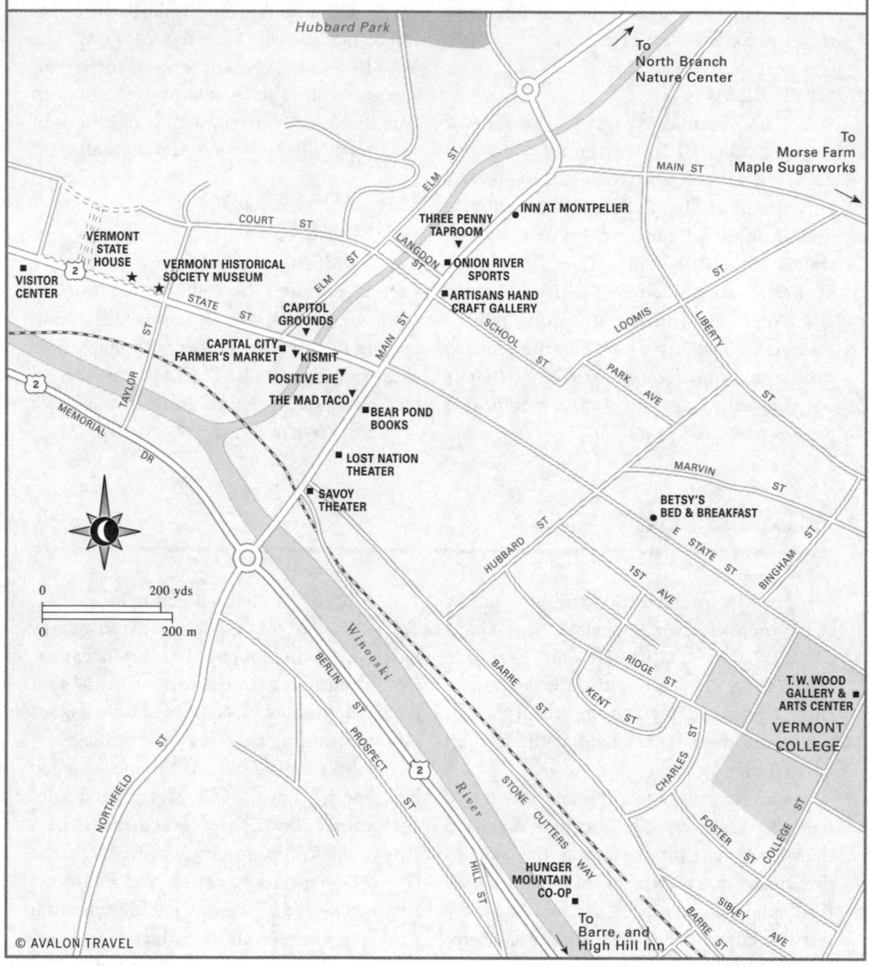

★ Morse Farm Maple Sugarworks

In Vermont, you are never far from a sugarhouse. On the edge of the city, seventh-generation Burr Morse has turned his farm into one of the premier maple syrup producers in the state. **Morse Farm Maple Sugarworks** (1168 County Rd., 800/242-2740, www.morsefarm.com, 9am-8pm daily late May-early Sept., 9am-6pm daily early Sept.-Christmas, 9am-5pm daily Christmas-late May, donations accepted) is a virtual museum of the industry, with old photographs and a "split-log" movie theater that shows a film of the sugaring process. A cavernous gift shop sells maple kettle corn and that most Vermont-y of treats, maple creemees (soft-serve maple ice cream cones).

Sugaring Off

Maple sap flows from a tap on a maple tree to produce maple syrup.

Spring in Vermont is better known as mud season, when frozen back roads melt into quagmires, and precipitation falls as a slushy wintry mix. But the period from mid-March until early April is also sugaring season, when a precise cycle of alternating freezes and thaws kick-starts the sugar maples' vascular systems and causes sap to flow. When that happens, sugarmakers collect the slightly sweet liquid by drilling tap holes in each tree and collecting the runoff in metal buckets or plastic tubing that runs through the forest like spider webs.

When they have enough sap, sugarmakers boil it in wide, shallow pans called evaporators, usually heated by wood gathered in the surrounding hills, and cook it down until it turns thick and golden—the ratio of sap to syrup varies from tree to tree, but averages around 40:1.

Sugaring is a social event in Vermont, and neighbors have a sixth sense for when someone's boiling. Over the course of an evening in the sugarhouse, friends will drop by for beer and conversation, along with shots of hot, fresh syrup, right out of the pan. Everyone's got a favorite sugaring snack, from hot dogs boiled in sap to syrup poured over vanilla ice cream, and you can discover yours at the yearly Maple Open House Weekend (www.vermontmaple.org, mid-Mar.), when sugarhouses around the state open their doors to visitors and prepare all the traditional treats. Don't miss sugar on snow, where syrup is cooked to a taffy-like consistency and served with a pickle.

Vermont Historical Society Museum

From the beginning of Vermont's history as an independent republic, its residents have struggled with the tension between "Freedom and Unity," the state motto that became a starting point for the complete renovation of the **Vermont Historical Society Museum** (109 State St., 802/828-2291, www.vermonthistory.org, 10am-4pm Tues.-Sat. May-mid-Oct., $7 adults, $5 students and seniors, children under 6 free, $20 families), a notably thoughtful journey back into the story of the state. Exhibits start with full-scale reconstructions of an Abenaki dwelling and the Revolutionary-era Catamount Tavern, and continue on to include Civil War artifacts, a room dedicated to Vermont-born president Coolidge, and even a collection on the early history of skiing. The gift shop has an extensive selection of books on Vermont history and culture.

Galleries

One of the best of Montpelier's galleries is also the oldest. The **T.W. Wood Gallery & Arts Center** (46 Barre St., 802/262-6035, www.twwoodgallery.org, noon-4pm Tues.-Sun.) has been showcasing the work of Vermont artists for more than 100 years, with a permanent collection of modern art and rotating shows by local contemporary artists.

Mary Stone's hand-sculpted clay animal whistles are just one of the unique crafts on display at the **Artisans Hand Craft Gallery** (89 Main St., 802/229-9446, www.artisanshand.com, 10am-6pm Mon.-Sat., noon-4pm Sun.), a hub for jewelry, pottery, woodwork, and metalwork from Vermont artisans.

ENTERTAINMENT AND EVENTS

With a destination-worthy beer list and a laid-back atmosphere, **Three Penny Taproom** (108 Main St., 802/223-8277, www.threepennytaproom.com) is Montpelier's best bar, and the adjoining restaurant serves appealing, dressed-up pub fare.

Montpelier's professional theater company, **Lost Nation Theater** (39 Main St., 802/229-0492, www.lostnationtheater.org) performs an eclectic mix of musicals, contemporary drama, and an annual fall Shakespeare production. The **Savoy Theater** (26 Main St., 802/229-0509, www.savoytheater.com) screens first-run and classic art films.

FOOD

Moody decor and sophisticated food have made **Kismet** (52 State St., 802/223-8646, www.kismetkitchens.com, 5pm-9pm Wed.-Fri., 8am-2pm and 5pm-9pm Sat., 9am-2pm Sun., $20-27, prix fixe $40) Montpelier's classic date-night restaurant; couples dine on tortellini with baked ricotta and pistachio butter, or crimini en croute (crimini bathed in garlic butter). Brunch is served on the weekends and is sublime: Think savory bread pudding with bone marrow broth, and eggs *en cocotte.*

Like its fraternal twin in Waitsfield, ★ **The Mad Taco** (72 Main St., 802/225-6038, www.themadtaco.com, 11am-9pm daily, $9-11) serves Mexican fare with an anarchic Yankee streak. The menu is the same as at the Waitsfield location, and tortillas come filled with classics like carnitas and pork *al pastor,* or culinary mashups: Try the smoked pork with kimchi and cilantro. The beer and the food are often local, and the hefty burritos are memorable.

Bringing a welcome serving of Southern cuisine to Montpelier's restaurant scene, **Down Home Kitchen** (100 Main St., 802/225-6665, www.downhomekitchenvt.com, 8am-2pm daily, $10-15) serves hearty, comforting food in a cheery space downtown. Meat and three, griddle cakes, and fried chicken are based in fresh, often local ingredients, with excellent coffee and beer to go alongside.

For years, **Bohemian Bakery** (78 Barre St., 802/461-8119, www.bohemianbakeryvt.com, 7:30am-1:30pm Wed.-Fri., 8am-2pm Sat.-Sun., $2-9) was based out of a tiny house in the northern woods, open to the public just one day a week, so sweets-lovers rejoiced when Bohemian opened a Montpelier shop in 2017. Favorites include the wonderfully flaky croissants, caramel-crispy kouign amann, and palm-sized fruit tarts, and there are savory pastries and hearty quiche for lunch.

FARMERS MARKETS

Artisans and growers come out of the woodwork for the **Capital City Farmers Market** (State St. at Elm St., 9am-1pm Sat. May-Oct.), one of the best in the state. Vendors include the highly sought-after (and scarce) **Lawson's Finest Liquids** brewery, which isn't open to the public.

ACCOMMODATIONS

$100-150

In the heart of downtown, **Betsy's Bed & Breakfast** (74 E. State St., 802/229-0466, www.central-vt.com/web/betsybb, $85-190) has 12 guest rooms spread between two Victorian mansions decorated with period antiques. The interiors are a bit timeworn and dark, but the friendly owners, Betsy and Jon, serve delightful breakfasts.

Drift off to the sounds of crickets and frogs (or falling snow) at ★ **High Hill Inn** (265 Green Rd., East Montpelier, 802/223-3623, www.highhillinn.com, $132-170). Comfortable rooms and a relaxed country setting make this hilltop inn feel like a getaway. The generous breakfast spread is a highlight.

$150-250

Two gracious federal-style buildings (with no fewer than 10 fireplaces) comprise the **Inn at Montpelier** (147 Main St., 802/223-2727, www.innatmontpelier.com, $150-250). The antiques-filled common areas lead into 19

Vermont's Northeast Kingdom

Wilder and more rural than the rest of the state, the northern part of Vermont between Jay Peak and New Hampshire is the Northeast Kingdom, often called simply The Kingdom. There's deep, dark forests here, mountains that rake huge piles of snow from the clouds, hippie communities, and some serious redneck credentials. Sights are scattered across the landscape, but this is the place to go for Vermont's best mountain biking, hallucinogenic performance art, beautiful scenery, and a small-town library with world-class art. Here are the very top picks for exploring the Kingdom.

Go Mountain Biking at Kingdom Trails (Kingdom Trail Association, 478 Rte. 114, East Burke, 802/626-0737, www.kingdomtrails.org, $15). Carriage paths, railroad right-of-ways, and single-track have been stitched together into a cyclist's wonderland, more than 100 miles of riding that ranges from fast and flowy to rocky and technical. There are trails for every ability, and it's easy to rent bikes on-site.

Line Up for the "World's Best Beer" at Hill Farmstead Brewery (403 Hill Rd., Greensboro Bend, 802/533-7450, www.hillfarmstead.com, noon-5pm Wed.-Sat.). True believers come from around the country to this rural brewery, bringing empty growlers to fill with Shaun Hill's creations. The brewery has repeatedly snagged the title of "best in the world," though many would dispute the honor, and the beer is undeniably fabulous.

Catch a Show at Bread and Puppet (753 Heights Rd., Glover, 802/525-3031, www.breadandpuppet.org, 10am-6pm daily June-Oct., free). Giant puppets, progressive politics, and a fierce ethos of "cheap art" have kept this wild and rural theater fresh since the 1970s. Bring a lawn chair and a sun hat, and join the crowd at Bread and Puppet's outdoor amphitheater.

Paddle Lake Willoughby (96 Bellwater Ave., Barton, 802/525-6205, www.vtstateparks.com/htm/crystal.htm, late May-early Sept.). A glacially carved lake flanked with high cliffs, this is a stunning body of water, especially when autumn foliage lights up the surface of the lake.

Browse the Stacks at the St. Johnsbury Athenaeum (1171 Main St., St. Johnsbury, 802/748-8291, www.stjathenaeum.org, 10am-5:30pm Mon., Wed., and Fri., 2pm-7pm Tues. and Thurs., 10am-3pm Sat.). A tiny library with lofty aspirations, this is one of a handful of athenaeums in New England—loaning libraries that take their name from ancient temples to Athena, the Greek goddess of wisdom. Hidden in the back is a magnificent art collection, including some fine examples from the Hudson School.

Eat and Drink at the Northeast Kingdom Tasting Center (150 Main St., Newport, 802/334-1790, www.nektastingcenter.com, 8am-8pm Mon.-Sat., 9am-3pm Sun.). Try cheese, locally brewed beer, and Kingdom-baked bread, but the real highlight of a trip to this tasting center is sampling ice cider, a sweet, nectar-like answer to old-world ice wine, made from frozen cider.

neat rooms, with canopy beds, colonial-style bureaus, and walls ranging from tomato-red to bold floral. A simple breakfast is served in the old-fashioned dining room, and in warm months, the gracious porch is the perfect place to watch the town drift by. Book well ahead during the legislative session (Jan.-Apr.).

INFORMATION AND SERVICES

Across from the State House, the **Capital Region Visitors Center** (134 State St., 802/828-5981, 6am-5pm Mon.-Fri., 9am-5pm Sat.-Sun.) has lots of brochures, maps, and advice on area attractions.

ATMs are available at many downtown locations, including at **Citizens Bank** (7 Main St., 802/223-9545). In an emergency, contact **Vermont State and Montpelier City Police** (1 Pitkin Ct., 802/223-3445).

GETTING THERE AND AROUND

Montpelier is located directly off I-89 at exit 8, and at the confluence of Route 2 and Route 302 from New Hampshire.

Amtrak (800/872-7245, www.amtrak.com) runs trains to Junction Road in Montpelier. Buses from **Green Mountain Transit** (802/864-2282, www.ridegmt.com) link Montpelier with Burlington on weekdays only. Taxi service is available from **Green Cab** (802/864-2424, www.greencabvt.com), and the **Green Mountain Transit Agency** (802/223-7287, www.gmtaride.org) operates bus routes around Montpelier and Barre.

Stowe

Upon arrival in Stowe's center, you might find that the curated cuteness of downtown—white church spire, alpine-style buildings, boutique shops—seems slightly clichéd. But this particular New England town is an original, the real deal, and helped define the genre of adorable mountain resorts. Tourists have been coming here since the Civil War, drawn to the remarkable scenery, rugged culture, and endless opportunities for outdoor adventure that continue to attract visitors from around the world. This is mountain living gone upscale, and if Stowe has acquired a commercial sheen since its founding in 1763, it's still got deep Vermont roots, with great dining and appealing accommodations that make it an excellent base for exploring the northern Green Mountains.

SIGHTS

Stowe Mountain Resort

Climbing the slopes of Mount Mansfield, Vermont's highest peak, **Stowe Mountain Resort** (7416 Mountain Rd., 800/253-3000, www.stowe.com, $92-124 adults, $82-114 seniors, $72-104 children) is one of the state's best downhill destinations. The base lodge is chic, the lifts are fast, and there's a massive snowmaking operation that keeps the mountain chugging even in chancy weather. A gondola links Mount Mansfield with the neighboring Spruce Peak, and even on busy weekends, the massive trail system means there's always some clear space to get in some turns.

In the summer, Stowe Mountain Resort operates an eight-person, high-speed **gondola skyride** (Mountain Rd./Rte.

Route 108 near Smugglers' Notch

108, 800/253-4754, www.stowe.com, 10am-4:30pm late June-mid-Oct., round-trip $28 adults, $17 youth 6-12, $84 families) up to the summit that takes in views of the village and surrounding mountains on the way.

Stowe Mountain Toll Road and Smugglers' Notch

It's also possible to drive to the summit of Mount Mansfield on the winding, unpaved **Stowe Mountain toll road,** which takes off from Route 108 at the **Toll House Conference Center** (5781 Rte. 108/ Mountain Rd., tolls $23 car and driver, $8 each passenger, children 4 and under free). The 4.5-mile-long road is closed to motorcycles, RVs, and bicycles, and climbs steeply to the "nose" of Mount Mansfield, where it's possible to park and continue to the "chin," the highest summit, on a 1.3-mile, one-way walking trail.

The views are spectacular, but for a scenic drive without the toll, just keep winding up **Route 108,** an incredibly twisty, curving road that's hemmed in by high cliffs, granite boulders, and trees that turn bright gold in the fall. Route 108 climbs through Smugglers' Notch, a mountain pass said to have been used to bring contraband from Canada during the years of Prohibition. Oversized vehicles should stay away, and all drivers should approach this road with great care, as hikers, rock climbers, and cyclists are often hidden behind the sharp corners.

Brewers and Distillers

Stowe is blessed with a wealth of locally made craft alcohols, starting with the Austrian lager beers at **Von Trapp Brewery & Bierhall** (1333 Luce Hill Rd., 802/253-5750, www.vontrappbrewing.com, 11:30am-9pm daily). Favorites include the malty Vienna Style Lager and the Helles Lager, and the Bierhall's menu of Austrian pub food—think cheddar and beer soup, hot soft pretzels, and many kinds of sausages—are perfect pairings for the entire lineup.

In contrast, the beers at **Idletyme**

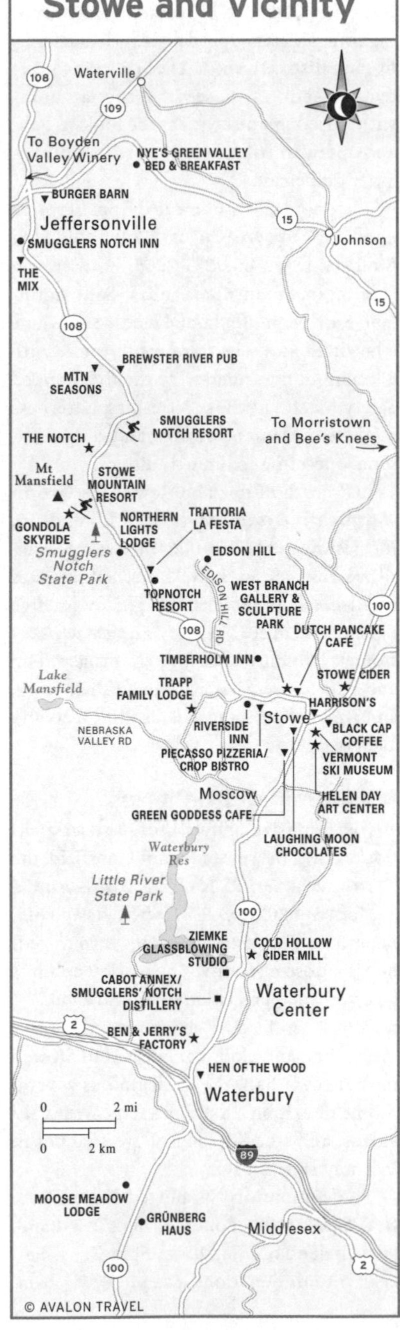

Brewing Company (1859 Mountain Rd./ Rte. 108, 802/253-4765, www.idletymebrewing.com, 11:30am-9pm daily) are defined only by their distinctiveness. The brewer is consistently creative, with seasonal specials along with a list of mainstays: Try the Pink 'n' Pale, an American pale ale brewed with a hint of bitter grapefruit.

Taste hard ciders fermented from Vermont apples at **Stowe Cider** (1799 Rte. 108/ Mountain Rd., 802/253-2065, www.stowecider.com, noon-6pm Thurs.-Sat., noon-5pm Sun.-Mon., flight of 4 ciders $6), where a husband-and-wife team gets creative with a lineup of dry ciders. Try the dry-hopped Safety Meeting, whose refreshing bitterness might tempt craft beer lovers, and sample seasonal one-offs and limited editions.

Just north of town on Route 100, **Green Mountain Distillers** (171 Whiskey Run, Morristown, 802/253-0064, www.greendistillers.com, noon-5pm Thurs.-Sat.) makes small-batch, organic vodka, gin, and maple liqueur, and in 2017, released an aged whiskey from its handmade pot still. The owners, Tim and Howie, are passionate about their work, and are amazing sources of distilling facts and alcohol lore.

Museums and Galleries

If you fantasize about laying the first ski tracks down the side of Mount Mansfield, the **Vermont Ski and Snowboard Museum** (1 S. Main St., 802/253-9911, www.vtssm.com, noon-5pm Wed.-Sun., donations encouraged) offers a dose of reality. The history exhibits give you an appreciation of just how gutsy it was to ski in the days before modern equipment, lifts, and clothing. Located in Stowe's former town hall, the museum has several rooms of exhibits, a plasma screen with ski videos, and a hall of fame of great names in Vermont skiing history.

The community-supported **Helen Day Art Center** (90 Pond St., 802/253-8358, www.helenday.com, 10am-5pm Tues.-Sat. year-round, donations accepted) has been dedicated to showcasing local art for more than 25 years. It inhabits the 2nd floor of a Greek Revival building in the center of town, with a sculpture garden out back.

A more extensive sculpture garden fills the grounds of the **West Branch Gallery and Sculpture Park** (17 Towne Farm Ln., 802/253-8943, www.westbranchgallery.com, 10am-5pm Tues.-Sun. year-round, free), where contemporary art has a bucolic backdrop about a mile north of town.

ENTERTAINMENT AND EVENTS

Nightlife

Mountain Road is lined with lively bars and restaurants for après-ski recovery, and most sport fireplaces, rustic decor, and the kind of comforting snacks that go well with beer. In addition to **Doc Ponds** and **The Bench** (see the *Food* section for listings), **Piecasso Pizzeria & Lounge** (1899 Mountain Rd., 802/253-4411, 11am-11pm daily, www.piecasso.com) is a local favorite, with lots of seats at the bar, creative pizza, and undeniably scrumptious chicken wings. This is the kind of bar where kids are welcome and comfortable.

Festivals and Events

The Trapp family keeps the hills alive (with the sound of classical music) by hosting **Music in our Meadow,** a series of outdoor performances in partnership with **Stowe Performing Arts** (802/253-7729, www.stoweperformingarts.com). And the **Stowe Theatre Guild** (67 Main St., 802/253-3961, www.stowetheatre.com) presents crowd-pleasing musicals throughout the year at the Stowe Town Hall Theatre.

Ski jumping and ice-sculpture carving shake Stowe out of the winter doldrums during the **Stowe Winter Carnival** (www.stowecarnival.com, late Jan.). A highlight is the Village Night Block Party, which fills the streets with bulky parkas and merriment.

SHOPPING

Sweets lovers can follow their noses to **Laughing Moon Chocolates** (78 S. Main St., 802/253-9591, www.laughingmoonchocolates.com, 9am-6pm daily), where confections are handmade on-site. True devotees can sign up for chocolate-dipping workshops ($125 for 2 people).

Artist Susan Bayer Fishman owns and runs **Stowe Craft Gallery** (55 Mountain Rd., 802/253-4693, www.stowecraft.com, 10am-6pm daily, until 7pm holiday season), an epic collection of many other artists' works—knickknacks like pewter measuring cups, glazed vases, and hand-carved backgammon sets.

SPORTS AND RECREATION

Winter Sports

Behind the Trapp Family Lodge, the **Trapp Family Lodge Touring Center** (700 Trapp Hill Rd., Stowe, 802/253-8511 or 800/826-7000, www.trappfamily.com, $25 adults, $20 seniors, $15 youth 12-18, $10 children 6-11, children under 6 free) has some 100 kilometers of cross-country ski trails through both groomed and ungroomed forest and meadowland. Plan your ski to pass by the **Slayton Cabin,** Trapp's hilltop warming hut, where you can cozy up with hot chocolate by the fire. Rentals are available on-site.

Or you can dash through the woods to the sound of sleigh bells and draft horses, as Trapp Family Lodge offers open sleigh rides each weekend ($25 adults, $15 children 4-12, children under 4 free), or book a private sleigh ride ($95 couple, $22 child).

For gravity-powered entertainment, rent a toboggan from **Shaw's General Store** (54 Main St., 802/253-4040, www.heshaw.com, 9am-6pm Mon.-Fri., 9am-5pm Sun.), or a more extreme sled from **Umiak Outdoor Outfitters** (849 S. Main St., 802/253-2317, www.umiak.com, 9am-6pm daily, $25 per day), which features the latest from Mad River Rockets and Hammersmith, and will point you to the vertiginous heights on which to test them. The best spot for sledding right in Stowe is Marshall's Hill, just behind the elementary school; to get there, turn onto School Street at **Black Cap Coffee** (144 Main St.).

Hiking and Biking

Leaving from the top of the Smugglers' Notch road, a steep, 1.1-mile hike leads to scenic **Sterling Pond,** a scenic body of water that is dazzling in autumn. To reach the trailhead from Stowe village, drive 8.9 miles north on Route 108, then park in the Smugglers' Notch Visitor Center parking lot on the left. The trail departs from just across the street, following blue blazes to the lake. Once there, an additional loop trail continues around the 1.4-mile perimeter of Sterling Pond.

An easier hike is the 1-mile walk to **Moss Glenn Falls,** which flows into a series of swimming holes that are perfect for hot afternoons. From Stowe village, drive 3 miles north on Route 100, then turn right on Randolph Road. Take the first right, on Moss Glenn Falls Road, then continue 0.6 mile to a parking lot on the left. Another great swimming hole (at the end of an even shorter trail) can be found at **Bingham Falls.** To reach the falls from Stowe village, drive north on Route 108 for 6.4 miles, and watch for the trailhead and pullouts to the east of the road. It's a 0.5 mile hike to the falls.

Stretching 5.3 miles from Stowe village to Top Notch Resort on Mountain Road, the paved **Stowe Recreation Path** (802/253-6148, www.stowerec.org) twists back and forth across the West Branch River, with plenty of places to stop to swim and picnic along the way. The access point in Stowe village is behind the Stowe Community Church at 137 Main Street, and dogs are allowed on leash. Bikes are available for rent at several locations in town, including **AJ's Ski and Sports** (350 Mountain Rd., 800/226-6257, www.stowesports.com, $9 per hour, $19 for 4 hours).

For biking that's more dirt, less asphalt, head to the excellent **Cady Hill Forest** (parking lot on Mountain Rd. across from Town and Country Resort, 876 Mountain Rd., www.stowelandtrust.org), with 11 miles of singletrack that ranges from moderate and flowy to technical and rocky. Maps of the trails can be found on the Stowe Land Trust parking lot, and paper versions are for sale at most of the town's bicycle shops. Some sections of Cady Hill are groomed for fat biking during the winter months.

FOOD

With a fabulous beer list and lots of polished copper, **The Bench** (492 Mountain Rd., 802/253-5100, www.benchvt.com, 4pm-close Mon.-Fri., 11:30am-close Sat.-Sun., mains $15-20) serves pizzas, salads, and grown-up comfort food in a relaxed setting. There are 25 beers on tap, and in the snowy months it's hard to beat a seat at the bar, where you'll have a view of the wood-fired brick oven that's used for much of the menu (including the delightful roast duck).

Run by the chefs behind the James Beard Award-winning Hen of the Wood in Burlington, ★ **Doc Ponds** (294 Mountain Rd., 802/760-6066, www.docponds.com, 4pm-midnight Tues.-Thurs., 11:30am-midnight Fri.-Mon., $7-19) serves a menu of hearty snacks and comfort food, with burgers, smoked meats, and ample pickled vegetables.

Excellent espresso, teas, and filling breakfast sandwiches make **PK Coffee** (1880 Mountain Rd., 802/760-6151, www.pkcoffee.com, 7am-5pm daily) a good stop on the way up to the mountain, and the counter is stocked with locally made pastries, granola, and other treats.

Ten minutes south of the village, **Michael's on the Hill** (4182 Rte. 100, 802/244-7476, www.michaelsonthehill.com, 5:30pm-9pm Wed.-Mon., $28-43) is worth the trip for a special dinner. An elegant menu of European-influenced food prepared with many local ingredients is served in a converted farmhouse.

If you're detoxing from all that comfort food, seek out the **Green Goddess Café** (618 S. Main St., 802/253-5255, www.greengoddessvt.com, 7:30am-3pm Mon.-Fri., 8am-3pm Sat.-Sun., mains $6-10), where breakfast and lunch include great salads, fresh juice, and plenty of vegetarian options alongside hearty sandwiches and egg dishes.

Also, it's worth nothing that many of the listings in other sections of this chapter—notably the **Von Trapp Brewery & Bierhall, Piecasso Pizzeria & Lounge,** and **Idletyme Brewing Co.**—are also very worthwhile restaurants.

ACCOMMODATIONS AND CAMPING

Under $100

For travelers on a budget, you can't beat a room at the **Riverside Inn** (1965 Mountain Rd., 802/253-4217, www.rivinn.com, $69-139), a homey, somewhat ramshackle farmhouse with charming owners and a great location. Motel-style rooms out back are newer and have coffeemakers and microwaves. It's a good choice for families and groups, as some rooms come equipped with several beds.

$100-150

The rustic and comfortable **Timberholm Inn** (452 Cottage Club Rd., 802/253-7603, www.timberholm.com, $110-235) is convenient to the mountain and village and includes a three-course homemade breakfast and warm cookies in the afternoon. A hot tub, shuffleboard, and movie area make this a welcoming haven when the weather doesn't cooperate. If you're planning to ski, ask about packages with lift tickets.

Even closer to the slopes is **Northern Lights Lodge** (4441 Mountain Rd., 802/253-8541, www.stowelodge.com, $99-200), which offers hot breakfasts, a hot tub, and a sauna to help you prepare for (and recover from) your activities of choice.

Over $250

★ **Edson Hill** (1500 Edson Hill Rd., 802/253-7171, www.edsonhill.com, $175-500), which was redesigned in 2014, is drop-dead gorgeous, from the picture-perfect interior to its setting on a hill with killer views. Rooms include breakfast in an enchanting dining room, and with a plush tavern, craft drinks, and a menu of creatively wrought comfort food, you many never want to leave. The 38-acre property includes stables and hiking trails, as well as cross-country skiing (equipment is provided).

With loads of pampering and fantastic recreation for adults and kids, ★ **Topnotch Resort** (4000 Mountain Rd., 800/451-8686, www.topnotchresort.com, $385-535) wins the luxury-for-families award, hands down. Grown-ups can chill out on the slopes at either of the beautifully kept mountainside pools (one indoors, one outdoors) or in the glorious new spa's treatment rooms. Meanwhile, the children's activity program is extensive and well organized, so both they and mom and dad feel entertained by the day's end. Not for families only, the resort also manages to make couples feel catered to, with romantic dining at Norma's, sumptuously decorated suites with oversized tubs, and couples' massages.

Camping

With 20 walk-in sites and 14 lean-tos, the campground at **Smugglers' Notch State Park** (6443 Mountain Rd., 802/253-4014, www.vtstateparks.com/smugglers.html, tent sites $18-20, lean-tos $25-27) has a great location on Mountain Road and historic structures built by the Civilian Conservation Corps (CCC).

INFORMATION AND SERVICES

The **Stowe Area Association** (51 Main St., 877/467-8693, 9am-6pm Mon.-Sat., 11am-5pm Sun., www.gostowe.com) runs a welcome center at the crossroads of Main Street and Mountain Road. Wi-Fi Internet can be accessed around the corner at **Stowe Free Library** (90 Pond St., 802/253-6145, 9:30am-5:30pm Mon., Wed., Fri., noon-7pm Tue. & Thu., 10am-3pm Sat.). Also at Main and Mountain is a branch of **People's United Bank** (1069 Mountain Rd., 802/253-8525, 8:30am-4:30pm Mon.-Fri.).

Medical needs can be filled at **Heritage Drugs** (1878 Mountain Rd., 802/253-2544) as well as **Kinney Drugs** (155 S. Main St., Cambridge, 802/644-8811, 8:30am-8pm Mon.-Fri., 8:30am-7pm Sat., 9am-5pm Sun., pharmacy 8:30am-7pm Mon.-Fri., 8:30am-4pm Sat.). In an emergency, contact the **Stowe Police Department** (350 S. Main St., 802/253-7126).

GETTING THERE AND AROUND

Stowe village is at the intersection of Route 108 and Route 100, 15 minutes north of I-89. **Amtrak** has service to Waterbury, where you can catch one of the frequent buses to Stowe with **Green Mountain Transit** (802/864-2282, www.ridegmt.com).

During the winter months, the free **Mountain Road Shuttle** (www.gostowe.com) connects the village and the resort, with stops at major hotels along the way.

Burlington

With a mix of small-town reserve and urban sophistication, Vermont's largest city is the state's cultural heart. There are forested trails, organic farms, and beaches within the city limits, and on snowbound winter mornings you can spot cross-country skis lined up outside the coffee shops.

Throughout the summer, the waterfront fills up with sailboats and kayaks, and locals ditch work to cool off at their favorite swimming spots. The warm months are a frenzy of activity in Burlington, with almost-weekly festivals that flood the town with music, art, and food lovers.

Perched above it all is the stately University of Vermont, whose 12,000 students swell the population by almost 30 percent. The school was founded in 1791 by Ira Allen (Ethan's brother), and academic life remains an important source of energy for the town. This is not a place with a town-gown divide—on a Saturday night in Burlington you can raise a glass, cut a rug, or take a moonlight ski with sugarmakers, sociologists, and senators.

SIGHTS

★ Waterfront Park

A few decades of renovations have turned the **Burlington Waterfront** (1 College St., 802/865-7247), once a bustling lumber port, into a pedestrian-friendly park filled with art and native plants. The view is dramatic when the sun sets over the Adirondacks, so bring a picnic and watch as sailboats, paddleboards, and kayaks drift by. The bike path runs right through the middle of things, so if you've got two wheels or want to rent them, the waterfront is a great starting point. While you're exploring, see if you can find the statue of ***The Lone Sailor*** tucked behind the **ECHO Leahy Center for Lake Champlain.** The monument was cast with bronze from eight U.S. Navy ships, a fitting tribute on the shores of Lake Champlain, which saw key naval battles in the Revolutionary War and the War of 1812.

On summer days when the city is stifling, the best seat in town may be at the easy-to-miss **Splash at the Boathouse** (0 College St., 802/343-5894, www.splashattheboathouse.com, 11am-10pm daily May-Oct.,

the Burlington Waterfront

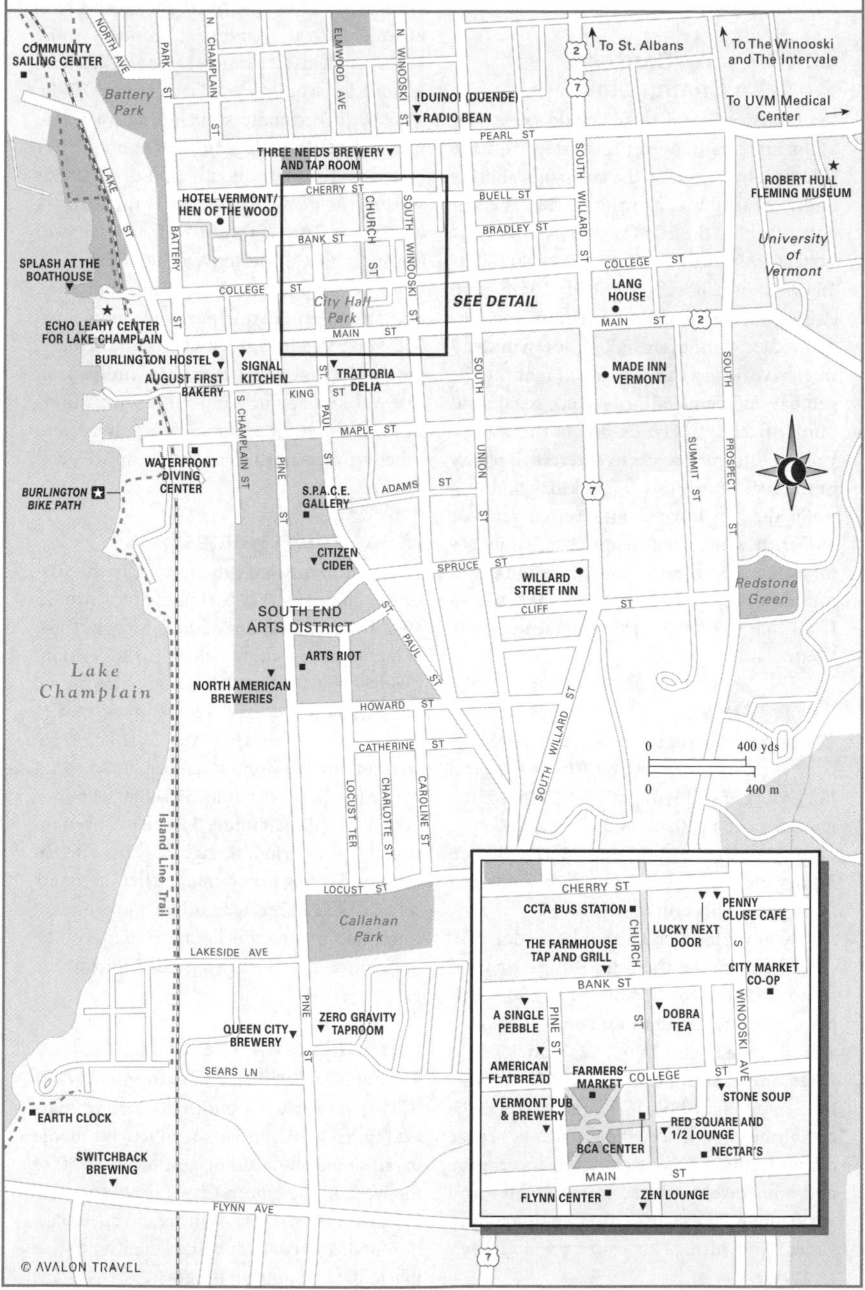
Burlington
COMMUNITY SAILING CENTER
Battery Park
!DUINO! (DUENDE)
RADIO BEAN
THREE NEEDS BREWERY AND TAP ROOM
HOTEL VERMONT/ HEN OF THE WOOD
SPLASH AT THE BOATHOUSE
ECHO LEAHY CENTER FOR LAKE CHAMPLAIN
BURLINGTON HOSTEL
AUGUST FIRST BAKERY
SIGNAL KITCHEN
TRATTORIA DELIA
City Hall Park
SEE DETAIL
To St. Albans
To The Winooski and The Intervale
To UVM Medical Center
ROBERT HULL FLEMING MUSEUM
University of Vermont
LANG HOUSE
MADE INN VERMONT
WATERFRONT DIVING CENTER
BURLINGTON BIKE PATH
S.P.A.C.E. GALLERY
CITIZEN CIDER
WILLARD STREET INN
Redstone Green
SOUTH END ARTS DISTRICT
ARTS RIOT
NORTH AMERICAN BREWERIES
Lake Champlain
Island Line Trail
Callahan Park
QUEEN CITY BREWERY
ZERO GRAVITY TAPROOM
EARTH CLOCK
SWITCHBACK BREWING
0 400 yds
0 400 m
CCTA BUS STATION
PENNY CLUSE CAFÉ
LUCKY NEXT DOOR
THE FARMHOUSE TAP AND GRILL
CITY MARKET CO-OP
A SINGLE PEBBLE
DOBRA TEA
AMERICAN FLATBREAD
FARMERS' MARKET
STONE SOUP
VERMONT PUB & BREWERY
RED SQUARE AND 1/2 LOUNGE
BCA CENTER
NECTAR'S
FLYNN CENTER
ZEN LOUNGE
© AVALON TRAVEL

$8-15) restaurant at the end of a dock on the waterfront. Snag an Adirondack chair for a stellar sunset view.

ECHO Leahy Center for Lake Champlain

With ancient coral reefs, whale skeletons, and a mythical monster in its depths, Lake Champlain is one of the most distinctive bodies of freshwater in the world. The scientists behind the **ECHO Leahy Center for Lake Champlain** (1 College St., 802/864-1848, www.echovermont.org, 10am-5pm daily, $16.50 adults, $14.50 seniors and students, $13.50 children 3-17, children under 3 free) have done a bang-up job of making the geology and fauna of the lake accessible and family friendly. "Hands-on" is the watchword at this small science center, with plenty of interactive exhibits to get kids good and wet while they learn about river currents or pull critters out of lake pools. There is plenty for nature-loving adults, too, like aquarium tanks full of the fish, turtles, snakes, and frogs that live beneath the surface of Lake Champlain.

Lake Tours

Check out Burlington from the water on the ***Spirit of Ethan Allen III*** (Burlington Boathouse, 348 Flynn Ave., 802/862-8300, www.soea.com, 10am, noon, 2pm, and 4pm daily May-Oct., $21 adults, $8.43 children 3-11), which has piped-in narration for its 1.5-hour sightseeing cruise.

If you prefer to hit the lake under sail, consider a trip on the beautiful gaff-rigged sloop ***Friend Ship*** (1 College St., 802/598-6504, www.whistlingman.com, May-Oct., $50 adults, $35 children 2-12), which offers three daily sailing cruises as well as two-, four-, and eight-hour private charters. It's a sublime experience when a steady breeze allows Captain Mike to shut off the engine and you travel to the sounds of water and wind alone. The cruises are two hours, and water is provided; bring your own food, beer, and wine.

University of Vermont and the Fleming Museum

University of Vermont (194 S. Prospect St., 802/656-3131, www.uvm.edu) educates some 12,000 students on a stately campus filled with historic brick buildings. Chartered in 1791 by a group of Vermonters, including Ira Allen, it was the fifth college in the country (after Harvard, Yale, Dartmouth, and Brown). For visitors, its prized attraction is the **Robert Hull Fleming Museum** (University of Vermont, 61 Colchester Ave., 802/656-0750, www.flemingmuseum.org, 10am-4pm Tues. and Thurs.-Fri., 10am-7pm Wed., noon-4pm Sat.-Sun., $5 adults, $3 students and seniors, children 6 and under free, $10 families), an art and archaeology museum with mummies, Buddhas, Mesoamerican pottery, and other artifacts from some of the world's great civilizations.

Ethan Allen Homestead

Today, Ethan Allen's name recalls the furniture company that was named for him in 1932, but Allen was one of the most colorful—and enigmatic—characters of early Vermont history. His modest Cape Cod-style home, known as the **Ethan Allen Homestead** (1 Ethan Allen Homestead Way, 802/865-4556, www.ethanallenhomestead.org, 10am-4pm daily May-Oct., $10 adults, $9 seniors, $6 children 5-17, children under 5 free), has been restored to the period, though only his kitchen table and a few other small Allen artifacts survive. The homestead offers a low-budget film exploring the conflicting accounts of the man himself, as well as a guided tour of the property.

Burlington Farmers' Market

The outdoor **Burlington Farmers' Market** (City Hall Park, www.burlingtonfarmersmarket.org, 8:30am-2pm Sat. May-Oct.) is a foodie paradise and one of the biggest social events of the week in the Queen City. Locals and visitors fill their baskets with fresh vegetables, hot food, and pastries while listening to live music and lounging on the grass. With dozens of vendors, you could browse all day, but don't miss the home-brewed soda at **Rookie's Root Beer** (the Dark Side is an addictive blend of espresso and root beer topped with molasses cream). If you're planning a picnic, pick up some excellent goat cheese at **Doe's Leap** to go with rye bread from **Slow Fire Bakery** or savory biscuits from **Barrio Bakery.** There are lots of sweet treats to choose from, but on a hot day you can follow the lines to **Adam's Berry Farm** for popsicles made from organic fruit, or to **The Farm Between** for what may be the world's best snow cones—try the black currant.

BCA Center

Art at the **BCA Center** (135 Church St., 802/865-7166, www.burlingtoncityarts.org, 11am-5pm Tues.-Thurs., 11am-8pm Fri.-Sat., also Sun. 11am-5pm May-Oct., free) explores contemporary themes with multimedia and interactive exhibitions in oversized gallery spaces. Some of its shows are more successful than others; all are provocative. A recent exhibit, for example, looked at perspectives from Iraq vets-turned-artists working in media including U.S. currency and flags and their own uniforms, to come to grips with their experiences in war.

Farm Tours

When flying into Burlington's airport, the city looks tiny, a tidy cluster of buildings surrounded by farms. It's worth getting out to one, because agriculture continues to be the cultural and financial mainstay of the state, and once you meet a few farmers you'll notice their names on menus all over town and leave with a deeper sense of place. Dairy continues to be the most significant agricultural product in the Champlain Valley, but locavore culture has made this fertile ground for a thriving community of small farmers who cultivate everything from grapes to grains.

A good place to start is **Vermont Farm Tours** (802/922-7346, www.vermontfarmtours.com, $75-125), which organizes visits to vintners, cheese makers, and other horticultural hot spots, as well as farm-oriented bike tours in the area. Chris Howell, the affable owner, also runs a monthly **Cocktail Walk** ($45) in Winooski that pairs local distillers and mixologists.

In July and August, the urban farming nonprofit **Intervale Center** (180 Intervale Rd., 802/660-0440, www.intervale.org) hosts **Summervale,** an agricultural hoedown each Thursday with music and food. They also organize free monthly tours of the on-site organic farms (call for details). Every Friday during the summer, the organic **Bread and Butter Farm** (200 Leduc Farm Dr., Shelburne, 802/985-9200, www.breadandbutterfarm.com) throws festive **Burger Nights,** with music, burgers (veggie and beef), hot dogs, and fixings from its cows and on-site bakery. The gorgeous spread is a 15-minute drive from downtown Burlington.

ENTERTAINMENT AND EVENTS

The best place to find out what's happening in the Queen City's nightclubs, theaters, and concert halls is in the free weekly paper *Seven Days* (www.7dvt.com) or on the Lake Champlain Region Chamber of Commerce website (www.vermont.org).

Bars

The last several years have seen an explosion of craft cocktail culture in Vermont, as creative bartenders bring the farm-to-table approach to mixing drinks using locally distilled spirits, artisanal bitters, and fresh ingredients of all kinds. Some of the best cocktail bars are also restaurants, like the superb **Juniper Bar at Hotel Vermont** (41 Cherry St., 802/651-0080, www.hotelvt.com, 7am-midnight daily), which stocks every single spirit made in Vermont and blends them into thoughtful drinks. Another fabulous restaurant bar is the one at **Pizzeria Verità** (156 St. Paul St., 802/489-5644, www.pizzeriaverita.com, 5pm-10pm Sun.-Thurs., 5pm-11pm Fri.-Sat.), whose Italian-inflected cocktails blend in a wide range of *amaro* liqueurs.

TOP EXPERIENCE

Burlington Breweries

Vermont has more breweries per capita than any other state, and many of its award-winning craft beers (and ciders!) are only available locally. It's a source of pride to beer-loving residents, who are always ready to debate the finer points of hop varieties and snap up tickets to Burlington's **Vermont Brewers Festival** (www.vtbrewfest.com, third weekend of July, $35) as fast as a case of Heady Topper (a notoriously hard-to-find canned beer made in Waterbury).

Conveniently, the downtown breweries are next door to one another, and the **Pine Street Arts District** is home to a cluster of young breweries that are easily reached by car or bus from the center. If all the options leave you thinking that you'd like a tour guide (and chauffeur), you can hop on the bus with **Burlington Brew Tours** (261 S. Union St., 802/760-6091, www.burlingtonbrewtours.com, $85), whose itineraries take you behind the scenes at some of the best breweries in town. Here are some favorites:

Zero Gravity Craft Brewery (115 St. Paul St., 802/861-2999, www.zerogravitybeer.com, 11:30am-close daily) has something for most beer lovers, starting with the flagship **Conehead,** a single hop wheat India pale ale that's brewed with Citra hops and is aromatic and hoppy without being overpowering. Another favorite is the **London Calling,** an English ordinary bitter that's malty and mellow—and not particularly bitter. The main location is tucked into the American Flatbread restaurant, but there's a newer outpost on Pine Street, **Zero Gravity Taproom** (716 Pine St., 802/497-0054, www.zerogravitybeer.com, noon-9pm Sun.-Mon. and Wed.-Thurs., noon-10pm Fri.-Sat.), which has all the same beers with an industrial-chic vibe.

Citizen Cider (316 Pine St., 802/448-3278, www.citizencider.com, noon-9pm Mon.-Thurs.) serves many varieties made from Vermont apples in a beautifully designed taproom. Tours tend to be impromptu but are a fascinating glimpse of the cider-making process. The five-glass flights are an excellent introduction to these unusual ciders: The sweetest of the bunch is the flagship **Unified Press,** but the ginger-spiked **Dirty Mayor** has a passionate following, as does the **Full Nelson,** which is dry hopped with Nelson Sauvin hops that give it a beer-like edge.

Queen City Brewery (703 Pine St., 802/540-0280, www.queencitybrewery.com, 2pm-7pm Wed.-Thurs., 2pm-9pm Fri., noon-7pm Sat., 1pm-5pm Sun.) makes European-style beers in a nondescript industrial building. The tasting room has more charm and is lined with old beer cans and historical images of Burlington. Try the hugely popular **Yorkshire Porter,** an English dark ale that's rich and full bodied, or **Argument,** an English India pale ale that's brewed true to style: strong and bitter.

Foam Brewers (703 Pine St., 802/540-0280, www.foambrewers.com, noon-10pm Mon.-Thurs., 11am-midnight Fri.-Sat., 11am-7pm Sun.) is a relatively recent addition to Burlington's beer scene, with hoppy, aromatic beers made by passionate beer geeks. A prime location on the Burlington waterfront, as well as pleasant outdoor seating, makes this a great place to linger over a flight, and the brewery serves charcuterie platters that make for perfect pairings.

And though it's not exactly a mixology destination, there is something transporting about a lazy afternoon at **Splash at the Boathouse** (0 College St., 802/658-2244, www.splashattheboathouse.com, 11am-10pm daily May-Oct.), where generic tropical bar decor complements the best views in town. Since Splash is built on a floating dock, you can drink your beer with your toes in the water while watching bare-chested yachties maneuver their powerboats in the marina's close quarters. (For Burlington's many beer-focused bars, see Callout.)

Live Music and Dancing

You can find something to shimmy to every day of the week in Burlington, where most bars stay open until 2am. There's always a full lineup at **Radio Bean** (8 N. Winooski Ave., 802/660-9346, www.radiobean.com), a bar and coffee shop packed with hipsters watching acts that range from traditional Irish to experimental jazz. **Honky Tonk Night** (10pm Tues.) is a good bet for swinging neo-country music.

On weekend nights, **Church Street Marketplace** is thronged with a lively college crowd that heads to **Red Square** (136 Church St., 802/859-8909, www.redsquarevt.com) or **Nectar's** (188 Main St., 802/856-4771, www.liveatnectars.com) to shake it off to DJ and live music.

It's always worth checking the lineup of high-quality indie groups that play at **Signal Kitchen** (71 Main St., 802/399-2337, www.signalkitchen.com) and **ArtsRiot** (400 Pine St., 802/540-0406, www.artsriot.com), who further their mission of "destroying apathy" by cooking up great shows and tasty, creative pub food. When bigger acts come through Burlington, though, they usually land at **Higher Ground** (1214 Williston Rd., South Burlington, 802/652-0777, www.highergroundmusic.com).

The Arts

A former vaudeville house, the **Flynn Center for the Performing Arts** (153 Main St., 802/863-5966, www.flynncenter.org) was restored to its art deco grandeur in 2000. It now serves as the cultural hub of the city, with musicals, dance performances, and shows by mainstream jazz and country acts from Diana Krall to Pink Martini.

The **South End Arts District** (802/859-9222, www.seaba.com) is home to many collective studios and galleries. They throw open their doors for the **First Friday Art Walk** (802/264-4839, www.artmapburlington.com) each month, which is free to attend; most galleries stay open 5pm-8pm. Don't miss the **S.P.A.C.E. Gallery** (266 Pine St., Ste. 105, 802/578-2512, noon-5pm Wed.-Sat.), which has a quirky mix of artist spaces that run the gamut from fine oil paintings to scary dolls.

Events

Burlington hosts a festival almost every weekend during the summer, and it's worth booking far ahead during those times, as hotels fill up quickly. For 10 days in early June, music lovers from around the region flock to the **Burlington Discover Jazz Festival** (www.discoverjazz.com, June). The town is filled with tunes, from ticketed events featuring big-name artists to free daily jazz sets in many restaurants, bars, and parks. And if you prefer brews to blues, don't miss July's **Vermont Brewers Festival** (802/760-8535, www.vtbrewfest.com, July), when a who's who of local and regional brewers sets up shop right in Waterfront Park. If you'd like to attend, check the website well in advance of your trip, as tickets often sell out the day they go on sale (usually in May).

One of the most energetic days on the lake is the picturesque **Dragon Boat Festival** (802/999-5478, www.ridethedragon.org, Aug.), a boat race in which teams of 20 paddle 40-foot brightly painted canoes to raise money for local charities. The winner is invariably the team that works the best together, not necessarily the strongest.

The summer wraps up with the **Grand Point North** (www.grandpointnorth.com, mid-Sept) festival, put on by hometown musical heroes **Grace Potter and the Nocturnals.** Two days of music feature an impressive lineup of bands on open-air stages on the Burlington Waterfront, and Sunday's final show is usually attended by a flotilla of kayaks and sailboats getting their tunes for free.

SHOPPING

Church Street Marketplace (2 Church St., 802/863-1646, www.churchstmarketplace.com, 10am-7pm Mon.-Thurs., 10am-8pm Fri.-Sat., 10am-6pm Sun.) is the pedestrian heart of Burlington, lined with restaurants, bars, and a blend of local and national stores. There's a handful of excellent outdoors gear stores, like **Outdoor Gear Exchange** (37 Church St., 802/860-0190, www.gearx.com, 10am-8pm Mon.-Thurs., 10am-9pm Fri.-Sat., 10am-6pm Sun.), which sells new and used equipment for every adventure imaginable, and the **Ski Rack** (85 Main St., 800/882-4530, www.skirack.com, 10am-7pm Mon.-Sat., 11am-5pm Sun.), whose collection of cross-country, backcountry, and alpine skis are the best in town. Both stores offer rental equipment for winter and summer sports.

Downtown Burlington also has two excellent locally owned bookstores: **Crow Bookshop** (14 Church St., 802/862-0848, www.crowbooks.com, 10am-9pm Mon.-Wed., 10am-10pm Thurs.-Sat., 10am-6pm Sun.) has a nice collection of used books and many local authors. **Phoenix Books** (191 Bank St., 802/448-3350, 10am-7pm Mon.-Wed., 10am-8pm Thurs.-Sat., 11am-5pm Sun., www.phoenixbooks.biz) has a broader selection of new books, including many options for regional travel.

SPORTS AND RECREATION

Walking and Biking

★ BURLINGTON BIKE PATH

Burlington is a great place to be a cyclist. If you've got wheels, the logical place to start is the **Burlington Bike Path** (Burlington Parks and Recreation, 802/864-0123, www.enjoyburlington.com), an eight-mile path that runs along the lake and connects several parks perfect for picnicking. A spur can connect via surface streets to **Ethan Allen Homestead** (1 Ethan Allen Homestead, 802/865-4556, www.ethanallenhomestead.org), where cyclists with dirt-appropriate tires can follow paths to the **Intervale,** a cluster of 11 organic farms strung out along the Winooski River.

At the far northern end of the path, you can continue onto the **Causeway,** an elevated path that has unparalleled views of the lake. On most summer weekends you can catch a **bicycle ferry** from the end of the causeway that will drop you and your bike on **South Hero Island.** For more information about the ferry, or to rent bikes, contact the nonprofit **Local Motion** (1 Steele St., 802/861-2700, www.localmotion.org, 10am-6pm daily May-Oct.), which is a great source of cycling maps, gear, and advice on where to ride.

WALKING TRAILS

You could stroll around downtown all day, but if you want to get your feet on some dirt there's some excellent natural areas right in town. The **Rock Point Center** (20 Rock Point Rd., 802/658-6233, www.rockpointvt.org, donations accepted) is owned by the Episcopal Church, which invites visitors to stroll around its forested property that juts dramatically out

view from the Burlington Bike Path on Lake Champlain

into the lake, making for showstopping sunsets. Stop by the diocese office for a free pass.

Rock Point's main rival for sunset watching is **Red Rocks Park** (Central Ave., South Burlington, 802/846-4108), which has well-maintained trails with great lake views. But in springtime, at least, you won't take your eyes off the ground, which is carpeted in wildflowers: look for Dutchman's-breeches, trillium, and columbine. For more information about parks, visit the **Burlington Parks and Recreation Department** website (www.enjoyburlington.com, 802/864-0123).

Boating

On sunny summer days, the lakefront fills with a cheerful flotilla of kayaks, canoes, and stand-up paddleboards, as locals and tourists alike head for the water. It's a wonderful way to explore the ins and outs of the shoreline, like the crags at Lone Rock Point and the forested peninsula just to the north of **North Beach** (60 Institute Rd. 802/862-0942). Look carefully at the rocks on the northern side of the outcropping and you'll see a clear divide between the pale, smooth dolomite rock that makes up the top of the cliff and the dark, crumbling shale at the base. It's an exposed thrust fault, where continental plates are colliding. You can rent a kayak or paddleboard right on the beach from **Umiak Outfitters** (802/651-8760, 11am-6pm daily mid-June-Labor Day, $20-30 for 2 hours).

Closer to downtown, the **Community Sailing Center** (234 Penny Ln., 802/864-2499, www.communitysailingcenter.org, hours vary, May-Oct, $15-55 per hour) has kayaks, paddleboards, and sailboats for use in Burlington Bay, and offers private and group classes if you want to brush up on your boat handling. Yogis ready to take their boat pose out for a spin should consider attending "Floating Yoga" classes taught on paddleboards (call for dates, $35).

FOOD

Before opening on the site of a national ham burger chain, **The Farmhouse Tap & Grill** (160 Bank St., 802/859-0888, www.farmhousetg.com, 11:30am-11pm Mon.-Thurs., 11:30am-midnight Fri., 10am-midnight Sat., 10am-11pm Sun., $16-24) asked the community to suggest names, and then held a vote on its favorites. The winner was "The Old McDonalds Farmhouse." Now known simply as The Farmhouse, this farm-to-table gastropub is popular for creative and comforting fare. The burgers are celebrated, but the starters, like the beef tartare with freshly made potato chips, are often standouts.

Right next door to the Zero Gravity Taproom, **The Great Northern** (716 Pine St., 802/489-5102, www.thegreatnorthernvt.com, 7am-9pm Mon.-Thurs., 7am-10pm Fri., 10am-10pm Sat., 10am-3pm Sun., $11-20) serves creative cuisine that pulls on local ingredients and global flavors. Brunch is a highlight here, with a lineup of hearty savory plates and stacks of pancakes topped with generous maple syrup.

Zabby & Elf's Stone Soup (211 College St., 802/862-7616, www.stonesoupvt.com, 7am-9pm Mon.-Fri., 9am-9pm Sat., $7-12), an intimate, sunlit café, serves hearty soups, salads, and excellent sandwiches on its own bread, along with an eclectic buffet with plenty of vegan and gluten-free options. The large front window is made for people-watching, and there's a decent wine and beer selection. When you add in one of the almond macaroons, you've got all the ingredients for a perfect afternoon.

★ **Hen of the Wood** (55 Cherry St., 802/540-0534, www.henofthewood.com, 4pm-midnight daily, $22-30) is the second location of Chef Eric Warnstedt's award-winning restaurant, and both turn out inspired, thoughtful food that draws diners from around the region. Chef Warnstedt blends a refined aesthetic with a serious throw-down of New England flavors. He places agriculture front and center, and the menu changes frequently, but oysters are a standout, as is the house-made charcuterie (Hen of the Wood offers a popular happy hour special of $1 oysters 4pm-5pm).

The food is as whimsical as the hosts are at ★ **Penny Cluse Cafe** (169 Cherry St., 802/651-8834, www.pennycluse.com, 6:45am-3pm Mon.-Fri., 8am-3pm Sat.-Sun., $6-12), named for the owner's childhood dog and decked out with an ever-rotating collection of posters and local art. Dig into gingerbread pancakes at breakfast, or hang out until lunch and order up Baja fish tacos and a Bloody Mary.

Butch + Babes (258 N. Winooski, 802/495-0716, www.butchandbabes.com, 5pm-9pm Sun.-Wed., 5pm-10pm Thurs.-Sat., brunch 9:30am-2pm Sun., $12-16) is a collaboration between a Chicago-raised restaurateur and a New England Culinary Institute-trained chef from Bangkok, with a pub-inspired menu that pulls from those sources willy-nilly. The results are surprisingly harmonious and refreshingly laid-back, in an atmosphere that channels the vitality and diversity of the Old North End neighborhood where it's located.

The folks at **American Flatbread** (115 St. Paul St., 802/861-2999, 11:30am-close daily, www.americanflatbread.com, pizzas $12-20) bought local before it was cool. This beloved pizza joint still serves thin-crust pizza topped with cheese, veggies, and meats from area farms. The specials are always worth a try, but the basic menu is filled with excellent options like the Punctuated Equilibrium, with olives, red peppers, and goat cheese. Wait times can get long on weekend nights, but if you can wedge yourself into the crowd at the bar, it's a convivial place to while away an evening.

On evenings that call for low light and house-made banana ketchup, atmospheric **¡Duino! (Duende)** (10 N. Winooski Ave., 802/660-9346, www.duinoduende.com, 4pm-midnight Sun.-Thurs., 4pm-1am Fri.-Sat., brunch 10am-4pm Sat.-Sun., $10-15) beckons. Its concept of "international street food" is interpreted loosely and with a taste for cultural mashups: Korean tacos with kimchi and coconut rice is a standout example. Duino is connected by an internal door to the **Radio Bean** bar, so check the music lineup before settling in for dinner.

Taiwanese chef Duval brings her fresh, local approach to cooking classic and regional Chinese dishes at this excellent restaurant, **A Single Pebble** (133 Bank St., 802/865-5200, www.asinglepebble.com, dim sum 11:30am-1:45pm Sun.; lunch 11:30am-1:45pm Mon.-Fri., 11:30am-3pm Sat.; dinner 5pm-late daily, $10-25), to ongoing acclaim. This is a favorite for special occasions and holidays, and the mock eel is legendary.

In the Old North End neighborhood, **Scout & Co.** (237 North Ave., www.scoutandcompanyvt.com, 7am-5pm Mon.-Fri., 8am-6pm Sat.-Sun.) serves excellent espresso alongside creative house-made ice cream in an airy space equipped with a browsing library of esoteric cookbooks.

ACCOMMODATIONS AND CAMPING

Under $100

A welcome exception to the lack of budget options downtown, the no-frills **Burlington Hostel** (50 Main St., 802/540-3043, www.theburlingtonhostel.com, May-Oct., $44-60 per person) is clean, safe, and walking distance from everything. Three of the eight-bed dorms are single gender, and several four-bed dorms are set aside for groups and families. There's Wi-Fi and a public computer, and weekly rates are available.

$150-250

In a sweet residential neighborhood overlooking the lake, **One of a Kind BNB** (53 Lakeview Terrace, 802/862-5576, www.oneofakindbnb.com, $175-275) is still walking distance from downtown. The owner, artist Maggie Sherman, has thoughtfully renovated the home, and the relaxed breakfasts are full of local options. There's no television or air-conditioning, but there is a friendly cat, an excellent garden, and a backyard tree swing.

The Willard Street Inn (349 S. Willard St., 802/651-8710, www.willardstreetinn.com, $150-265) is as beautiful inside as it is outside; the sprawling Victorian manse lays claim to impeccably decorated rooms. Each is filled with thoughtful details—a hand-carved antique chest here, a gas fireplace with antique mosaic tile there. Terry bathrobes and a full breakfast served in the marble-floored solarium come with every stay. Children over 12 are welcome.

Over $250

The newest, chicest digs in town are surely at ★ **Hotel Vermont** (41 Cherry St., 802/651-0080, www.hotelvt.com, from $275), an urban oasis that blends a rustic aesthetic with Scandinavian-influenced modern style. From woolly blankets to rough-hewn granite, seemingly everything you touch here is sourced regionally and with beautiful taste. The friendly staff includes a beer concierge and an outdoor activities director, and there are bicycles, snowshoes, and even an ice fishing shack available for guest use.

Made INN Vermont (204 S. Willard St., 802/399-2788, www.madeinnvermont.com, from $230) is perched on a hill above downtown, a bed-and-breakfast that's a temple of curated quirk with artistic flair and a contemporary sensibility. Owner Linda Wolf has filled her historical home with curiosities and comforts, and rooms are stocked with cans of Heady Topper, chalkboard walls, and views of the lake below. Atop the peaked roof and equipped with a telescope, the enclosed widow's walk is where you can watch stars and sails drift by. Breakfast is sumptuous. And well-behaved pets are welcome.

Camping

With a prime location by the lake and the bike path, **North Beach Campground** (60 Institute Rd., 802/862-0942, www.enjoyburlington.com, tent sites $37, hookups $41-45) is also just two miles north of downtown, making it an excellent base for exploring the city.

INFORMATION AND SERVICES

The **Lake Champlain Chamber of Commerce** (877/686-5253, www.vermont.org) runs an information booth (9am-9pm daily, mid May-mid Oct.) during summer months on Church Street at the corner of Bank Street. Also look for a copy of the **Blue Map** (www.bluemap.com), a detailed tourist map of downtown and the Greater Burlington Area.

For emergency and hospital services, head to **Fletcher Allen Hospital** (Colchester Ave., 802/847-0000), but **Vermont Children's Hospital** (111 Colchester Ave., 802/847-5437) is equipped to handle younger patients' needs. Fill prescriptions at **Lakeside Pharmacy** (242 Pearl St., 802/862-1491, www.lakerx.org, 8:30am-7pm Mon.-Fri., 9am-3pm Sat.) or **Rite Aid** (158 Cherry St., 802/862-1562, 8am-9pm Mon.-Fri., 9am-6pm Sat., 9am-5pm Sun.), which also offers faxing services and has a second location (1024 North Ave., 802/865-7822). A handful of banks are in the downtown blocks of Burlington's retail area along Church Street. In that same area, ATMs seem to be on every block. In nonmedical emergencies, contact the headquarters for the **Burlington Police Department** (1 North Ave., 802/658-2704).

Internet access is offered at almost all cafés and at the **Fletcher Free Library** (235 College St., 802/863-3403, www.fletcherfree.org, 10am-6pm Mon. and Thurs.-Sat., 10am-8pm Tues.-Wed., noon-6pm Sun.). **FedEx Office Center** (199 Main St., 802/658-2561, 6am-midnight Mon.-Fri., 8am-9pm Sat., 9am-9pm Sun.) also offers fax services and shipping services.

GETTING THERE AND AROUND

Burlington is on I-89, and flights from many major cities land at **Burlington International Airport** (BTV, 1200 Airport Dr., South Burlington, 802/865-7571, www.btv.aero), which is served by half a dozen airlines. Reservation desks for major rental car companies are available at the airport.

Amtrak (800/872-7245, www.amtrak.com) sells tickets for trains to Burlington, but the station is 20 minutes away in Essex Junction (29 Railroad Ave., Essex Junction).

Greyhound Bus Lines (800/231-2222, www.greyhound.com) runs buses to Burlington from Montreal and Boston that arrive at the airport, and **Megabus** (www.us.megabus.com) has regular service to several cities around the Northeast,including Boston and New York City.

Green Mountain Transit (802/864-2282, www.ridegmt.org) has bus routes throughout Burlington and the surrounding area, including buses downtown from the airport and train station. Bus fare is $1.25. Taxi stands are also available at the airport and the train station; to call a cab from other locations, contact **Green Cab VT** (802/864-2424, www.greencabvt.com). Burlington is also served by **Uber** (www.uber.com) and **Lyft** (www.lyft.com), mobile-app services connecting riders with private drivers/vehicles, but coverage is less complete than in bigger cities.

Ferry

From New York, it's possible to get to Burlington via ferry from Port Kent. Several boats a day are run by **Lake Champlain Transportation** (King Street Dock, 802/864-9804, www.ferries.com, mid-June-late Sept., $8 adults, $3.10 children, children under 6 free, $30 vehicle and driver one-way), which take about an hour to cross the lake. The round-trip threading through the lake's islands is also one of the most economical ways to enjoy Champlain's scenery.

SHELBURNE

A sweet cluster of inns and shops, it would be easy to miss Shelburne entirely, but beyond the picturesque downtown is a gracious landscape of well-kept farms and vineyards. The sprawling Shelburne Farms is a grand example of a historic agricultural estate, with walking trails and barns, and Shelburne Museum is a trove of art and ephemera. And even without visiting the major sites, it's a pleasant place to spend a fall day picking apples and tasting wine.

Shelburne Farms' head cheesemaker, Kate Turcotte

Sights

★ SHELBURNE FARMS

Shelburne Farms (1611 Harbor Rd., 802/985-8686, www.shelburnefarms.org, 9am-5:30pm daily mid-May-Oct., $8 adults, $6 seniors, $5 children 3-17, children under 3 free) is a bewitching property that's a wonderful stop for a stroll through the wooded paths and rolling farm fields, past elegant barns with patinated copper roofs. The farm was the country retreat of the Webb family, and if you find it inspires hazy historical fantasies about roaming the estate with members of the American aristocracy and their glamorous guests, you're not the only one.

These days, though, you're more likely to bump into school kids than scions, as Shelburne Farms is now a nonprofit that works for sustainability in the food system. All income from the property goes to education and conservation efforts, including those from the inn and on-site restaurant.

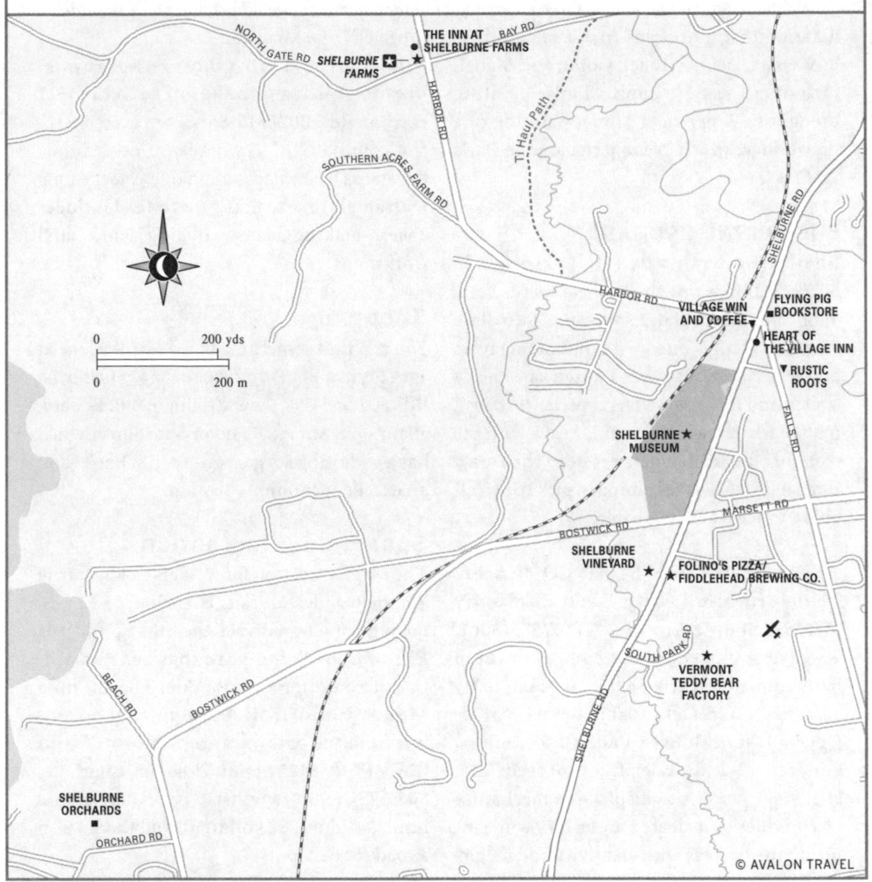

Sights change with the season: Spring means maple sugaring and lambing, and you can bundle up for horse-drawn sleigh rides in the winter. The on-site cheese-making operation is active year-round, however.

SHELBURNE MUSEUM

The **Shelburne Museum** (5555 Shelburne Rd., 802/985-3346, www.shelburnemuseum.org, 10am-5pm daily May-Dec., 10am-5pm Wed.-Sun. Jan.-Apr., $24 adults, $14 youth 13-17, $12 children 5-12, children under 5 free, $58 family day pass, Nov.-Apr. $10 adults, $5 youth 5-17, children under 5 free) is less a museum than a city-state founded by a hoarder with exquisite taste. Its 38 buildings are full of extraordinary art and historical gewgaws, not to mention a Lake Champlain steamship and its own covered bridge. This is the work of art collector Electra Havemeyer Webb, who relocated buildings from across the country to display her collection, opening the museum in 1947. The buildings are as intriguing as their contents, and include a 19th-century jailhouse, a Methodist meetinghouse, and a beautifully restored round barn, one of just two dozen built in Vermont. While the entire campus is open from May through October, access to limited exhibits is now possible from November through April.

Webb's own home was a Greek Revival mansion that now holds first-rate paintings by Cassatt, Degas, Monet, Corot, and Manet, including the first impressionist painting brought to America, a Monet painting of a drawbridge, which Webb purchased in Paris for $20.

SHELBURNE ORCHARDS

Shelburne Orchards (216 Orchard Rd., 802/985-2743, www.shelburneorchards.com, 9am-6pm Mon.-Sat., 9am-5pm Sun. late Aug.-late Oct.) is lined with undulating rows of trees that produce over a dozen varieties of apples, and it's a marvelous experience to visit in the early fall when the air is heavy with the scent of ripe fruit. The trees keep their own timetables, so before coming to pick fruit, call ahead to see what's available.

VERMONT TEDDY BEAR COMPANY

The **Vermont Teddy Bear Company** (6655 Shelburne Rd./Rte. 7, 802/985-3001, www.vermontteddybear.com, 9am-6pm daily mid-June-early Sept., 9am-5pm daily early Sept.-mid-Oct., 10am-2pm daily mid-Oct.-mid-June, tours $4 adults, $3 seniors, children 12 and under free) succeeds at a challenging task—to display the mechanics of a production-oriented toy factory while infusing the process with creativity and magic. Even for nonbelievers, the company does a darn good job, and there's little point in resisting the charm. The gift shop is stocked with bears and bear things, from children's books to artwork and tiny gift boxes of "bear poo." Or you can create your own toy at the Make a Friend for Life station, where you select a bear body, then fill it with fluff from a machine whose settings include Joy, Giggles, and Imagination.

Events

Past performers at the **Concerts on the Green** (5555 Shelburne Rd., 802/985-3346, www.shelburnemuseum.org) music series include Willie Nelson, Emmylou Harris, and Crosby, Stills, and Nash. Musicians play on select summer weekends on the grounds of the Shelburne Museum.

Shelburne Farms hosts the annual **Vermont Cheesemakers Festival** (1611 Harbor Rd., 802/986-8686, www.vtcheesefest.com, late July), where you can sample the state's best wedges all in one place. Along with ample time to graze, the festival includes cheese-making demos, cooking demos, and workshops.

Shopping

You can find something to read by the lake at **The Flying Pig Bookstore** (5247 Shelburne Rd., 802/985-3999, www.flyingpigbooks.com, 10am-6pm Mon.-Sat., noon-5pm Sun.), which has a wide range of general-interest books and an excellent children's section.

Sports and Recreation

The main attraction for walkers in Shelburne are the wonderful trails at Shelburne Farms, but a great alternative is the hike up **Mount Philo,** a low-lying peak that has views of the surrounding countryside. The 1.9-mile **Mount Philo Trail** loops up to the summit from the parking area of **Mount Philo State Park** (5425 Mount Philo Rd., Charlotte, 802/425-2390, www.vtstateparks.com/philo.html, $4 adults, $2 children), and there's also a road to the top.

Food

As renowned for the food as for the setting, the **Inn at Shelburne Farms** is worth a trip to the area— from maple syrup to lamb, the inn's kitchen uses many ingredients that are produced onsite, and the menu changes with the unfolding summer season. Dinners are spectacular, but stopping by for breakfast is a good way to experience the inn without splashing out for an expensive treat... and the inn's light-as-a-feather scones are a local legend. Shelburne has a handful of restaurants clustered in the downtown area, but it's worth heading to the southern edge of town to find **Folino's Pizza** (6305 Shelburne Rd., 802/881-8822, www.folinopizza.com, noon-9pm daily, $10-18), which serves crisp, wood-fired pizza with views of the vineyard next door. Try the rhapsody-inspiring flatbread with bacon, scallops, and lemon zest. Folino's is strictly BYO, but it's got a freezer full of pint glasses and shares a building with **Fiddlehead Brewing** (802/399-2994, www.fiddleheadbrewing.com, noon-9pm Sun.-Fri., 11am-9pm Sat.), which offers free tastings of its beers on tap as well as growler and growlette fills.

Right across the street is **Shelburne Vineyard** (6308 Shelburne Rd., 802/982-8222, www.shelburnevinyard.com, 11am-6pm daily May-Oct., 11am-5pm daily Nov.-Apr.), where the $7 tastings include a souvenir wineglass and a taste of 8-10 wines. Don't miss the award-winning Marquette Reserve.

In the village center, **Rustic Roots** (195 Falls Rd., 802/985-9511, www.rusticrootsvt.com, brunch 9am-3pm Wed.-Sun., dinner 6pm-7:30pm Fri.-Sat., $14-25) serves thoughtful food with European flair in a restored home, using many local ingredients. For a coffee with something sweet, **Village Wine and Coffee** (5288 Shelburne Rd., 802/985-8922, www.villagewineandcoffee.com, 7am-6pm Mon.-Sat., 8:30am-4pm Sun.) is a favorite stop by the town's main intersection.

Accommodations

The gorgeously preserved ★ **Inn at Shelburne Farms** (1611 Harbor Rd., 802/985-8498, www.shelburnefarms.org, May-Oct., $160-525) is situated right on the lake and may have the best sunset views in the Champlain Valley. The inn's restaurant prepares beautiful meals with ingredients grown organically on-site.

Tucked into a sweet Victorian in the center of town, **Heart of the Village Inn** (5347 Shelburne Rd., 802/985-9060, www.heartofthevillage.com, $220-400) charms with thoughtful touches like locally made chocolates. The homemade breakfasts are sumptuous, with hot and cold options available daily.

Information and Services

The **Shelburne Museum** (5555 Shelburne Rd., 802/985-3346, www.shelburnemuseum.org, 10am-5pm daily May-Dec., 10am-5pm Wed.-Sun. Jan.-Apr.) has a visitor information center stocked with maps and brochures; no admission fee is required.

A **Rite Aid Pharmacy** (30 Shelburne Shopping Park, 802/985-2610, 9am-6pm Mon.-Sat. for both store and pharmacy) is located in the center of downtown. In an emergency, contact the **Shelburne Police** (5420 Shelburne Rd., 802/985-8051).

Getting There and Around

Shelburne is on Route 7, a two-lane highway that runs parallel to Lake Champlain. **Green Mountain Transit** (802/864-2282, www.ridegmt.org) has frequent bus service between Burlington and Shelburne Monday-Saturday, with stops at the Shelburne Museum and Vermont Teddy Bear Company.

New Hampshire Seacoast and Lakes Region

A perfect sliver of coast leads to a thick, inland forest dotted with lakes, a varied region with deep history, a fascinating natural world, and a laid-back vacation culture.

Craggy peaks and fierce politics are the face New Hampshire turns toward the world, so the lakes and seacoast can come as a bit of a surprise.

And with just 18 miles of coastline, there's a lot to see and do by the water. Portsmouth is a stately blend of colonial history and Yankee grit, equally appealing for a trip through New England history as for an afternoon of "deck punch" and sunshine by the Piscataqua River, with the town's active fishing fleet bobbing at your feet.

All the pomp and tradition are offset by the hubbub of nearby Hampton Beach, where Portsmouth's brick architecture gives way to an oceanside strip scented with fried dough and teenage hormones.

Leave the coast behind, and the landscape closes into a rolling forest, broken by some of New Hampshire's endless lakes—the state claims nearly 1,000. Ranging from thumbprint ponds to vast bodies of water, they're pure nostalgia, lined with ice cream shops, lakeside cottages, penny arcades, and old-fashioned bandstands.

PLANNING YOUR TIME

Unless you're a die-hard history buff, two days is enough to see Portsmouth's main sites, though it's worth adding in a third if you'd like to explore the nearby Isles of Shoals. Since Hampton Beach is a love-it-or-hate-it sort of destination, opt for a couple of wild days or skip it altogether. And while there's plenty of lakes for a lifetime of puddle jumping, a few days will suffice for most, time enough to swim, take in a drive-in movie, and listen to the sounds of loons or power boats (depending on your lake of choice).

Previous: Hampton Beach; Lake Wentworth. **Above:** lobsters in Portsmouth.

Look for ★ to find recommended sights, activities, dining, and lodging.

Highlights

★ **Strawbery Banke Museum:** A whole neighborhood of historic homes brings colonial-era America to life with costumed docents and fascinating stories (page 86).

★ **Cruising the Isles of Shoals:** Shrouded in mist and a bit of historic mayhem, this cluster of rocky islands has long drawn pirates, dreamers, and outcasts (page 88).

★ **Lake Winnipesaukee Cruises:** People come from all over to take in the breathtaking views of Lake Winni aboard impressive vessels (page 95).

★ **Squam Lakes Natural Science Center:** Among New England's best places to learn about the natural world, families can meet mountain lions, bears, and more at this rambling outdoor nature center (page 103).

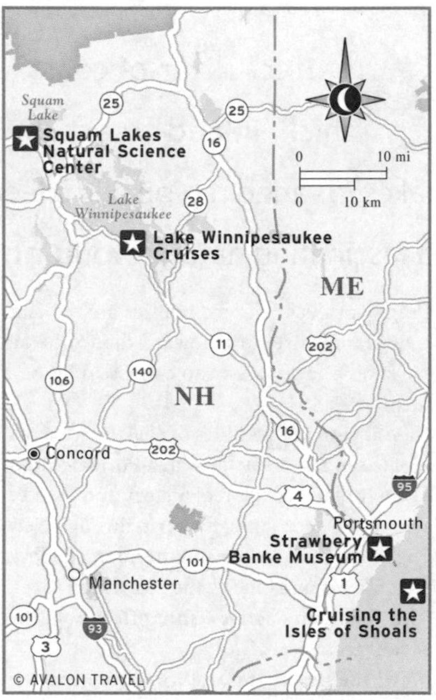

New Hampshire Seacoast and Lakes Region

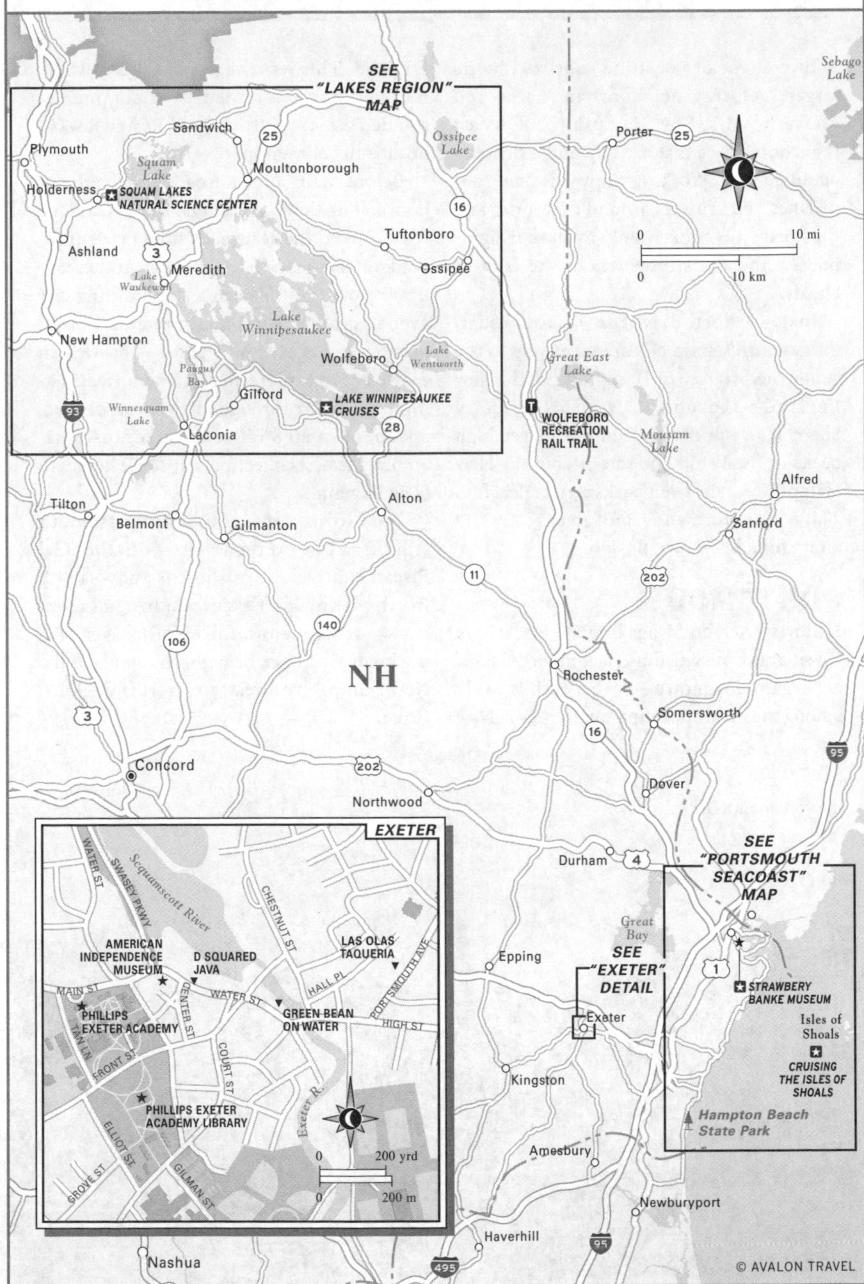

SEE "LAKES REGION" MAP
Sandwich
Plymouth
Squam Lake
Moultonborough
Holderness
SQUAM LAKES NATURAL SCIENCE CENTER
Ossipee Lake
Porter
Sebago Lake
Ashland
Tuftonboro
Meredith
Lake Waukewan
Ossipee
Lake Winnipesaukee
New Hampton
Wolfeboro
Lake Wentworth
Paugus Bay
Great East Lake
Gilford
Winnesquam Lake
LAKE WINNIPESAUKEE CRUISES
Laconia
WOLFEBORO RECREATION RAIL TRAIL
Mousam Lake
Alfred
Tilton
Belmont
Gilmanton
Alton
Sanford
NH
Rochester
Somersworth
Concord
Northwood
Dover
Durham
SEE "PORTSMOUTH SEACOAST" MAP
Great Bay
Epping
SEE "EXETER" DETAIL
STRAWBERY BANKE MUSEUM
Exeter
Isles of Shoals
CRUISING THE ISLES OF SHOALS
Kingston
Hampton Beach State Park
Amesbury
Newburyport
Haverhill
Nashua
0 10 mi
0 10 km
EXETER
WATER ST
SWASEY PKWY
Squamscott River
CHESTNUT ST
AMERICAN INDEPENDENCE MUSEUM
D SQUARED JAVA
LAS OLAS TAQUERIA
HALL PL
PORTSMOUTH AVE
MAIN ST
CENTER ST
PHILLIPS EXETER ACADEMY
GREEN BEAN ON WATER
HIGH ST
TAN LN
FRONT ST
COURT ST
PHILLIPS EXETER ACADEMY LIBRARY
Exeter R.
ELLIOT ST
GROVE ST
GILMAN ST
0 200 yrd
0 200 m
© AVALON TRAVEL

Portsmouth and the Seacoast

A thin sliver of coastline squeezed by its larger seafaring neighbors in Maine and Massachusetts, New Hampshire's seacoast is anchored by a historic city and a thriving ocean culture. Working shipyards send submarines and cruisers around the world, and the horizon is broken only by harbor lighthouses and the silhouettes of the Isles of Shoals.

Just a short drive down the coast, Portsmouth's staid culture gives way to the sunburned frenzy of Hampton Beach, New England's raucous answer to the Jersey Shore. It's a world away from the rugged high peaks of the White Mountains, but the New Hampshire waterfront packs a great deal into a bit of shoreline, and it's all an easy day trip away from downtown Boston.

PORTSMOUTH

Historic brick buildings line the Piscataqua River, and a busy fishing fleet moors just off an elegant downtown—Portsmouth is easily among the most appealing small cities in New England. This was the site of the Strawbery Banke colony, founded by a commerce-minded group of settlers in 1630, and it was a beautifully chosen spot.

Before roads and railroads left riverboats bobbing at their moorings, the Piscataqua River linked the seacoast with a maze of inland waterways, rich in timber and other natural resources. It's been a shipbuilding city ever since, and Portsmouth retains a blend of moneyed grace and workaday hustle. An easy place to explore on foot, there's fascinating architecture throughout the heart of town, and the open-air Strawbery Banke Museum is among the best collection of historic homes in New England.

True to its roots, though, Portsmouth still turns toward the water—both the tidal Piscataqua and the offshore islands—so it's worth planning an excursion by mail ferry, kayak, or gundalow, the historic river sailing boats that once brought the spoils of the New Hampshire forests to a port with global reach.

the Portsmouth Decks

Portsmouth Seacoast

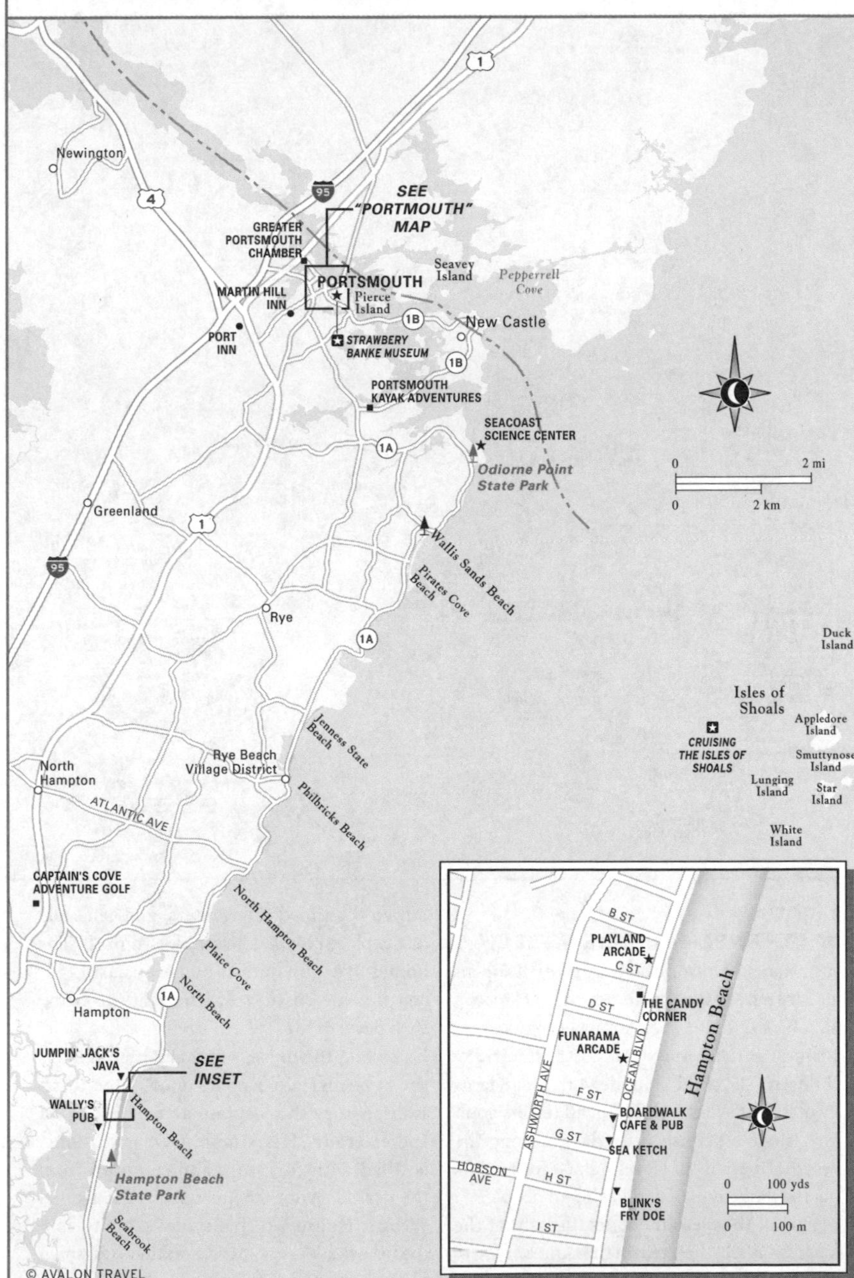

Newington
SEE "PORTMOUTH" MAP
GREATER PORTSMOUTH CHAMBER
PORTSMOUTH
Seavey Island
Pepperrell Cove
MARTIN HILL INN
Pierce Island
New Castle
PORT INN
STRAWBERY BANKE MUSEUM
PORTSMOUTH KAYAK ADVENTURES
SEACOAST SCIENCE CENTER
Odiorne Point State Park
0
2 mi
0
2 km
Greenland
Wallis Sands Beach
Pirates Cove Beach
Rye
Duck Island
Isles of Shoals
Appledore Island
CRUISING THE ISLES OF SHOALS
Smuttynose Island
Lunging Island
Star Island
White Island
Jenness State Beach
Rye Beach Village District
North Hampton
ATLANTIC AVE
Philbricks Beach
CAPTAIN'S COVE ADVENTURE GOLF
North Hampton Beach
Plaice Cove
North Beach
Hampton
JUMPIN' JACK'S JAVA
SEE INSET
WALLY'S PUB
Hampton Beach
Hampton Beach State Park
Seabrook Beach
© AVALON TRAVEL
B ST
PLAYLAND ARCADE
C ST
THE CANDY CORNER
D ST
FUNARAMA ARCADE
OCEAN BLVD
ASHWORTH AVE
F ST
BOARDWALK CAFE & PUB
G ST
SEA KETCH
HOBSON AVE
H ST
BLINK'S FRY DOE
I ST
0
100 yds
0
100 m

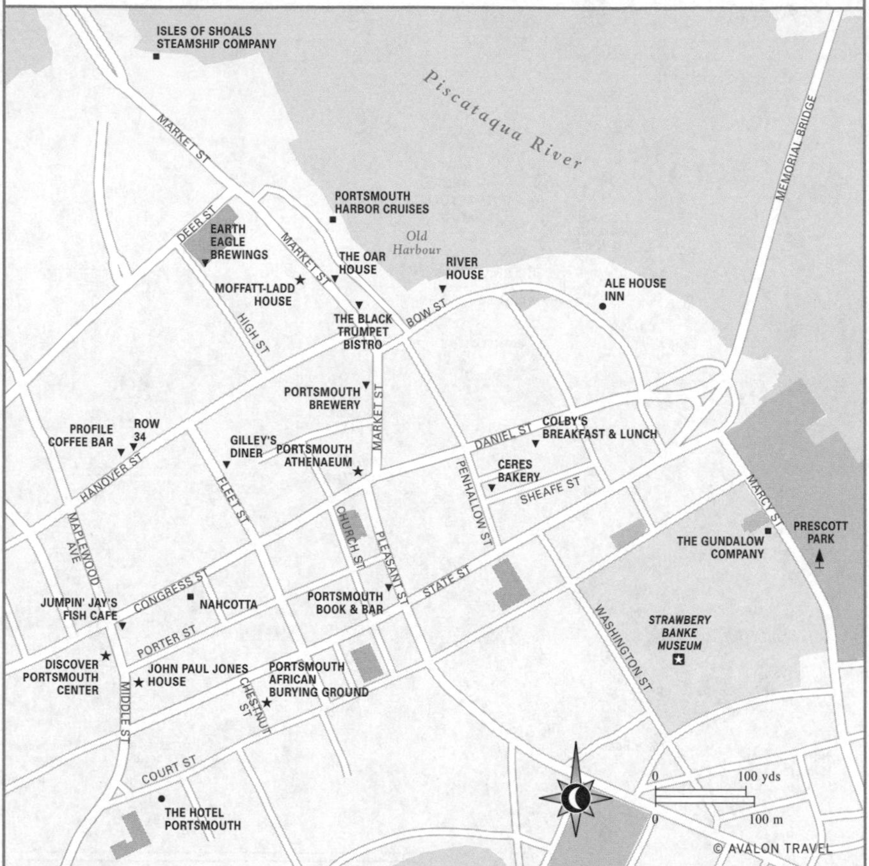

Sights

★ STRAWBERY BANKE MUSEUM

A cluster of 32 historic homes makes the open-air **Strawbery Banke Museum** (14 Hancock St., 603/433-1100, www.strawberybanke.org, 10am-5pm daily May-Oct., $19.50 adults, $9 children 5-17, children under 4 free, $48 family of 2 adults and 2 children, all tickets good for visits on 2 consecutive days) among the best destinations in New England for exploring the daily lives of early colonial people.

Part of the pleasure of visiting is that the museum is self-directed; in the summer you're invited to wander around, poke into houses, talk to costumed interpreters, and generally just explore colonial history for yourself. The homes are "inhabited" by enthusiastic docents, some costumed, who work to bring each place to life.

Among the museum's many highlights is the Wheelwright House, once home to an 18th-century ship captain active in the East Indies trade. His simple Georgian home is filled with furniture and ceramics from the period. Another must-see is the Daniel Webster House, which includes exhibits from the time that the great 19th-century statesmen spent in Portsmouth in the early part of his career. And if you are interested in seeing the actual items unearthed in the restoration of all the homes in the museum, stop by the **Jones Center,** which displays the findings from archaeological work on the neighborhood.

PORTSMOUTH HARBOR TRAIL

Strawbery Banke is just the beginning of historic properties on view in the city; if house museums are your thing, you could easily spend a week marveling at the variety and quality of those preserved here. The **Greater Portsmouth Chamber of Commerce** (500 Market St., 603/610-5510, www.goportsmouthnh.com) has linked up some of the highlights on the Harbor Trail, a walking path that loops through the historic downtown—pick up a map at the chamber of commerce office, or at the information booth on Market Square.

While it's easy enough to explore on your own, the **walking tours** offered by the **Portsmouth Historical Society** (10 Middle St., 603/436-8433, www.portsmouthhistory.org, $15) are very worthwhile. Led by knowledgeable, local docents, the tours offer broad context for the sites along the way. If you're planning to visit historic homes, it's a good introduction before exploring each place. Tours depart from the Portsmouth Historical Society, which maintains rotating exhibits on local history.

One fascinating stop on the Harbor Trail is the **Portsmouth Athenaeum** (9 Market Sq., 603/431-2538, www.portsmouthathenaeum.org, 1pm-4pm Tues. and Thurs., 10am-4pm Sat., free), one of New England's most fascinating private libraries, with a collection that illustrates the founders' broad-minded approach to documenting history. Treasures include the hatchet from the infamous Smuttynose murders and a purported whale eyeball that's rumored to be a whale testicle, but the building itself is gorgeous.

And if you're visiting just one historic house in the city, make it the **Moffatt-Ladd House** (154 Market St., 603/436-8221, www.moffattladd.org, 11am-5pm Mon.-Sat., 1pm-5pm Sun. June-mid-Oct., $8 adults, $2.50 children), built by a wealthy colonial merchant. The Georgian-style mansion is carefully restored, with wallpaper, paint, and decor much like those used by generations of inhabitants. And if you didn't know that there was a National Register of Historic Trees, the docents will fill you in—the enormous horse chestnut tree in front of the house was planted in 1776 by a signer of the Declaration of Independence.

A pleasant place to end the walk is at the riverside **Prescott Park** (105 Marcy St., www.prescottpark.org), which overflows with perennial blooms throughout the summer months. It's also the location for many free, outdoor movies, concerts, and other events—you can even go on the website to reserve blanket space right in front of the stage.

PORTSMOUTH BLACK HERITAGE TRAIL

In recent years, Portsmouth has worked to acknowledge the history of enslaved people who lived and worked in the city through colonial times and beyond. Focusing on their stories, the **Portsmouth Black Heritage Trail** (www.blackheritagetrailnh.org) visits taverns, homes, and two burial grounds, including the moving **Portsmouth African Burying Ground** (1 Junkins Ave., 603/610-7226, www.africanburyinggroundnh.org), which was rediscovered in 2003. The site is now inscribed with words from the 1799 Freedom Petition that a group of enslaved Africans submitted to the New Hampshire legislature, an eloquent document requesting that "we may regain our liberty and be rank'd in the class of free agents, and that the name of SLAVE be no more in a land gloriously contending for the sweets of freedom." A self-guided tour is available from the website, and the Portsmouth Historical Society also leads walking tours of the Black Heritage Trail.

SEACOAST SCIENCE CENTER

Kids can get their hands salty at the coastal **Seacoast Science Center** (570 Ocean Blvd.,

Rye, 603/436-8043, www.seacoastsciencecenter.org, 10am-5pm daily, $13 adults, $8 seniors and military, $5 children 3-12, children under 3 free), with indoor exhibits and outdoor programs that take advantage of the rocky tide pools that are just outside. Indoor tanks and touch pools explore the wildlife of the Gulf of Maine, as well as the researchers who work with marine wildlife. One advantage of the Seacoast Science Center's long-established marine rescue program is that when local fishermen and lobstermen find odd creatures—like the rare blue, yellow, or calico lobsters—they will often land on public display in one of the center's rotating tanks, so there's usually something remarkable for even repeat visitors. Memorial Day-Columbus Day, visitors in cars must also pay admission to **Odiorne State Park** (603/436-7406, www.nhstateparks.org, $4 adults, $2 children), where the science center is located.

★ ISLES OF SHOALS

A haven for fishermen, pirates, artists, and Unitarians, the nine rocky islands scattered off Portsmouth Harbor are thick with legend. This was a colonial-era escape from the Puritan strictures of the mainland, a prime spot for buried pirate treasure, and, they say, where Blackbeard honeymooned with his final bride. The 19th-century poet Celia Thaxter was raised in the Isles of Shoals, and later wrote of the islands that "there is a strange charm about them, an indescribable influence in their atmosphere, hardly to be explained, but universally acknowledged."

But the islands' most famous event is of the true crime genre—in 1873 two sisters were brutally murdered by an axe-wielding itinerant fisherman on the island of Smuttynose. A third woman managed to elude the killer and bring him to justice, but the story continues to haunt the area, inspiring florid books and movies ever since (for the best account, look up Celia Thaxter's contemporary piece in *The Atlantic*).

Tours of the islands with the **Isles of Shoals Steamship Company** (315 Market St., Portsmouth, 603/431-5500, www.islesofshoals.com, several tours daily, 2.5-4.5-hour cruises, $28-35 adults, $25-35 seniors, $18-25 children) milk all of the mist-enshrouded legends, and some include time to explore Star Island. You're free to wander off, but guided tours cover the stories, from the 1614 arrival of Captain John Smith to a lineup of local ghosts.

Entertainment and Events

There's often live music at the laid-back **Portsmouth Book & Bar** (40 Pleasant St., 603/427-9197, www.bookandbar.com, 10am-10pm Sun.-Thurs., 9am-midnight Fri.-Sat.), a bookstore with comfortable seats, strong coffee, and a solid menu of local beers and wine. In a cavernous space downtown, **The Portsmouth Brewery** (56 Market St., 603/431-1115, www.portsmouthbrewery.com, 11:30am-12:25am daily) has held court for years with a range of well-executed beers that range from traditional to highly creative. There's a full menu and bar snacks, and there's usually food specials during the 5pm-7pm Mon.-Fri. happy hour. Smaller and infinitely funkier, **Earth Eagle Brewings** (165 High St., 603/502-2244, www.eartheaglebrewings.com, 11:30am-10pm Sun.-Thurs., 11:30am-midnight Fri.-Sat.) specializes in gruits, beers that use herbs to provide the bitter background usually supplied by hops. An outdoor patio and live music on weekends make this a friendly, offbeat place to while away the night.

In the summer months, though, evenings in Portsmouth start at **The Decks,** a series of patios that jut out above the Piscataqua River, a great spot for catching the breeze and lovely sunset views. Most of the restaurants near the junction of Bow Street and Ceres Street have great decks, and many have their own version of "deck punch," usually a tropically inspired blend of rum and something sweet. One favorite is **The River House** (53 Bow St., 603/431-2600, www.riverhouse53bow.com, 11am-9pm daily), which also has a very respectable seafood chowder. Just around the corner, **The Oar House** (55 Ceres St., 603/436-4025, www.portsmouthoarhouse.

com, 11:30am-9pm Mon.-Fri., 11:30am-10pm Sat., 10am-3pm Sun.) commands equally great views, with live music on Friday and Saturday nights. The website **Seacoast Happy Hours** (www.seacoasthappyhours.com) is a great resource for daily drinks and food specials.

On the first Friday of every month, the local art association sponsors a **Gallery Walk** (www.artroundtown.org), in which galleries around downtown break out wine and cheese for simultaneous openings. Additionally, Strawbery Banke Museum sponsors several different theme weekends throughout the year, including a summer Maritime Weekend, Halloween ghost tours, and the popular **Candlelight Stroll** (603/433-1100, www.strawberybanke.org, Dec.), in which the streets of the museum are filled with hundreds of lit candles, and interpreters lead visitors in traditional holiday festivities.

Shopping

Downtown Portsmouth is packed with shops, with many clustered around Market Square, then following Market Street to the water. Just off that route is the stylish gallery-boutique **Nahcotta** (110 Congress St., 603/433-1705, www.nahcotta.com, 10am-6pm Mon.-Sat., 11am-5pm Sun.), which features a great deal of work by New England artists. When it comes to shopping in Portsmouth, visitors are divided between the browsable shops in the historic center and the outlet stores just across the Piscataqua River in Kittery.

Sports and Recreation

HIKING AND BIKING

Following the coast through a former military installation, **Odiorne State Park** (570 Ocean Blvd., Rye, 603/436-7406, www.nhstateparks.org, $4 adults, $2 children) has a network of walking trails that weave between salt marsh, beaches, and rocky outcroppings. On the western side of the park, there's a breakwater and pleasant sandy beach looking across the harbor, while the northeastern extreme has a picnic area surrounded by water.

In 2017, Portsmouth launched a **city bike program** (202/999-3924, bike.zagster.com/portsmouthnh) with six bike stations in the downtown area. To access the bikes, users download a free app, then pay a small membership fee. Bikes are free for up to two hours, then $3 per hour for the rest of the day. They're great for cruising around town, and there are some good, longer rides from Portsmouth—one favorite is the New Castle Loop, an eight-mile route that follows Route 1B from downtown across a series of linked islands, the largest being New Castle.

BOATING

The Piscataqua River once bristled with sails, as merchants brought lumber and other goods between the seaport and inland communities. Many of the boats were cargo barges with a shallow draft, and a mast that could be lowered to slide under bridges. That tradition lives on at **The Gundalow Company** (60 Marcy St., 603/433-9505, www.gundalow.org, $25-35), whose *Piscataqua* is a floating lesson in local sailing heritage. Trips range from history sails along the Portsmouth waterfront to longer, upriver sails, and some scheduled trips include free admission for children.

Less expensive and with multiple departures each day through the summer, **Portsmouth Harbor Cruises** (64 Ceres St., 800/776-0915, www.portsmouthharbor.com, $15-25 adults, $13-22 seniors, $11-18 children) has fully narrated trips aboard the comfortable *Heritage*, including history cruises, upriver cruises, and sunset tours that catch the city at its most enchanting.

You can get out on the water in decidedly smaller craft through **Portsmouth Kayak Adventures** (185 Wentworth Rd., 603/559-1000, www.portsmouthkayak.com, 2- to 3-hour guided tours $45-75, kayak rentals from $45), which leads guided trips around the Piscataqua River estuaries as well as out on the open ocean of Portsmouth Harbor.

BEACHES

Ten minutes outside of Portsmouth, **New Castle Beach** (301 Wentworth Rd., New

Castle, admission $4) has sand for lounging and picnic tables, as well as great views of Portsmouth Harbor boat traffic and a pair of pretty lighthouses. Restrooms are available through the summer months, and a small playground is on-site.

With somewhat warmer water and more facilities, **Wallis Sands State Beach** (1050 Ocean Blvd., Rye, 603/436-6404, www.nhstateparks.org, parking $15) is a favorite with families. A long stretch of sand looks out toward the Isles of Shoals, a lifeguard is on duty 10am-5pm, and the park is stocked with snack bars, showers, and a bathhouse. Low tide reveals a network of tidepools among beds of glistening seaweed.

Food

In a sleekly hip space downtown, ★ **Row 34** (5 Portwalk Pl., 603/319-5011, www.row34nh.com, 11:30am-10pm Mon.-Thurs., 11:30am-11pm Fri.-Sat., 10:30am-10pm Sun., $15-35) is a shrine to the raw bar, with piles of glistening ice mounded under fresh oysters, clams, and shrimp. Some of the oysters come from the restaurant's own farm in Duxbury, Massachusetts, and the servers are uncommonly knowledgeable about the subtleties of oyster provenance and flavor. It's fascinating to try a lineup of oysters from neighboring farms, as the bivalves vary dramatically, but the regular menu is solid as well, with classic seafood preparations and a few non-maritime options. Every day until 5pm, $1 oysters are on special.

Another favorite for seafood is **Jumpin' Jay's Fish Café** (150 Congress St., 603/766-3474, www.jumpinjays.com, 5pm-9pm Sun.-Thurs., 5pm-10pm Fri.-Sat., $20-30), whose careful preparations belie the casual atmosphere. The crab cakes are superb, and the haddock piccata is something of a legend around town, with a bright lemon, caper, and white wine sauce served over mashed potatoes.

A sip of Portland (Oregon) in the middle of Portsmouth, **Profile Coffee Bar** (15 Portwalk Pl., 603/501-1801, www.profilecoffeebar.com, 6:30am-6pm daily, $2-9) serves the best cups in town. Cold brew nitro, espresso, and pour overs are made with Counter Culture coffee beans, and the small menu of breakfast sandwiches, soups, and salads is excellent. If you're looking for a place to settle in with a laptop, this is the spot.

Not a gourmet destination, per se, **Gilley's Diner** (175 Fleet St., 603/431-6343, www.gilleyspmlunch.com, 11am-2am daily, $2-6) is all about steamed hot dogs and nostalgia. The tiny diner is in a lunch cart built by the Worcester Lunch Car Co., the original 1940 structure banged onto a trailer-like extension. Order your dog "with everything" and it will come buried in a delightfully sloppy pile of mustard, relish, onions, mayonnaise, ketchup, and pickles.

For a romantic night out, it's hard to beat the **Black Trumpet Bistro** (29 Ceres St., 603/431-0887, www.blacktrumpetbistro.com, 5pm-9:30pm Sun.-Thurs., 5pm-10pm Fri.-Sat., $19-35), which has been a leader in bringing sustainable seafood to New England restaurants. It's in an atmospheric building by the waterfront that's all brick and polished wood, while the menu brings broad influences to bear on local fish and meat. Seafood paella is very well done here, and the hangar steak wins raves.

A bright, casual eatery with very hearty servings, **Colby Breakfast & Lunch** (105 Daniel St., 603/436-3033, 7am-2pm daily, $5-12) is cozy and compact. You might have to wait for a table on busy mornings, but piles of blueberry pancakes, generously sauced huevos rancheros, and classic sandwiches make it worth your while.

With a bakery case full of goodies and a menu of sandwiches, soups, and wraps, **Ceres Bakery** (51 Penhallow St., 603/436-6518, www.ceresbakery.com, 7am-5pm Mon.-Sat., 7am-4pm Sun., $2-9) is a longtime local favorite with colorful charm. Sometimes the seating fills up, but the bakery is a short walk away from Prescott Park, making this an excellent spot to pick up picnic fare on a sunny day.

Accommodations

Hotels and inns in central Portsmouth tend to be quite expensive, especially those that are walking distance from downtown sights. Airbnb is a good alternative here, and many owners of historic homes rent out a room or two during high season. Finding a place to park on the street, however, can be a challenge, so it's worth ensuring that your rental has a spot for guests. A cluster of chain hotels by the interstate is another option for travelers on a budget.

$150-250

Outside of the crush of the center, **Port Inn** (505 Rte. 1 Bypass, 855/849-1513, www.portinnportsmouth.com, $159-259) is a good option for families who don't lean toward inns—motel-style rooms are spacious, and the inn is equipped with a heated, outdoor pool. The dog-friendly property has a self-serve breakfast bar that's a solid step above the average motel options, with local granola, cappuccinos, and Belgian waffles.

A 0.5 mile stroll from downtown sights, ★ **Martin Hill Inn** (404 Islington St., 603/436-2287, www.martinhillinn.com, $145-220) is a pair of historic homes surrounded by pretty gardens. Decor leans toward B&B-traditional, with judicious flounces, throw pillows, and the occasional four-poster bed, but rooms are comfortable and updated, each with private bath and flat-screen television. The innkeepers serve a hearty, two-course breakfast between 8:30 and 9:30 in the morning, and set out treats like freshly baked cookies, chocolates, and a decanter of sherry, along with fixings for tea and coffee.

The stylish **Ale House Inn** (121 Bow St., 603/431-7760, www.alehouseinn.com, $129-600) is built into a former brewery warehouse that's over a century old, and it has the feel of a beautifully renovated loft (as well as the very recognizable put-a-bird-on-it aesthetic of the Lark Hotel chain). Amenities include use of the hotel's bicycles, parking, air-conditioning, and in-room iPads, and the downtown location is unbeatable. The same hotel group owns **The Hotel Portsmouth** (40 Court St., 603/433-1200, www.thehotelportsmouth.com, $169-500), which combines the same amenities and design focus with an inn-like feel (rates at this property also include breakfast).

Information and Services

For more information on the city, contact the **Greater Portsmouth Chamber of Commerce** (500 Market St., 603/610-5510, 9am-5pm Mon.-Fri., 10am-5pm Sat.-Sun. mid May-mid Oct.; 9am-5pm Mon.-Fri. mid Oct.-mid May, www.goportsmouthnh.com) which also runs an information booth (10am-5pm daily mid May-mid Oct.) on the main corner of Market Square. Portsmouth offers free Wi-Fi Internet access throughout the downtown Market Square area.

Getting There

Portsmouth is located off I-95, on the northern border of the New Hampshire seacoast. **C & J Bus** (800/258-7111, www.ridecj.com) has service between Portsmouth and **Boston** (from 1 hr., 20 min., one-way ticket $17) and **New York City** (5 hrs., one-way ticket $79).

HAMPTON BEACH

Fried clams, penny arcades, sunburns, and mini golf—Hampton Beach is a rowdy and ramshackle beach town with the volume cranked to 11. Go for the people-watching or just dive into the honky-tonk fun, drifting up and down the main drag alongside a crowd of slow-cruising teenagers checking out each other's tans.

And when you've got enough sun, hit the arcades for some skee-ball, pinball, and vintage video games, then get your fortune told by a beachfront psychic.

Sights

HAMPTON BEACH STATE PARK

Miles of sandy beach are the starring attraction at **Hampton Beach State Park** (Ocean Blvd., 603/926-8990, www.nhstateparks.org), and on sunny days, the waterfront fills with families. Restroom facilities are dotted along the street side of the beach, and there's a huge parking lot on the south end of the beach that is a good alternative to searching for street parking (160 Ocean Blvd., 603/227-8700, all-day parking $15).

PENNY ARCADES

There used to be far more, but the Hampton Beach arcade scene has been reduced to two holdouts. The 1905 **Funarama Arcade** (169 Ocean Blvd., 603/926-2381, 10am-11pm daily) is the largest arcade in Hampton Beach, with a good mix of newer games and nostalgic favorites. A bit grimy and neglected, this is the land of Skee-Ball and PAC-MAN, and includes some one-off treasures like a vintage, coin-operated puppet show. Pinball aficionados should opt for **Playland Arcade** (211 Ocean Blvd., 603/926-3831, 10am-11pm daily), which has a huge collection of games and a classic selection of chintzy prizes.

MINI-GOLF

Shipwrecks, waterfalls, and a full 18 holes makes **Captain's Cove Adventure Golf** (814 Lafayette Rd., 603/926-5011, www.smallgolf.com, 10am-10pm daily in season) a favorite with the mini-golf crowd, and there's a concession stand that doles out mammoth servings of ice cream (there's often golfing discounts available online).

Entertainment and Events

Back in the 1930s, the historic **Hampton Beach Casino Ballroom** (169 Ocean Blvd., 603/929-4100, www.casinoballroom.com) featured big-band headliners from Count Basie to Duke Ellington. It's been a bit of a downhill journey, but the historic 2,000-seat ballroom is still a great place to see a show. Locals play live at **Wally's Pub** (144 Ashworth Ave., 603/926-6954, www.wallyspubnh.com), where you'll never have difficulty securing a seat or a cold beer. Some nights can get a little raucous (the tail end of Monday night beer pong tournaments, for example).

The strip is home to countless events over the course of the summer. Perhaps the most eagerly anticipated is the **Master Sand Sculpting Competition** (603/929-6301, www.greggrady.com, late June), in which 250 tons of sand are delivered to the beach for sculptors to turn into castles, mermaids, and pop stars.

Shopping

There are souvenir shops up and down Ocean Boulevard, but the classic Hampton Beach

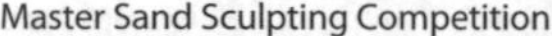
Master Sand Sculpting Competition

souvenir would be a pile of saltwater taffy and caramel corn from **The Candy Corner** (197 Ocean Blvd., 603/926-1740, 9am-11pm daily), which also does a brisk trade in fudge of all varieties.

Food

Beachgoers line up for great slabs of golden fried dough from **Blinky's Fry Doe** (191 Ocean Blvd., 603/926-8933, 9am-1am daily, $2-9), a longtime institution across the street from the beach. The standard offering comes showered with powdered sugar and cinnamon, but there's a laundry list of options, including several savory varieties.

Find coffee and a menu of light breakfast items at **Jumpin' Jack's Java** (333 Ocean Blvd., 603/758-1559, www.jumpinjacksjava.com, 5am-6pm Mon.-Sat., 6am-3pm Sun., $2-8), which also has decent non-fried take-out options that are convenient for ocean-side picnics.

A big, shady porch is the draw at **Boardwalk Café and Pub** (139 Ocean Blvd., 603/929-7400, www.boardwalkcafe.net, 11am-late daily, $10-32), whose huge menu has something for everyone. This is a prime place to stake out for watching the crowd, and there are some healthy options to offset the fried seafood mainstays.

Slightly more sedate, **Sea Ketch** (127 Ocean Blvd., 603/926-0324, www.seaketch.com, 7:15am-11:45pm daily, $11-25) serves classic surf and turf dinners and straight-from-the-market seafood on outdoor porches and a rooftop deck.

Information

The **Hampton Area Chamber of Commerce** (603/926-8717, www.hampton-chamber.com) runs a visitors information center located at the Seashell (180 Ocean Blvd.). More information is available from the **Hampton Village District** (22 C St., 603/926-8717, www.hamptonbeach.org).

Getting There and Around

Ocean Boulevard is the heart of Hampton Beach, but the center of town can get terribly snarled with traffic and crowds. Parking is a major cottage industry here, with small lots on every street that range $5-15 for the day, depending on proximity to the strip. There's no direct public transit from Boston to Hampton Beach, but it's possible to catch a **Coach Company** (800/874-3377, www.coachco.com, one-way $13) bus to the Newburyport Park and Ride, then take a taxi for the remaining 10-mile trip to Hampton Beach. Taxi service is available from **Merrimack Taxi Co.** (978/687-0911).

EXETER

For a brief period between 1775 and 1789, the attractive town of Exeter was the capital of New Hampshire. To this day, the town celebrates its link to the colonial period, when it was a bustling trade center and hotbed of Revolutionary sentiment. Nowadays, the town is best known as the site of Phillips Exeter Academy, one of the best private high schools in the country and the archetype of the New England prep school.

Sights

PHILLIPS EXETER ACADEMY

It's difficult to tell where the town ends and the prestigious **Phillips Exeter Academy** prep school (20 Main St., 603/772-4311, www.exeter.edu) begins. The academy was founded in 1781 by local doctor and Harvard graduate John Phillips, under the sound principle, "Goodness without knowledge is weak and feeble, yet knowledge without goodness is dangerous." With a campus more impressive than many small colleges, the school is a mix of Georgian colonial buildings and more modern structures radiating out in waves from downtown Exeter.

If you're wandering through the campus, don't miss the **Philips Exeter Academy Library** (2-36 Abbot Hall, 603/777-3328, 8am-4pm Mon.-Fri.), whose spectacular design was created by the architect Louis Kahn (it's also the second-largest secondary school library in the world).

AMERICAN INDEPENDENCE MUSEUM

The smart little **American Independence Museum** (1 Governors Ln., 603/772-2622, www.independencemuseum.org, 10am-4pm Tues.-Sat. May-Nov., $6 adults, $5 seniors, $3 students, children under 6 free) brings America's fight for independence to life. It includes two historic properties: the home of one of Exeter's rebel families and the tavern where many political theories were hashed out at the time. Inside are interactive exhibits exploring the causes and characters of the Revolution. The stars of the museum's collection are an original draft of the Constitution and a Dunlap copy of the Declaration of Independence, but they're only on display during the yearly Independence Day festivities.

Entertainment and Events

"George Washington" addresses the crowds at the annual **American Independence Festival** (603/772-2622, www.independencemuseum.org, mid-July), which takes place on the grounds of the American Independence Museum and is held in mid-July to celebrate the date that the Declaration of Independence was first read in Exeter, on July 16, 1776. Costumed interpreters also circulate through the event, which features helicopter rides, fireworks, music, craft vendors, and a specially brewed Independence Ale from Redhook Brewery.

Food

A downtown coffee shop that's popular with students, **D2 Java** (155 Water St., 603/583-5646, www.dsquaredjava.com, 7am-8pm Mon.-Sat., 8am-6pm Sun., $2-7) has the best espresso in town, a short menu of breakfast items, and a case stocked with treats from local bakers, including gluten-free and vegan options.

Mexican American staples like burritos and nachos are the draw at **Las Olas Taqueria** (30 Portsmouth Ave., 603/418-8901, www.lasolastaqueria.com, 11am-9pm Mon.-Sat., 11am-8pm Sun., $7-10), a bright, basic space with counter service. Build-your-own options include organic pork and locally sourced chorizo, and servings are generous.

A favorite for super-fresh lunches, **Green Bean on Water** (33 Water St., 603/778-7585, www.nhgreenbean.com, 11am-7pm daily, $8-12) specializes in sandwiches on house-baked ciabatta, big salads, and soups—there's a rotating menu of more than 60 varieties. The outdoor seating is welcome on sunny days, with views to the Exeter River from the back patio.

Getting There

Exeter is located on Route 101, inland from Hampton Beach and Portsmouth. It's on the Downeaster rail line from **Amtrak** (800/872-7245, www.amtrakdowneaster.com), linking the city with **Boston** (1 hr., one-way ticket $11) and **Brunswick,** Maine (2 hrs., one-way ticket $26), with several stops in between.

The Lakes Region

Hundreds of lakes are scattered through the forested landscape of central New Hampshire, from tiny fishing ponds to the sprawling shoreline of Lake Winnipesaukee. The lakeshore communities are just as varied, and include tranquil getaways, historic villages, and old-school vacation towns soaked in tanning oil and beer. A getaway for New Englanders since the 19th-century, the Lakes Region retains a nostalgic charm, but most visitors come to whip around the lakes on speedboats, snap up souvenir T-shirts, and hit the boardwalk at Weirs Beach.

If that's not your box of fudge, it's easy to get beyond the crowds to search for loons, explore the natural world, or hike one of the many low-lying mountains that rise up between the lakes, where it's easy to get away from the crowds.

PLANNING YOUR TIME

Visting the Lakes Region isn't about bagging sites per se; it's more about getting out on the water—whether that means by inner tube, canoe, speedboat, or cruise ship. As far as that goes, you can't go wrong with the **M/S *Mount Washington*,** the queen of Winnipesaukee and the best way to get a feel for the history of the lake. If you want to experience all the bustle and excitement of Lake Winni, base yourself in the quaint town of Meredith, which is close enough to the action of Weirs Beach without being *too* close. If it's solitude you're after, go straight to Squam Lake—and while you are there, take in the excellent live animal displays and nature cruises offered by the **Squam Lakes Natural Science Center.**

LAKE WINNIPESAUKEE

Four-season, water-bound activities are everywhere you look around Winnipesaukee, the largest lake in New Hampshire and the third-largest in New England (after Champlain and Moosehead). Known universally to residents as Lake Winni, the lake is a full 72 square miles of spring-fed water, with upwards of 200 miles of shoreline. Come summer, tourists descend on the lake from all over New England for boating, swimming, and cruises.

The villages surrounding the lake help everyone self-sort: Families and packs of Harley riders know just where to go. If you're looking for kitschy fun, the boardwalks of Weirs Beach have more than their fair share of waterslides, public beaches, arcades, and a great drive-in theater. Meanwhile, spots like Meredith and Wolfeboro offer quieter pleasures like antiquing, searching out galleries, and simply enjoying the scenery.

Laconia and Weirs Beach

If the villages clustered around Lake Winnipesaukee were a family, Weirs Beach would be the fun-loving cousin who gets a little wild on the weekends. Throngs gather on its beach and boardwalk every summer, and it buzzes all through the warm months. It's been that way since about 1848, when the railroad running from Boston to Montreal reached Weirs Beach. By the turn of the 19th century, four express trains left Boston's Union Station each day for Weirs Beach. The train service ended in 1960, but the annual migration did not: Each year, thousands of tourists still make their way here to ride the lake steamship, eat glorious piles of fried food, and pick up a tan or tattoo.

★ LAKE WINNIPESAUKEE CRUISES

The feeling strikes almost as soon as you catch a glimpse of Lake Winni's vast, folded shoreline—*why am I on dry land right now?* The grande dame of the lake is the **M/S *Mount Washington*** (211 Lakeside Ave., Weirs Beach, 603/366-5531 or 888/843-6686, www.cruisenh.com, May-Oct., $32-50 adults, $16-25 children 5-12, children under 5 free), so named—the tour guides will tell you—because when the sky is clear you can see New Hampshire's tallest peak from the deck (M/S stands for motor ship). The current cruise ship is actually the second *Mount Washington* to cruise the lake. The first ship, built in 1872, was destroyed by a fire in 1939. Her replacement is an 1888 steamship that was completely overhauled and rebuilt in 1940. The ship is a whopping 230 feet long, and re-creates the era of the old paddlewheel steamships, even though she is now propelled by twin diesel engines.

The same company also has two smaller boats in its fleet that are ideal for those wanting to avoid crowds or poke into some of the smaller bays the *Mount* can't get into. The **M/S *Sophie C.*** ($28 adults, $14 children) is the only U.S. Mail Boat on an inland waterway, and passengers can hitch a ride on the two-hour run to a scattering of island communities and summer camps.

Lakes Region

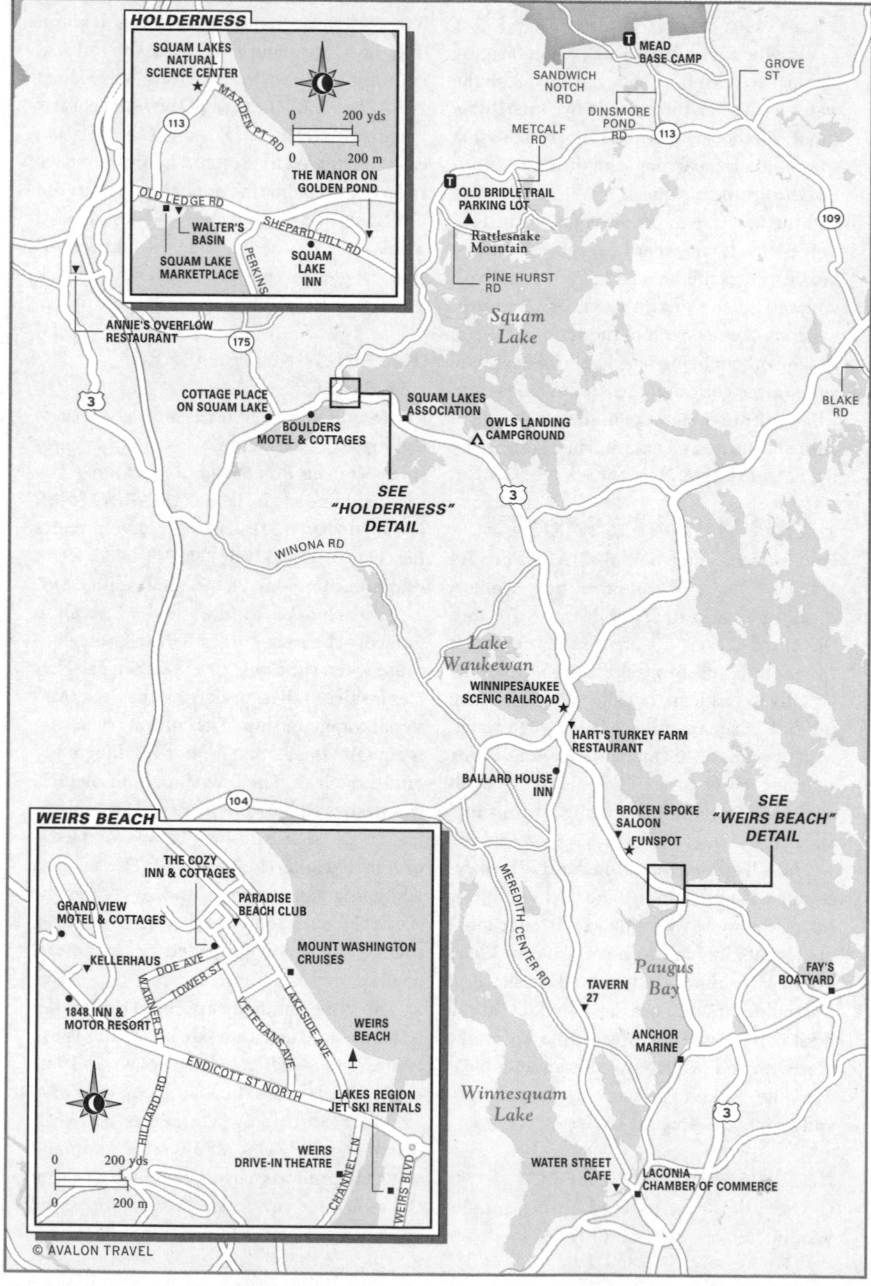
HOLDERNESS
SQUAM LAKES NATURAL SCIENCE CENTER
MARDEN PT RD
113
0 200 yds
0 200 m
THE MANOR ON GOLDEN POND
OLD LEDGE RD
SHEPARD HILL RD
WALTER'S BASIN
SQUAM LAKE MARKETPLACE
PERKINS
SQUAM LAKE INN
MEAD BASE CAMP
SANDWICH NOTCH RD
GROVE ST
DINSMORE POND RD
METCALF RD
113
109
OLD BRIDLE TRAIL PARKING LOT
Rattlesnake Mountain
PINE HURST RD
Squam Lake
ANNIE'S OVERFLOW RESTAURANT
175
3
COTTAGE PLACE ON SQUAM LAKE
BOULDERS MOTEL & COTTAGES
SQUAM LAKES ASSOCIATION
OWLS LANDING CAMPGROUND
BLAKE RD
SEE "HOLDERNESS" DETAIL
3
WINONA RD
Lake Waukewan
WINNIPESAUKEE SCENIC RAILROAD
HART'S TURKEY FARM RESTAURANT
BALLARD HOUSE INN
104
BROKEN SPOKE SALOON
FUNSPOT
SEE "WEIRS BEACH" DETAIL
MEREDITH CENTER RD
Paugus Bay
TAVERN 27
FAY'S BOATYARD
ANCHOR MARINE
Winnesquam Lake
3
WATER STREET CAFE
LACONIA CHAMBER OF COMMERCE
WEIRS BEACH
THE COZY INN & COTTAGES
PARADISE BEACH CLUB
GRAND VIEW MOTEL & COTTAGES
MOUNT WASHINGTON CRUISES
KELLERHAUS
DOE AVE
TOWER ST
WARNER ST
LAKESIDE AVE
VETERANS AVE
1848 INN & MOTOR RESORT
WEIRS BEACH
ENDICOTT ST NORTH
HILLIARD RD
LAKES REGION JET SKI RENTALS
0 200 yds
0 200 m
WEIRS DRIVE-IN THEATRE
CHANNEL LN
WEIRS BLVD

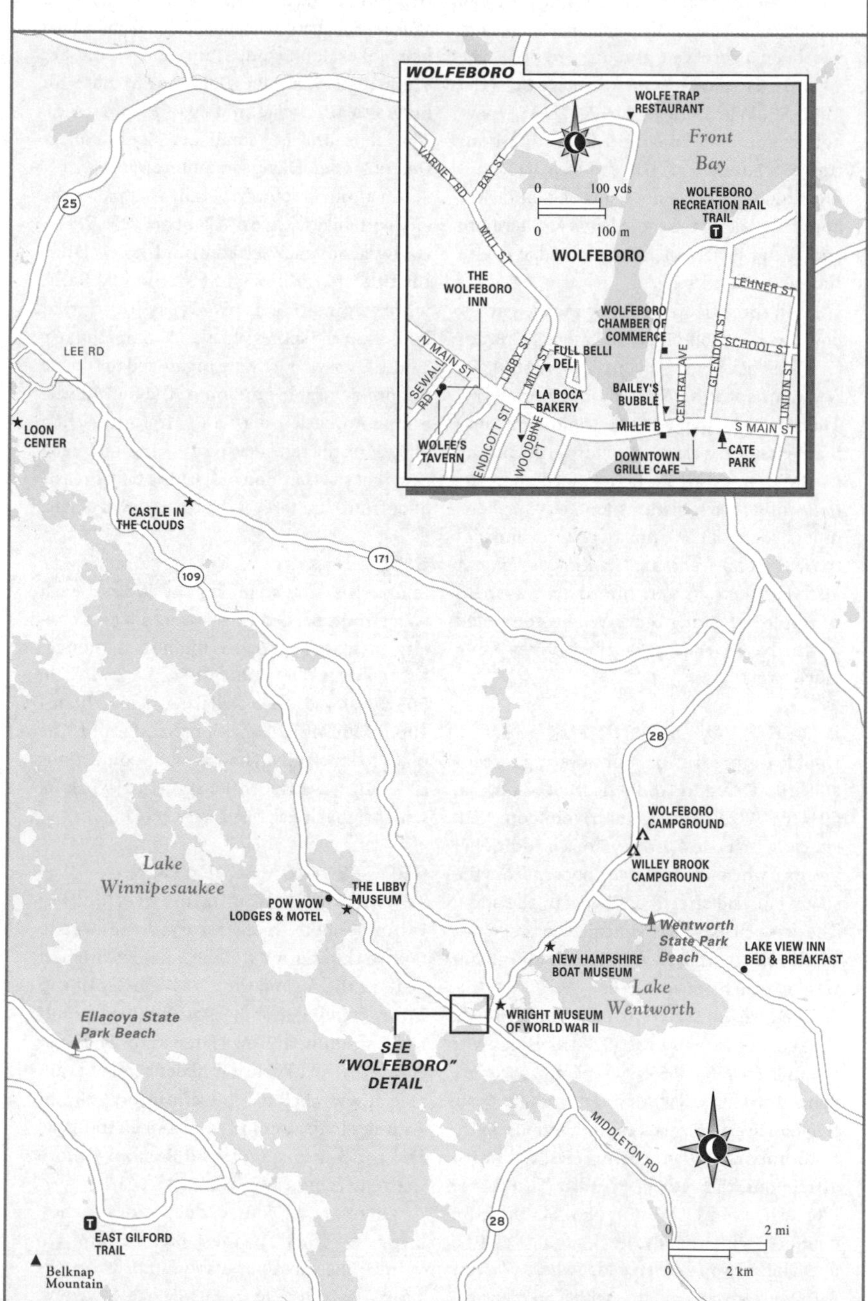
WOLFEBORO
WOLFE TRAP RESTAURANT
Front Bay
VARNEY RD
BAY ST
0 100 yds
0 100 m
WOLFEBORO RECREATION RAIL TRAIL
MILL ST
WOLFEBORO
THE WOLFEBORO INN
LEHNER ST
WOLFEBORO CHAMBER OF COMMERCE
N MAIN ST
LIBBY ST
MILL ST
FULL BELLI DELI
SCHOOL ST
GLENDON ST
SEWALL RD
CENTRAL AVE
UNION ST
LA BOCA BAKERY
BAILEY'S BUBBLE
ENDICOTT ST
WOODBINE CT
MILLIE B
S MAIN ST
WOLFE'S TAVERN
DOWNTOWN GRILLE CAFE
CATE PARK
25
LEE RD
LOON CENTER
CASTLE IN THE CLOUDS
171
109
28
WOLFEBORO CAMPGROUND
WILLEY BROOK CAMPGROUND
Lake Winnipesaukee
THE LIBBY MUSEUM
POW WOW LODGES & MOTEL
Wentworth State Park Beach
NEW HAMPSHIRE BOAT MUSEUM
LAKE VIEW INN BED & BREAKFAST
Lake Wentworth
Ellacoya State Park Beach
WRIGHT MUSEUM OF WORLD WAR II
SEE "WOLFEBORO" DETAIL
MIDDLETON RD
28
EAST GILFORD TRAIL
Belknap Mountain
0 2 mi
0 2 km

SIGHTS

Part of the original Boston & Maine Railroad that used to bring tourists to the region has been preserved and turned into the **Winnipesaukee Scenic Railroad** (154 Main St., Wiers Beach, 603/745-2135, www.hoborr.com, late May-mid-Oct., 1-/2-hour trips $18/20 adults, $14/16 children 3-11, children under 3 free). It now runs one- and two-hour rides along the shore between Meredith and Weirs Beach, including a bridge over a slice of the lake itself.

With three floors of classic arcade games, bowling, mini golf, bingo, and more, **Funspot** (579 Edicott St. N., Laconia, 603/366-4377, www.funspotnh.com, 10am-10pm Sun.-Thurs., 10am-11pm Fri., 10am-midnight Sun.) is a Weirs Beach classic. Proudly proclaiming itself the largest arcade in the world, there *actually* might be something for everyone here, unless you don't like fun, of course. Funspot trivia: Pivotal scenes in *The King of Kong: A Fistful of Quarters* were filmed here, as then-unemployed gamer Steve Wiebe competed for the best-ever score on the Donkey Kong video game.

ENTERTAINMENT AND EVENTS

Double features run on four towering screens at **Weirs Drive In** (76 Endicott St., Laconia, 603/366-4723, www.weirsdrivein.com, $28 per car with up to 4 people, $6 each additional person), where you can grab popcorn from the snack bar and stretch out beneath the stars. The drive-in uses FM frequencies to broadcast sound, so you'll need a portable radio if you want to watch outside the car.

The heart of the Weirs Beach party scene is **Paradise Beach Club** (322 Lakeside Ave., Laconia, 603/366-3665, www.paradisebc.com, 8pm-1am Thurs.-Sat. May-Oct.), which hosts frequent live performances and a serious dance floor lined with (faux) palm trees. On warm afternoons, the outdoor **Phukitz Tiki Bar** is like a slice of Key West in New Hampshire, complete with a sandy beach, lounge chairs, and a bicycle-operated blender where you can earn your frozen daiquiris with a bit of sweat.

For something completely different, **Broken Spoke Saloon and Museum** (1072 Waston Rd., Laconia, 603/366-5511, www.brokenspokesaloon.com, 11am-1am Wed.-Sat., 11am-10pm Sun. June-Oct.) is a favorite with bikers (leather-clad, not spandex-wearing). The "museum" is a small, artfully lit collection of Harley-Davidson motorcycles.

An annual motorcycle rally that packs the city with bikes, **Laconia Motorcycle Week** (www.laconiamcweek.com, mid-June) claims the title of World's Oldest Motorcycle Rally, with origins in a 1916 "Gypsy Tour" that landed on the shores of Lake Winnipesaukee. Those Gypsy Tours were organized to "create a more favorable opinion of the motorcycle and motorcycle rider," and after more than 100 years, the rally may be working—it's been said that the tradition of flashing bare breasts at or from a motorcycle has died down of late.

SHOPPING

Shops line "the strip" on the Weirs Beach waterfront, packed with souvenirs and novelty gifts. Set back on the main road, though, **Kellerhaus** (259 Endicott St., Weirs Beach, 603/366-4466, www.kellerhaus.com, 10am-10pm Mon.-Fri., 8am-10pm Sat.-Sun.) is the place to stock up on house-made confections like fudge, pecan brittle, and truffles, along with bright sweets from self-serve bins.

SPORTS AND RECREATION

Several small mountains overlooking Winnipesaukee make for good vantages to take in the enormity of the lake. The highest peak in the region, the 2,384-foot **Belknap Mountain** is one of the most-climbed mountains in southern New Hampshire. The **East Gilford Trail** (detailed trail description available at www.belknaprangetrails.org) climbs 1.9 miles to the summit from a small trailhead and parking area on Wood Road in Gilford (parking is quite limited, so start early).

There are, of course, dozens of beaches, large and small, in the Lakes Region. On Winni, the most popular (and crowded) is **Weirs Beach** (Rte. 3, 603/524-5046, www.

city.laconia.nh.us), which has the advantage of being easily accessible and close to the action. Quieter and more family-friendly, **Ellacoya State Park** (280 Scenic Dr., Gilford, 603/293-7821, www.nhstateparks.org, $5 adults, $2 children 6-11) has a long, sandy beach with views of the mountains and welcome patches of shade beneath stands of trees. Admission is capped, and on busy weekends, the beach can fill to capacity.

If it floats and it's fun, you can probably rent it in Weirs Beach. Zip around on a **Jet Ski** from **Lakes Region Jet Ski Rentals** (1184 Weirs Rd., Laconia, 603/366-5566, www.lakesregionjetski.com, 1 hour from $85, half day from $299), or opt for a more sedate **pontoon boat** from **Anchor Marine** (1285 Union Ave., Laconia, 603/366-4311, www.anchormarine.net, 2-hour pontoon boat rental $135). A short drive south in Gilford, **Fay's Boat Yard** (71 Varney Point Rd., Gilford, 603/293-8000, www.faysboatyard.com, half-day rentals from $25) is the place to go for canoes, kayaks, and sailboats.

FOOD

Ten minutes north of Weirs Beach, you can tuck into year-round Thanksgiving dinners at ★ **Hart's Turkey Farm Restaurant** (233 Daniel Webster Hwy., Jct. Rtes. 3 and 104, Meredith, 603/279-6212, www.hartsturkeyfarm.com, 11:15am-8:30pm daily, $10-28), where dark and light meat come with all the fixings, from cranberry sauce to gravy and stuffing. The regular menu is long and features an astonishing variety of turkey items: turkey nuggets, turkey marsala, turkey livers, turkey croquettes, turkey tempura . . .

Beyond the gift shop at **Kellerhaus** (259 Endicott St., Weirs Beach, 603/366-4466, www.kellerhaus.com, 10am-10pm Mon.-Fri., 8am-10pm Sat.-Sun.) is an ice cream wonderland. The self-serve ice cream sundae bar features a laundry list of flavors, but the joy is in the toppings, from house-made marshmallow fluff to fudge and caramel sauce.

A tapas bar with live piano music, **Tavern 27** (2075 Parade Rd., Laconia, 603/528-3057, www.tavern27.com, 5pm-9pm Wed.-Thurs., 11am-9pm Fri.-Sun., $17-22) has a menu of small plates that use many locally sourced ingredients, some from the restaurant's own organic vegetable garden. Save room for dessert—the bread pudding comes highly recommended.

Every Friday, seemingly all Laconia turns up at **Water Street Cafe** (141 Water St., Laconia, 603/524-4144, www.water-street-cafe.com, 6am-2pm Mon.-Thurs. and Sat., 6am-8pm Fri., 7am-1pm Sun., $5-25) for all-you-can-eat fresh haddock or clams. It's a great deal—as are the homemade seafood chowders and farm-fresh egg omelets at breakfast.

ACCOMMODATIONS

Decorated with grandfather clocks, maple wood floors, and tufted sofas, **The Cozy Inn & Cottages** (12 Maple St., Weirs Beach, 603/366-4310, www.cozyinn-nh.com, cottages $135-245, rooms $60-125) offers 16 cottages (either poolside or with lake views) and rooms in two separate buildings. Cottages have kitchens, air-conditioning, and grills, and the rooms in the main houses are simple but tidy and comfortable. It's a short downhill walk to the center of Weirs Beach.

The family-owned **1848 Inn and Motor Resort** (258 Endicott St., North Weirs Beach, 603/366-4714, www.1848inn.com, Apr.-Nov., $79-125) has clean rooms as well as cottages with kitchens and an outdoor swimming pool, a game room, and a picnic area. It's located within walking distance to Weirs Beach. Another good option for cottages is **Grand View Motel & Cottages** (291 Endicott St., North Weirs Beach, 603/366-4973, www.grandviewmotel-nh.com, Apr.-Oct., $129-189), which also offers neatly kept cottages with views of the lake, and grounds with grills, fire pits, and a fenced-in pool.

Simple and tranquil, **Ballard House Inn** (53 Parade Rd., Meredith, 603/279-3434, www.ballardhouseinn.com, $129-239) is a welcome break from the action in Weirs Beach without going too far away—it's just a few miles north of town. The house-made breakfast is a highlight, and the innkeepers furnish the common spaces with cookies, hot drinks, beer, and wine for guests. Some rooms have gorgeous views of the lake and mountains.

INFORMATION

The **Lakes Region Chamber of Commerce** (383 S. Main St., Laconia, 603/524-5531, 9am-3pm Mon.-Fri., www.lakesregionchamber.org) has year-round travel information in its main office, as well as a self-serve rack of brochures on Weirs Boulevard in Weirs Beach.

GETTING THERE

Laconia and Weirs Beach are located on Route 3, on the western shore of Lake Winnipesaukee. **Concord Coach Lines** (800/639-6317, www.concordcoachlines.com) links Meredith, a few miles north of Weirs Beach, with **Boston** (2 hrs., 30 min., $24.50), **Portland** (5 hrs., 10 min., $45.50), and **Concord** (1 hr., $12).

Wolfeboro

Waving flags, white churches, and a compact main street make Wolfeboro a nostalgic place to while away a summer weekend on Lake Winnipesaukee. Locals like to call the town the "oldest summer resort in America"—Governor John Wentworth drew a fashionable crowd to the area after building a summer home in 1769—and it retains an old-fashioned charm.

Catch a concert in a lakeside gazebo, see a stars-and-stripes take on World War II, or take a cruise on a vintage wooden lake boat, while slowing down to the pace of life on the "quiet side" of the lake.

SIGHTS

The tank bursting out of the brick facade of the **Wright Museum of World War II** (77 Center St., 603/569-1212, www.wrightmuseum.org, 10am-4pm Mon.-Sat., noon-4pm Sun. May-Oct., $10 adults, $8 seniors and veterans, $6 students, children under 8 free) sets the tone for the museum's extensive collection, which offers a more upbeat take on the era than the average war museum. There's an impressive array of cars, motorcycles, tanks, and airplanes, as well as ephemera that helps illustrate daily life in the United States during the conflict.

Gleaming vintage boats are the starring attraction at the diminutive **New Hampshire Boat Museum** (395 Center St./Rte. 28, Wolfeboro Falls, 603/569-4554, www.nhbm.org, 10am-4pm Mon.-Sat., noon-4pm Sun. late May-mid-Oct., $7 adults, $5 seniors, $3 students, children under 7 free), whose collection includes some of the glamorous vessels that cruised Lake Winnipesaukee a century ago.

Twenty-five minutes outside of Wolfeboro, **Castle in the Clouds** (455 Old Mountain Rd., Moultonborough, 603/476-5900, www.castleintheclouds.org, 10am-5:30pm daily mid-May-late Oct., $17 adults, $14 seniors, $10 children 5-17, children under 5 free) is a spectacular Arts and Crafts mansion set high on a hilltop with views of the entire Lakes Region. It's the former home of a shoe mogul, whose original estate once covered 6,300 acres, stretching from the mountains to the edge of the lake. The view itself is worth the trip to the house, but the interior is beautifully restored, with decor and furnishings based on images of the original house or on written descriptions. The surrounding grounds are now managed by the **Lakes Region Conservation Trust** (LRCT, www.lrct.org), with 30 miles of hiking trails that are accessible without paying the entrance fee to the house. Maps of the hiking trails are available on the LRCT website, or can be purchased at the Castle in the Clouds gift shop. Hiker parking is by Shannon Pond on Ossipee Park Road.

A quirky natural history museum built from the collection of an early 20th-century doctor, **The Libby Museum** (755 N. Main St., 603/569-1035, www.thelibbymuseum.org 10am-4pm Tues.-Sat., noon-4pm Sun. June-mid-Oct., $5 adults, youth under 17 and veterans free) has a fascinating rainy-day collection of stuffed animals and Native American artifacts. Free wild animal shows are held at 2pm each Wednesday in July and August.

ENTERTAINMENT AND EVENTS

Nighttime entertainment can be tough to come by in these quiet parts, but there's usually a good crowd at **Wolfe's Tavern** (90 N. Main St., 603/569-3016, www.wolfeboroinn.com, 7am-9pm daily) at the Wolfeboro Inn. The authentic New England-style pub (with several fireplaces, and pewter beer mugs strewn across the ceiling) serves food, but later in the evening, it's all about the beer. If you drink all 70 kinds available—no more than two per visit, alas—you'll get to kiss the moose head and hang your own personalized pewter mug on the ceiling.

Saturday evenings July-early September, a crowd gathers near the water for the **Wolfeboro Community Bandstand Concerts** (Cate Park, www.wolfebrorobandstand.org, 7pm-9pm, free), featuring a range of performers that lean local. Held by the New Hampshire Boat Museum, the **Vintage Race Boat Regatta** (603/569-4554, www.nhbm.org, Sept.), features dozens of boats that range from magnificent to strange, a rare chance to see the historic vessels in action.

SPORTS AND RECREATION

Running 11 miles from Wolfeboro to the village of Wakefield, the **Wolfeboro Recreation Rail Trail** (trailhead on Depot St. by the Wolfeboro Chamber of Commerce, www.nhstateparks.org) leaves right from the center of town, following the mostly flat rail bed through the forest. The trail surface is crushed gravel that's easy to ride even with narrow tires, and highlights of the trail are a pair of causeways that cross Lake Wentworth and Crescent Lake. Bikes are available to rent at **Nordic Skier Sports** (47 N. Main St., 603/569-3151, www.nordicskiersports.com, 9am-5pm Mon.-Sat., half-day rental $20).

On a small lake just east of Winni, **Wentworth State Park** (Rte. 109, 603/569-3699, www.nhstateparks.org, $4 adults, $2 children 6-11, children under 6 free) features a sandy beach on the land where Governor Wentworth once spent summer vacations. There are picnic tables and a bathhouse, and the water tends to be warmer than Lake Winnipesaukee, making this an excellent place to swim.

With a design based on a 1928 Hacker-Craft, the ***Millie B*** (11 S. Main St., 603/569-4554, www.nhbm.org, 45-minute tour $22 adults, $20 seniors, military, and youth 13-16, $10 children 5-12, children under 5 free) is 28 feet of sleek mahogany with an unusual triple cockpit, and is owned and operated by the New Hampshire Boat Museum. The tours combine local sights with wildlife watching and a bit of history, but the real highlight is just cruising around in a gorgeous boat that's a throwback to the glory days of wooden boats.

FOOD

It's all ice cream, all the (summer)time at **Bailey's Bubble** (5 Railroad Ave., 603/569-3612, www.baileysbubble.com, 11am-9pm Mon.-Fri., 11am-10pm Sat.-Sun., $2-4). Open May-September, the locally loved stand scoops up banana splits, brownie sundaes, and flavors like maple walnut and cherry chip, plus homemade hot fudge. A New Hampshire classic is Moose Tracks, with a blend of vanilla ice cream, peanut butter, and chocolate.

With a menu of hefty sandwiches, **Full Belli Deli** (15 Mill St., 603/569-1955, 10:30am-6pm Mon.-Fri., 10:30am-4pm Sat., 10:30am-3pm Sun., $8-12) is a good option for lunch or a picnic. You might find that the sandwiches are big enough to share, and it's worth calling in an order on busy days, when the line can stretch to the door.

Simple egg breakfasts, wraps, and waffles bring in a steady crowd for breakfast at the **Downtown Grille Café** (33 S. Main St., 603/569-4504, www.downtowngrille.cafe, 7am-3pm daily, $5-11), while lunch is a lineup of sandwiches and burgers. It's an easygoing spot with counter service, and if you're lucky you'll snag a table on the back deck with views of the lake.

A short distance outside of the compact

downtown, **Wolfetrap** (19 Bay St., 603/569-1047, www.wolfetrapgrilleandrawbar.com, 11am-late daily, $9-25) is an escape from the crush on busy days, with waterfront seating on a back bay of Lake Winnipesaukee. There's a reasonable raw bar with shucked oysters and clams, but the main draw is a menu of fried and grilled seafood (the crab cakes win raves).

Scratch-baked pastries and breads at **La Boca Bakery** (50 N. Main St., 603/569-5595, www.labocabakery.com, 9am-4pm Wed.-Sat., 8am-1pm Sun., $3-8) are well made and not too sweet, with croissants, cupcakes, and personal-size cheesecakes.

ACCOMMODATIONS AND CAMPING

With a gorgeous location between two lakes, ★ **Pow-Wow Lodges & Motel** (19 Governor Wentworth Hwy., 603/515-7011, www.powwowlodges.com, suites $145-165, cottages from $1,250 per week) is a great place to get out on the water, and rowboats, canoes, kayaks, and paddleboards are available for guest use. Suites each come with two beds and a private deck, microwaves, refrigerators, coffeemakers, and air-conditioning, while some have a full kitchenette. When things quiet down for the evening, you may hear calling loons from nearby Mirror Lake.

A good value that's 10 minutes away from the center of Wolfeboro, **Lake View Bed & Breakfast** (20 Martin Hill Rd., 603/515-6415, www.lakeview-inn.com, $160) certainly delivers on the promise of lake views, with spectacular vistas from some rooms. Big breakfasts of scones, with cooked-to-order plates of eggs and French toast, are highlights. The innkeepers have six friendly dogs, and some guests have been bothered by their sometimes energetic barking.

Lines of Adirondack chairs line the private beach at **The Wolfeboro Inn** (90 N. Main St., 603/569-3016, www.wolfeboroinn.com, $150-300), which is walking distance from the center of town. Rooms are smart, if unremarkable, and there's plenty of room to linger on the property—around fire pits, by the shore, and over cookies, lemonade, and tea each day in the lobby.

Set back in the forest behind Lake Wentworth, **Wolfeboro Campground** (61 Haines Hill Rd., 603/569-9881, www.wolfeborocampground.com, $29-33) has wooded sites, clean restrooms, and a group campfire area, as well as a screened-in gazebo in a pleasant garden. If that's full, the nearby **Willey Brook Campground** (883 Center St., 603/569-9493, www.willeybrookcampground.com, $29-37) is just about the same, with perhaps a shade more lawn than forest.

INFORMATION

The **Wolfeboro Area Chamber of Commerce** (32 Central Ave., 603/569-2200, www.wolfeboro.com, 10am-3pm Mon.-Sat., 10am-noon Sun.) runs a comprehensive information center in the town's historic old train station.

GETTING THERE

Wolfeboro is at the intersection of Route 28 and Route 109, on the eastern shore of Lake Winnipesaukee. There's no direct public transit to Wolfeboro, but buses from **Concord Coach Lines** (800/639-3317, www.concordcoachlines.com) link **Boston** with **Meredith** (2 hrs., 30 min., $23.50). From there, taxi service to Wolfeboro is available from **Big Lake Taxi & Limousine** (603/875-3365, www.biglaketaxiandlimo.com, $125).

Squam Lakes

Beyond the bustle of Lake Winnepesaukee, the forest closes in around a scattershot of ponds, lakes, and potholes—New Hampshire has almost 1,000 lakes altogether. Of these, Squam Lakes are among the most appealing. Morning breaks with the eerie loon call, or with the shushing rhythm of canoe paddles.

There's not much to the town itself—a stamp-sized post office and a general store hold down the main crossroads—but that's just the idea. It's a place to pack a picnic lunch, maybe pick up some bait, then spend the day exploring the shoreline, spotting birds, or visiting the rambling outdoor science museum.

★ SQUAM LAKES NATURAL SCIENCE CENTER

New England's last known mountain lion was killed in Maine in 1938, but you can still see one of the beautiful cats at the excellent **Squam Lakes Natural Science Center** (23 Science Center Rd./Rte. 113, Holderness, 603/968-7194, www.nhnature.org, 9:30am-5pm daily May-Oct., $19 adults, $16 seniors, $14 youth 3-15, children under 3 free), hands-down the best in New England. The center has dozens of local animals, including a bobcat, several black bears, otters, and flying raptors arranged in spacious enclosures along a 0.75-mile wooded nature trail. (Most of the animals were injured and unable to survive in the wild.)

Where it really excels, though, is in the interactive exhibits that accompany each animal—they're imaginative and educational for kids and adults alike. (Case in point is the "long jump" that compares your personal best with the mountain lion's.) The center also has an informative exhibit on the star of the northern lakes: the common loon.

The science center also runs a series of highly regarded, 90-minute **lake cruises** ($27 adults, $25 seniors, $23 youth, children 3 and under free) that focus on everything from bald eagles to loons, geography, and lake ecosystems. Combo tickets for the science center and lake cruises are also available ($40 adults, $35 seniors, $31 youth).

If hanging out on the lakes for a while makes you suddenly crazy for loons, learn more about the water bird with the eerie call at the **Loon Center** (183 Lee's Mill Rd./off Rte. 25, Moultonborough, 603/476-5666, www.loon.org, 9am-5pm Mon.-Sat. mid-May-June, 9am-5pm daily July-early Oct., 9am-5pm Thurs.-Sat. early Oct.-mid-May, free), a half-hour drive from Holderness. This homegrown museum explains such mysteries as why loons' eyes are red, why chicks ride on their parents' backs, and what that ghostly cry actually means. A 1.5-mile nature trail along the shores of Moultonborough Bay, a branch of Lake Winni, takes in coves where loons are known to nest in spring.

SHOPPING

In small New England communities, a good general store can make the town, and **Squam Lake MarketPlace** (862 Rte. 3, Holderness, 603/968-8588, www.squammarket.com,

river otter at the Squam Lakes Natural Science Center

7am-5pm daily) is a one-stop destination for gossip, advice, food, and cabin-cutesy souvenirs. The made-to-order breakfast sandwiches are a treat, and the store packs customized picnic boxes that range from a simple lunch of sandwiches and canned drinks to more elaborate spreads including lobster rolls, bottles of bubbly, and cheese boards (with a loaner cooler for the day).

Dozens of artists display their work at **Squam Lakes Artisans** (900 Rte. 3, Holderness, 603/968-9525, www.squamlakesartisans.com, 10am-5pm daily mid-May-early Sept., 10am-5pm Fri.-Mon. early Sept.-mid-Oct.), whose collection ranges from elegant canvases to folksy quilts and crafts.

SPORTS AND RECREATION

The nonprofit **Squam Lakes Association** (534 Rte. 3, Holderness, 603/968-7336, www.squamlakes.org, 9am-5pm daily) rents canoes, kayaks, and paddleboards by the hour and the day ($15-20 per hour, $50-65 per day), and the staff is happy to help with paddling basics. The Squam Lakes Association also operates a series of backcountry and island campsites that are amazing for overnight canoe trips if you're equipped for sleeping out of doors.

The most popular hike near Squam Lakes is the 2-mile round-trip to the summit of **West Rattlesnake Mountain,** which departs from the Old Bridle Path trailhead on Route 113. To reach the trailhead, travel 5.5 miles north from the intersection of Route 113 and Route 3, parking on the right-hand side of the road in a small pullout. The yellow-blazed trail leads through a forest of red oaks and red pines, then breaks from the trees for gorgeous views of Squam Lakes from a rocky summit.

For a longer day on the trail, the **Squam Range Traverse** is a classic, 13.1-mile point-to-point that summits the seven named peaks in the Squam Range, starting from Mead Base Camp to the north of Squam Lakes, and describing an arc that moves south and west on the Crawford Ridgepole Trail. Hiking maps and guides can be purchased at the **Squam Lakes Association,** and an excellent trail description is available at **Hike New England** (www.hikenewengland.com).

FOOD

Laid-back and sunny, the dining room at the ★ **Squam Lake Inn** (28 Shepard Hill Rd., Holderness, 603/968-4417, www.squamlakeinn.com, 5pm-8pm Wed.-Sun., $18-33) turns out consistently excellent meals that are among the most appealing in the region. The well-balanced menu blends seafood and classic meat dishes, including oysters fresh from the coast, salmon grilled on a cedar plank, flatiron steak, and ribs. The meltingly tender scallops are a highlight, as is the bright and refreshing frozen key lime pie.

The only waterfront dining on Squam is at **Walter's Basin** (Rte. 3, Holderness, 603/968-4412, www.waltersbasin.com, 11:30am-9:30pm Sun.-Thurs., 11:30am-10pm Fri.-Sat., $11-26), a restaurant and pub serving a mishmash of comfort foods, including great piles of fried fish, meatloaf, and hearty sandwiches. The dining room inside is open year-round, whereas outdoor seating runs May-October, and is as apt to see guests arrive by boat as by foot.

Ten minutes from the edge of Squam Lakes, **Annie's Overflow Restaurant** (138 Rte. 175A, Holderness, 603/536-4062, www.overflowrestaurantplymouth.com, 6am-2pm daily, $4-10) is a cheerful little diner with hearty servings. Breakfasts are egg classics and piles of pancakes, while the lunch menu ranges from Reuben sandwiches to old-fashioned beef liver and onions.

For formal occasions in the New Hampshire forest, ★ **The Manor on Golden Pond** (Rte. 3, Holderness, 603/968-3348, www.manorongoldenpond.com, seatings 6pm-8pm daily, reservations recommended, $28-41) is the place to be. The elegant estate house serves grand, European-style cuisine in the white linen-filled Van Horn room, with a refined wine list to accompany meals.

ACCOMMODATIONS AND CAMPING

Sweet and welcoming, ★ **Cottage Place on Squam Lake** (1132 Rte. 3, Holderness, 603/968-7116, www.cottageplaceonsquam.com, $129-269) is the kind of place families return to year after year, setting up shop in compact cabins just across the road from a private beach. The units are being overhauled one by one with plenty of antiques, but the feel is more old-fashioned than fussy. Perks include an outdoor fire pit, grills for guests to use, and inexpensive kayak and canoe rentals. While the cottages are the starring attraction, the property also includes a handful of more modern motel units and a lodge for larger groups.

You'll find 10 very pretty guest rooms (each with lake-themed decor) at **Squam Lake Inn** (Rte. 3 and Shepard Hill Rd., Holderness, 603/968-4417, www.squamlakeinn.com, $160-300). The century-old Victorian farmhouse building outfits each chamber with exceptional linens and Wi-Fi, and offers a full breakfast (from four-grain blueberry pancakes to eggs Benedict). Common areas include a charmingly decorated library and a lovely wraparound porch.

The rustic (and rather outdated) **Boulders Motel** (981 Rte. 3, Holderness, 603/968-3600, www.bouldersmotel.com, $79-299) gets mixed reviews, but snagging a cottage with a screened-in porch means you can enjoy your morning coffee overlooking the lake. There's a fire pit on the beach, grills, and a swimming raft that make this an especially good choice for families, and muffins and hot drinks are included in the price.

Somewhat rundown and dominated by season-long RVers, **Owls Landing Campground** (245 Rte. 3, Holderness, 603/279-6266, www.owlslanding.com, sites $30-40) is nevertheless a serviceable and affordable place to sleep. A campground store on-site is good for stocking up on campfire marshmallows, and kid-friendly perks include a swimming pool and rec room with pool tables.

INFORMATION

For more information on the area, contact the **Lakes Region Tourism Association** (603/286-8008, www.lakesregion.org).

GETTING THERE

Squam Lakes are a pair of lakes linked by a short outlet at Holderness, flanked by Route 3 and Route 113. No public transportation is currently available to Squam Lakes.

New Hampshire's White Mountains

Alpine peaks tower over wooded valleys, mountain rivers, and a lifetime of hiking trails in New Hampshire's White Mountains.

It's a place of howling winter storms, fiercely pitched trails, and flowers that grow nowhere else in the world. A highlight of the 2,200-mile Appalachian Trail, the White Mountains are New England's top wilderness destination.

What really sets these mountains apart, though, is how easy it is for visitors of any ability (or motivation) to get to a peak. In the 19th century, Americans fell hard for the wilderness of New Hampshire, which became a favorite destination for escaping hot, crowded cities. They took to the hills in woolen knickers and hiking gowns, capturing images of the sublime landscape and weather on portable easels and with early cameras. Those first tourists left paths that can still be followed today: They forged scenic roads that wind to mountain peaks, built a railway that runs straight to the top of Mount Washington, and slept in grand hotels offering all the views with none of the sweat. Another legacy is a series of backcountry huts maintained by the Appalachian Mountain Club (AMC), off-grid stations that in the summer become small communities that welcome hikers from around the world.

To discover the best of the White Mountains, simply choose a trail, pick a road, or take a seat on the cog railway to get a taste of New England rock laid bare.

PLANNING YOUR TIME

Two great ranges hold down opposite sides of the White Mountains, and a series of valley highways wind from peak to peak. On the northeastern side is Mount Washington and the Presidential Range, mountains that are most easily accessed from Gorham or the Conways, where many of the region's services, hotels, and attractions are based.

On the west side, along I-93, is the Franconia Range. Here the peaks are smaller (though by no means unimpressive), and the highway is studded with family-style attractions and trailheads. Running along the southern edge of both

Previous: horses in Franconia; covered bridge over Pemigewasset River. **Above:** Flume Gorge.

Look for ★ to find recommended sights, activities, dining, and lodging.

Highlights

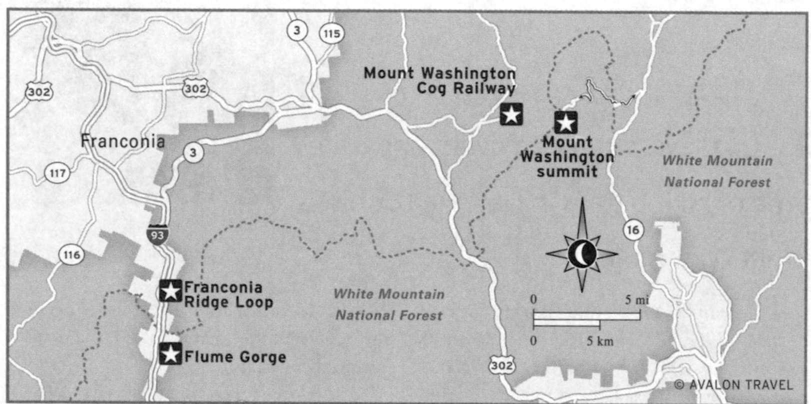

★ **Mount Washington Summit:** Explore wind-whipped ridges, learn about Mount Washington's extreme weather, and take in views across three states (page 115).

★ **Mount Washington Cog Railway:** Chug to the top of the highest peak in the East in colorful carriages pushed by coal and biodiesel engines (page 118).

★ **Flume Gorge:** Walk to dramatic waterfalls and covered bridges on an easygoing, family-friendly trail (page 125).

★ **Franconia Ridge Loop:** Trek through the second-highest range in New Hampshire, topping out several peaks with views across a forested valley (page 128).

ranges, the Kancamagus Highway—or "the Kanc"—cuts through the most dramatic terrain in the White Mountains, following the Swift River past rolling hills and notches. The towns of Franconia and Littleton are the principal gateways to the Franconia Range, with trailheads, campgrounds, and accommodations.

Mount Washington and the Presidential Range

A series of bare peaks pushing high above the tree line, the Presidential Range is the heart of White Mountain National Forest, a rugged spine that culminates in Mount Washington, the highest summit in the northeastern United States. While the area isn't vast—the entire Presidential Range can be hiked in one punishing 23-mile day—it has the feel of true wilderness.

Even in summer, the temperature difference between the peak of Mount Washington and neighboring valleys averages around 30 degrees. The tree line, the elevation where trees go from stunted to nonexistent, is around 4,400 feet in the White Mountains, in contrast to 11,000-12,000 feet in Colorado's Rocky Mountains; that difference shows how harsh the conditions are in New Hampshire's relatively low-lying alpine areas. The weather observatory on that peak has recorded some of the world's most extreme weather, including the highest wind speeds on record, and the Presidentials get hammered by winter storms that coat them in thick layers of rime ice, snow, and frost.

Anyone with time and strong legs can find lonely trails and solitude in the White Mountains, and it can be a sublime experience. But it's delightfully fun to enjoy the Presidential Range in 19th-century style, chugging up the slope in "The Cog," bagging a few stony summits, then taking high tea in the Princess Room at Bretton Woods.

NORTH CONWAY AND CONWAY

In the shadow of the towering Presidential Range, this pair of mountain towns is the gateway to White Mountain adventures. North Conway's cute and historic downtown quickly gives way to an uninspiring cluster of outlet stores and inns, and it can get jammed on busy hiking and skiing weekends. But it's not really about the town—above all, this is the place to stock up on gear, plan your route, and rise early for a trip into New Hampshire's high places, then come back to recover over hearty mountain food and beer. North Conway and Conway are just five miles apart, with services stretching along Route 16, so this section includes listings for both towns.

Sights

A beloved destination for New Hampshire's rock climbers, **Cathedral Ledge** is a spectacular band of granite cliffs within **Echo Lake State Park** (68 Echo Lake Rd., Conway, 603/356-2672, www.nhstateparks.org, 9am-7pm daily mid-May-mid-Oct., $4 adults, $2 children 6-11) that have wonderful views of the surrounding mountains—it's a prime spot for picnics. To reach the top of the ledge, visitors can drive a scenic, mile-long road, or hike up the steep **Bryce Path** from the same parking lot (2.4-miles round-trip). An easier hike within the park is the mostly flat, mile-long loop around **Echo Lake,** which departs from the visitors center (with a beach that's perfect for cooling off).

During the heyday of 19th-century travel to the White Mountains, rail lines threaded around the range, with spurs to each of the grand hotels. Most of the tracks are quiet, but the **Conway Scenic Railway** (38 Norcross Circle, North Conway, 603/356-5251, www.

New Hampshire's White Mountains

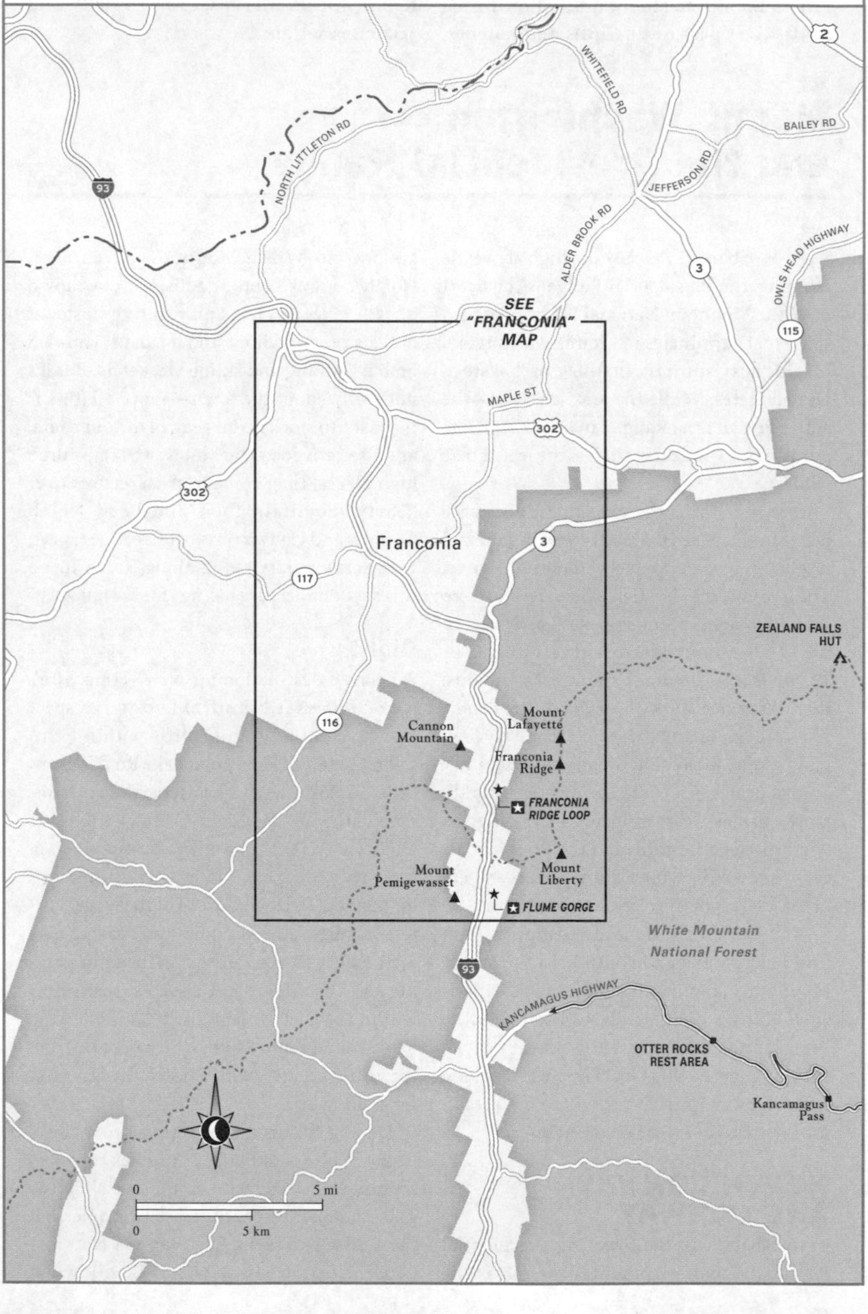

2
WHITEFIELD RD
BAILEY RD
NORTH LITTLETON RD
93
JEFFERSON RD
ALDER BROOK RD
OWLS HEAD HIGHWAY
3
115
SEE "FRANCONIA" MAP
MAPLE ST
302
302
Franconia
3
117
ZEALAND FALLS HUT
116
Cannon Mountain
Mount Lafayette
Franconia Ridge
FRANCONIA RIDGE LOOP
Mount Pemigewasset
Mount Liberty
FLUME GORGE
White Mountain National Forest
93
KANCAMAGUS HIGHWAY
OTTER ROCKS REST AREA
Kancamagus Pass
0
5 mi
0
5 km

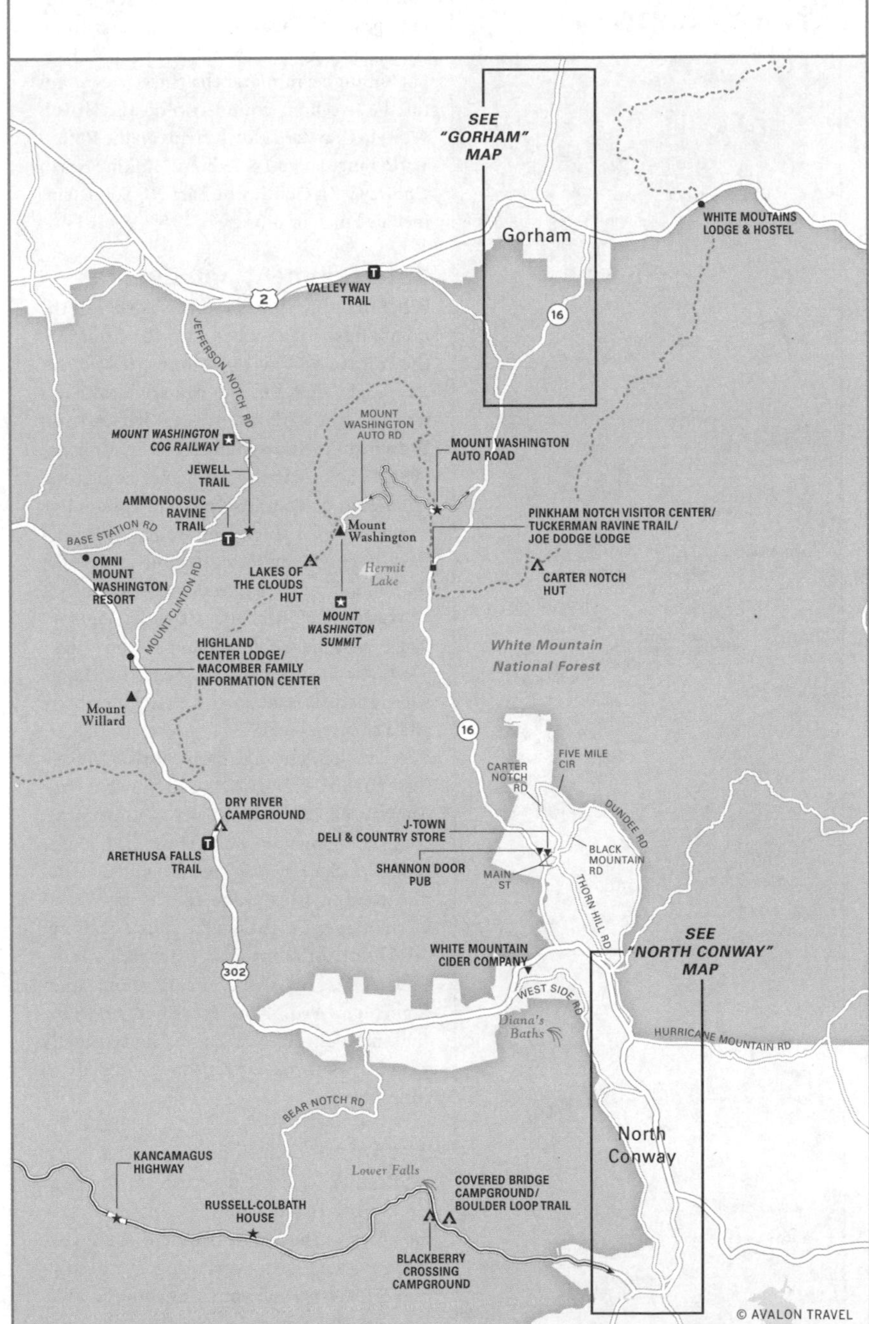

SEE "GORHAM" MAP
Gorham
WHITE MOUTAINS LODGE & HOSTEL
VALLEY WAY TRAIL
2
16
JEFFERSON NOTCH RD
MOUNT WASHINGTON AUTO RD
MOUNT WASHINGTON COG RAILWAY
JEWELL TRAIL
AMMONOOSUC RAVINE TRAIL
MOUNT WASHINGTON AUTO ROAD
BASE STATION RD
Mount Washington
PINKHAM NOTCH VISITOR CENTER/ TUCKERMAN RAVINE TRAIL/ JOE DODGE LODGE
OMNI MOUNT WASHINGTON RESORT
LAKES OF THE CLOUDS HUT
Hermit Lake
CARTER NOTCH HUT
MOUNT CLINTON RD
MOUNT WASHINGTON SUMMIT
HIGHLAND CENTER LODGE/ MACOMBER FAMILY INFORMATION CENTER
White Mountain National Forest
Mount Willard
16
CARTER NOTCH RD
FIVE MILE CIR
DRY RIVER CAMPGROUND
DUNDEE RD
J-TOWN DELI & COUNTRY STORE
ARETHUSA FALLS TRAIL
SHANNON DOOR PUB
MAIN ST
BLACK MOUNTAIN RD
THORN HILL RD
WHITE MOUNTAIN CIDER COMPANY
SEE "NORTH CONWAY" MAP
302
WEST SIDE RD
Diana's Baths
HURRICANE MOUNTAIN RD
BEAR NOTCH RD
North Conway
KANCAMAGUS HIGHWAY
Lower Falls
COVERED BRIDGE CAMPGROUND/ BOULDER LOOP TRAIL
RUSSELL-COLBATH HOUSE
BLACKBERRY CROSSING CAMPGROUND
© AVALON TRAVEL

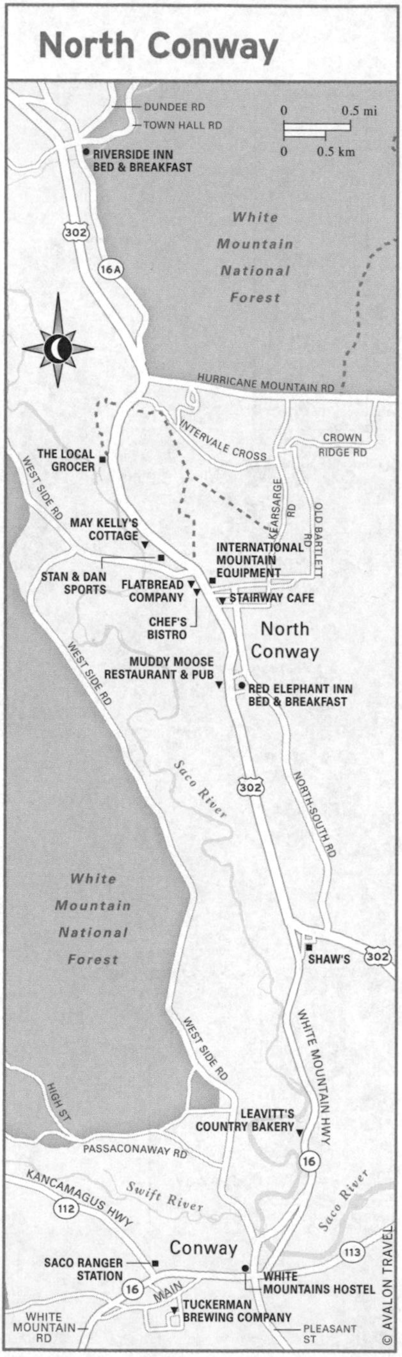

conwayscenic.com, $17.50-140) sends vintage passenger trains from the charming, 1874 train station in North Conway Village. For rolling terrain and the finest views, opt for the five-hour round-trip on the **Notch Train** to Crawford Notch. Trips on the **Valley Train** range about 1-1.75 hours, linking North Conway with Conway or Bartlett. Some trips include lunch or dinner.

Entertainment and Events

What nightlife there is in this corner of the mountains is firmly based in the Conways, the cultural hub of the Whites. It's not really "night" life, but you can try local beers well into the early evening at **Tuckerman Brewing Company** (66 Hobbs St., Conway, 603/447-5400, www.tuckermanbrewing.com, noon-6pm daily, tours 2pm and 4pm daily), which brews a lineup of stouts, ales, and IPAs. A good way to meet some locals is at the Sunday night Irish session at **May Kelly's Cottage** (3002 Rte. 302, Conway, 603/356-7005, www.maykellys.com, 4pm-9pm Tues.-Thurs., noon-10pm Fri.-Sat., noon-8pm Sun.), which has a pleasant porch for afternoon beers and a convivial feel.

A favorite watering hole is **Muddy Moose Restaurant & Pub** (2344 Rte. 302, North Conway, 603/356-7696, www.muddymoose.com, 11:30am-9pm Sun.-Thurs., 11:30am-10pm Fri.-Sat.), whose antler chandelier and raw wood interior evoke an oversized summer cottage. Up the road in little Jackson, the **Shannon Door Pub** (Rte. 16, Jackson, 603/383-4211, www.shannondoor.com, 4pm-10pm Mon.-Wed., 4pm-11pm Thurs. and Sun., 4pm-midnight Fri.-Sat.) has live music nightly Thursday-Saturday and a fun, country Irish atmosphere.

Shopping

While there are plenty of shops for poking around in the Conways, the most useful stores in the White Mountains are gear shops stocked with everything you need to walk, ride, or climb your way into the hills. The Conways have a plethora: **International**

Mountain Equipment (2733 Rte. 302, North Conway, 603/356-7013, www.ime-usa.com, 9am-6pm Sun.-Thurs., 9am-9pm Fri., 8am-8pm Sat.) is a well-stocked gear shop run by the International Mountain Climbing School, which also rents hiking and camping equipment. **Stan & Dan Sports** (2936 Rte. 302, North Conway, 603/356-6997, www.stananddansports.com, 9am-6pm Mon.-Sat., 9am-5pm Sun.) is a go-to for bike and ski gear.

Sports and Recreation

HIKING

A good choice for hiking with kids, the gentle, 0.6-mile walk to **Diana's Baths** between North Conway and Bartlett ends in an enchanting series of waterfalls ideal for cooling off in wading pools (the baths vary greatly with water level, though, and by late summer the waterfalls can be mere trickles). To reach the parking area from North Conway, take Route 302 north out of town, then turn left on River Road (which becomes West Side Rd. after a mile) for 2.5 miles. A large parking lot is on the left with a self-service, cash-only parking fee station ($5).

Steeper and a bit more ambitious is the **Black Cap Hiking Trail** (Hurricane Mountain Rd., Intervale), a 2.4-mile round-trip that passes through a forest of beech and spruce trees on the way to a rocky summit with great views of the surrounding mountains (it's particularly spectacular in fall).

Food

A year-round favorite is ★ **May Kelly's Cottage** (3002 Rte. 302, 603/356-7005, www.maykellys.com, 4pm-9pm Tues.-Thurs., noon-10pm Fri.-Sat., noon-8pm Sun., $9-22), which serves hearty Irish classics and American pub fare in a relaxed, old-world setting. With fabulous mountain views and shaded tables, the outdoor patio is perfect for an early evening meal, while the interior is decked with a pleasant jumble of Americana and Irish bric-a-brac. Shepherd's pie, soups, and hearty salads all come with homemade, grainy bread, and regulars love the fried potato cakes with spinach and horseradish sauce. On Sunday evenings, a fun group of Irish musicians holds a relaxed live session, playing around a table over beers.

Fresh, simple breakfasts and hearty lunches at ★ **Stairway Café** (2649 Rte. 302, North Conway, 603/356-5200, www.stairwaycafe.com, 7am-3pm daily, $7-18) are the main draw, but the atmosphere is pretty great too—the decor strikes a curious balance between country kitchen and rock and roll (imagine a bacon-and-egg skull on a floral print menu). Both the breakfast and lunch menus are served all day and include plenty of basic egg plates, burgers, and sandwiches, along with offbeat additions like wild game sausage and Maine lobster Benedict.

The unassuming **Leavitt's Country Bakery** (564 Rte. 302, Conway, 603/447-2218, 4am-5pm Mon.-Sat., 4am-1pm Sun., $2-7) turns out great piles of doughnuts, fritters, and Bismarck pastries—regular visitors fill boxes full of sweets before leaving the Whites. With no seating and little fuss, Leavitt's is perfect for picking up pre-hike treats and coffee, and it also prepares a mean breakfast sandwich to go.

Part of a small chain of earthy pizza joints with a focus on natural, organic ingredients, **Flatbread Company** (2760 Rte. 302, North Conway, 603/356-4470, www.flatbreadcompany.com, 11:30am-9pm Sun.-Thurs., 11:30am-9:30pm Fri.-Sat., $9-13) pulls thin-crust pies from a wood-fired oven, topped with homemade pepperoni and sausage, piles of fresh vegetables, and tomato sauce that bubbles away in a cauldron by the fire. The very casual spot is rustic and a little loud, a good choice for larger groups and families with children.

With a bit more polish and creative food, **Chef's Bistro** (2724 Rte. 302, North Conway, 603/356-4747, www.chefsbistronh.com, 11am-9pm daily, $9-28) serves eclectic dinners ranging from a vegetarian Thai curry to Asian beef salad and bistro-style steaks with great piles of hand-cut fries. Lunch is simpler, with unfussy and appealing sandwiches, burgers, and salads. This is an especially good place for those with dietary restrictions, and the restaurant has a basic kids' menu.

Conway is the main base for services in the area, with a **Shaw's grocery store** (1150 Eastman Rd., Conway, 603/356-5471, 7am-11pm Mon.-Sat., 7am-10pm Sun.); **The Local Grocer** (3358 Rte. 302, North Conway, 603/356-6068, www.nhlocalgrocer.com, 8am-7pm daily) is a smaller store that stocks natural and organic options.

Accommodations

UNDER $100

Compare blisters with fellow travelers at the **White Mountains Hostel** (36 Washington St., Conway, 866/902-2521, www.wmhostel.com, dorms $34, private rooms $64), a super-friendly spot with a communal kitchen, comfortable common areas, and very clean (if rather plain) quarters. The six-bed dorms include female-only, male-only, and coed options, and the private rooms are an excellent choice for families—each has a full bed, and some have an additional twin or bunk bed (prices are for two adults, and there's a supplemental charge of $20 per adult or $10 per child).

$100-150

A family-owned motel with plain and tidy rooms, **Colonial Motel** (2431 Route 16, North Conway, 603/356-5178, www.thecolonialmotel.com, $80-160) is a convenient choice (and a pretty solid deal). Rooms have mini fridges; hot drinks are served in the morning; and the motel is easy walking distance from downtown and the railway station. Dogs are welcome for an additional $10 per night.

$150-250

With a central location in North Conway, the ★ **Red Elephant Inn Bed & Breakfast** (28 Locust Ln., North Conway, 603/356-3548, www.redelephantinn.com, $129-239) combines the best of a classic bed-and-breakfast—giant breakfast spread, a friendly atmosphere, and cozy common spaces—with the amenities and style of a more luxurious inn. Complimentary afternoon wine and snacks are just the thing after a day spent on the trails, and the big library is stocked with local maps and books to read by the unheated outdoor pool. A hot drink and snack bar is available throughout the day for guests to help themselves, and rooms balance a warm wood-and-plaid White Mountains aesthetic with bits of art deco flair that keep things fresh and contemporary.

Fireplaces in every room and elegant four-poster beds make the **Riverside Inn Bed & Breakfast** (372 Rte. 16, Intervale, 866/949-0044, www.riverside-inn-bed-breakfast.com, $119-225) one of the more romantic places to stay in the White Mountains, with a central location that's four miles outside of North Conway. A river runs through the serene backyard, which is stocked with well-placed lawn chairs and a hammock, and the cooked-to-order breakfasts use lots of local ingredients, organic veggies, and seasonal fruits. Fresh cookies are served at afternoon teas in the old-fashioned sitting room.

Information

The White Mountain National Forest **Saco Ranger Station** (33 Rte. 112, Conway, 603/447-5448, 8am-5pm daily late May-mid-Oct., 8am-4:30pm daily Oct.-May) has maps, advice, and updated weather reports. Small visitors information centers cover non-trail-related questions in **North Conway** (2617 Rte. 16, North Conway, 603/356-5947, 10am-6pm daily) and **Conway** (250 Main St., Conway, 603/447-2639, 10am-5pm Sun.-Thurs., 10am-2pm Fri.-Sat.).

Getting There

The Conways are at the junction of several main access roads: Route 302 from Maine, Route 16 from southern New Hampshire, and the eastern end of the Kancamagus Highway. **Concord Coach Lines** (800/639-3317, www.concordcoachlines.com) links North Conway by bus with **Boston** (3 hrs., 50 min., round-trip $59).

The Presidential Traverse

Strictly for extremely fit, experienced hikers, the **Presidential Traverse** is a 23-mile hike that goes up and over every peak in the Presidential Range—tellingly, this hike is often referred to as the **Death March.** Many hikers begin and end in the dark (although the classic Death March is a long day hike, it's possible to break it up with a night in the **Lakes of the Clouds** hut). Most hikers go north to south, taking the **Valley Way Trail** from the Appalachia parking lot (Rte. 2, 5 miles west of the intersection with Rte. 16) up Mount Madison before ticking off a who's who of American presidents, ending with Mount Jackson, then descending into Crawford Notch. The one-way hike requires a car on either end, or you can use the **AMC Hiker Shuttle** (603/466-2727, www.outdoors.org, early June-Oct., $23). More information can be obtained at the **Pinkham Notch Visitor Center** (361 Rte. 16, 603/466-8116, www.outdoors.org, 6:30am-10pm daily).

PINKHAM NOTCH

A scenic pass at the base of Mount Washington, Pinkham Notch is wrapped in peaks, with the Presidential Range commanding the western horizon and the ski slopes of Wildcat Mountain and the Carter Range to the east. More mountain outpost than actual town, this is a starting point for peak-bagging hikes and time above tree line, with an Appalachian Mountain Club hiker information center to get you safely on the trail.

Sights

MOUNT WASHINGTON AUTO ROAD

You'll see the bumper stickers as soon as you start driving around New England: "This Car Climbed Mount Washington." And you'll earn breathtaking views with every turn of the **Mount Washington Auto Road** (Rte. 16, Pinkham Notch, 603/466-3988, www.mountwashingtonautoroad.com, variable hours early May-late Oct., $29 car and driver, $9 each adult, $7 each child, children under 5 free, $17 motorcycle and driver, no bicycles or hitchhiking). The 7.6-mile trip goes by at a snail's pace, taking about 30 minutes on the way up, 40 on the way down, and it's not for everyone—both drivers and passengers who are unnerved by heights may be better off in one of the guided van tours (from $36 adults, $31 seniors, $16 children 5-12, children under 5 free).

For hikers who'd like to make a one-way trip up or down Mount Washington, there's an annoyingly expensive **one-way shuttle** ($31 adults, $26 seniors, $13 children 5-12); hitchhiking is prohibited. At the bottom of the road, the **Red Barn Museum** (1 Mount Washington Auto Rd., 603/466-3988, 10am-4pm daily late May-early Oct., free) displays objects relating to the auto road's past, including antique cars and a carriage that used to climb the mountain.

★ MOUNT WASHINGTON SUMMIT

Learn about the scientists who live and work at the top at the **Mount Washington Observatory Weather Discovery Center** (summit building, 10am-5pm daily, $2 adults, $1 children 7-17, children under 7 free), which has interactive displays explaining the mountain's wild weather and telling the story of the day in 1934 when a record-breaking 231 miles-per-hour wind was recorded at the summit. There's also a good visual guide to the alpine plants that grow on the summit, including the dwarf cinquefoil, a tiny flower that grows only in the alpine zones of the Presidential Range and Franconia Ridge.

Those willing to join the observatory's membership program can register for a tour of the **weather station** (www.mtwashington.org, 603/356-2137, ext. 211, membership $50 individual, $75 couple or family) itself; unfortunately, the station is closed to the public, though the observatory recently began partnering with the Mount Washington Cog

Railway so that several railway trips a week include a tour of the weather station (call for details).

The oldest surviving building on the summit is the **Tip Top House,** a rustic stone lodge built in 1853 as a hotel, which then became the office for *Among the Clouds*, a mountain newspaper that chronicled social events, train schedules, weather, and gossip in 1888-1915. Tiny bunks, communal tables, and a few dusty reproductions of the newspaper are on display.

Sports and Recreation

TOP EXPERIENCE

HIKING

The most iconic hike in the White Mountains may be the **Tuckerman Ravine Trail,** a 4.2-mile route to the summit of Mount Washington that leaves from the **Pinkham Notch Visitor Center** (361 Rte. 16). Doing this hike as a round-trip is a full-day outing of at least six hours, and it's especially important to bring extra clothes, water, and a headlamp for this strenuous trail. After some initial switchbacks through thick forest, the trail rises fairly gradually to **Hermit Lake Shelter** after 2.4 miles, where you'll find lean-tos, tent platforms, and potable water from a hand-operated pump.

After the lake the trail begins to climb in earnest, then aims straight up the western edge of Tuckerman Ravine, earning elevation and views with every step. Upon cresting the valley headwall, the trail reaches a junction that's clearly signed for the Mount Washington summit (0.6 mile) and Lakes of the Clouds (0.8 mile), the most spectacular of the White Mountains' AMC huts and a pleasant spot to stop for hot drinks (and sometimes freshly baked treats from the hut staff). For a return trip to Pinkham Notch that's easier on the knees, it's possible to descend via the more moderate **Boott Spur** or **Lion Head Trails,** or just book a spot on the one-way hiker shuttle from the top.

Before setting out, it's important to stop by the **Pinkham Notch Visitor Center** (361 Rte. 16, 603/466-8116, www.outdoors.org, 6:30am-10pm daily) to pick up detailed maps and get the most recent updates about weather and trail conditions.

SKIING

A ski resort with broad exposure to the northwest, **Wildcat Mountain** (542 Rte. 16, Pinkham Notch, 603/466-3326, www.

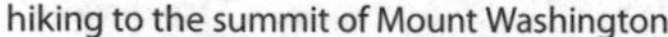
hiking to the summit of Mount Washington

skiwildcat.com, $75-79 adults, $50-54 seniors and youth 7-17, children under 7 free with adult) is known for snagging the area's biggest snowfalls. There's 2,112 feet of vertical drop and 48 runs dominated by intermediate options, and many of the trails have spectacular views across the valley to Mount Washington.

Food

Family-style meals at the **Pinkham Notch Visitor Center** (361 Rte. 16, 603/466-8116, www.outdoors.org, breakfast 6:30am-9am $15, lunch 9:30am-4pm $5-12, dinner Mon.-Thu. 6pm, Fri.-Sun. 5:30pm-7:30pm $29, open seven days) are just about the only game in town, but the food is plentiful and it's a great way to meet fellow hikers. Breakfast and dinner are all-you-can-eat affairs—weekend dinners are buffets, and weeknights are served family-style with a single seating. The à la carte lunch menu is deli style and designed for the trail, with packable sandwiches and snacks.

Accommodations and Camping

$100-150

One of the two front-country lodges operated by the AMC, the **Joe Dodge Lodge** (Rte. 16, Pinkham Notch, 603/466-2727, www.outdoors.org, room with dinner and breakfast from $92 pp) is something of a hostel experience, and a good fit for families. Both private rooms and bunk rooms share bathrooms, and there's often a blazing fire in the living room and library. Meals are served family style at big tables, and knowledgeable staff members lead guided hikes and give talks on the natural world.

CAMPING

In the White Mountain National Forest, backcountry camping is allowed below the tree line, as long as tents are over 200 feet from trails and water. The national forest also operates a number of excellent campgrounds: Six miles south of Gorham, **Dolly Copp Campground** (Rte. 16, 877/444-6777, mid-May-mid-Oct., reservations accepted, some sites first-come, first-served, $22) is one the largest in the forest, with vault toilets, campfire rings, and ranger-run programs. No showers are on-site, but coin-operated showers are available five miles south at the AMC's **Pinkham Notch Visitor Center** (361 Rte. 16).

Information and Services

On Route 16, the AMC's **Pinkham Notch Visitor Center** (361 Rte. 16, 603/466-8116, www.outdoors.org, 6:30am-10pm daily) has plenty of the same, along with a small trading post for supplies. If you're coming to use the visitors center's coin-operated showers, plan to bring a stack of quarters.

Getting There and Around

Roughly 40 minutes north of Conway, Pinkham Notch is on Route 16. Parking is available at the visitors center, and **Concord Coach Lines** (800/639-3317, www.concordcoachlines.com) links Pinkham Notch by bus with **Boston** (4 hrs., 14 min., round-trip $64).

Pinkham Notch Visitor Center is the starting point for one of the two **AMC Hiker Shuttle** (www.outdoors.org, early June-Oct., $23, $19 AMC members) routes, which access many popular trailheads in the area, especially those that lead to the AMC's mountain huts.

BRETTON WOODS AND CRAWFORD NOTCH

Look carefully at the southern flank of Mount Washington, and you may see tiny puffs of smoke and steam emerging from a toy-sized train—the Mount Washington Cog Railway is climbing to the summit. Along with a grand, 19th-century hotel, the cog railway is a remnant of the heyday of White Mountain tourism, when New England's urban residents fell for big peaks and wilderness.

But if the name Bretton Woods sounds familiar, it's likely due to a financial accord that involved the world's leading economists and (reportedly) a great deal of alcohol. In

July 1944, the Bretton Woods Conference was held in the Mount Washington Hotel as World War II still raged. With a spectacular view of Mount Washington, delegates from 44 Allied Nations fought a series of bloodless battles that determined the postwar financial landscape, drank late into the night, and established the dollar as the world's standard reserve currency.

It's fascinating to explore that history in the hotel—now with the drably corporate name of Omni Mount Washington Resort—and on the cog, which makes several chugging trips up Mount Washington each day. And for those who'd prefer to hike the mountain, this is an excellent place to set out, with trails leaving from Bretton Woods and Crawford Notch State Park.

Sights

★ MOUNT WASHINGTON COG RAILWAY

When Chicago meatpacking baron Sylvester Marsh first presented his idea for a railway to the top of Mount Washington, the state legislature told him he might as well "build a railway to the moon." In the spirit of the times, he was undeterred and began work on the world's first mountain-climbing train using materials hauled through thick forest by oxen teams. When the railway began service in 1869, it was the first in the world to employ toothed gears, or cogs, that meshed with a pinion on the track to prevent the train from slipping backward. In those early years, the railway was powered with staggering quantities of wood, which gave way to coal in 1908.

These days the historic coal-fired trains alternate with more eco-friendly biodiesel engines, and though the railway is slower (and more expensive) than the auto road, it's wonderfully fun to chug your way up Mount Washington as the steam whistle echoes off the surrounding peaks. The trains of the **Mount Washington Cog Railway** (Base Rd., off Rte. 302, Bretton Woods, 603/278-5404, www.thecog.com, 3-hour round-trip on steam/biodiesel, $75/$69 adults, $69/65 seniors, $39 children 4-12, children under 4 free, one-way tickets $48, discount with military ID) run late April-November; daily service June-October tapers to weekends during April-May and November. After reaching the top of Mount Washington, it's worth asking the engineer for a peek inside the engine to see the coal bin, brakes, levers, and gauges. Trips allow for one hour on the summit, so if you'd like to spend the day hiking, you'll

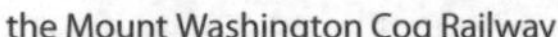

the Mount Washington Cog Railway

have to book a standby return ticket—though you're guaranteed to get down by the end of the day, it's not possible to reserve a spot on any given train.

Entertainment and Events

The **Omni Mount Washington Resort** (Rte. 302, Bretton Woods, 603/278-1000, www.mountwashingtonresort.com) has a suite of restaurants with varying quality, but it's the hotel's high tea and cocktail hours that are destination worthy. For alpine elegance, you can't beat tea in the **Princess Room** (3pm Fri.-Sat., $20 adults, $12 children 10 and under): Grown-ups sip their brews along with ceviche, savory tartlets, scones, and sweets, while kids get mini marshmallows in their hot chocolate, and a menu of tiny sandwiches, savory muffins, macarons, and strawberry tarts. The elegant room is named for Princess Caroline, the eccentric, glamorous wife of the hotel's original owner.

As charming as those princess-worthy tea parties can be, though, the finest seats in the hotel are on the broad back veranda, where comfortable wicker chairs are pointed straight at the southern slope of Mount Washington. Sunsets are spectacular here, and sharp-eyed visitors can spot the glint and smoke of the cog railway as it chugs up the slope. Guests on the veranda can order from the ★ **Rosebrook Bar** (noon-10pm, $9-15), and sip wine, beer, and cocktails along with savory nibbles that would seem overpriced in a different venue.

Sports and Recreation

TOP EXPERIENCE

HIKING

Two trails ascend Mount Washington from the cog railway station; allow a full day for a round-trip hike on either. The most direct route is the 4.4-mile **Ammonoosuc Ravine Trail,** which climbs steeply to Lakes of the Clouds, then continues up a rocky path to the summit; in addition to passing scenic ponds and the AMC hut, this trail has gorgeous views as it works its way up the southwest face of the mountain. Somewhat longer and more gradual, the 5.1-mile **Jewell Trail** ascends the western slope of Mount Clay, then skirts the summit to join a ridge trail to the top of Mount Washington. This is another stunner on clear days; it's delightful to hike parallel to the cog railway for views of the brightly colored trains with an endless backdrop.

Not all the hikes in the White Mountains are quite so strenuous. One favorite option for families is the 3.2-mile round-trip hike up **Mount Willard,** which earns fabulous views of Crawford Notch, with more gradual slopes (for that reason, this hike tends to be crowded on busy days in the Whites, so don't expect solitude). Park at the railroad depot information center adjacent to the **AMC Highland Center** on Route 302.

Find the highest single-drop waterfall in New Hampshire at the end of the **Arethusa Falls Trail,** a 2.6-mile round-trip hike along Bemis Brook. Park on the west side of Route 302 about a mile south of Dry River Campground in Crawford Notch State Park. The hike is fairly steep but well suited for families with older kids, and it's possible to extend it into a 4.7-mile loop by returning via **Frankenstein Cliff Trail,** which has lovely views of the valley. The falls' musical name is said to be taken from a poem by Percy Bysshe Shelley about a Greek nymph who was transformed into a flowing spring, and the lines evoke the spot beautifully:

Arethusa arose
From her couch of snows
In the Acroceraunian mountains,
From cloud and from crag,
With many a jag,
Shepherding her bright fountains.
She leapt down the rocks,
With her rainbow locks
Streaming among the streams;
Her steps paved with green
The downward ravine
Which slopes to the western gleams

SKIING

New Hampshire's biggest ski area is **Bretton Woods Mountain Resort** (99 Ski Area Rd., Bretton Woods, 603/278-3320, www.brettonwoods.com, lift tickets $78-89 adults, $25-89 seniors, $58-68 youth 13-17, $43-53 children 5-12), which looks out at the southern edge of Mount Washington and the Presidential Range, with 97 trails, from beginner to expert. There's 464 acres of terrain here and 10 lifts, which usually run mid-November-mid-April. The ski hill is part of the Omni Mount Washington Resort group, and tickets are discounted for hotel guests.

Food

Nonguests can join the convivial dining hours at the AMC's **Highland Center at Crawford Notch** (Rte. 302, Crawford Notch, 603/278-4453, www.outdoors.org, breakfast 6:30am-10am, $15 adults, $10.50 children 3-12, à la carte lunch 11am-4pm, dinner 6pm-8pm, $29 adults, $14 children 3-12). Breakfast is an all-you-can-eat buffet spread that's aimed at hikers heading into the hills, and dinner is either buffet-style or family-style (on family-style nights, dinner is at 6pm sharp). For breakfast and dinner, it's important to call ahead, as meals can book up on busy nights—lunch is for stocking up on trail food, with no reservations required.

Another solid choice is **Fabyan's Station** (Rte. 302, 603/278-2222, www.brettonwoods.com, 11:30am-9pm daily, hours may be limited in off-season, $11-14), which serves basic pub fare in a historic railroad station that was once the depot for Crawford Notch. Burgers, sandwiches, and salads aren't standout, but the atmosphere is good and the alternatives are sparse. Like almost everything else in Bretton Woods, the restaurant is owned by Omni Mount Washington Resort, which also operates a fancy dining room and an on-site pub (which are decent options if you're staying, but aren't really worth the trip).

Accommodations and Camping

$100-150

Adjacent to the Appalachian Mountain Club's visitors center is the **Highland Center at Crawford Notch** (Rte. 302, Crawford Notch, 603/278-4453, www.outdoors.org, pp with shared bath, dinner and breakfast included, from $90 adults, $80 youth 12-17, $45 children 11 and under), the sibling to the Joe Dodge Lodge in Pinkham Notch. It's friendly and rustic, with fireplaces for post-hike lounging,

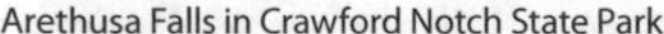

Arethusa Falls in Crawford Notch State Park

The Appalachian Mountain Club's White Mountain Huts

The Appalachian Mountain Club (AMC) has maintained a system of nine backcountry huts in the White Mountains since 1888, making the wilderness accessible for hikers without the gear and experience to rough it on their own. Spending a night at one of the AMC huts is a great deal like alpine summer camp, with bunk beds, communal meals, and a convivial atmosphere among the tired hikers. While rates can seem high (especially given the rustic experience), you're paying for meals hiked in by hardy college students in a wild, scenic place, and staying in the backcountry is an unforgettable experience.

The most famous—and perhaps most spectacular—among the AMC huts is **Lakes of the Clouds,** set by a cluster of alpine ponds just a ridgeline away from the top of Mount Washington. The trail to pretty **Zealand Falls Hut** is far less challenging, a relatively gradual 2.8-mile hike that ends at a perfect river swimming spot. Less popular (and crowded) than those two all-stars, **Carter Notch Hut** is the easternmost hut in the AMC system, a 1914 stone structure set between Wildcat Dome and Carter Mountain.

One of the AMC's most easily accessible huts from the Franconia Range side is **Lonesome Lake Hut,** which is a 1.6-mile hike from the trailhead in Lafayette Campground, with fabulous views of the mountains, naturalist programs, and rustic coed bunk rooms. Another favorite in the Franconia area is **Greenleaf Hut,** which is at the end of a moderate, 2.7-mile walk and offers an equally spectacular perspective on the rugged terrain.

Rates include dinner the night of arrival and breakfast the morning after, and **reservations** (603/466-2727, www.outdoors.org, $105-131) can be made online or by phone. Visitors must bring their own sleeping bags, though additional wool blankets are provided, and guests share simple, often solar-powered bathrooms with cold running water. The most popular huts, and especially Lakes of the Clouds, are often booked months in advance, but there's almost always last-minute space if you're flexible about where you stay.

and a cafeteria where meals are served family style. Most rooms at the lodge use shared baths, but there are a few private bathrooms available for those who prefer not to share sinks. If you're staying at the Highland Center, you get free access to the gear room, which has all the warm layers and hiking boots you need for tackling some peaks.

OVER $250

Of the dozens of grand hotels that dotted the mountains at the turn of the 20th century, the 1902 ★ **Omni Mount Washington Resort** (Rte. 302, Bretton Woods, 603/278-1000 or 800/843-6664, www.mountwashingtonresort.com, $179-469) is the most perfectly preserved, and discovering the gorgeous historical touches throughout the building could easily occupy a rainy afternoon. A gracious veranda runs the length of the rambling hotel, with comfortable chairs that look straight out on Mount Washington. Even if you're not staying here, stopping by for a drink on the deck—or an utterly charming high tea in the Princess Room—is a wonderful experience, and a gracious counterbalance to the White Mountains' rugged scenery.

If you come for the night, be sure to head outside to watch the stars from the outdoor fireplace or pool, and enjoy the period feel of the rooms—while the usual contemporary amenities have been added, the rooms are still thoroughly old-fashioned. For much of the year, the most desirable are those facing the mountain, which get stunning sunrise views, but for trips during foliage season, book the front of the hotel, which looks across the valley at a slope crowded with flaming maple trees. Bretton Woods, as it's still called by many, is a city unto itself, complete with a post office in the basement, golf courses, a zip line, riding stables, and a handful of restaurants on-site. While much of Bretton Woods is beautifully done, meal service is inconsistent, and the main dining room seems overpriced for quality. Many visitors prefer to duck into the downstairs pub, which is less grand but more reliable.

CAMPING

For good access to the cog railway and hikes on the Crawford Notch side of Mount Washington, Crawford Notch State Park's **Dry River Campground** (2057 Rte. 302, Bartlett, 877/647-2757, www.nhstateparks.org, May-Oct., $23) is a good option, with 36 primitive sites, good bathroom facilities, and showers.

Information

The AMC **Macomber Family Information Center** (3575 Rte. 302, Crawford Notch, 603/466-2727, 9am-4pm daily, closes earlier in off-season) is a popular trailhead and hiker information spot. The AMC also has a trail information and weather hotline (603/466-2721).

Getting There and Around

Both Crawford Notch and Bretton Woods are located on Route 302, and visitors need their own form of transportation to get there. For hikers who want to do longer, one-way hikes, it's worth looking into the **AMC Hiker Shuttle** (www.outdoors.org, early June-Oct., $23), which has a fixed route that accesses many popular trailheads in the area, especially those that lead to the AMC's mountain huts. There's also local service from **Garey's Taxi** (603/991-4546, www.gareystaxi.weebly.com).

GORHAM

A useful stop for food and supplies on the way to the Whites, Gorham is also a reasonable home base for trips into the mountains. Though the sprawling downtown is a bit faded, the northern edge of the Presidential Range provides a dramatic backdrop. Gorham has taken the moose as an unofficial mascot—the rest of New Hampshire might contest its claim—and tours set out daily in search of the lumbering creatures.

Sights

As wary New England drivers know, moose come out at dusk. With that in mind, **Gorham Moose Tours** (69 Main St., 603/466-3103, www.gorhammoosetours.org, 2.5-3-hour tours depart 7pm daily, $25 adults, $15 children 5-12, $5 children under 5) strikes out into the forest as the sun goes down. Tours are on 14-person vans, and the odds of spotting moose are high—in a good year with plentiful moose, the animals are sighted on every outing. A driver will search out moose-y spots and share an encyclopedia of moose facts along the way, but here are a few good ones: The animals weigh in at 1,500 pounds and can measure nine feet long, and a moose can carry up to 120,000 ticks.

In many ways, the White Mountains were easier to reach a century ago than today—frequent trains made the trip from Boston a breeze, with whistle stops at lodges and hotels. The small, volunteer-run **Gorham Historical Society & Railroad Museum** (25 Railroad St., 603/466-5338, www.gorhamnewhampshire.com, 10am-3pm Tues.-Sat. May-Oct., free) preserves artifacts from that era in Gorham's 1907 railway station. Call before visiting, as hours can vary with volunteer availability.

Shopping

In Gorham, stop by **Gorham Hardware & Sport Center** (96 Main St., 603/466-2312, www.nhhockeyshop.com, 8am-5pm Mon.-Fri., 8am-4pm Sat., 8am-1pm Sun., hours may vary seasonally) for hiking, climbing, skiing, and camping setups.

For groceries in Gorham, you'll find a **Save-A-Lot** (491 Main St., 603/752-1248, 8am-8pm daily) discount grocery and **Walmart Supercenter** (561 Main St., 603/752-4621, 7am-10pm daily).

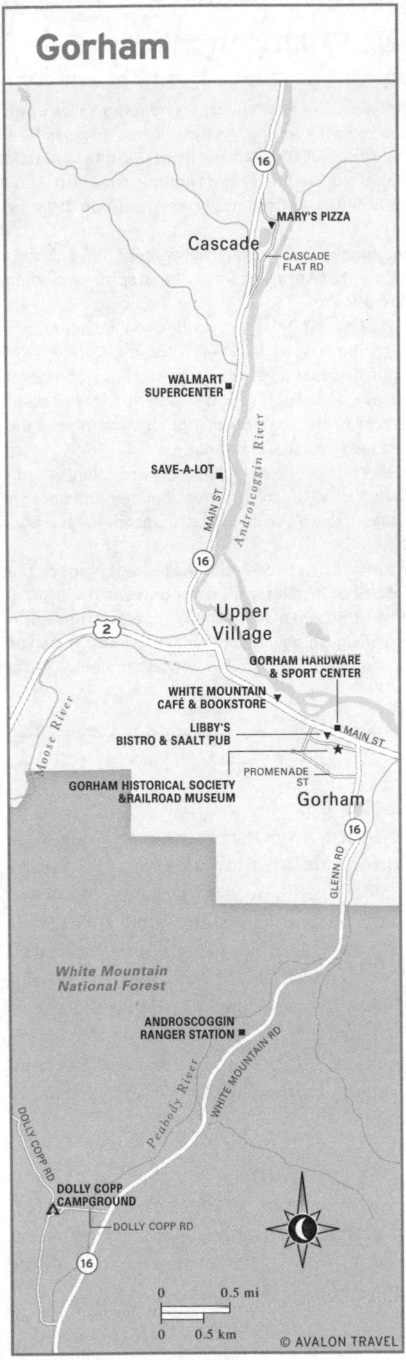

Food

Amid the generic chains lining Route 2 through Gorham, **White Mountain Café & Bookstore** (212 Rte. 2, 603/466-2511, www.whitemountaincafe.com, 7am-4pm daily, $4-11) stands out with personality and charm. Head to the counter for sandwiches, burritos, pastries, and salads, then settle in at a small café table or the sunny front lot. The café also has solid espresso and wireless Internet, making it a good spot to sit a spell and catch up on emails.

For pizza lovers of a certain age, it's hard not to love **Mary's Pizza** (9 Cascade Flats Rd., 603/752-6150, www.maryspizzanh.com, lunch 11am-2pm Wed.-Sat., dinner 4pm-9pm Mon.-Sat., $6-18), an old-school Italian American joint that recalls the years before "flatbread" began to appear covered with gourmet toppings. Pizzas and pastas are simple and come piled with lots of cheese, meat, and vegetables, with decor to match—think red and white-checkered vinyl tablecloths, red Coke glasses, and a jukebox stocked with country and rock-and-roll CDs.

If you've taken some time to explore Gorham, then ★ **Libby's Bistro & SAaLT Pub** (111 Rte. 16, 603/466-5330, www.libbysbistro.org, bistro 5pm-8pm Fri.-Sat., $10-24, pub 5pm-9pm Wed.-Sun., $9-15) will come as something of a surprise. The more upscale bistro and the clubby, convivial pub both have outstanding food, as well as a full bar menu. Even the burgers have creative flair, like the Korean burger topped with kimchi coleslaw and chili mayo or the Peruvian fish sandwich daubed with spiced tartar sauce, but the kitchen really gets going with the global mains: Ricotta gnocchi with veal meatballs, Mumbai cakes, and Middle Eastern-spiced fried chicken strike a balance between thoughtful and satisfying.

Accommodations

UNDER $100

Four miles east of Gorham, ★ **Rattle River Lodge and Hostel** (592 Rte. 2, Shelburne, 603/466-5049 or 715/557-1736, www.whitemountainslodgeandhostel.com, $35 with

Driving the Kancamagus Highway

Between Conway and Lincoln, 35 miles of tightly inscribed switchbacks, swooping valleys, and perfect mountain views make the Kancamagus Highway among the most iconic drives in New England. Route 112, affectionately known as "the Kanc," rolls through the heart of White Mountain National Forest, following the twists and curves of the Swift River and climbing to almost 3,000 feet—at 2,855 feet, the Kancamagus Pass has fabulous views, especially when autumn turns the surrounding forest into a riot of color.

There are plenty of places to stop along the way on the Kancamagus Highway—look for clusters of cars along the side of the road, which often signals a favorite local swimming spot—including a series of scenic overlooks, hiking trails, and historic sites.

Driving from Conway to Lincoln, mile zero is at the White Mountain National Forest ranger station, making it easy to find landmarks along the way. Six miles after leaving Conway, the **Boulder Loop Trail** is a moderate, three-mile hike that takes 2-3 hours and has good views of rocky ledges and forest. A series of interpretive signs illustrates the geologic history, flora, and fauna of the White Mountains. At 7.0 miles, **Lower Falls** is a popular spot for swimming in the Swift River, and has bathrooms and a picnic area near a small, scenic fall.

You can peer into daily life in 19th-century New Hampshire at 12.7 miles in the volunteer-run **Russell-Colbath House,** which is open when staff is available. It's small but free, and docents are happy to share the mysterious story of Thomas Colbath's years-long disappearance and possible reappearance.

Keep winding up to the **Kancamagus Pass,** which at 2,855 feet is the highest point on the road, then you'll find the **Otter Rock Rest Area** at 26 miles, with restrooms and a short trail to another lovely swimming area in the Swift River. Detailed maps of the sights along the Kancamagus Highway are available online (www.kancamagushighway.com) or at the **Saco Ranger Station** (33 Rte. 112, Conway, 603/447-5448, 8am-5pm daily late May-mid-Oct., 8am-4:30pm daily Oct.-May).

breakfast) is an excellent option for budget travelers, and as it's popular with thru-hikers on the Appalachian Trail, it's a good place to hear tales from the woods. The coed rooms have 2-6 beds, and the huge, home-cooked Belgian waffle breakfasts are perfect fuel for a day on the trail. The rambling 19th-century building is both gracious and homey, with a patio, pond, and fire pit.

The basic **Moose Brook Motel** (65 Lancaster Rd., Gorham, 603/466-5400, www.moosebrookmotel.com, $79-109) has simple, clean accommodations with nostalgic wood paneling. Each room is stocked with a coffeemaker, there's (slow) wireless Internet, and the pool looks pretty inviting after a day on the trail. Children are free, and dogs are an additional $5.

$100-150

A step up from the other motels along Main Street, **Mount Madison Inn and Suites** (365 Main St., Gorham, 603/466-3622, www.mtmadisoninnandsuites.com, $129-159) is a comfortable, motel-style spot with unexpected perks. Chief among those is the completely awesome bouncy castle, but there's also a heated pool, hot tub, gas-powered grills, an outdoor fireplace, and a guest computer and laundry that are helpful for anyone coming off the trail.

Information

The town runs a **Gorham Information Booth** (69 Main St., 603/466-3103, www.gorhamnh.org) on the town green with all the usual brochures.

Getting There and Around

At the intersection of the east-west Route 2 and the north-south Route 16, Gorham is the entry point to the Mount Washington Valley for visitors arriving from northern Maine and Vermont.

Concord Coach Lines (800/639-3317, www.concordcoachlines.com) links Gorham by bus with **Boston** (4 hrs., 30 min., round-trip $67). The **AMC Hiker Shuttle** (www.outdoors.org, early June-Oct., $23) connects the Gorham gas station (350 Main St.) with trailheads throughout the mountains.

The Franconia Range

A north-south ridgeline running from Mount Lafayette to Mount Flume, the Franconia Range is second only to the Presidential Range among New Hampshire's peaks. While the Presidential Range outdoes the highest of these by a cool 1,000 feet, the Franconia Range is just as rugged. And there's no road to the top of these mountains, so if you sweat to the Mount Lafayette summit, you won't need to share the view with crowds in flip-flops.

In the valley below, Franconia Notch State Park offers easy access to hiking trails, waterfalls, and a deep, natural gorge. This was the home of New Hampshire's most recognizable landmark, the "Old Man of the Mountain," but the series of granite ledges came tumbling down in 2003, despite elaborate efforts to hold the stony face together.

The towns of Littleton and Franconia are the main bases for visiting Franconia Notch, and the road into the park is high drama, twisting between high peaks and cliff faces. Franconia Notch itself is a bustling vacation spot, with an enormous campground, a lake with a swimming beach, a mountain tram, and trail after trail heading up into the hills.

FRANCONIA

Sights

FRANCONIA NOTCH STATE PARK

Following the valley (and highway) between the Kinsman Range and the Franconia Range, this beautiful state park has a bit of everything—including beaches, a campground, lots of hiking, and kid-friendly trails. Set just at the base of Cannon Mountain, **Echo Lake Beach** (Exit 34C, Franconia Notch State Park, 603/823-8800, $4 adults, $2 children 6-11, children under 6 free) is sandy and scenic, with a lifeguard on duty during the day; it's possible to rent canoes, kayaks, and paddleboats here for $20 per hour.

The fast-moving traffic through the valley doesn't give much time for taking in the views, but you can move at your own pace on the **Franconia Notch State Park Recreation Path,** an 8.8-mile bike and pedestrian trail that slopes gently downhill from the base of Cannon Mountain to the Flume Gorge. There's trailhead parking at both ends—to reach the Cannon Mountain trailhead, take exit 34B; you'll see the trailhead on the left. Bike rentals are available at each end from **Sport Thoma** (371 Rte. 3, Lincoln, 603/745-8151 *or* Aerial Tramway Lodge, Exit 34B, Franconia, 603/823-8800, www.sportthoma.com, bike rental half-day $35, full-day $50, shuttle-only $20), whose prices include transfer on the one-way shuttle. (Most people drop a car at Flume Gorge, take a shuttle to the top, then ride back down.)

★ FLUME GORGE

Narrow, wooden walkways lead through this natural chasm, accessible from a **visitors center** (852 Rte. 3, Lincoln, 603/745-8391, www.nhstateparks.org, 8:30am-5pm daily early May-late Oct., until 5:30pm mid-June-early Sept., $16 adults, $13 children 6-12, children under 6 free) just a few minutes south of Franconia Notch State Park. Its high Conway granite walls shelter covered bridges, mossy

Franconia

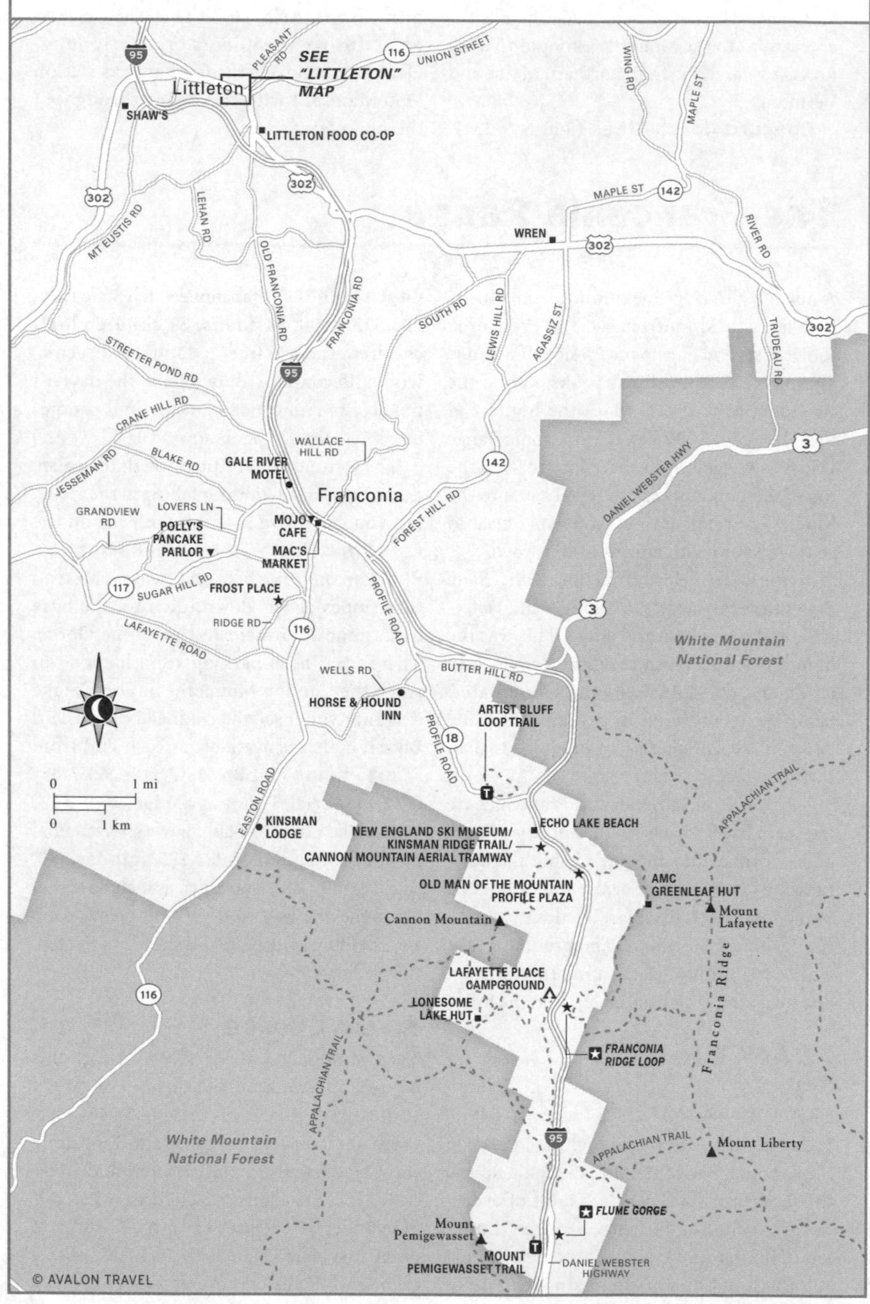
SEE "LITTLETON" MAP
Littleton
SHAW'S
LITTLETON FOOD CO-OP
PLEASANT RD
UNION STREET
WING RD
MAPLE ST
MAPLE ST
RIVER RD
WREN
LEHAN RD
MT EUSTIS RD
OLD FRANCONIA RD
FRANCONIA RD
SOUTH RD
LEWIS HILL RD
AGASSIZ ST
TRUDEAU RD
STREETER POND RD
CRANE HILL RD
WALLACE HILL RD
JESSEMAN RD
BLAKE RD
GALE RIVER MOTEL
Franconia
DANIEL WEBSTER HWY
GRANDVIEW RD
LOVERS LN
POLLY'S PANCAKE PARLOR
MOJO CAFE
MAC'S MARKET
FOREST HILL RD
SUGAR HILL RD
FROST PLACE
RIDGE RD
LAFAYETTE ROAD
PROFILE ROAD
White Mountain National Forest
WELLS RD
BUTTER HILL RD
HORSE & HOUND INN
ARTIST BLUFF LOOP TRAIL
0 1 mi
0 1 km
EASTON ROAD
KINSMAN LODGE
APPALACHIAN TRAIL
NEW ENGLAND SKI MUSEUM/ KINSMAN RIDGE TRAIL/ CANNON MOUNTAIN AERIAL TRAMWAY
ECHO LAKE BEACH
OLD MAN OF THE MOUNTAIN PROFILE PLAZA
AMC GREENLEAF HUT
Mount Lafayette
Cannon Mountain
LAFAYETTE PLACE CAMPGROUND
LONESOME LAKE HUT
FRANCONIA RIDGE LOOP
Franconia Ridge
APPALACHIAN TRAIL
White Mountain National Forest
APPALACHIAN TRAIL
Mount Liberty
FLUME GORGE
Mount Pemigewasset
MOUNT PEMIGEWASSET TRAIL
DANIEL WEBSTER HIGHWAY
© AVALON TRAVEL

walls, and waterfalls, including the spectacular 45-foot-high Avalanche Falls. The gorge was formed before the last ice age, when a fin of basalt was forced into the vertically fractured granite; the basalt weathered away more quickly than the surrounding granite, leaving a winding slot in its place. A two-mile trail leads through the gorge, with a few places to duck off the path and explore, such as the Wolf's Den, a narrow, one-way route that involves squeezing yourself through cracks in the rock and crawling on hands and knees. As the story goes, Flume Gorge was discovered by 93-year-old Jess Guernsey when she was looking for a new spot to drop a fishing line, and it still holds the thrill of discovery: It's cool between the rock walls, and birch trees worm out of stony cracks. Don't miss the visitors center's display case full of old-timey Flume Gorge postcards that 19th-century vacationers sent to their friends back home.

CANNON MOUNTAIN

Get your bearings from the top of this bare granite dome—on a clear day, views stretch to four states and Canada, and you can enjoy the scene from an observation deck. You'll also find a café at the top of Cannon Mountain and walking trails that cross the 4,080-foot summit. Zip up to the top in fewer than 10 minutes on the **Aerial Tramway** (260 Tramway Dr., 603/823-8800, www.cannonmt.com, 9am-5pm daily late May-mid-June, 8:30am-5:30pm daily mid-June-mid-Oct., round-trip $18 adults, $16 children 6-12; one-way $13 adults, $10 children 6-12, children under 6 free), or you can hike to the top on the **Kinsman Ridge Trail,** a 2.2-mile one-way hike that leaves from the tramway parking lot and has great perspectives on Franconia Notch.

FROST PLACE

From 1915 to 1920, Robert Frost lived in a small house with views of the mountains, and his spirit lives on at the secluded farmstead, now a museum and poetry center. Each year, the museum invites a poet to live in the house for six weeks, writing and working in Frost's former home of **Frost Place** (Ridge Rd., 603/823-5510, www.frostplace.org, 1pm-5pm Thurs.-Sun. late May-June, 1pm-5pm Wed.-Mon. July-mid-Aug., 10am-5pm Wed.-Mon. Sept.-mid-Oct., $5 adults, $4 seniors, $3 students 12 and above, children under 12 free), which retains a peaceful, contemplative feel. The museum has signed first editions of Frost's poetry, as well as other memorabilia from his life, and there's a 0.5 mile nature trail winding through the property with poems from the Franconia years. The trail, grounds, and peaceful front porch of the house are always open to the public.

OTHER SIGHTS

Relive the glory days and the fall of New Hampshire's rocky mascot at the **Old Man of the Mountain Profile Plaza** (Tramway Dr., Exit 34B from I-93), where you can line up just right and get a glimpse of what the cliffs looked like before they collapsed in 2003. You can watch ski technology progress from furry boots and wool knickers to high-tech jumpsuits at the diminutive **New England Ski Museum** (Tramway Dr., 603/823-7177, www.newenglandskimuseum.org, 10am-5pm daily late May-end of ski season, free), whose koan-like motto is "preserving the future of skiing's past." The museum has medals and trophies from New Hampshire-native skier Bode Miller and a short movie about his career.

Entertainment and Events

The mountain meadows north of the notch are filled with violet blossoms every year in time for the **Lupine Festival** (603/823-8000, www.franconianotch.org, mid-June), a street festival and art show with events throughout the region. By governor's decree, each year in early July, Frost Place holds **Frost Day** (603/823-5510, www.frostplace.org), with readings of poetry by the poet-in-residence and musical performances at the farmstead.

Hiking

For hikes in the area, stop by the hiker cabin at **Lafayette Place Campground** (Franconia

Notch State Park, 603/823-5884, www.nhstateparks.org, 8am-3pm daily) for updated trail conditions, maps, and alpine weather reports—even when valley weather is blissful, the exposed alpine trail can get howling wind and whiteout fog.

★ FRANCONIA RIDGE LOOP

For the ultimate Franconia hike, plan for at least six hours on the 8.2-mile **Franconia Ridge Loop,** a rugged New Hampshire classic that goes up and over three peaks: Little Haystack Mountain, Mount Lincoln, and Mount Lafayette. The trail starts on the east side of I-93, opposite Lafayette Place Campground, and starts straight up the fall line, climbing 3,480 feet in around four miles, passing a series of scenic waterfalls on the way up Little Haystack. The ridgeline trail between Mount Lincoln and Mount Lafayette is a highlight, a knife-edge ridge that's all exposed rock and perfect views.

Earn your views with (somewhat) less work on the **Mount Pemigewasset Trail,** a moderate, 3.3-mile out-and-back that takes roughly 2-3 hours to complete from the Flume Gorge Visitor Center parking lot. Much of the way is wooded and shady, and the trail crosses a series of pretty brooks, but the summit is bare rock, and though the mountain tops out at 2,557 feet, it feels like a real adventure. For more information on this hike, ask at the on-site visitors center.

Easy enough for younger children, the 1.5-mile **Artist Bluff Loop Trail** looks out toward Cannon Mountain and Franconia Notch from the valley floor. To access the trailhead from Littleton or Franconia, take exit 34C from I-93, then take Route 18 west for 0.5 mile and park in the large lot on the right. This trail is particularly nice in early spring, when wildflowers bloom along the edge of Echo Lake.

Skiing

With the longest vertical drop in New Hampshire, **Cannon Mountain** (Exit 34C, 603/823-7771, www.cannonmt.com, lift tickets $75 adults, $62 youth 13-17, $52 seniors and children 6-12) has a mix of groomed trails and glades that are dominated by intermediate runs. The aerial tramway means riders get to the top with a bit less windchill than elsewhere in the White Mountains, but Cannon is very exposed to harsh weather, and can be an extremely cold place to ski and ride when the temperatures drop.

Artist Bluff Loop Trail

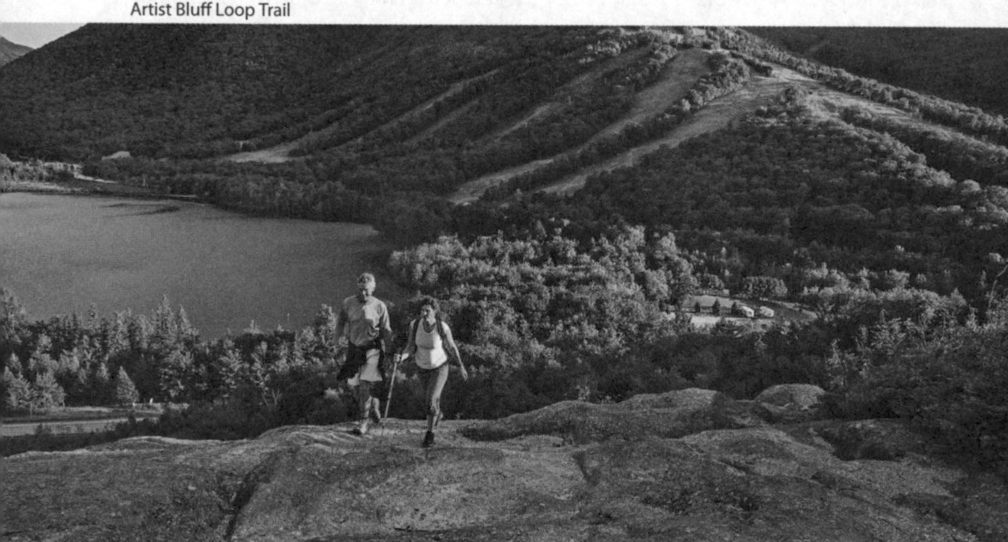

Food

For takeout sandwiches, strong coffee, ice cream, and pizza, the colorful **Backpack Cafe** (334 Main St., 603/823-5697, www.backpackcafenh.com, 7am-4pm Tues.-Thurs., 7am-7pm Fri.-Sat., 8am-11:30am Sun., $3-12) is the place in town. Limited counter seating is available inside, and there are a few tables on the sunny front porch.

The elegant dining room at the ★ **Horse & Hound Inn** (205 Wells Rd., 800/450-5501, www.horseandhoundnh.com, reservations recommended, 5pm-8pm Wed.-Sun. late May-late Oct., 5pm-8pm Fri.-Sun. late Nov.-Apr., $20-33) has a refined menu that changes with the season, using plenty of fresh, local ingredients, some of which come from the on-site garden. A recent menu included lobster corn custard, fresh handkerchief pasta with wild mushrooms, and a roasted half rack of lamb with mint pesto. On warm days, the outdoor terrace is serene and sunny, and the more casual tavern has a full bar and wonderfully cozy, historical feel.

Two miles west of Franconia, ★ **Polly's Pancake Parlor** (672 Rte. 117, Sugar Hill, 603/823-5575, www.pollyspancakeparlor.com, 7am-3pm daily, $7-13) serves legendary stacks of three-inch cakes with house-made maple syrup (the "fake stuff" is available on request, but it's sure to come with a tart helping of side eye). Buckwheat, cornmeal, and whole wheat flours are stone-ground on-site, and while some nostalgic visitors note that the newly renovated building doesn't have the down-home charm of the original, it has loads of seating, which reduces the impressive lines on weekend mornings.

Find basic groceries in Franconia at **Mac's Market** (347 Main St., 603/823-7795, 7am-8pm daily), which is small, but has beer, wine, and deli products.

Accommodations and Camping

UNDER $100

Find country hospitality at the ★ **Kinsman Lodge** (2165 Easton Rd., 603/823-5686, www.kinsmanlodge.com, $55 s, $95 d), which Chet and Sue Thompson run with a minimum of fuss in a rambling historic building. Guest rooms share superclean bathrooms in the hallway, and the accommodations are simple but comfortable. After a hot day of hiking, it's hard to beat a rocking chair on the broad, shady porch, or a seat in the library, which is stocked with books and games. A big breakfast is served in the sunny dining room.

$100-150

Simple motel rooms and cottages have views of Mount Lafayette and Franconia Notch at **Gale River Motel** (1 Main St., 603/823-5655, www.galerivermotel.com, rooms $90-105, cottages $140-220), where fairly basic accommodations are set on a six-acre property with a shuffleboard, pool, and barbecue area. Rooms have coffeemakers, fridges, wireless Internet, and televisions; the lobby always has freshly baked cookies, cocoa, and tea; and the friendly owner is happy to lend out a DVD player and board games. This motel attracts many guests with pets and kids.

Six miles south of Cannon Mountain, the rustic and pet-friendly **Pemi Cabins** (460 Rte. 3, Lincoln, 800/865-8323, www.pemicabins.com, $72-130) are right on the Pemigawasset River, and some cabins have screened-in porches that look out over the water. Each one is a little different, but most have wood-burning fireplaces, a small sitting area, and cable television, while some have little kitchenettes. The owners can provide home-baked muffins or s'more fixings upon request.

$150-250

As in the wonderful restaurant on-site, lodgings at the ★ **Horse & Hound Inn** (205 Wells Rd., 800/450-5501, www.horseandhoundnh.com, $130-195) are full of well-polished rustic charm. Hardwood floors, locally handmade maple furniture, organic soaps, and beautiful linens are right in keeping with the inn's nostalgic, lodge-like feel. There's a bottle of brandy for nightcaps, a library stocked with books and games, and a fireplace that roars away on cold nights; a breakfast of freshly baked pastries, egg dishes, granola, and fruit is served.

CAMPING

The sites at **Lafayette Place Campground** (1 Franconia Notch State Park, 603/823-9513, www.nhstateparks.org, $25) are right in the heart of the action, with quick access to the trails and destinations within Franconia Notch State Park and hiker information on-site. The location also means the campground has quite a bit of road noise, contained by the high valley walls, but the 97 sites have showers, a camp store, and fire rings, and are ideal for an early start up the Franconia Ridge.

Information and Services

The **Franconia Notch Chamber of Commerce** (603/823-8000, www.franconianotch.org), on I-93 just north of the notch, runs an unstaffed **information center** stocked with brochures, open 24 hours a day. The booth is right next door to the **Abbie Greenleaf Library** (439 Main St., 603/823-8424, 2pm-6pm Mon.-Tues., 10am-noon and 2pm-6pm Wed., 2pm-5pm Thurs.-Fri., 10am-1pm Sat.). Another good source of outdoors info is the hiker cabin at **Lafayette Place Campground** (Franconia Notch State Park, 603/823-5884, www.nhstateparks.org, 8am-3pm daily).

Getting There

Franconia is located off I-93, which continues south through Franconia Notch State Park. **Concord Coach Lines** (800/639-3317, www.concordcoachlines.com) links Franconia by bus with **Boston** (3 hrs., 20 min., round-trip $58).

LITTLETON

With a sweetly old-fashioned Main Street that runs along the Ammonoosuc River, Littleton is farther from the action in Franconia Notch, but there's (a little) more to do here after a day in the mountains. The town's claim to fame may be fading from memory—this was the hometown of writer Eleanor H. Porter, author of the book *Pollyanna*—but Littleton keeps the spirit alive with a yearly festival that celebrates the famously chipper main character.

Sights

Littleton's not big on sights, per se, but if you're walking around downtown there's two small-town landmarks worth the stroll. The **Riverwalk Covered Bridge** (18 Mill St.) was built in 2004, but has the elegant trusswork of the original variety, and the **Pollyanna Statue** (92 Main St.) is a permanent monument to exuberance and joy.

Entertainment and Events

The **Schilling Beer Co.** (18 Mill St., 603/444-4800, www.schillingbeer.com, noon-11pm Sun.-Thurs., noon-midnight Fri.-Sat.) brews small-barrel batches of European-style beers that range from more familiar Hefeweizens to offbeat pours; on a recent summer afternoon, the family-owned brewery was pouring a sour brown wild ale, Leipzig-style gose, and Czech black lagers in a historic riverside barn.

Littleton author Eleanor H. Porter created the super-chipper Pollyanna in a pair of children's novels, and the town has adopted the character as a kind of local mascot. The official **Pollyanna Glad Day** (www.golittleton.

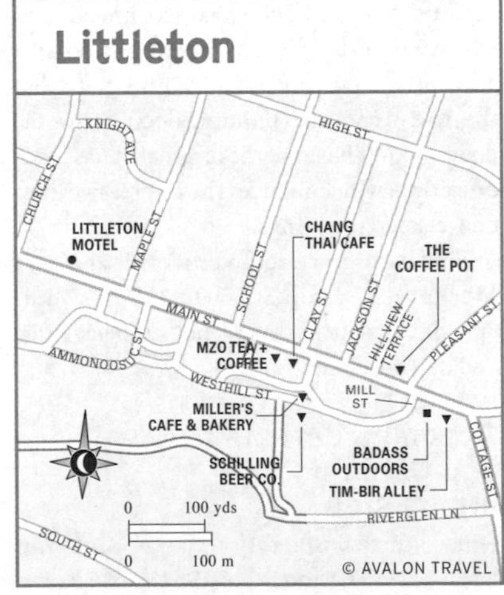

com, early June) celebrates her optimistic legacy with readings, awards, and festivities.

Shopping

Shopping in this area usually means picking up an extra layer for a hike, so stores lean more toward gear than souvenirs. In Littleton, stop by the little, employee-owned **Badass Outdoors** (17 Main St., 603/444-9445, 11am-5pm Tues.-Thurs. and Sun., 10am-6pm Fri.-Sat.). Bethlehem, a cute little town five miles down Route 302 from Littleton, has a supercool shop stocked with work by local artists and artisans, a worthwhile exception to the mostly gear rule; visit **WREN** (2011 Main St., Bethlehem, 603/869-9736, www.wrenworks.org, 10am-5pm daily) to pick up truly local gifts, which are otherwise hard to find in the area.

Food

In addition to its brews, the ★ **Schilling Beer Co.** (18 Mill St., 603/444-4800, www.schillingbeer.com, noon-11pm daily, $9-18) serves Neapolitan-style pizza from a wood-fired oven, and when the riverside patio is open, it's easily the most pleasant, relaxing place to eat in town.

For hearty American breakfasts and lunch at old-fashioned prices, ★ **The Coffee Pot** (30 Main St., 603/444-5722, www.thecoffeepotrestaurant.com, 6:30am-4pm Mon.-Fri., 6:30am-2pm Sat., 6:30am-noon Sun., $4-10) is beloved, with tightly packed tables, a diner counter, and paper place mats advertising local lawn mower repair services. The blueberry pancakes are chock-full of fruit and served with maple syrup, hearty sandwiches are made using house-baked bread, and a fresh fruit pie is always on the menu.

Exposed brick walls, white tablecloths, and refined service make **Tim-Bir Alley** (7 Main St., 603/444-6142, 5pm-9pm Fri.-Sun., $19-30) the most romantic place to eat in Littleton, and the small, handwritten menu changes frequently to reflect the season. Tournedos of beef, ocean fish with fresh herbs, and wild mushroom soup were included on a recent springtime menu, and it's a genuine challenge not to fill up on the breadbasket full of fresh-baked biscuits and butter.

The back porch of **Miller's Cafe and Bakery** (16 Mill St., 603/444-2146, www.millerscafeandbakery.com, 9am-3:30pm Sun. and Tues.-Fri., 9am-9pm Sat., $5-9) overlooks the Ammonoosuc River just as it makes its way under a bright-red covered bridge, so the views alone make this a charming place for breakfast or lunch. Sandwiches, quiche, salads, and a bakery case full of toothsome, old-fashioned sweets are hearty and simple.

Find big-city style and beans from a local roaster at **Blue Jay Coffee & Tea Bar** (81A Main St., 603/575-5433, 9am-6pm Mon.-Sat., 9am-5pm Sun., $3-8), along with a long menu of loose leaf teas and locally baked pastries. Comfy chairs and wireless Internet make this a good place to catch up on the world outside the White Mountains.

A few doors down, **Chang Thai Café** (77 Main St., 603/444-8810, www.changthaicafe.com, 11:30am-3pm and 4:40pm-9pm daily, lunch $9-13, dinner $9-19) is a casual, laid-back place with a menu that includes the American Thai classics—pad thai, drunken noodles—as well as some unexpected additions, like Massaman avocado curry with black tiger shrimp. Lunch specials are a great deal, and the café serves bento boxes with teriyaki and sushi.

Stock up on groceries at **Shaw's** (625 Meadow St., 603/444-1017, 7am-9pm daily) or the **Littleton Food Co-Op** (43 Bethlehem Rd., 603/444-2800, www.littletonfoodcoop.com, 8am-8pm daily), which has a very good selection of local and organic products, a bulk department, and prepared foods.

Accommodations and Camping

UNDER $100

Just off I-93, the pragmatically named **Exit 41 Travel Inn** (337 Cottage St., 603/259-3085, www.exit41travelinn.com, $90-110) is designed as a decent place to get off the road—but that said, the motel is friendly, clean, and kempt, with an outdoor swimming pool and a (very) small continental breakfast.

Walking distance from downtown restaurants, the **Littleton Motel** (166 Main St., 603/444-5780, www.littletonmotel.com, $68-108, 2-room suites $98-158) has old-fashioned, wood-paneled rooms and country charm. Guests gather around the fire pit, and the rooms all have flat-screen televisions and coffeemakers. Children under the age of 16 are free.

$100-150

In a mauve-colored historic home on Main Street, you can't miss **The Beal House** (2 W. Main St., 603/444-2661, www.thebealhouse-inn.com, $129-169), a friendly inn with quaint and pleasant rooms. There's an appealing tavern on-site, and rates include a self-serve continental breakfast of fruit, fresh pastries, and granola.

CAMPING

Five miles from downtown, the forested **Crazy Horse Family Campground** (788 Hilltop Rd., 603/444-2204, www.crazy-horsenh.com, tent sites from $35, sites with hook-ups from $39, 2-bedroom trailer $110) is open year-round, with a summer camp's worth of amenities—a swimming pool, nature trails, a playground, and fire pits—and there's wireless Internet on-site. Pets are welcome (dogs on leash).

Information

In downtown Littleton, stop by the **information center** (124 Main St., 603/444-0616, 9am-4pm Fri.-Sat., 11:30am-3pm Sun. late May-June, 9am-4pm Mon.-Sat., 11:30am-3pm Sun. July-Oct.) run by the **Littleton Area Chamber of Commerce** for a self-guided walking tour of town and information on area businesses. During the months the center is closed, information is available at the **chamber office** (2 Union St., 603/444-0616, www.littletonareachamber.com, 9am-5pm Mon.-Fri.).

Getting There

Littleton is located off I-93, Route 302, and Route 116. **Concord Coach Lines** (800/639-3317, www.concordcoachlines.com) links Littleton by bus with **Boston** (3 hrs., 30 min., round-trip $60.50).

Coastal Maine

Look for ★ to find recommended sights, activities, dining, and lodging.

Highlights

★ **Portland Museum of Art:** This excellent museum houses an extensive collection of impressionist and American art, including nautical themed paintings by Winslow Homer (page 151).

★ **Popham Beach State Park:** Stretch out on a dreamy swatch of sand, or plot a low-tide walk across the flats to tiny Fox Island (page 170).

★ **Lobster Feast:** Dig into great piles of steamed lobster and clams and get a taste of Maine (page 179).

★ **Pemaquid Point Light:** Every rocky peninsula and outcropping's got its very own lighthouse, from hidden gems to crowd favorites (page 181).

★ **Farnsworth Art Museum:** See the Maine coast through the eyes of the state's most beloved painter, Andrew Wyeth, who captured the moods and melancholy of Penobscot Bay and beyond (page 184).

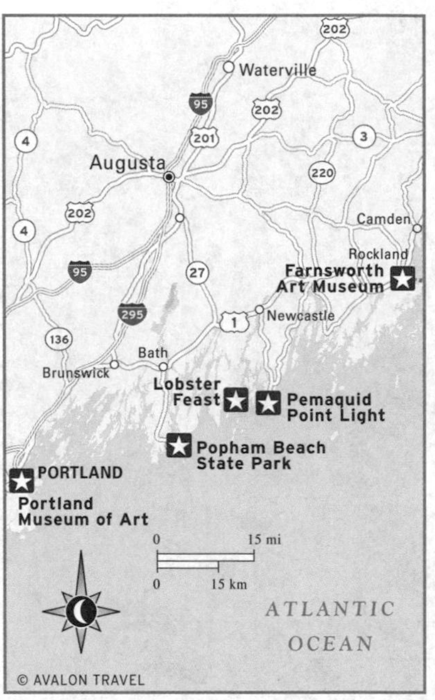

Trace a route along Maine's 3,500-mile waterfront, and you'll find fishing towns, far-flung beaches, and one of New England's most vibrant small cities.

Within day-tripping distance from Boston, the south coast is a classic vacation getaway for city crowds who come to sail and socialize in grand seaside inns. This is the pinnacle of Maine beach chic, with perfect sand, gentle surf breaks, and elegant waterside dining. A few lighthouses up the coast, Portland is the cultural capital of the state, with a fabulous setting and quality of life that draw creative talent from around the country. Framed by a pair of scenic parks, downtown overflows with boat-to-table restaurants, microbreweries, and art.

After Portland, the shoreline goes wild, fracturing into deep coves and bays; proud shipwright towns stand back from the sea on tidal rivers that sent merchant vessels and warships to every corner of the globe. Roads to the shore dead-end at seasonal lobster shacks where you can dine "in the rough" as fishers unload the day's catch.

From Rockland's working waterfront to pretty Camden, the towns lining Penobscot Bay are home to lobster-boat captains, sailors, and summer people, and their harbors shelter grand old schooners and elegant luxury yachts. This is the beginning of Down East, the far stretch of the Maine coast that extends to the most easterly point in the United States. From Penobscot Bay, the coast gets increasingly remote, the towns divided by long passages of deep forest and rugged shoreline leading onward to the scenic jewel of Acadia National Park.

PLANNING YOUR TIME

Even more than other destinations in New England, the true high season in Maine is during schools' summer vacation, when families descend on beaches in hordes. Visiting in late June or late August offers the best weather without the crowds, though many locals say September is the finest month, with still-warm days and cooler nights. At any time of year, however, the weather can be unpredictable, and Maine can seemingly pass through multiple seasons in a single day, with sunshine giving way to fog and rain before turning again.

Previous: York Beach; Ogunquit Coast. **Above:** statue of Paul Bunyan in Bangor.

Experiencing the highlights of coastal Maine takes at least a week, especially when summer crowds turn Route 1 into a series of bottlenecks. Allot this much time and you can take in the region in a series of clusters (with less time, perhaps focus on one, and avoid Route 1 when possible for expediency).

Spend a couple of days exploring south coast lighthouses, beaches, and restaurants from the Kennebunks—Kennebunkport and Kennebunk—or Portland, with time to visit the outdoors or go outlet shopping in Freeport. Make your second destination one of the towns of Maine's Mid-Coast, such as Brunswick, Bath, Wiscasset, and Damariscotta. Plenty of museums and historic downtowns are along Route 1, but don't miss the chance to get off the main road, following quiet highways to island communities and seaside lobster shacks.

After making its way through inland forests, Route 1 finds the coast in Penobscot Bay, where a trio of wonderful towns is perched on picturesque harbors: Rockland, Rockport, and Camden are ideal places to trade your car for a kayak or a berth on a historic schooner and explore the islands dotting the coast.

ORIENTATION

Perched just before the coastline crumbles into a squiggly line of bays and peninsulas, Portland is the cosmopolitan hub and gateway to Maine's endless shoreline. Beyond the city, other destinations on the Maine coast lie along Route 1, a two-lane highway lined with banks of wildflowers and thick forest. Traffic slows to a crawl in each of the towns along the way, where coastal roads sheer off into fishing villages and deep inlets.

The Southern Coast

A beach-lover's utopia, this region more than doubles its population in summer—and for good reason. Its shoreline is peppered with craggy beaches boasting soft sand and unforgettable sunsets, nature preserves, and bird and wildlife sanctuaries.

But there are plenty of man-made reasons to visit, too. The area was originally settled not two decades after the *Mayflower* hit Plymouth Rock, and that shows in its pervasive sense of history, from Kennebunkport's 17th-century homes to Kittery's old naval museums. More modern treasures are abundant, too, from Kennebunk's clam shacks to the antiques shops of Wells, the cafés and top-notch restaurants of Ogunquit, and the bargain outlets of Kittery. June-October, the region's streets get congested with vacationing families and urbanites; the best times to soak up the area's pleasures are in early to mid-autumn.

KITTERY

Just across the Piscataqua River from downtown Portsmouth, Kittery is mostly a destination for shoppers—there's a massive collection of outlet stores and malls sprawling along Route 1. If you're looking for classic Maine, keep heading up the coast, but Kittery's got a few interesting spots beyond the bargain-seeking mayhem, including a small naval museum that explores the town's seafaring past. For a pleasant drive that feels a world away from Route 1, simply duck off the main road onto Route 103, which winds through coast and forest on the scenic route to York Harbor.

Sights

Nautical buffs ought not miss the **Kittery Historical and Naval Museum** (200 Rogers Rd. Extension, 207/439-3080, www.kittery-museum.com, 10am-4pm Wed.-Sat., 1pm-4pm Sun. June-Oct., $5 adults, $3 children

Coastal Maine

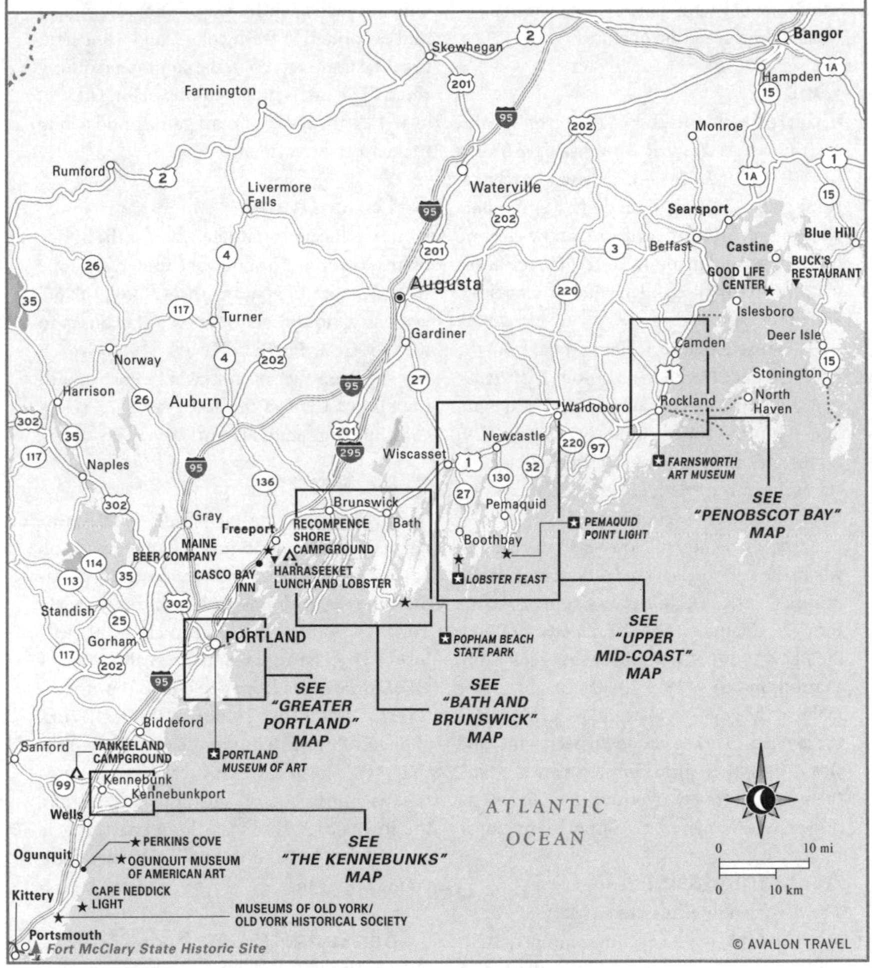

7-15, children under 7 free, $10 families,), full of seafaring gear, loads of intricate scrimshaw, ship models, and a collection of painted seascapes.

Armed and ready through the colonial period, the American Revolution, the War of 1812, the Civil War, and the Spanish American War, **Fort McClary** (Rte. 103, Kittery Point, 207/490-4079, www.fortmcclary.org, 10am-sunset daily Memorial Day-Columbus Day, $4 adults, $1 seniors) is perfectly situated to protect the Portsmouth Harbor from naval attacks, but these days it's mostly a good spot for a walk, or a picnic with views across the water to the Portsmouth Naval Shipyard.

Shopping

You can't miss **Kittery Outlets** (306 Rte. 1, 207/439-4367, www.thekitteryoutlets.com, 9am-9pm daily), where more than 120 stores draw bargain-minded shoppers from around the region, and which shouldn't be confused with the adjacent **Kittery Premium Outlets** (375 Rte. 1, 207/439-6548, www.premiumoutlets.com, 9am-9pm daily), which has a somewhat fancier selection of stores.

Food

If you're headed to the beach or on a hike, grab picnic fixings at **Beach Pea Baking Co.** (53 Rte. 1, 207/439-3555, www.beachpeabaking.com, 7:30am-6pm daily, $6-9), where all breads are fresh-baked and sandwiches are overstuffed and made-to-order. There's also a tempting pastry case filled with tarts, cookies, and other treats.

An old-school favorite for seafood from the fryer, **Bob's Clam Hut** (315 Rte. 1, 207/439-4233, www.bobsclamhut.com, 11am-9pm Sun.-Thurs., 11am-9:30pm Fri.-Sat., $7-29) serves enormous portions of fried whole belly clams, beautifully tender haddock, and a very respectable creamy chowder.

Kittery's version of "lobster in the rough," where the seafood is served outdoors and with minimal fuss, is **Chauncey Creek Lobster Pier** (16 Chauncey Creek Rd., Kittery Point, 207/439-1030, www.chaunceycreek.com, 11am-8pm daily, $8-35), with bright picnic tables at the edge of a peaceful river. Make like the locals and bring your own beer, wine, and side dishes, then pick a lobster from the tank (it's worth noting that lobsters tend to be a bit pricier here than more far-flung destinations).

Accommodations

The pet-friendly **Coachman Inn** (380 Rte. 1, 800/824-6183, www.coachmaninn.net, $120-200) is a basic motel that's a good alternative to pricier accommodations in neighboring Portsmouth and York. It's walking distance from the Kittery outlets and several fast-food chains, and there's a useful family suite, with a pair of twin beds in the second bedroom. A basic continental breakfast is served in the lobby, and fully accessible rooms are available upon request.

With views across the Piscataqua River, the ★ **Portsmouth Harbor Inn & Spa** (6 Water St., 207/439-4040, www.innatportsmouth.com, $150-250) is an inviting place to land, as well as a good base for visiting Portsmouth, which is just 0.5 mile away. Rooms are simple and decorated in fresh colors, and wonderful breakfasts are served in the communal dining room. The inn is nicely equipped for a day in, as well, with DVDs, board games, and a long menu of spa treatments.

Getting There

Kittery is located on Route 1, across the bridge from Portsmouth, and just under an hour from Portland. **Greyhound** (214/849-8966, www.greyhound.com) has regular buses to Kittery from Portland (1 hr., $19); to reach Kittery from the south, travel to Portsmouth then hop a **COAST** bus (603/743-5777, www.coastbus.org) across the bridge.

THE YORKS

Picture-perfect Maine village meets sunburned Vacationland in The Yorks, made up of the adorable York Village, the carnival atmosphere at York Beach, and the more sedate York Harbor and Cape Neddick. Confused? Just call it "The Yorks" and forget about it—it's all of three miles from one end to the other.

First settled by colonists in 1624, York chugged along as a modest seaside town until the 19th century, when it earned a reputation as a posh coastal vacation spot. Among the towns of Maine's southern coast, this is among the best choices for families with young children.

Cape Neddick Light

Otherwise known locally as Nubble Light, the stark-white **Cape Neddick Light** (Nubble Rd., Rte. 1A, off Short Sand Beach, York Beach, 207/363-1040, www.lighthouse.cc/capeneddick) and rocky grounds are a favorite with photographers, as it's easy to capture dramatic shots with a big sweep of ocean and sky. The lighthouse itself is on a small, rocky island some dozen yards off the coast, and is off-limits to the public. Viewers congregate on the grounds of Sohier Park (Nubble Rd., York) instead, snacking on ice cream, scrambling over the rocks, or just gazing past the lighthouse to the horizon.

Museums of Old York

Small and meticulous, York Village is a historian's dream, filled with colonial homes, a library and schoolhouse, and a cemetery. Many landmarks are open for tours through the **Old York Historical Society** (3 Lindsay Rd., York, 207/363-4974, www.oldyork.org, 10am-5pm Tues.-Sat., 1pm-5pm Sun. late May-early Sept., 10am-5pm Thurs.-Sat., 1pm-5pm Sun. early Sept.-mid-Oct., all-day/one site tickets $15/8 adults, $10/5 children under 16). Start at the historical society, where you can purchase tickets and pick up a map of town, then walk to the landmarks, many of which are staffed by local docents.

York Beaches

LONG SANDS BEACH

Easily walkable from the shops and restaurants that line Route 1A, **Long Sands Beach** is a 1.5-mile stretch of pale sand that invites daylong beach planet sessions. Bring quarters for the metered parking that's available along the waterfront—it's $1 per hour south of **Sun and Surf Restaurant** (264 Rte. 1A), and $2 per hour north of the restaurant. Sheltered from the wind by Cape Neddick, the beach is among the best around for **surfing,** with (often) gentle waves that are good for beginning riders. Rent a board and 3/2 wetsuit from **Liquid Dreams Surf Shop** (171 Long Beach Ave., 207/351-2545, www.liquiddreamssurf.com, 8am-8pm daily, rentals $8 per hour, $20 half day), which also offers **surf lessons** (2-hour group lessons $70, private $105, includes board and wetsuit). During the hours of 9am-5pm Memorial Day-Labor Day, surfing is limited to the marked "surf zone," but it's a free-for-all after hours or in the off-season.

SHORT SANDS BEACH

A quarter mile of sand between the cliffs in York, **Short Sands Beach** is a favorite with young families, who love the sheltered water and adjoining playground. Every handful of years, rough tides will expose a historic shipwreck that's (mostly) buried beneath the sand here, thought to be a "pinky," a maneuverable square-rigged fishing boat that was popular along the coast in the 18th century. If you're lucky enough to see the ship appear, keep your distance, as it's considered an archaeological site. Parking in the on-site lot is $1 per hour, though it's worth arriving early during the summer months if you're hoping for a spot.

Both of the beaches are on the route of the **Beach Trolley** (207/363-9600, www.yorktrolley.com, $4), making this a great spot to park the car for the day and explore on foot.

Food

No pilgrimage to Nubble Light is complete without a stop off at **Dunne's Ice Cream** (214 Nubble Rd., York Beach, 207/363-1277, noon-9pm daily), formerly known as Brown's Ice Cream, whose enormous list of flavors includes New England treats like Maine blueberry, Indian pudding, and Maine whoopie pie.

The other classic stop for vacation food is **Flo's Hot Dogs** (1359 Rte. 1, Cape Neddick, www.floshotdogs.com, 11am-3pm Thurs.-Tues., $2-5), an unassuming little shack at the edge of Route 1. Like the sign says, though, Flo's has "the most famous hot dogs with hot sauce on Route 1 from Maine to Key West," and there's often a line—locals say the secret is in the tasty relish that tops the "house special," along with mayonnaise and celery salt. Cash only.

Tucked in a basement with a nautical theme, the **Ship's Cellar Pub** (480 York St., York, 207/363-5119, www.yorkharborinn.com, 11:30am-11:30pm Mon.-Thurs., 11:30am-midnight Fri.-Sat., 3pm-11:30pm Sun., $24-35) is a cozy spot to while away an evening over classic dishes like broiled scallops or seafood pie. All portholes and glossy wood, it's the next best thing to dinner on a boat, and the pub has frequent live music during the busy months, as well as a popular happy hour 4pm-6pm weeknights.

With a welcome emphasis on fresh ingredients and preparations, ★ **Frankie & Johnny's** (1594 Rte. 1, Cape Neddick, 207/363-1909, www.frankie-johnnys.com, 5pm-9pm Thurs.-Sun., $27-40) has beautiful vegan and vegetarian options on an eclectic menu that pulls from all over the globe. Meat eaters rave about the rack of lamb and the chicken piccata, and even the house salad impresses with a rainbow of veg. Cash and reservations only; bring-your-own beer and wine.

Accommodations and Camping

No frills but with an unbeatable location, **Seaturn Motel** (55 Longbeach Ave., York, 207/363-5137, www.seaturnmotel.com, $95-245) offers a clean, tidy place to recover from trips to the beach, which is right across the street. Rooms are compact, but stocked with a mini fridge and microwave, and rates include parking on-site. Oh, and there's a pool.

In a quiet spot that's still walking distance to Long Sands Beach, ★ **The Lighthouse Inn & Carriage House** (20 Nubble Rd., York Beach, 207/363-6072, www.thelighthouseinn.com, $89-199) is a great base for exploring the Yorks, with a pool and hot tub to retreat from the crowded beach. Decor is bright and updated, and the thoughtful owners supply extras like "beach wagons," so you can hit the sand with all your gear. Rates include an above-par continental breakfast.

Staking out its own peninsula, the **Stage Neck Inn** (8 Stage Neck Rd., York, 207/363-3850, www.stageneck.com, $175-450) has a small private beach, with lots of cozy places to watch the ocean rise and fall. There are tennis courts and walking paths on-site, and rates include an ample, if forgettable, self-serve buffet breakfast.

Exclusively for RVs and trailers, **Libby's Oceanside Camp** (725 York St., York, 207/363-4171, www.libbysoceancamping.com, sites with hook-ups $60-100) looks right out over the water, with picnic tables and fire pits that are perfect for long ocean sunsets. The **Beach Trolley** passes right by, so you can leave your rig parked and explore on foot. Adjacent to the bridge between York and Ogunquit, **Cape Neddick Oceanside Campground** (63 Shore Dr., Cape Neddick, 207/363-4366, 2-person tent sites $41) has tightly packed spaces with some shade, reasonably clean facilities with coin-operated showers, and a pleasantly rocky waterfront to explore.

Getting There and Around

The Yorks are linked by Route 1A, paralleled by both Route 1 and I-95. While Route 1A is indisputably the scenic route, it can get terribly clogged during the summer season, so expect delays. If at all possible, it's worth parking your car and getting around on the **Beach Trolley** (207/363-9600, www.yorktrolley.com, $4), which links up many of the towns' sites and beaches. There is currently no bus or train transport to York.

OGUNQUIT AND WELLS

Neighboring Ogunquit and Wells used to be a single town, until a knock-down, drag-out fight about streetlights caused the people of Ogunquit to rise up and secede. Things have simmered down since then, and the two towns have distinctive personalities—Ogunquit's gorgeous beachfront has become a favorite escape for New England's LGBT community, while Wells moves at a more relaxed pace, with nature preserves that ramble through pine forest and salt marsh.

That 1980 secession vote aside, it's really a nice combination. Ogunquit has a party scene that doesn't quit all summer, and sunny days bring a crowd to the three-mile sandy beach. Just up the coast, then, the Rachel Carson National Wildlife Refuge is a welcome break, with plenty of walking trails and paddling for afternoons of exploring.

Marginal Way

The 1.25-mile paved walking path that skims Ogunquit's harbor was bequeathed to the town in 1923, winding from Ogunquit beach to a rocky cove. It's a dramatic walk, with crashing surf to one side and salt-kissed coastal plants to the other. Bayberry bushes and roses, in white and seemingly every shade of pink, perfume the path in summertime, when it's one of Ogunquit's most popular destinations.

Perkins Cove

Known in its early days as Fish Cove, this stubby peninsula was once the focal point of the area's fishing and trade industry—one holdover from the era is a footbridge that cranks up and down to allow ships to pass beneath. These days it's pure vacationland, with art galleries, chowder houses, gift shops, and studios, all with lovely views of the water. This is the place to pick up salt water taffy and watch the lobster boats come and go—preferably early or late in the day, when the area isn't so crowded. Parking can be difficult in busy summer months, so it's worth parking downtown and catching a trolley to the cove.

Ogunquit Museum of American Art

This jewel of a museum, the **Ogunquit Museum of American Art** (542 Shore Rd., 207/646-4909, www.ogunquitmuseum.org, 10am-5pm daily, $10 adults, $9 seniors and students, children under 12 free) is displayed like a work of art, perched on a cliff above the ocean. The temporary exhibits often feature some of Maine's great painters like Andrew Wycth and Rockwell Kent, and the permanent collection includes a beautifully chosen selection of watercolors, oils, sculpture, and drawings. Save some time to see the outdoor sculpture garden.

Sports and Recreation

RACHEL CARSON NATIONAL WILDLIFE REFUGE AND WELLS RESERVE

Stretching 50 miles along the coast, the remarkable **Rachel Carson National Wildlife Refuge** protects salt marshes and estuaries that are essential for the migratory birds that travel the Atlantic seaboard on their yearly journeys. Stop by the refuge's **visitors center** (321 Port Wells Rd., Wells, 207/646-9226, www.fws.gov, office hours 8am-4:30pm Mon.-Fri.) to learn about the wildlife that thrives here, then hike the mile-long **Carson Trail,** which has a series of overlooks across the salt marsh, with signs that explore local species and conservation.

The adjacent **Wells Reserve** (342 Laudholm Farm Rd., Wells, 207/646-1555,

Perkins Cove

www.wellsreserve.org, 7am-sunset daily, $5 adults, $1 children 6-16, children under 6 free) is smaller, but has more ways to get around. A network of trails extends from the main entrance through the forest and salt marshes to Laudholm Beach, which narrows to a sliver at high tide, then widens into an expanse of nubbly rocks and tidepools. There are guided walks on many days, covering themes from the intertidal zone to the history of waterfront farming in Maine.

BEACHES

Ogunquit's crowning glory is the 3.5-mile-long **Ogunquit Beach** (Beach St., Ogunquit, parking $4 per hour, $30 per day), among New England's very finest. Soft sand is fringed by low dunes on a long peninsula that runs between the sea and the Ogunquit River. The southern end of the beach is the main access point, but there's also parking and an access road at the opposite end, called **North Beach** (Ocean Ave., Ogunquit, parking $4 per hour, $25 per day), which tends to be a bit quieter. There are bathroom facilities at both ends.

On the other side of the town line, Wells's beaches hold their own. The main destination is **Wells Beach** (Atlantic Ave., Wells, parking $12 half day, $20 full day), a long, sandy stretch that's popular with families and has lifeguards and restroom facilities in several locations. (If you can find a spot, there's free parking for Wells Beach at the ocean end of Mile Road, near Forbes Restaurant.) For fewer crowds and a bit more distance from the downtown shops, head to **Drake's Island Beach** (Island Beach Rd., Wells, parking $12 half day, $20 full day), which also has lifeguards and restrooms.

Food

OGUNQUIT

Excellent coffee and pastries make **Bread and Roses Bakery** (246 Main St., 207/646-4227, www.breadandrosesbakery.com, 7am-9pm daily, $2-7) a favorite for breakfast, but it's an equally worthwhile stop for picnic sandwiches. If you haven't tried pie made from wild Maine blueberries, this is the perfect place to get initiated.

Eat outside a little flotsam-covered shack at **Beach Plum Lobster Farm** (615 Main St., 207/646-7277, 9am-7pm daily, $5-25), which keeps it simple with lobsters and steamers (clams) served alongside corn on the cob and copious melted butter. Call ahead and the shop will package up your order to go, the fixings for a pretty luxe seaside picnic.

The food at ★ **The Front Porch Piano Bar & Restaurant** (9 Shore Rd., 207/646-4005, www.thefrontporch.com, 5pm-11pm daily, bar open late, $13-38) is every bit as good as it needs to be—think solid entrées like baked salmon, steak, and hearty salads. But the real draw is the piano bar atmosphere, which invites increasingly raucous show tune sing-alongs as the night wears on. There are no reservations at this popular spot, but you can call 45 minutes ahead to get your name on the waiting list.

WELLS

The classic seafood at **Fisherman's Catch** (134 Harbor Rd., 207/646-8780, www.fishermanscatchwells.com, 11:30am-9pm daily, $7-20) keeps it bustling through the summer months, when diners gather around picnic tables on the restaurant's large, screened-in porch. The restaurant has all the usual orders, but the chowder and the blueberry pie win raves.

Meet local policemen (or local anyone, for that matter) at **Congdon's Doughnuts** (1090 Post Rd., 207/646-4219, www.congdons.com, 6am-2pm daily, $2-9), which has been slinging vast quantities of the sweet treats since 1945. There's also a hearty breakfast and lunch menu, including some of the best breakfast sandwiches in town.

Set in a charming 18th-century house, ★ **Joshua's** (1637 Post Rd., 207/646-3355, www.joshuas.biz, 5pm-10pm daily, $27-35) creates special meals using locally sourced ingredients, and is a wonderful choice for an evening out. The menu changes frequently, but always features some good vegetarian options, as well as truly phenomenal crab cakes.

Accommodations and Camping

An impeccable budget option that's a fabulous deal in the shoulder season, **Towne Lyne Motel** (747 Main St., Ogunquit, 207/646-2955, www.townelynemotel.com, $69-214) is right on the trolley line, making it an easy spot for hitting the beach or the town. Rooms are stocked with fridges, microwaves, and coffeemakers, and updated bathrooms and decor make this a cut above the average motel.

The welcoming **Dragonfly Guest House** (254 Shore Rd., Ogunquit, 207/216-4848, www.dragonflyguesthouse.com, $125-275) is walking distance from Perkins Cove, Marginal Way, and the beach, but still manages to feel relaxed in the heart of the summer season. Perks include afternoon cookies and a great breakfast, and the bed-and-breakfast runs frequent specials with discounted massages and theater tickets.

Pet-friendly and simple, **The Beaches Motel & Cottages** (773 Post Rd., Wells, 207/216-4065, www.beachesofmaine.com, motel rooms $55-145, 6-person cottages $74-245) has adorably vintage cottages that are a short drive from the beach. The tidy grounds include a pool, a barbecue area, and a fire pit that's perfect for evenings under the stars.

Less than a mile from the shore, **Beach Acres Tent Sites & Park** (563 Post Rd., Wells, 207/646-5612, www.beachacres.com, tents $40, hookups $45-54) is spacious, if not particularly private, and its location on the trolley route makes it a good place for exploring car free. A pool, picnic tables, playgrounds, and barbecue facilities make this a popular choice for families.

Getting There and Around

Ogunquit and Wells are located on Route 1, about 50 minutes south of Portland. The Amtrak **Downeaster** (800/872-7245, www.amtrakdowneaster.com) stops in Wells on the route between Boston and Portland, and there's also a **Greyhound** (800/231-2222, www.greyhound.com, service from Portland $15, Boston $30) station in town.

During the summer season, the **Shoreline Explorer** (207/459-2932, www.shorelineexplorer.com) trolley links up the main sites and beaches, making this an appealing place to visit without a car. Taxi service is available from **Brewster's Taxi & Travel Services** (201/646-2141).

The Kennebunks

The two towns that make up southern Maine's toniest seaside destination—Kennebunk and Kennebunkport—are filled with luxurious inns that turn platoons of beach chairs toward the sea. A great, sweeping curve of beach in Kennebunk is one of the best on the southern coast, with plentiful sand and sunrise views of the bay. And the Kennebunk River, a spidering tidal waterway that divides the pretty villages, also offers places to swim and sit away from the blustering waves of the sea.

While the Kennebunks' reputation is for blue bloods and well-heeled preppies (an image bolstered by the presence of the bi-presidential Bush clan in an eye-catching compound on Ocean Avenue), it's not much more expensive than destinations up the coast. Streets are lined with old-fashioned colonial and federal homes, the whitewashed facades and bright shutters of which are classic New England. Ways to get on the water here include helming a sailboat, paddling into knee-high rollers on a surfboard, or searching for whales on the offshore banks—this is among the best places in the state for spotting them.

The Kennebunks

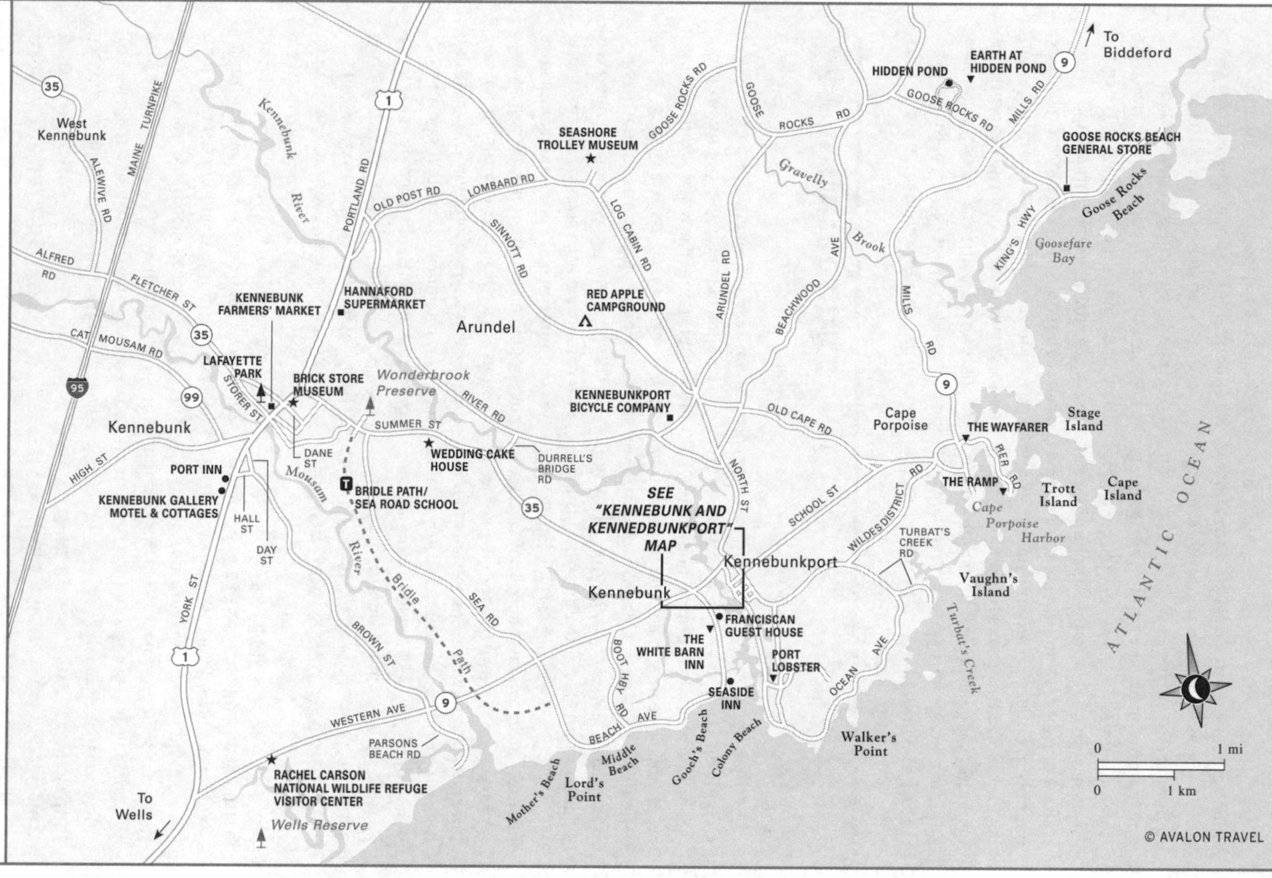

West Kennebunk
ALEWIVE RD
ALFRED RD
MAINE TURNPIKE
95
35
HIGH ST
CAT MOUSAM RD
FLETCHER ST
Kennebunk
99
KENNEBUNK FARMERS' MARKET
LAFAYETTE PARK
STORER ST
PORT INN
KENNEBUNK GALLERY MOTEL & COTTAGES
YORK ST
1
To Wells
HALL ST
DAY ST
DANE ST
BRICK STORE MUSEUM
HANNAFORD SUPERMARKET
Kennebunk River
PORTLAND RD
Mousam River
BRIDLE PATH/ SEA ROAD SCHOOL
Wonderbrook Preserve
SUMMER ST
OLD POST RD
Arundel
WEDDING CAKE HOUSE
RIVER RD
LOMBARD RD
SINNOTT RD
Bridle Path
BROWN ST
WESTERN AVE
PARSONS BEACH RD
RACHEL CARSON NATIONAL WILDLIFE REFUGE VISITOR CENTER
Wells Reserve
9
SEA RD
DURRELL'S BRIDGE RD
SEASHORE TROLLEY MUSEUM
RED APPLE CAMPGROUND
KENNEBUNKPORT BICYCLE COMPANY
LOG CABIN RD
GOOSE ROCKS RD
Mother's Beach
Lord's Point
Middle Beach
BEACH AVE
BOOT HBY RD
SEE "KENNEBUNK AND KENNEDBUNKPORT" MAP
Kennebunk
THE WHITE BARN INN
FRANCISCAN GUEST HOUSE
Kennebunkport
NORTH ST
ARUNDEL RD
Gooch's Beach
Colony Beach
SEASIDE INN
PORT LOBSTER
SCHOOL ST
OLD CAPE RD
BEACHWOOD AVE
Gravelly Brook
GOOSE ROCKS RD
OCEAN AVE
Walker's Point
WILDES DISTRICT RD
TURBAT'S CREEK RD
Cape Porpoise
MILLS RD
HIDDEN POND
Turbat's Creek
Vaughn's Island
THE RAMP
Cape Porpoise Harbor
THE WAYFARER
PIER RD
EARTH AT HIDDEN POND
GOOSE ROCKS RD
KING'S HWY
MILLS RD
Trott Island
Stage Island
Goosefare Bay
GOOSE ROCKS BEACH GENERAL STORE
To Biddeford
Cape Island
Goose Rocks Beach
ATLANTIC OCEAN
0 1 mi
0 1 km
© AVALON TRAVEL

SIGHTS

You won't find the usual local historical paraphernalia at the **Brick Store Museum** (117 Main St., Kennebunk, 207/985-4802, www.brickstoremuseum.org, 10am-5pm Tues. and Thurs.-Fri., 10am-8pm Wed., 10am-4pm Sat., noon-4pm Sun., $7 adults, $6 seniors, $3 children 6-16, $20 families). Instead, the staff gets creative with frequently rotated themed displays such as The Kennebunks During the Civil War and Kennebunks A-Z. The museum also runs a walking tour of the historic district at 11am every Friday throughout the summer, and a tour of historic homes around nearby Mother's Beach at 2pm on Thursday; maps of the sites are also available if you'd prefer to explore the areas on your own (guided tours $5, maps $5).

Step back into the golden days of narrow-gauge rail at the **Seashore Trolley Museum** (195 Log Cabin Rd., Kennebunkport, 207/967-2800, www.trolleymuseum.org, 10am-5pm daily summer, Sat.-Sun. only May and Oct., closed Nov.-Apr. except during Christmas Prelude, $12 adults, $10 seniors, $9.50 children 6-15, $5 children 3-5, children under 3 free). With a collection of more than 200 trolleys (some of which you can ride through nearby woods from the museum), plus a gift shop dedicated entirely to streetcars, the museum is well suited to enthusiastic kids and train aficionados alike.

The 1825 **Wedding Cake House** (104 Summer St., Kennebunkport) has become an essential sight for many visitors, who stop along the road to peer through the fence (the house is no longer open to the public). On a street with trim and tidy colonial gems, the overwrought Carpenter Gothic exterior *is* eye-catching, though the building sinks deeper into disrepair with each passing winter.

ENTERTAINMENT AND EVENTS

Nightlife

While there's plenty of nightlife in the Kennebunks to go around, the main event is sunset, when boat drinks and microbrews flow at packed waterside bars. For a local vibe, flotsam-inspired decor, and Geary's beer on draft, the **Pilot House** (4 Western Ave., Kennebunk, 207/967-9961, 11am-1am Mon.-Sat., 11am-midnight Sun.) is right by a marina and often has live music on weekend afternoons. The cavernous **Federal Jack's** (8 Western Ave., Kennebunk, 207/967-4322, www.federaljacks.com, 11:30am-1am daily) is less atmospheric but has plenty of seating on deep balconies overlooking the water. A little farther into Kennebunk, **Old Vines Wine Bar** (173 Port Rd., Kennebunk, 207/967-2310, www.oldvineswinebar.com, 5pm-10pm daily) makes up for an inland location with a rooftop patio, gorgeously crafted cocktails, and the best wine list in town. On the other end of the spectrum, the **Arundel Wharf** (43 Ocean Ave., Kennebunkport, 207/967-3444, 11:30am-9pm daily) is more rum-and-Coke than Riesling, but you'll be served on a floating dock in the Arundel River.

Festivals and Events

Free **Concerts in the Park** (Lafayette Park, Kennebunk, 6:30pm-7:30pm Wed.) feature classic rock and jazz bands mid-June-mid-August; bring a picnic blanket to spread out on the grass. In early June, the **Kennebunk Food and Wine Festival** (www.kennebunkportfestival.com) gathers local celebrity chefs and winemakers for a series of tastings and themed dinners. Later that month, **Launch! Maritime Festival** (www.gokennebunks.com) celebrates the Kennebunks' nautical heritage with seafood cook-offs, boat parties, and the annual Blessing of the Fleet.

SPORTS AND RECREATION

Whale-Watching

Humpback, finback, and minke whales congregate and feed at offshore banks, where they luxuriate in a whale's dream buffet of tiny sea creatures. Try to catch a glimpse aboard ***Nick's Chance*** (4 Western Ave., Kennebunk, 207/967-5507, www.firstchancewhalewatch.com, 4.5-hour trip $48 adults, $28 children

3-12), an 87-foot vessel that makes daily trips mid-June-September and weekend trips in the shoulder season. The boat goes up to 20 miles offshore, so even if the weather on the beach is balmy, bring plenty of warm clothing (and your favorite seasickness remedy). No refunds are given for trips when no whales are spotted, but passengers get a free pass for a second outing. The same company also runs 1.5-hour cruises on a **lobster boat** that's a fun, inexpensive way to explore the coast and see what's on the other end of all those colorful lobster buoys ($20 adults, $15 children 3-12).

Beaches

The 1.5-mile stretch of coastline known as **Kennebunk Beach,** located where the Kennebunk River reaches the ocean and about 1.2 miles away from Dock Square, is actually a series of three beaches, scalloped curves neatly separated by small, rocky outcroppings. Farthest east and easily the most popular of the three, **Gooch's Beach** is long and easy to access (if you've already secured a parking place downtown, it's easy to reach Gooch's Beach by bicycle or on foot: Leave Dock Square heading west on Western Avenue, then turn left onto Beach Avenue), but dwindles to a thin strip of sand at high tide. Next in line is **Middle Beach,** a quieter portion where the sand gives way to smooth stones that keep away sunbathers and sandcastle builders. **Mother's Beach** is small and sandy, with a good playground that makes it a hit with young families. A $25 parking fee for Kennebunk Beach is charged mid-June-mid-September. The local Intown Trolley also makes stops at the three beaches.

On busy summer weekends, it's often worth making the trip to **Goose Rocks Beach** in Cape Porpoise. Wide and scenic, the beach is rimmed with dune grass and perfect for strolling or taking a dip into the bracingly cold water. Parking at the beach is limited, and passes are required 8am-6pm late May-early September; buy a sticker at **Goose Rocks Beach General Store** (3 Dyke Rd., Kennebunkport, 207/967-2289, 7:30am-2pm Mon.-Thurs., 7:30am-7pm Fri.-Sat. May-June, 7:30am-7pm daily July-Sept., $15). A pass doesn't guarantee you'll find a spot, though, and the store advises showing up before 8:30am for the best chance at parking.

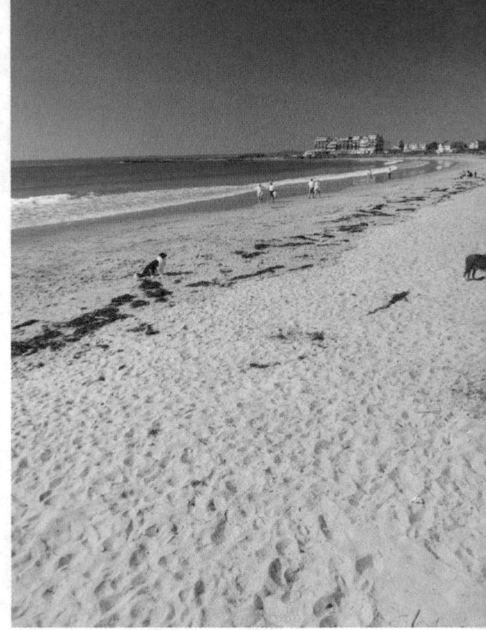

Kennebunk Beach

Biking

Back roads and trails around the Kennebunks invite endless exploration on two wheels. Though the way is narrow, winding, and sometimes clogged with sightseers, the eight-mile one-way ride down Ocean Avenue from Kennebunkport to **Cape Porpoise** via Wildes District Road is among the most scenic in town; the jewel-box seaside village has a few good seafood restaurants and an ice cream shop for mid-ride recovery. A gentler option is the flat, dirt **Bridle Path** that runs two miles along the Mousam River; the main access point and parking is at **Sea Road School** (29 Sea Rd., Kennebunk).

The 65-mile **Eastern Trail** (www.easterntrail.org) stretches along the coast from Kittery to South Portland, including 22 miles of smooth, off-road trail between Kennebunk and Bug Light in South Portland (parking available at Kennebunk Town Hall). Rent a hybrid, road, or mountain bike at **Kennebunkport Bicycle Company** (34 Arundel Rd., Kennebunkport, 207/385-4382, www.kennebikeport.com, 10am-5pm Mon.-Sat., 8am-3pm Sun., bikes from $20 half day, $26 full day), which also offers guided tours of local trails.

Boating

All eyes are on 55-foot schooner *Eleanor* when she cruises down the coast with gaff-rigged sails flying, and a trip with Captain Woody feels like stepping back into the grand old days of New England sailing. ***Eleanor*** (43 Ocean Ave., Kennebunkport, 207/967-8809, www.schoonereleanor.com, $50 day cruise, $60 sunset sail) makes two-hour outings daily May-September, and passengers are welcome to bring snacks and drinks aboard.

Hiking

Kennebunk Beach makes a great place to start the day with a sunrise walk. Just outside of downtown Kennebunk, **Wonder Brook Reserve** (www.kennebunklandtrust.org, parking on Plummer Ln.) has 2.5 miles of footpaths through shady upland forest and banks of rustling ferns.

Old, sandy roads-turned-walking-trails run through pine barrens and grassland at **Kennebunk Plains** (Rte. 99, www.nature.org), which The Nature Conservancy bought to protect the endangered Morefield's leather flower, threatened northern blazing star plants, and endangered grasshopper sparrows. The reserve also has a treasure trove of **wild blueberries,** and late summer brings a luxurious crop of the tiny, intensely flavored fruit (it's essential to stay on the trail when picking, however, as some of the plains' most vulnerable birds make their nests on the ground Apr.-Sept.).

Paddling

Paddle the Kennebunk River or follow the shoreline to **Goat Island Light** on a guided kayak outing with **Coastal Maine Kayak & Bike** (8 Western Ave., Kennebunk, 207/967-6065, www.coastalmainekayak.com, 3-hour tours $85, kayak rentals from $45 half day, $60 full day), which also has a fleet of stand-up paddleboards. The Arundel River winds through scenic forest as it leaves the coast and is the most popular place for independent kayak trips, but outings must be timed to the tides (some paddlers have found themselves stuck in the mud).

Surfing

Unless there's a hurricane sending giant swells to shore (and sending expert surfers to the beach), the Kennebunks' waves are relatively gentle and beginner friendly. Learn your way around the break at Gooch's Beach with one of the instructors from **Aquaholics Surf Shop** (166 Port Rd., Kennebunk, 207/967-8650, www.aquaholicsurf.com, 1.5-hour private lesson $110 for 1 person, $170 for 2, $230 for 3, rental boards from $25 half day, $35 full day), which also rents soft- and hard-top boards.

FOOD

Kennebunk

The main competition for best lobster roll in town is ★ **The Clam Shack** (2 Western Ave., 207/967-3321, www.theclamshack.net, 11am-8pm daily May-Oct., $12-25), which has gotten top scores from a who's who of food magazines and television shows. The riverside spot charges a premium for its version, but stuffs the toasted hamburger buns with a pound of lobster in large, meaty chunks bathed in your choice of mayonnaise or butter.

It's a travel truism that nothing says "tourist trap" like a giant board screaming: "Locals eat here!" The thing about the **Pilot House** (4 Western Ave., 207/967-9961, 11am-1am Mon.-Sat., 11am-midnight Sun., $8-22), though, is that locals really do spend their time on the riverside patio or bellied up to the inside bar outfitted with outboard motors and fishing gear. Geary's beer on tap, a convivial atmosphere, and a decent menu of fried grub (which many regulars like to cap off with a Jell-O shot, or three) make this a fine place to nurse a pint at the end of the day, listening to conversations about tourist foibles and fishing.

Grab a few basic foods, along with deli sandwiches and some prepared items at **H. B. Provisions** (15 Western Ave., 207/967-5762, www.hbprovisions.com, 6am-10pm daily). For a more extensive selection, a **Hannaford Supermarket** (65 Portland Rd., 207/985-9135, 7am-10pm Mon.-Sat., 7am-9pm Sun.) is on Route 1. Meet local bakers, farmers, and artisans at the **Kennebunk Farmers' Market** (3 Wells Ct., www.kennebunkfarmersmarket.org, 8am-1pm Sat. May-Nov.), rain or shine.

Kennebunkport

There's nowhere to sit at **Port Lobster** (122 Ocean Ave., 207/967-2081, www.portlobster.com, 9am-6pm daily, $9-16), but you can bring your takeout lunch across the street to the edge of the Arundel River and find park benches and views of the local fishing fleet. This seafood shop buys lobster and fish straight from the boat, and its lobster roll is simple and to the point: toasted white hot dog bun and tender meat just kissed with mayonnaise. The short menu also includes crab rolls, seafood salads, and chowder that come highly recommended.

Funky and offhandedly cool, **Bandaloop** (2 Dock Sq., 207/967-4994, www.bandaloop.biz, 5pm-10pm Tues.-Thurs., 5pm-11pm Fri.-Sat., $19-31) is an airy, energetic place to catch dinner made from organic, all-natural, and local foods served by a young, hip waitstaff. The menu changes frequently but includes creative dishes like tandoori-grilled salmon and pan-seared halibut with pepitas and pineapple chutney. Bandaloop also has beautifully prepared vegan options and is easily the best choice in town for non-meat options.

The lighthearted **Salt & Honey** (24 Ocean Ave., 207/204-0195, www.thesaltandhoney.com, breakfast and lunch 8:30am-2pm Fri.-Mon., dinner 4:30pm-9pm Wed.-Mon., breakfast $9-22, lunch $7-18, dinner $15-26) has fresh food and ambience offering a refreshing change from the seafood shack scene. Fish tacos and crab cakes are immensely popular, and you can start the day like a high roller with a lobster omelet dripping with caramelized onions and Havarti cheese.

A long-standing fine dining destination, **The White Barn Inn** (37 Beach Ave., 207/967-2321, www.whitebarninn.com, 6pm-9:30pm Mon.-Thurs., 5:30pm-close Fri.-Sun., four-course prix fixe $109, nine-course tasting menu $155, wine pairing $48-85) has won seemingly every award and honor a restaurant can earn in the United States. It has impeccable service, and the 19th-century barn setting makes a luxurious backdrop for the food, which balances classic and creative flavors.

With offbeat offerings ranging from Lemon Pink Peppercorn to Malbec & Berries, **Rococo Artisan Ice Cream** (6 Spring St., 207/251-6866, www.rococoicecream.com, 11:30am-11pm Mon.-Fri., 11am-11pm Sat.-Sun., $4-6) is the sweetest game in town. Lucky for wafflers, the shop serves ice cream in "flights" that include four small scoops of different flavors.

CAPE PORPOISE

Though it's only three miles down the road from the center of Kennebunkport, the village of Cape Porpoise is a place apart, with salt marshes and just a few places to eat in between the vacation homes lining the waterfront.

On a coast where flotsam-chic is a competitive sport—everything from clam shacks to inns are draped in fishing net, buoys, and other marine paraphernalia—**The Ramp** (77 Pier Rd., Kennebunkport, 207/967-8500, www.pier77restaurant.com, 11:30am-9pm daily, $14-25) might take the prize. Crushed shells cover the ground and rowboats stand guard over the parking lot. The menu of pub classics and seafood is solid, but it's the Portuguese-style mussels that win raves.

Out a bit farther, **Earth at Hidden Pond** (354 Goose Rocks Rd., Kennebunkport, 207/967-6550, www.earthathiddenpond.

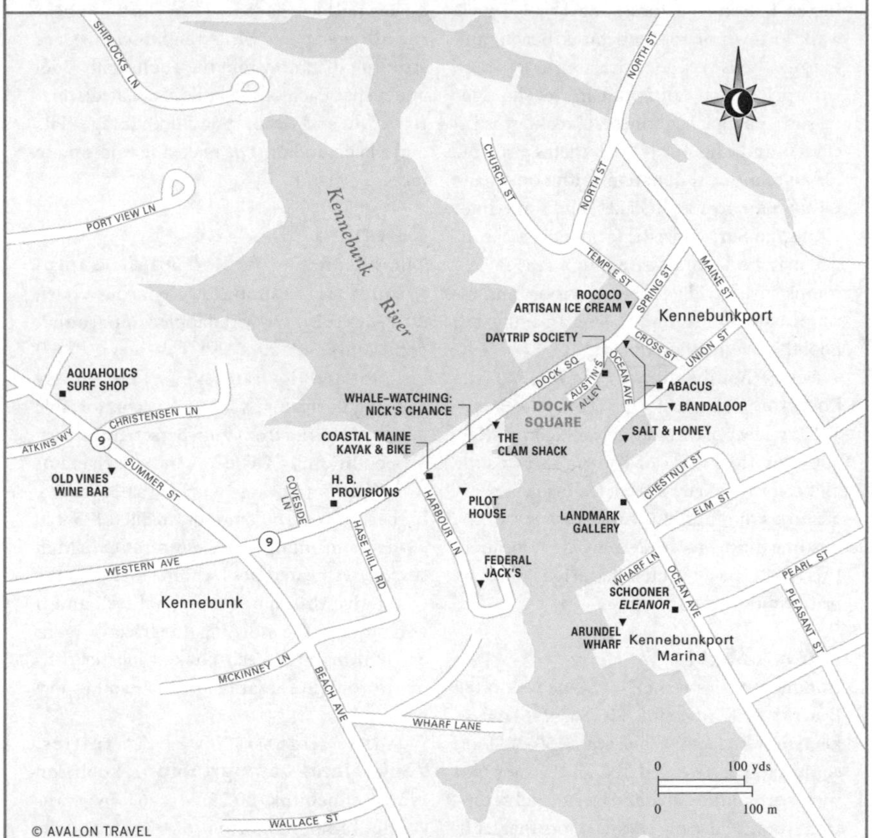

com, 5:30pm-9:30pm daily, $40-65) is a top contender for a night of splashing out with its exquisite food and modern-design-meets-rustic-chic decor. Its menu of contemporary cuisine is rooted in local products and flavors, and while any spot in the restaurant makes a lovely place to spend the evening, two private screened-in shacks (first-come, first-served) are the most stunning places to enjoy a meal.

ACCOMMODATIONS AND CAMPING

$100-150

There's nothing fancy about **Kennebunk Gallery Motel & Cottages** (65 York St., Kennebunk, 207/985-4543, www.kennebunk-cottages.com, May-Oct., $45-164), but the friendly staff and location just outside of town make it an excellent find. Larger cottages have small, simple kitchens, and a volleyball court and pool keep things cheery.

$150-250

Set on the serene grounds of a Lithuanian Franciscan monastery, the nonprofit **Franciscan Guest House** (26 Beach Ave., Kennebunk, 207/967-4865, www.francis-canguesthouse.com, $61-195) is a converted boardinghouse that hosts retreats and a regular crowd of Lithuanian summer people. The dated, very simple rooms are not for everybody—same goes for faux wood paneling and flaxen-haired figurines—but it's a 0.5 mile walk to town or to Kennebunk Beach, and the guesthouse is a good deal for the location, with prices that fall to $61 in the shoulder season. A simple, continental breakfast is included, and a hot breakfast buffet is available for an additional donation, with homemade Lithuanian bread, pancakes, and sometimes Ukininku Suris, a rustic farmer cheese; dinner may be served during high season. All rooms have a fridge, cable television, and in-room bathrooms, and there's an unheated pool that's a treat for lounging.

Perfectly tidy and well maintained, the **Port Inn** (55 York St., Kennebunk, 855/849-1513, www.portinnkennebunk.com, $105-300) has flourishes of contemporary style and color that keep it from feeling generic. A generous, hot buffet breakfast is served in a bustling dining room, and, given the location, this spot feels a bit more luxurious than the price would suggest.

Over $250

Common spaces at the ★ **Seaside Inn** (80 Beach Ave., Kennebunk, 207/967-4461, www.kennebunkbeachmaine.com, $150-369) are somewhere between dated and homey, but rooms are comfortable and bright, and ocean-front rooms have big sliding doors that let in the sound of rolling waves and the scent of the sea. For access to the beach, this spot is unmatched, with a private, sandy path that leads straight to the water. The breakfast buffet is classic, old-fashioned Maine: whole grain oatmeal, French toast with blueberries and syrup, and bowls of fresh fruit in a convivial dining room.

The closest thing in adult life to an indulgent, sleep-away summer camp may be **Hidden Pond** (354 Goose Rocks Rd., Kennebunkport, 888/967-9050, www.hiddenpondmaine.com, bungalows from $299, cottages from $499), a dreamy resort tucked into a quiet patch of woods. Guests ride cruiser bikes down the dirt roads between bungalows and gather each night to toast s'mores at a lakeside bonfire. The two-bedroom cottages have small kitchens and are clustered near the all-ages pool, while the bungalows are strolling distance from the adults-only pool and a spa. Each of the buildings has distinctive style and decor, but chic, vintage flair and a keen eye for style make the whole place picture-perfect.

Camping

The hospitable ★ **Red Apple Campground** (111 Sinnott Rd., Kennebunkport, 207/967-4927, www.redapplecampground.com, tents $51, RVs $60, full-service $65) has neat and tidy campsites set on a grassy clearing in the forest, as well as comfortable **cabins** ranging from four-person units with air-conditioning, cable TV, and a refrigerator to six-person options with a small kitchen, barbecue area, and outdoor fire pit ($175-220 , 3-day minimum, 1-week minimum in high season). A heated pool, camp store, and rec room give this spot a convivial feel, and if you order in the morning, the friendly owners will bring a fresh-cooked lobster dinner to your site at far below Kennebunkport prices.

With slightly fewer amenities, **Yankeeland Campground** (1 Robinson Way, Kennebunk, 207/985-7576, www.yankeelandcampground.com, $34/36 for 2 adults in partial/full-hookup sites, $5 extra adult, $3 extra child) is still an appealing option, especially at the lower price.

INFORMATION

All the usual pamphlets, along with maps and good advice, are available at the **chamber of commerce** (16 Water St., Kennebunk, 207/967-0857, www.gokennebunks.com, 9am-4pm Mon.-Fri.).

GETTING THERE AND AROUND

Kennebunk and Kennebunkport are on opposite sides of the Kennebunk River on Route 9, roughly 40 minutes south of Portland.

There's currently no public transportation to the Kennebunks.

Intown Trolley (207/967-3638, www.intowntrolley.com, June-Oct., $16 adults, $6 children 3-17, children under 3 free, $45 family of 2 adults and up to 4 children) follows a fixed route through town that takes in Kennebunk and Kennebunkport's main sights and beaches, with narration. Fares are good for one whole day, making this a useful option if you plan on doing a lot of sightseeing. **Shuttle-Bus** (207/282-5408, www.shuttlebus-zoom.com) operates buses around the southern coast. Fares and schedules vary.

Portland

Perched at the aft end of Casco Bay, Portland's the last bit of solidly built earth before the coastline splinters into the bays, inlets, and islands of Mid-Coast Maine. Look closer, though, and the city itself seems all shoreline: heads, breakwaters, and lighthouses wrap in on themselves, pinching Portland's peninsular center between Back Cove and the Fore River. Downtown bristles with schooner masts and wharves that give way to a rugged, working waterfront.

That blend of picturesque charm and real-world maritime culture infuses the city, and wherever you go in the Old Port and peninsula, the sea is not far away. Cobblestone streets are lined with galleries, museum, and boutiques celebrating Maine's seafaring traditions, and many of the city's chic bars and restaurants have a boat-to-table philosophy boasting chefs on a first-name basis with fishers, long-liners, and sea captains. The effect is utterly entrancing: When the weather is fine and Casco Bay sparkling, and the air smells of salt and fresh seafood, many visitors find themselves at Old Port brewpubs or on the deck of a sailing ship thinking up ways to move to Portland.

SIGHTS

To orient yourself in Portland, find its two major thoroughfares: Commercial Street runs between the Old Port and working waterfront, which anchor the heart of Portland's peninsula. The Arts District centers around Congress Street, with a collection of fine art galleries, studios, and the excellent Portland Museum of Art. Meanwhile, to the west, up-and-coming areas Munjoy Hill and West Bayside are primarily residential, with a handful of art galleries and cafés.

Lighthouses

With a craggy shoreline that's often wrapped in thick fog, it's no wonder the Portland area needs half a dozen lighthouses to keep boats off the rocks. Even with their blinking beacons, the city's seen centuries of dramatic and often tragic wrecks: the *Annie C. Maguire* ran aground right at the base of Portland Head Light on Christmas Eve 1886. Set on pretty capes and outcroppings, lighthouses are part of the Maine landscape at its most picturesque, but even on sunny days, their powerful lenses and stout architecture serve as a reminder that sailing Maine's waters has always been a dangerous undertaking.

The most iconic lighthouse in Portland is Portland Head Light, in nearby Cape Elizabeth, but there are some worthy beacons that can be spotted from the city. Watch for the squat **Bug Light** at the edge of the Portland Breakwater, **Ram Island Ledge Lighthouse** on its own tiny island, and **Spring Point Ledge Lighthouse,** which looks like a stubby, cast-iron spark plug and has excellent views of the bay.

★ Portland Museum of Art

The I. M. Pei-designed **Portland Museum of Art** (7 Congress Sq., 207/775-6148, www.portlandmuseum.org, 10am-6pm Sat.-Wed., 10am-8pm Thurs.-Fri., hours fluctuate in

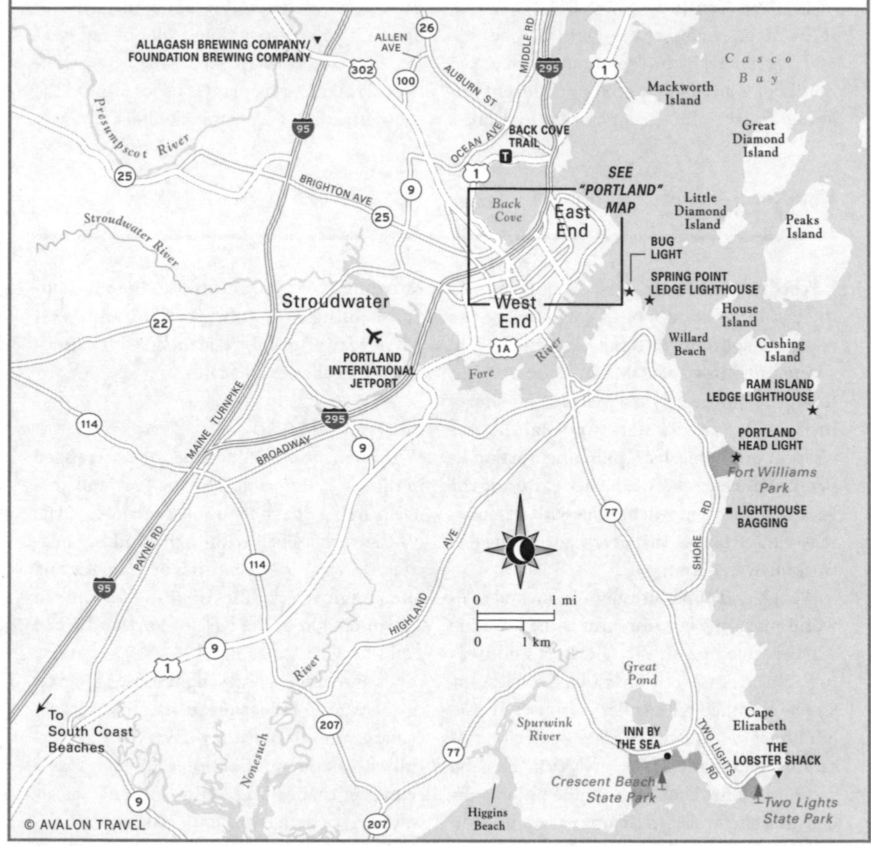

off-season, $15 adults, $13 seniors, $10 students, children under 15 free, free to all 4pm-8pm Fri.) is a world-class collection of impressionist and American work. A highlight for many visitors is work by Maine artist Winslow Homer, whose dramatic images of rescues at sea, windy shorelines, and small boats are seen as among the best American landscapes. Other noteworthy artists include Mary Cassatt, Claude Monet, Edward Hopper, and Auguste Renoir, but don't miss the dramatic engravings, lithographs, and paintings by Maine artist Rockwell Kent, many of whose mythic landscapes and woodcuts were made on the nearby island of Monhegan.

Institute of Contemporary Art at the Maine College of Art

For a more modern slice of the art scene, check out the **Institute of Contemporary Art at the Maine College of Art** (522 Congress St. or 87 Free St., 207/879-5742 or 207/669-5029, www.meca.edu, 11am-5pm Wed. & Fri.-Sun, 11am-7pm Thurs., 11am-8pm first Fri. of the month, free). The school's galleries draw cutting-edge installations from local and global artists, both established and aspiring.

Maine Historical Society

Rotating exhibitions at the **Maine Historical Society** (489 Congress St., 207/774-1822, www.mainehistory.org, 10am-5pm Mon.-Sat., noon-5pm Sun., $8 adults, $7 seniors and students, $2 children 6-17) illustrate the state's past through collections, exhibits, and lectures. Particularly riveting are the exhibits pertaining to the shelling that Portland received at the hands of the British during the Revolutionary War, when the port, then known as Falmouth, was burned to the ground in October 1775. The British captain offered mercy if the townspeople would swear allegiance to King George. No oath came, and the city was destroyed—only to be rebuilt over the next two decades.

Wadsworth-Longfellow House

Next door, the **Wadsworth-Longfellow House** (487 Congress St., 207/774-1822, www.mainehistory.org, tours noon-5pm daily May, 10am-5pm Mon.-Sat., noon-5pm Sun. June-Oct., $15 adults, $12 seniors and students, $3 children 6-17, $30 family of 2 adults and up to 3 children) was built in 1786 and achieved fame as the childhood home of poet Henry Wadsworth Longfellow. It's been restored to the time of the early 1800s, when Longfellow lived there. Tours lasting 45 minutes take in the life of the poet, as well as other members of the Longfellow family, such as Revolutionary War general Peleg Wadsworth.

Portland Observatory

Tired of waiting for boats to round Spring Point Ledge and come into view, Captain Lemuel Moody built the **Portland Observatory** (138 Congress St., 207/774-5561, www.portlandlandmarks.org, tours 10am-4:30pm daily May-Oct., sunset tours 5pm-8pm Thurs. late July-early Sept., $10 adults, $8 seniors and students, $5 children 6-16, $30 families) in 1807 so he could see harbor arrivals—and pass along the news to other shipowners for a tidy $5 annual fee. Climb the cheery red tower for Cap'n Moody's coveted lines of sight across Casco Bay and beyond, a vantage point especially sublime at sunset, when the waterfront and islands seem to glow on the sparkling water.

Victoria Mansion

Fans of Italianate architecture (or anyone who likes a pretty building) can swing by the **Victoria Mansion** (109 Danforth St., 207/772-4841, www.victoriamansion.org, tours 10am-3:45pm Mon.-Sat., 1pm-4:45pm Sun. May-Oct., 1pm-5pm Tues.-Sun. late Nov.-early Jan., $16 adults, $14 seniors, $5 students 6-17, children under 6 free, $35 families). Built by a hotel magnate between 1858 and 1860, the mansion is considered the greatest surviving example of pre-Civil War architecture in the country. Ahead of its time, it employed central heating, running water, and gas lighting in an era when such efficiencies were virtually unknown luxuries. These days the house is particularly impressive at Christmastime, when it's decorated from baseboards to ceilings with ornaments and wreaths.

ENTERTAINMENT AND EVENTS

Bars

Even if it weren't for all its breweries, Portland would have an amazing bar scene. Some of the most popular places to grab a drink are also restaurants, like **Eventide Oyster Co., Duckfat,** and **Terlingua,** but there are a few that go right to the point.

Nordic chic and Scandinavian-themed small bites prevail at the stylish **Portland Hunt & Alpine Club** (75 Market St., 207/747-4754, www.huntandalpineclub.com, 3pm-1am daily), and a happy hour lineup of four $6 cocktails is available until 6pm daily. Unless you're really looking, you'll walk right by **Novare Res Bier Cafe** (4 Canal Plaza, 207/761-2437, www.novareresbiercafe.com, 4pm-1am Mon.-Thurs., 3pm-1am Fri., noon-1am Sat.-Sun.), which is tucked down an alley between Union and Exchange Streets. Between the shady beer garden and cave-like interior, it works in any weather, and has an enormous list of beers from around the world. Drinkers who like their music on vinyl and decor eclectic will *love* **Maps** (64 Market St., 207/272-9263, 4pm-midnight Wed.-Sun.), which feels like a basement

Portland

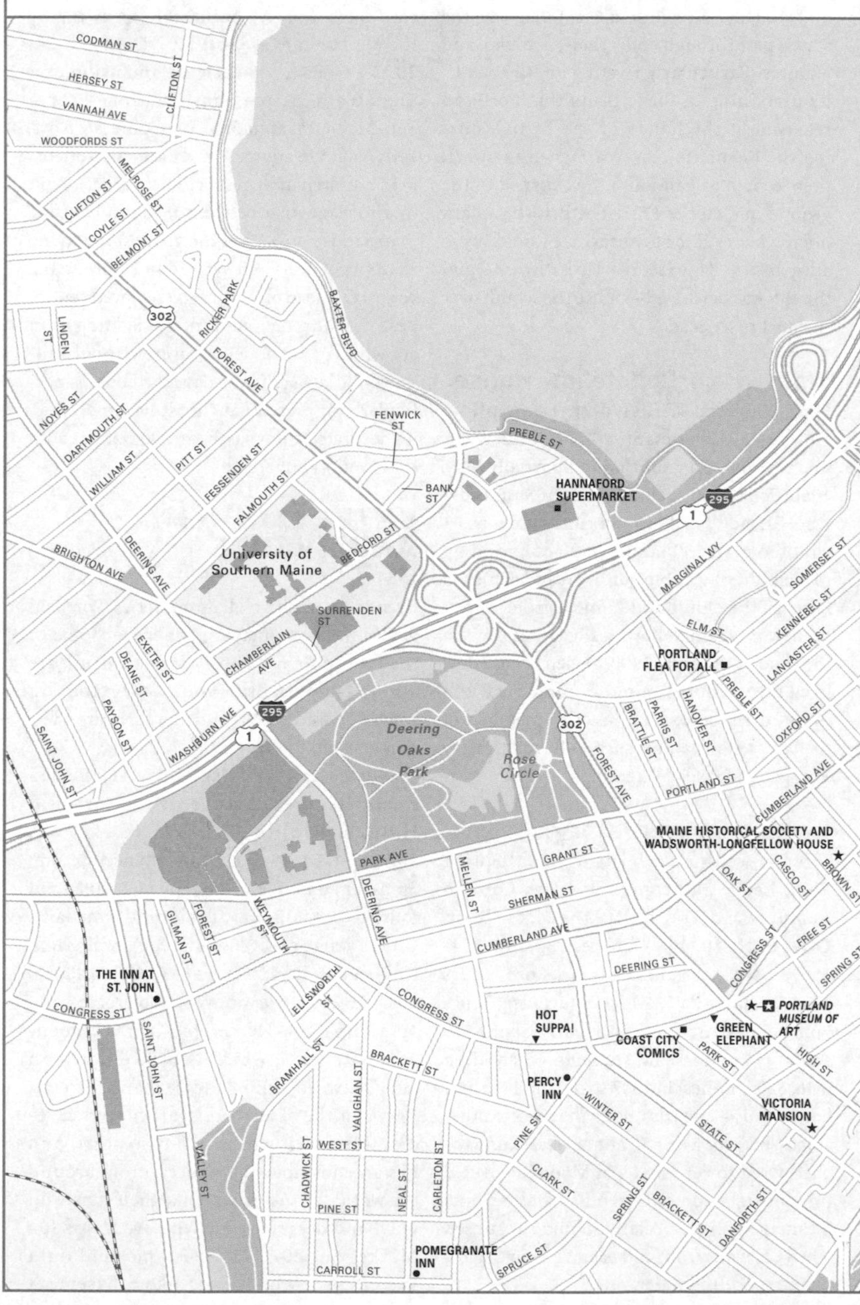

COASTAL MAINE
PORTLAND

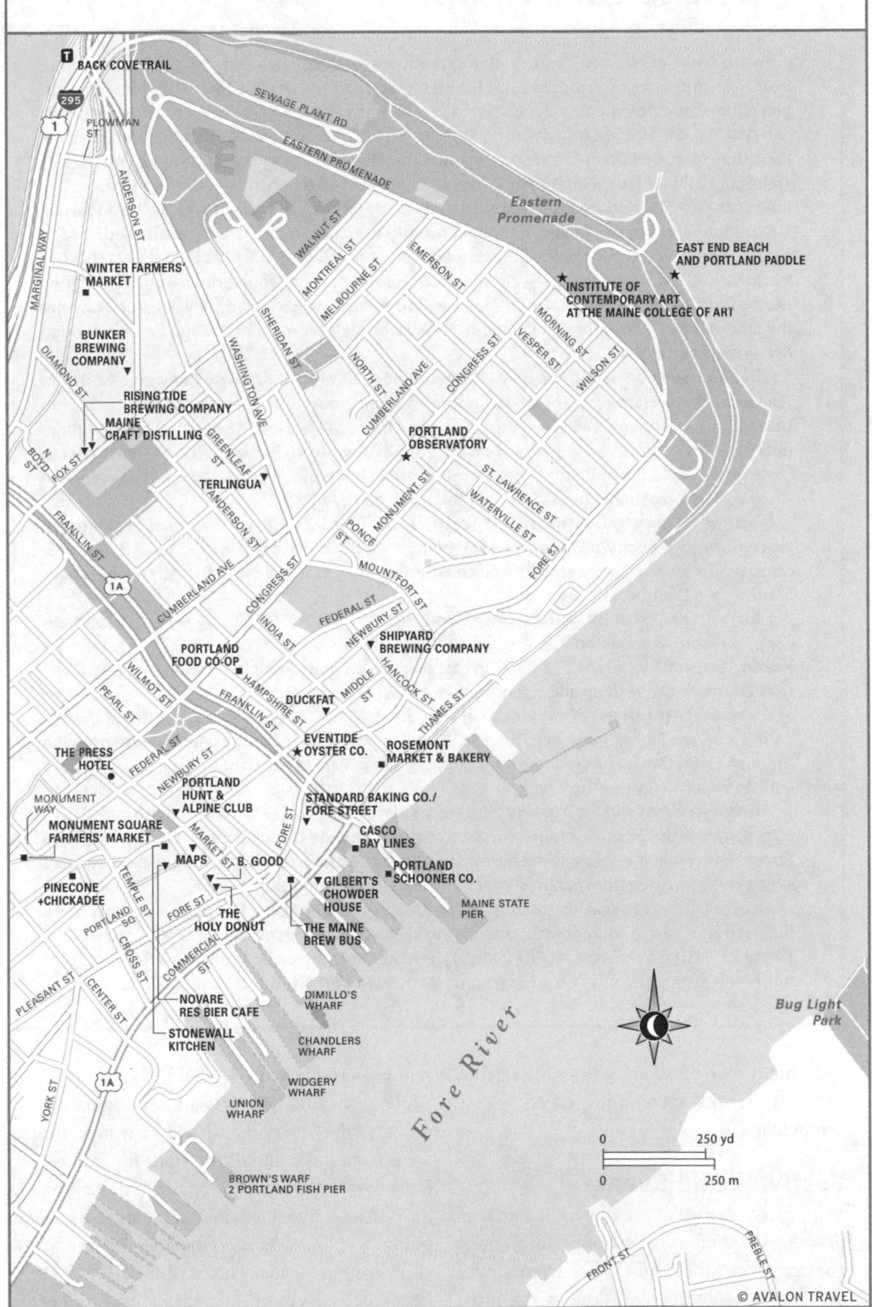
BACK COVE TRAIL
SEWAGE PLANT RD
EASTERN PROMENADE
Eastern Promenade
EAST END BEACH AND PORTLAND PADDLE
INSTITUTE OF CONTEMPORARY ART AT THE MAINE COLLEGE OF ART
WINTER FARMERS' MARKET
BUNKER BREWING COMPANY
RISING TIDE BREWING COMPANY
MAINE CRAFT DISTILLING
PORTLAND OBSERVATORY
TERLINGUA
SHIPYARD BREWING COMPANY
PORTLAND FOOD CO-OP
DUCKFAT
EVENTIDE OYSTER CO.
ROSEMONT MARKET & BAKERY
THE PRESS HOTEL
PORTLAND HUNT & ALPINE CLUB
STANDARD BAKING CO./ FORE STREET
MONUMENT SQUARE FARMERS' MARKET
CASCO BAY LINES
MAPS
B. GOOD
PORTLAND SCHOONER CO.
PINECONE +CHICKADEE
GILBERT'S CHOWDER HOUSE
MAINE STATE PIER
THE HOLY DONUT
THE MAINE BREW BUS
NOVARE RES BIER CAFE
STONEWALL KITCHEN
DIMILLO'S WHARF
CHANDLERS WHARF
WIDGERY WHARF
UNION WHARF
BROWN'S WARF 2 PORTLAND FISH PIER
Fore River
Bug Light Park
0 250 yd
0 250 m
© AVALON TRAVEL

Portland's Best Pints

Even in beer-loving New England, Portland stands out for the quality and variety of its breweries, from hole-in-the-wall startups to established brewers. It's the perfect place to explore the cutting edge of American beer, with a cluster of locations that are walking distance from downtown.

Rising Tide Brewing Company (103 Fox St., 207/370-2337, www.risingtidebrewing.com, noon-7pm Mon.-Sat., noon-5pm Sun., free tours 3pm daily, additional tours 1pm and 5pm Fri.-Sat., 1pm Sun., flights of four beers $8) has a diverse list of beers on tap, including the flagship Daymark American Pale Ale, a gorgeously balanced brew made with locally grown rye. The tasting room is cavernous and a bit gritty, and in summer months the outdoor beer garden is flanked by food trucks. Even devoted beer geeks should head next door to **Maine Craft Distilling** (101 Fox St., 207/798-2528, www.mainecraftdistilling.com, noon-5pm Sun.-Thurs., noon-7pm Fri.-Sat., free tastings), which uses many local ingredients in its offerings, which include whiskey, rum, gin, and the unusual Black Cap Barley Spirit, made entirely with Maine-grown barley and filtered through Maine maple charcoal.

Shipyard Brewing Company (86 Newbury St., 207/761-0807, www.shipyard.com, 11am-5pm Mon.-Wed., 11am-6pm Thurs.-Sat., noon-4pm Sun., tours 5pm Tues. mid-May-Oct., $7 with tastings, reserve online well in advance, flight of 4 beers $4) started in Kennebunkport, but the heart of Maine's largest brewery is just on the edge of downtown Portland. The tasting room has more of a finished brewpub feel, with barrels of aging beers stacked high against the walls, and a huge selection of brews (and a few craft sodas) on draft.

Bunker Brewing Company (17 Westfield St., Unit D, 207/613-9471, www.bunkerbrewingco.com, 3pm-8pm Wed.-Thurs., noon-10pm Fri.-Sat., noon-6pm Sun., flights of 3 beers $3) offers mainstay Machine Czech Pilz, and constantly turns out funky one-offs and collaborations like the Long Island Potato Stout.

Foundation Brewing Company (1 Industrial Way, 207/370-8187, www.foundationbrew.com, 3pm-7pm Thurs., noon-7pm Fri.-Sat., self-guided tours, 4-ounce pour $2, 10-ounce pour $4) is teeny-tiny and friendly, with a rotating cast of beers on draft that's been winning raves. Don't miss Zuurzing, a refreshing and bright sour farmhouse ale.

Austin Street Brewery (1 Industrial Way, Ste. 8, 207/200-1994, www.austinstreetbrewery.com, 3pm-7pm Thurs., noon-7pm Fri.-Sat., 5-ounce pours $2) is another diminutive spot with brews that run the gamut from the citrusy, piney Patina Pale to the dark-as-espresso Milk Stout with its sweet, richly toasted flavor.

Allagash Brewing Company (50 Industrial Way, 207/878-5385, www.allagash.com, 11am-6pm daily, check website for tour hours and registration, free tastings) turns out beers beloved across New England, especially the refreshing Allagash White and a rich-tasting tripel that packs a malty wallop. Aside from tastings, beer is not sold for consumption on-site.

An excellent way to soak up (so to speak) the Maine brewing scene is on a tour, so you can sip flights to your heart's content without worrying about cabs, buses, or wobbly bikes. **The Maine Brew Bus** (111 Commercial St., 207/200-9111, www.themainebrewbus.com, tours from $65) runs fun, highly regarded tours to the best taprooms in town, with food and drinks included.

apartment owned by a fashionable friend, but with drinks, cake, and grilled cheese sandwiches.

Festivals and Events

With such a deluge of art venues, it's no surprise Portland offers a slew of performances, concerts, openings, and other events over the course of every year. One of the most regular—and festive—is the **First Friday Art Walk** (www.firstfridayartwalk.com, 5pm-8pm on first Fri. of every month). In early June, the waterfront pulls out all the stops for the **Old Port Festival** (www.portlandmaine.com), an outdoor event packed with musicians, public art, and a Ferris wheel at the water's edge. Another favorite is the **Maine Brewers Festival** (www.mainebrewersfestival.com) in early November, which assembles the best of local beer in one place.

SHOPPING

Pretty shops line the cobblestone streets of Portland's Old Port. For the most efficient browsing, make your way along Exchange and Congress Streets. One local favorite is the sweetly hipster **Pinecone + Chickadee** (6 Free St., 207/772-9280, www.pineconeandchickadee.com, 10am-6pm daily), which stocks unique clothing, vintage finds, and doohickeys that make perfect gifts. Comic book lovers from around the East come to **Coast City Comics** (634 Congress St., 207/899-1505, www.coastcitycomics.com, 11am-8pm daily) for its collection not only of comics but also pinball and arcade games and vintage toys so fun the store could charge admission. Vintage and antiques hounds shouldn't miss the **Portland Flea-For-All** (585 Congress St., 207/370-7570, www.portlandfleaforall.com, noon-6pm Fri., 10am-6pm Sat., 10am-5pm Sun., hours can change without notice so call to confirm) for treasures covering three sprawling floors. Loved for classic jams and jellies, **Stonewall Kitchen** (182 Middle St., 207/879-2409, www.stonewallkitchen.com, 10am-8pm Mon.-Sat., 10am-6pm Sun.) is one of Maine's most recognizable brands, and the company store in Portland is a wonderland of free samples and things to buy.

SPORTS AND RECREATION

Beaches

With great sunset views and a skinny strip of sand, **East End Beach** is pleasant for walking and kayaking, and, more to the point, it's Portland's only public beach. It's set on the southern end of the **Eastern Promenade,** where monuments, cliffs, and smooth trails make for a haven from the city. If you have a day to spend on the sand, however, it's worth getting out of town to Cape Elizabeth's gorgeous **Crescent Beach.**

Boating

Take a turn hoisting the gaff-rigged sails—or let someone else do the work—on a two-hour cruise aboard the *Bagheera* or *Wendameen*, the 72- and 88-foot schooners operated by **Portland Schooner Co.** (Maine State Pier, 56 Commercial St., 207/766-2500, www.portlandschooner.com, 2-hour sailing trip $44 adults, $22 children 12 and under).

Hiking and Biking

Walking and biking paths wind through Portland's streets, and much of the scenic waterfront is pedestrian accessible. One of the finest places to walk or bike is **Back Cove Trail,** a 3.6-mile paved trail that circles a small estuary just north of downtown. Hop on (and leave your car) at Payson Park, the northern access point, or Preble Street. If you're headed from north to south, the Back Cove Trail connects to the **Eastern Promenade,** a slender waterfront park that caps Portland's East End neighborhood; 2.1 miles end-to-end, the park has walking trails, a popular swimming beach, and showstopping sunrise views. **Portland Trails** (207/775-2411, www.trails.org) maintains a website with maps and directions to many of the city's best offerings.

Paddling

Rent a kayak (or stand-up paddleboard) from **Portland Paddle** (East End Beach, Eastern Promenade, 207/370-9730, www.portlandpaddle.net, kayaks $30 for 2 hours, $40 half day, $55 full day, SUP $25 for 1 hour, $35 for 3 hours) to explore Casco Bay on your own. Paddlers with basic skills can poke along the coast and beaches, while more experienced kayakers can visit uninhabited islands, the historic Fort Gorges, and offshore communities. The company also offers guided tours: Family paddles, moonlight outings, and sunset trips are just a hair more expensive than renting the equipment alone (tours from $40 adults, $35 children 10-16).

FOOD

From old-school seafood joints to achingly hip bistros, Portland punches far above its weight in the restaurant department, and deciding where to apportion your limited meals in the city can be agonizing. Oysters and cocktails? Super-fresh salads packed with ingredients from local farms? How about a creamy bowl of chowder within earshot of the waterfront's clanging masts and foghorns?

Seafood

A refreshing throwback to Portland's pre-hipster, rough-hewn days, **Gilbert's Chowder House** (92 Commercial St., 207/871-5636, www.gilbertschowderhouse.com, 11am-10pm daily, $7-21) slings fresh corn and clam chowders in a thoroughly unpretentious space. The crisp, flaky haddock sandwiches are another treat, as is the open terrace behind the restaurant; when the restaurant is packed, order a cup of soup to go and find a spot on the nearby wharves for a very Maine picnic.

The interior of the ★ **Eventide Oyster Co.** (86 Middle St., 207/774-8538, www.eventideoysterco.com, 11am-midnight daily, $16-25) is almost too gorgeous: bright teal walls setting off a mammoth chunk of granite filled with crushed ice and sea creatures. The oysters—which mostly come from Maine, with a few out-of-state additions—are the obvious choice and centerpiece, and come with anything from "Kim Chee Ice" to classic mignonettes and cocktail sauce. Other options include small plates like duck confit salad and tuna crudo, but Eventide is famed for its lobster roll, a luscious combination of sweet lobster meat, brown butter, and chives in a soft Chinese-style steamed bun.

Bakeries

From dark chocolate with sea salt to maple bacon, the flavors of the soft, crisp-crusted treats at **The Holy Donut** (7 Exchange St., 207/775-7776, www.theholydonut.com, 7:30am-4pm Mon.-Thurs., 7:30am-8pm Fri.-Sat., 7:30am-5pm Sun., $2-5) are some of the best around—for doughnut lovers, this shop is a pilgrimage place. Arrive early to get the best selection, and avoid coming at the end of the day, as the doors close when the last doughnut sells.

A rustic, French aesthetic means great piles of croissants and fruit galettes at **Standard Baking Co.** (75 Commercial St., 207/773-2112, www.standardbakingco.com, 7am-6pm Mon.-Fri., 7am-5pm Sat.-Sun., $3-9), a beloved local institution walking distance from the Old Port. Breads and pastries are made with organic wheat flour from regional growers, and all the delightfully crusty loaves are naturally leavened.

Casual Fare

Just a few doors down, you'll find fresh fare to offset any doughnut guilt: **B. Good** (15 Exchange St., 207/747-5355, www.bgood.com, 11am-9pm Mon.-Thurs., 11am-10pm Fri.-Sat., 11am-8pm Sun., $7-12) is a chain with a couple-dozen locations across the East, but the concept of healthy food with local roots means the ingredients are sourced from Maine farmers and producers. Come for bowls of kale and quinoa, bright salads, simple burgers, and healthy smoothies, and find a seat upstairs when the place is hopping—a quiet bar and window-side tables overlook the action on Exchange Street.

Cheerful and welcoming, **Hot Suppa!** (703 Congress St., 207/871-5005, www.hotsuppa.com, 7:30am-2pm Sun.-Mon., 7am-2pm and 4pm-9:15pm Tues.-Sat., breakfast $5-11, lunch $7-12, dinner $15-24) serves an eclectic selection of comfort food with Southern flair, like pork belly with red beans and rice, catfish and grits, chicken and waffles, and some of the best corned beef hash in New England. Waits can get long, so aim to come early or late.

Named for a map-dot Texas town that hosts a yearly chili cook-off, **Terlingua** (52 Washington Ave., 207/808-8502, www.terlingua.me, 11:30am-9pm Mon.-Thurs., 11:30am-10pm Fri.-Sat., 10am-9pm Sun., $14-20) is a warm, vivid antidote to all that seafood. The barbecue fare at this laid-back restaurant is executed with a reverence for smoke and meat and Tex-Mex flair, from butternut squash empanadas to red and green chilis. Menu items like Frito pie (in the bag) lean cheeky, and regulars wash it all down with the killer house margaritas and solid beer choices.

Just down the road is another local favorite: ★ **Duckfat** (43 Middle St., 207/774-8080, www.duckfat.com, 11am-10pm daily, $8-14) serves a casual lineup of panini, salads, and golden french fries redolent of—you guessed it—duck fat. Decor is exposed brick and magnetic poetry tiles, and the poutine topped with cheese curds, gravy, and a fried egg would fortify you for a week of lighthouse bagging. If at all possible, save room for one of the shop's luxurious milkshakes, and come prepared to wait most nights.

Fine Dining

Vegetarians weary of meat-heavy Yankee fare shouldn't miss **Green Elephant** (608 Congress St., 207/347-3111, www.greenelephantmaine.com, 11:30am-2:30pm and 5pm-9:30pm Mon.-Sat., 5pm-9pm Sun., $12-15), a top-notch Asian bistro with stenciled green walls and chandeliers. The spicy ginger noodles are a favorite with regulars, as are the tofu tikka masala and crispy wontons filled with soy cheese and spinach.

Often credited with putting Portland on the international foodie map, ★ **Fore Street** (288 Fore St., 207/775-2717, www.forestreet.biz, 5:30pm-10pm Sun.-Thurs., 5:30pm-10:30pm Fri.-Sat., bar from 5pm daily, $28-40) could rest on its locally sourced, handcrafted laurels for a decade. That makes it all the more refreshing that the kitchen continues to turn out such high-quality fare. An open kitchen keeps the industrial-chic space from seeming too hushed as diners tuck in to seafood roasted in a wood-fired oven or house-made charcuterie paired with a serious wine list.

Markets

Conveniently located in the Old Port, **Rosemont Market & Bakery** (5 Commercial St., 207/699-4560, www.rosemontmarket.com, 9am-7pm Mon.-Sat., 9am-6pm Sun.) is "human sized" and stocked with regional vegetables, cheese, meat, and house-made baked goods as well as pizza and sandwiches. The **Portland Food Co-Op** (290 Congress St., 207/805-1599, www.portlandfood.coop, 8am-8pm daily) has aisles stuffed with local and organic products plus healthy, premade food. More basic options are available at **Hannaford Supermarket** (295 Forest Ave., 207/761-5965, 7am-11pm daily), at the edge of Back Cove.

Portland has three farmers markets overflowing with everything from local veggies to goat yogurt and kimchi. A carnival atmosphere commands at the downtown **Monument Square Market** (456 Congress St., 7am-1pm Wed. Apr.-Dec.), while the market at **Deering Oaks Park** (7am-1pm Sat. late Apr.-Nov.) is a bit more relaxed. The **Winter Farmers' Market** (84 Cove St., 9am-1pm Sat. Dec.-Apr.) also has live music and food trucks.

ACCOMMODATIONS

Though Portland has some wonderful top-end offerings, a lack of reasonably priced accommodations in the city makes sites like Airbnb and VBRO good options for travelers on a budget.

$100-150

Ask a local about **The Inn at St. John** (939 Congress St., 207/773-6481, www.innatstjohn.com, $75-250), and he or she will likely recall its seedy years when the West End was decidedly down-market. It's been overhauled one room at a time, however, retaining flourishes of Gilded Age glamour and gaining much-needed updates like wireless Internet, coffeemakers, and a bit of contemporary style. Continental breakfast is served in a downstairs dining room, and the rooms vary widely, from more luxurious king rooms boasting en suite baths and views of the street to somewhat garret-like singles with shared baths. The narrow, steep stairs are not for everyone.

$150-250

Set on a quiet side street in the West End, the **Percy Inn** (15 Pine St., 207/871-7638, www.percyinn.com, $89-219) is in a renovated 1830s federal-style brick house that feels like pure, old-fashioned Portland. The house has some quirks and could use a bit of updating, but the overall effect is lovely; rooms are named for famous writers, and the fire-lit library and spacious common room are welcoming.

Over $250

Somewhere between bohemian whimsy and design-chic, ★ **Pomegranate Inn** (49 Neal St., 207/772-1006, www.pomegranateinn.com, $200-359) is settled on a pretty corner in a historic neighborhood and full of visual treasures. Every room has unique hand-painted walls, and antiques are displayed alongside modern art. A 3rd-floor lounge is stocked with games, and a quiet back patio makes an ideal spot for enjoying the daily cookies, tea, and coffee. "The Pom" is now operated by Lark Hotels and serves the group's characteristic small-plate breakfast that will charm your socks off (and leave some hungry travelers looking for a bit more).

Flying typewriters and wordy art are reminders that **The Press Hotel** (119 Exchange St., 207/808-8800, www.thepresshotel.com, $225-450) was once the home of the *Portland Press Herald*, and the journo-chic theme runs throughout the property. Excellent service gives the large property a boutique feel, and the Inkwell coffee and wine bar feels like just the place to type up some hotel poetry of your own—local touches are everywhere and, all in all, Press offers some of the coolest new digs in New England.

INFORMATION

The remarkably helpful and informative **visitors bureau** (207/772-5800, www.visitportland.com) has a website full of information and links, and runs information centers on the waterfront at 14 Ocean Gateway Pier (207/772-5800, 9am-5pm Mon.-Fri., 9am-4pm Sat.-Sun., winter hours vary) and in the Jetport Terminal next to baggage claim (207/775-5809, 8am-midnight Mon. and Thurs.-Fri., 10am-midnight Sat.-Sun., winter hours vary).

GETTING THERE

Air

Maine's largest airport is **Portland International Jetport** (1001 Westbrook St., 207/774-7301, www.portlandjetport.org), with service from American, Delta, JetBlue, Southwest, and United. There you'll find national car rental agencies Alamo, Avis, Budget, Enterprise, Hertz, and National, and the **Greater Portland Transit District METRO** (207/774-0351, www.gpmetrobus.net), which has a bus from the airport to downtown Portland (Route #5, 6-15 buses daily).

Train

The Amtrak **Downeaster** (800/872-7245, www.amtrakdowneaster.com) runs from Boston to Portland five times a day, with two trains making an extended trip to Freeport and Brunswick. The Portland stop is at the **Portland Transportation Center** (100 Thompson's Point Rd.), two miles outside of downtown. Trolleys link **Wells Regional Transportation Center** with the Kennebunks, and the **Freeport station** is within walking distance of downtown shops.

Bus

Concord Coach Lines (100 Thompson's Point Rd., 800/639-3317, www.concord-coachlines.com) operates buses from Boston and New York City; long-distance routes connect to Portland, then continue to many towns along Route 1, including Brunswick (16 Station Ave.), Bath (Mail It 4 U, 10 State Rd.), Rockland (Maine State Ferry Terminal, 517A Main St.), and Camden/Rockport (Maritime Farms, 20 Commercial St./Rte. 1, Rockport).

Greyhound (950 Congress St., 207/772-6588 or 800/231-2222, www.greyhound.com)

has services to Portland from Boston and around New England.

GETTING AROUND

Portland's local bus company is **Metro** (114 Valley St., 207/774-0351, www.gpmetrobus.net, $1.50 adults, $0.75 seniors, children under 6 free, $5 all-day pass), which runs out of its downtown station to points including the airport. Compared to most capital cities, Portland has a decent amount of metered street parking, which doesn't guarantee you'll find any right away (particularly in the summer), but the odds are good. That said, the city has pay lots and garages set up every few blocks. Local taxis to call are **ABC Taxi** (207/772-8685) and **Town Taxi** (207/773-1711).

CASCO BAY ISLANDS

There are 136 islands, give or take, scattered across the broad Casco Bay—enough that they were long called the Calendar Islands, a name that evokes the dreamy possibility of spending an entire year skipping from isle to isle. The islands on Casco Bay can feel wonderfully remote, though they're just a quick ferry ride from downtown Portland, and they're well worth a day trip or overnight escape.

Peaks Island

The most accessible of the Casco Bay islands, Peaks Island is like a Portland neighborhood surrounded by water, and with many ferry departures each day, it's the easiest way to get out on the water. Most visitors leave their cars on the mainland, then rent a golf cart or bicycle for a day of exploring.

SIGHTS AND ACTIVITIES

Circle the island by bicycle on the **Peaks Island Loop,** a four-mile, mostly flat route that winds between residential neighborhoods and the waterfront. Bikes are available to rent, with helmets and maps of the island, from **Brad's Bike Rental and Repair** (115 Island Ave., 207/766-5631, 10am-6pm daily, rentals $10 per hour, $30 all day), a short walk from the ferry terminal.

Oddly wonderful and wonderfully odd, the **Umbrella Cover Museum** (62 B Island Rd., 207/766-4496, www.umbrellacovermuseum.com, 10am-1pm and 2pm-5pm Tues.-Sat., 10am-12:30pm Sun. June-early Sept.) is a deep dive into the sheaths, envelopes, and slipcovers that umbrellas come in. Tours sometimes include impromptu "umbrella songs" by the accordion-playing curator.

For the best perspective on the rugged coast, grab a paddle. Guided kayak tours are available from **Maine Island Kayak** (207/766-2373, www.maineislandkayak.com, half-day tour from $65), whose guides meet the arriving ferryboat from Portland.

FOOD

Dining options are limited on Peaks Island, but **The Cockeyed Gull Restaurant** (78 Island Ave., 207/766-2800, 11:30am-8:30pm daily, hours and days vary in winter $8-25) has seafood standards and great views of the water from its deck. Another possibility is **The Inn on Peaks Island** (33 Island Ave., 207/766-5100, www.innonpeaks.com, 11am-9pm Sun.-Thurs., 11am-10pm Fri.-Sat., $9-26), whose menu ranges from basic burgers and sandwiches to upscale entrées like lobster risotto.

GETTING THERE

Casco Bay Lines (56 Commercial St., 207/774-7871, www.cascobaylines.com, approximately 1 per hour, $7.70 adults, $3.85 children and seniors) has year-round ferry service from downtown Portland to Peaks Island.

Great Chebeague Island

Farther away from Portland both geographically and in spirit, this is a quiet place to explore by bike, or picnic on one of the island's appealing beaches. If you're looking for an overnight escape, the island's single hotel is an ideal place to get away from it all.

SIGHTS AND ACTIVITIES

For two hours on either side of low tide, the ocean exposes a slender sandbar linking Great Chebeague with **Little Chebeague Island,** an uninhabited islet that's covered in thick forest. To reach the sandbar, follow Indian Point Road to a sandy beach that looks out at Little Chebeague Island.

Close to the Chebeague Island Inn, **Hamilton Beach** is the island's best for swimming and sunbathing, with warmer water then elsewhere on Chebeague.

FOOD AND ACCOMMODATIONS

The island's main social hub is the **Slow Bell Café** (2 Walker Rd., 207/846-3078, 5pm-midnight Thurs.-Sun. Memorial Day-Labor Day, $9-20), a bar and restaurant with a laid-back, castaway feel. Seafood, salads, and sandwiches are casual and well made.

Though there's just one place to stay on the island, the lovely ★ **Chebeague Island Inn** (61 South Rd., 207/856-5155, www.chebeagueislandinn.com, $175-450) more than compensates for the lack of variety. A great, shady porch faces the water, with rocking chairs and warm blankets for morning coffee, and there are beach towels and umbrellas to borrow for a trip to the shore. Nonguests are welcome at the inn's **restaurant** (breakfast 7:30am-9:30am, lunch 11:30am-2:30pm, light fare 2:30pm-9pm, dinner 5:30pm-8pm, daily, $15-35), which serves elegant preparations using many local ingredients.

GETTING THERE AND AROUND

Casco Bay Lines (56 Commercial St., Portland, 207/774-7871, www.cascobaylines.com, 1 hr., 20 min., $11 adults, $5.50 children and seniors) has year-round ferry service from downtown Portland to Chebeague Island, with several departures each day. **Chebeague Transportation Company** (Cousins Island Wharf, Yarmouth, 207/846-3700, www.chebeaguetrans.com, 15 min., $16 adults, $4.50 children 6-11) has regular service from Yarmouth. Parking is available at the company's lot in Cumberland, with a bus shuttle to the wharf.

Getting There and Around

A network of ferries connects Portland with the islands speckling Casco Bay. **Casco Bay Lines** (56 Commercial St., 207/774-7871, www.cascobaylines.com, passenger ferry $7-12, mail boat run $16 adults, $14 seniors, $8 children) runs trips to seven islands, from a quick hop to Peaks Island to the longer trip to Chebeague. The ferry service still delivers the mail to offshore communities, and you can tag along on the **mail boat run,** which lasts 2.5-3.5 hours; while the boat doesn't linger long enough for you to explore the islands, you'll get great views, and the crew narrates the whole experience on a loudspeaker (bring your own food and drinks).

CAPE ELIZABETH

Just a short drive from the city of Portland, this seaside community offers views back across Casco Bay, and one of Maine's most recognizable lighthouses. While this is a quick day trip for most visitors, it's equally appealing as a home base for visiting the city, where you can nip into town for dinner, then return to the quiet of night by Crescent Beach.

Sights

PORTLAND HEAD LIGHT

The most iconic among Portland's lighthouses is the **Portland Head Light** (1000 Shore Rd., www.portlandheadlight.com, museum and gift shop 10am-4pm daily, park sunrise-sunset daily); its slender proportions and red-roofed keeper's house are perfectly offset by jagged outcroppings and crashing waves. It was the first lighthouse completed by the U.S. government and has been guiding ships on Casco Bay since 1791; the rocky head is rich with history, including shipwrecks and daring, stormy rescues, and some believe it's haunted by the benevolent ghost of a former lighthouse keeper. One frequent visitor was hometown poet Henry Wadsworth Longfellow, who liked to drink with the lighthouse keeper and later wrote:

> Steadfast, serene, immovable, the same
> Year after year, through all the silent night
> Burns on forevermore that quenchless flame,
> Shines on that inextinguishable light!

For the real Maine beach experience, it's worth heading out of town. Eight miles south of Portland, **Crescent Beach** (66 Two Lights Rd., 207/767-3625, www.maine.gov, 9am-sunset daily, $8 adults, $2 seniors, $1 children 5-11) is all dune grass and soft sand, a gorgeous place to watch the fishing fleet cross the horizon.

OTHER SIGHTS

A favorite spot for lighthouse bagging is **Two Lights** (Two Lights Rd.), a pretty pair of private lighthouses with a small beach and rocks perfect for hopping around and scouting for sea creatures. Confusingly, neither of the two lights is visible from Two Lights State Park, so just continue down the road until it ends in a small parking lot. Since neither lighthouse is open to the public, the views (and photo opportunities) aren't quite as good as elsewhere, but the neighboring Lobster Shack takes up the slack.

Food

Adjoining the Two Lights lighthouses, **The Lobster Shack** (225 Two Lights Rd., 207/799-1677, www.lobstershacktwolights.com, 11am-8pm daily Mar.-Oct., $12-18) has some of Maine's most beloved lobster rolls. The interior is decked out in marine bric-a-brac, and the outdoor picnic tables overlook crashing waves and the lighthouses—but be vigilant about seagulls to avoid losing bits of your meal. While the lobster roll is the main attraction here, The Lobster Shack also serves the standard lineup of market-price seafood, and a homemade strawberry rhubarb pie that gets rave reviews.

Accommodations

Set back from Crescent Beach, ★ **Inn by the Sea** (40 Bowery Beach Rd., 207/779-3134, www.innbythesea.com, $450-700) has a perfect location and gorgeous grounds. The luxurious resort has family-friendly bungalows and cottages as well as beautiful rooms in the main inn and perks like outdoor pools, a fireplace stocked with s'mores, and a spa. What sets the inn apart from other top-notch properties, though, is a remarkable focus on conservation: The on-site wetlands and meadows were overhauled to create habitat for the endangered New England cottontail rabbit, the inn runs environmental science education programs, and the chef works with local fishers to source from underutilized fish populations. It's also easy to leave the inn with an unusual memento of your stay—the staff fosters friendly dogs from the local humane society that can be adopted by guests; hundreds find new homes each year.

Getting There

Cape Elizabeth is 20 minutes south of Portland on Route 77, which loops past the cape's main destinations. There's currently no public transit from Portland to the sights in Cape Elizabeth.

FREEPORT

Just 20 minutes up the coast from Portland, Freeport is a shipbuilding and fishing village turned New England-themed outlet shopping destination, a transformation that's left some interesting quirks, with boutiques, outlets, and even a McDonald's restaurant tucked into historic homes. Visitors tend to love it or hate it, but whether you're planning an all-day shopping itinerary or just want a home base for exploring Portland, it's a good place to stay, with more affordable accommodations than the city.

Sights

The undisputed headliner of Freeport's retail scene is the **L.L. Bean Flagship Store** (95 Main St., 877/755-2326, www.llbean.com), which is open 24 hours a day, 365 days a year. If the appeal of buying waterproof boots at 3am isn't enough to tempt you, the indoor trout pond or archery and clay shooting lessons might.

With some of Maine's most beloved brews, **Maine Beer Company** (525 Rte. 1, 201/221-5711, www.mainebeercompany.com, 11am-8pm Mon.-Sat., 11am-5pm Sun.) has a tasting room that keeps eight of its beers on tap—and you can watch the beer-in-progress through a big window onto the brewing facility.

Shopping

Aside from the behemoth L.L. Bean outlet, much of Freeport's big-name shopping is clustered in the **Freeport Village Station** (1 Freeport Village Station, www.onefreeportvillagestation.com, 10am-7pm Sun.-Thurs., 10am-8pm Fri.-Sat.) or along **Main Street,** including the Gap, Patagonia, Bass, and the North Face. Most stores open at 9am or 10am and remain open until 6pm or 7pm.

For a town that's made shopping its raison d'être, it only makes sense that **Black Friday**—the massive sales day following Thanksgiving—would be a kind of official carnival, with midnight trains of shoppers arriving from Boston to live music and a celebratory atmosphere.

Sports and Recreation

HIKING AND BIKING

There are five miles of walking trails at **Wolfe's Neck Woods State Park** (426 Wolfe's Neck Rd., 207/865-4465, www.maine.gov, 9am-sunset daily, $6 adults, $4 seniors), which encompasses rocky shoreline, wetlands, and fields. A pair of ospreys returns each year to nest on an island just off the shore, and the park's **White Pines Trail** offers a good vantage point over their territory from spring until they begin their long autumn trip to South America.

WINTER SPORTS

The **L.L. Bean Outdoor Discovery School** (15 Casco St., 888/552-3261, www.llbean.com/adventures) offers cross-country skiing and snowshoeing outings, and there are several parks groomed for cross-country skiing within the city limits. With views of the snowy shore and ocean, **Winslow Park** (30 Main St.) is good for both cross-country and snowshoeing, and although **Wolfe's Neck Woods State Park** is officially closed, the ungroomed access road and trails are ideal for a winter outing.

Food

Downtown Freeport is packed with national chain restaurants—like that "olde New Englande" McDonald's—but there are plenty of local spots to recover from your shopping.

One favorite is the hunting lodge-like **Broad Arrow Tavern** (162 Main St., 207/865-9377, www.harraseeketinn.com, 11:30am-10pm daily, $15-30), where Maine classics line up alongside brick-oven pizza, hearty salads, and soups.

Get a taste of Freeport's maritime past at **Harraseeket Lunch and Lobster** (36 Main St., South Freeport, 207/865-3535, www.harraseeketlunchandlobster.com, 11am-8:45pm daily Apr.-Oct. or end of season, $9-25), which leans a bit pricey for an outdoor lobster shack but has an unbeatable location at the edge of the marina.

For a quick, healthy lunch of sandwiches and salad, L.L. Bean's **1912 Café** (95 Main St., inside the store, 9am-7pm daily, $6-12) is a convenient option in the heart of the action, or head outside of town for a great bistro meal at **Conundrum** (117 Rte. 1, 207/865-0303, www.conundrumwinebistro.com, 4:30pm-10pm Tues.-Sat., $14-30), a cozy wine joint in the shadow of the "Big Indian," a beloved local landmark.

Accommodations and Camping

Clean and family-run **Casco Bay Inn** (107 Rte. 1, 207/865-4925, www.cascobayinn.com, $101-175) may not be fancy, but it's a short drive to downtown Freeport and a good value, with coffeemakers and fridges in the rooms as well as a basic continental breakfast.

Wonderfully friendly hosts and a hearty fresh breakfast make the **Nicholson Inn** (25 Main St., 207/618-9204, www.nicholsoninn.com, $130 s, $160 d) a relaxing option with a good location, period furnishings, and private baths, though young children may not be allowed. Prices drop in the off-season.

Once the home of Arctic explorer and Bowdoin grad Donald MacMillan, the **White Cedar Inn Bed and Breakfast** (178 Main St., 207/865-9099, www.whitecedarinn.com, $199-379) combines Victorian charm with modern touches like comfy beds, a guest pantry, common spaces, and a great breakfast, all within walking distance of downtown.

A shady cluster of quiet roads on 626 waterfront acres makes **Recompence Shore Campground** (134 Burnett Rd., 207/865-9307, www.freeportcamping.com, $28-52) a haven from the bustling downtown, with fun lobster bakes most Saturday nights and rustic **waterfront cabins** (from $155).

Getting There

Freeport is located off I-295 and Route 1, 18 miles north of Portland. The Amtrak **Downeaster** (800/872-7245, www.amtrakdowneaster.com) stops in Freeport on the daily, round-trip route that links Boston and Brunswick, and there's also a **Greyhound** (800/231-2222, www.greyhound.com) station in town. To reach Freeport from Portland, use the **Metro BREEZ Express Bus Service** (www.gpmetrobus.net, one-way fare $1.50-3), which has a stop by L.L. Bean.

Mid-Coast

The scattershot coast that spreads south from Route 1 is anchored by a pair of solid brick towns, and they're a study in contrasts. Brunswick is home to Bowdoin College, which rambles outward from a picturesque campus filled with elite undergraduates and grand buildings named for famous alums. Nine miles west, Bath is all union halls, shipyards, and hulking ironworks, an industrial town that once launched the world's grandest schooners.

Look closer, however, and the distinction blurs. Until it closed in 2011, the local naval air station meant that downtown pubs and cafés were likely to have as many service members as students, keeping Brunswick from feeling too precious. And while Bath's riverfront still rings with the sound of shipbuilding and workers, the pretty center is full of cafés, shops, and bookstores run by the liberal-leaning, creative community.

On a state-sized map of Maine, both towns seem to be a breath away from the sea, but it would be easy to pass through Bath and Brunswick with nothing but river views. To experience the best parts of this scenic stretch of coast, drive south, looping into the long peninsulas; the tangled coastlines are classic Maine, with fishing villages, lobster shacks, and sheltered bays that appear around every bend in the road, making for idyllic driving at a leisurely pace.

BRUNSWICK

Sights

The pretty campus of **Bowdoin College** (255 Maine St., 207/725-3000, www.bowdoin.edu) is all soaring oaks and grassy quads, and would be a worthwhile place to stroll even without the college's two fascinating museums. The tiny **Peary-MacMillan Arctic Museum** (9500 College Station, 207/725-3416, www.bowdoin.edu/arctic-museum, 10am-5pm Tues.-Sat., 2pm-5pm Sun., free) traces the Arctic adventures of two Bowdoin graduates and explorers, Donald MacMillan and Robert Peary. In addition to stuffed arctic animals and one of the original dog

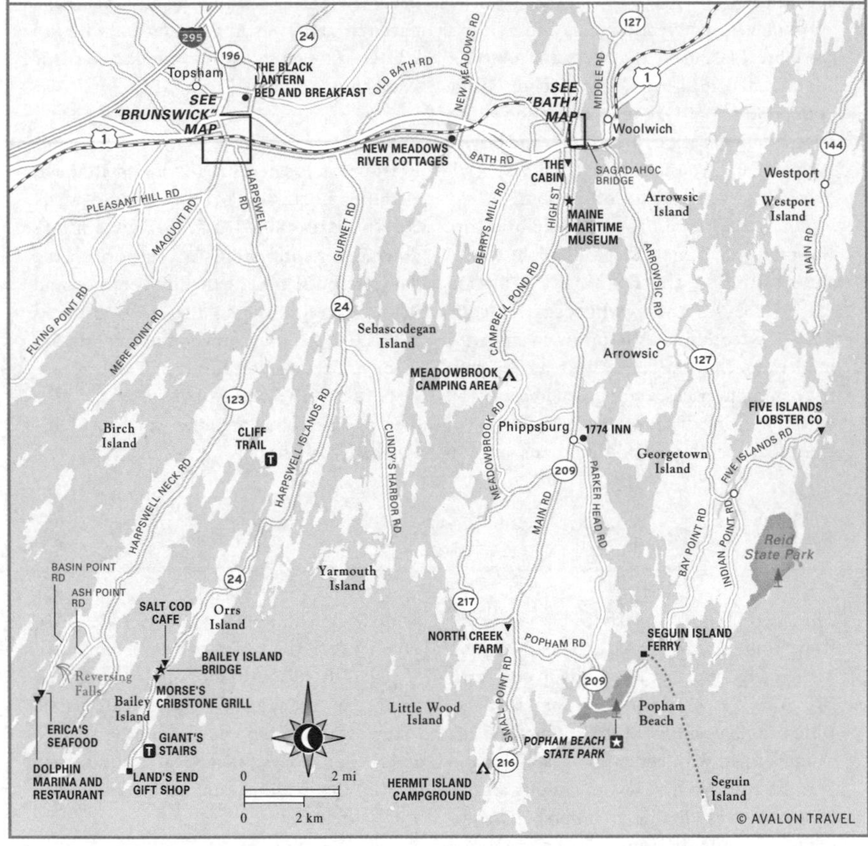

sledges from the Peary expedition, a display honors Matthew Henson, an African American explorer who was the first known person to set foot at the pole and whose contributions to exploration went unrecognized until late in his life, when he was accepted to the New York Explorers Club at age 70. The other highlight on campus is the **Bowdoin College Museum of Art** (9400 College Station, 207/725-3275, www.bowdoin.edu/art-museum, 10am-5pm Tues.-Wed. and Fri.-Sat., 10am-8:30pm Thurs., noon-5pm Sun., free), where an eclectic—and sometimes exquisite—permanent collection is on display alongside exhibits encompassing everything from Renaissance painting to edgy critiques of contemporary culture.

Food

While great views and a picturesque setting count for a great deal with most casual foodies, among devoted lobster roll hounds there's a special thrill that comes with discovering a diamond in the rough. **Libby's Market** (42 Jordan Ave., 207/729-7277, 3am-5pm Mon., 3am-7:30pm Tues.-Fri., 8am-7pm Sat., 4:30am-5pm Sun., $6-20) is a classic example: The unprepossessing convenience store has a short-order counter and a couple of picnic tables outside, but aside from a great pile of

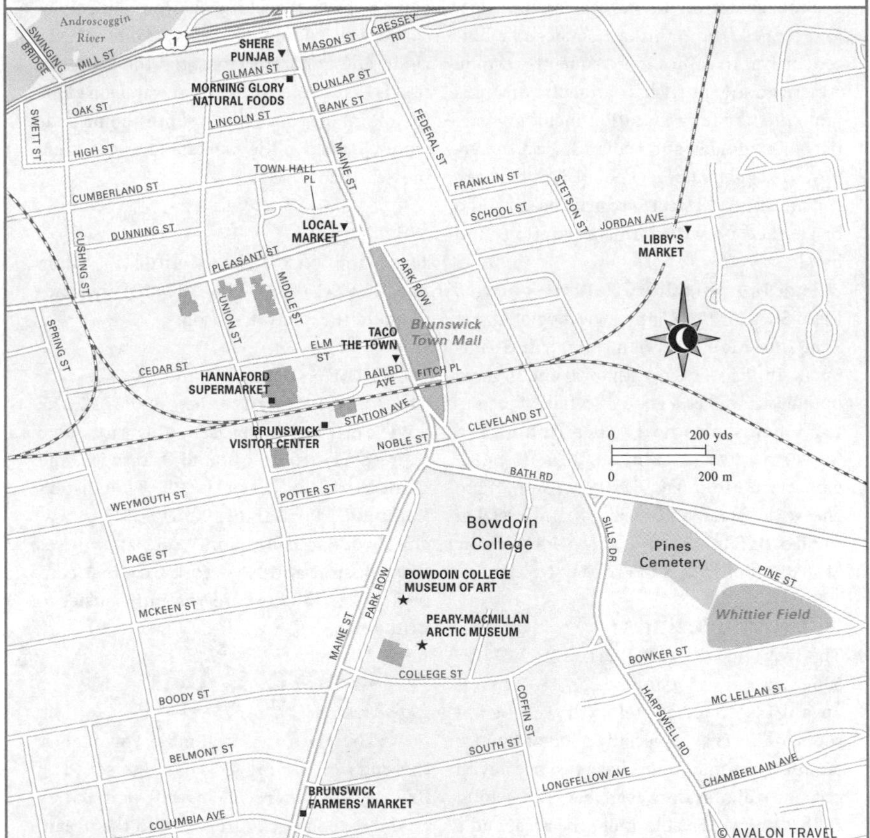

lobster traps and early, fisher-friendly hours, passersby would never guess it's a lobster roll mecca. The classic rolls come in small, medium, or large, and the meat is more finely chopped than usual, with a heavier dose of mayo. A real locals' favorite.

The best Mexican food in the Mid-Coast is served from a shiny truck just a few blocks from the Bowdoin campus. **Taco the Town** (205 Maine St., 207/632-4740, 10am-3pm Tues.-Sat., $4-9) has burritos, quesadillas, and classic tacos served with four kinds of house-made salsa. Cool off with a sweet, cinnamon-spiced *horchata* or a "cochata," a delightfully innovative coffee-*horchata* blend.

Tucked into the back of a little gourmet and kitchen store, ★ **Local Market** (148 Maine St., 207/729-1328, www.localmarket04011.com, 9:30am-6pm Mon.-Sat., 9:30am-5pm Sun., $6-12) has a pair of big communal tables and a deli counter with sandwiches, salads, and soups prepared with plenty of fresh, local, and organic ingredients. The Cobb salad gets raves, as do hearty sandwiches made with bread from Portland's Standard Baking Co.

The North Indian food at **Shere Punjab** (46 Maine St., 207/373-0422, www.sherepunjabme.com, 11am-3pm and 5pm-9pm Mon.-Thurs., 11am-9pm Fri.-Sat., noon-10pm Sun., $8-16) is full of rich flavors and spices—though the chef deftly tempers the heat for all palates. The vast menu includes a good selection of vegetarian options, and ranges from familiar classics like butter chicken to dishes less frequently seen on American menus such as aromatic, steamed lamb *dilruba* (a preparation including garlic, onion, ginger, and Indian spices), or syrupy, fried *gulabjamun* (a popular, milk-based Indian dessert). Decor is casual and cozy, and brightened up with Punjabi paintings and handicrafts.

Little **Morning Glory Natural Foods** (60 Main St., 207/729-0546, www.moglonf.com, 9am-7pm Mon.-Fri., 9am-6pm Sat., 10am-5pm Sun.) is stocked with local and organic options, as well as a good selection of picnic-ready items; also nearby is a **Hannaford Supermarket** (35 Elm St., 207/725-6683, 6am-11pm Mon.-Sat., 6am-9pm Sun.). Find cheese, lobsters, and locally baked bread at the **Brunswick Farmers' Market** (Maine St., 8am-2pm Tues. and Fri. May-Nov.).

Accommodations

The **Travelers Inn** (130 Pleasant St., 207/729-3364, www.travelersinnme.com, $65-133) is an old-fashioned motel with well-kempt rooms. This is an especially good option for families, as some rooms have two beds, with cribs or rollaway cots available. The helpful staff is knowledgeable about the area, and a basic continental breakfast of bagels, fruit, coffee, and juice is served in the lobby.

Just across the Androscoggin River from downtown Brunswick, the **Black Lantern Bed and Breakfast** (57 Elm St., Topsham, 207/725-4165, www.blacklanternbandb.com, $125-160) is walking distance from a scenic bit of riverbank, and is a gracious, welcoming place to stay. Comfortable beds, en suite baths, hearty breakfasts, and old-fashioned charm are highlights, as are Judy and Tom, the super-friendly innkeeps.

With a location in the heart of downtown, the **Brunswick Hotel & Tavern** (4 Noble St., 207/837-6565, www.thebrunswickhoteland-tavern.com, $175-350) is often filled with families visiting the nearby college, and it's a comfortable place to enjoy the town. A gracious porch has rocking chairs and plenty of shade, well-appointed rooms are on the luxurious side of comfortable, and the train station is easy walking distance away. Don't look for a mint on your pillow, but the homemade whoopie pies on the nightstand earn fervent praise.

Information

The **Brunswick Visitor Center** (16 Station Ave., 207/721-0999, 10am-6:30pm daily) is adjacent to the Amtrak station.

Getting There

The Amtrak **Downeaster** (800/872-7245, www.amtrakdowneaster.com) runs two trains a day from Boston to Brunswick, and **Concord Coach Lines** (100 Thompson's Point Rd., Portland, 800/639-3317, www.concordcoachlines.com) operates buses from Boston and New York City that connect to Portland, where you can transfer to Brunswick.

HARPSWELL AND BAILEY ISLAND

Leave the main road behind as you explore the ends of the ragged coastline south of Brunswick, where Harpswell and Bailey Island extend rocky fingers into the ocean. It's easily worth the trip for the views and a walk along the shore, but each destination has excellent seafood if you need another excuse.

Sights

Passing blocky ledges that catch crashing surf, the 0.5 mile **Giant Stairs Trail** (parking at 19 Ocean St., Bailey Island) picks its way along the coast to **Thunder Hole**—a common enough name for formations that boom in heavy waves. You'll see crystallized quartz pressed into the metamorphosed sedimentary rock, split by seams of dark basalt that have worn away from between the chunks of stone.

It would be easy to pass over **Cribstone Bridge** from Orr's Island to Bailey Island without a second glance, but the 1,150-foot span is an engineering marvel. The only bridge of its kind in the United States (or the world—accounts differ), it's built with granite "cribstones" from a quarry in Yarmouth, the heavy stones laid without mortar in a latticework that allows the powerful tides to sweep through unhindered. Some 10,000 tons of granite were used to build the 1928 bridge, which is a Historic Civil Engineering Landmark, and forever changed life in Bailey Island.

Food

A pair of seafood stops anchors each side of the cribstone bridge to Bailey Island. The **Salt Cod Cafe** (1894 Harpswell Island Rd., Orr's Island, 207/833-6210, 8am-5pm daily late May-early Oct., hours vary at beginning and end of season) has blueberry pie and quick bites that can be eaten by the shore. Across the bridge is **Morse's Cribstone Grill** (1495 Harpswell Island Rd., Bailey Island, 207/833-7775, 11:30am-8pm Mon.-Thurs., 11:30am-9pm Fri.-Sat., noon-8pm Sun., $8-30), whose deck has perfect views back toward the water. Morse's serves the usual seafood fare, plus "twin" lobster dinners for ambitious eaters.

With views to Bailey Island and beyond, **Dolphin Marina and Restaurant** (515 Basin Point Rd., Harpswell, 207/833-6000, 11:30am-8pm daily, $12-28) would be a sublime place to dine on a plate of rocks, so the nice quality of the international seafood menu is an added bonus. Many entrées come with a mystifying (but welcome) blueberry muffin on the side.

If you'd prefer your eats from a takeout window, the nearby **Erica's Seafood** (6 Malcolm Dr., Harpswell, 207/833-7354, www.ericasseafood.com, 11am-7pm daily May-Oct., $7-16) is a popular shack with haddock sandwiches, lobster rolls, and crisp, slender fries. The outdoor picnic tables are right by a working wharf, so you can watch the day's catch arrive on local fishing boats.

Getting There

Part of a network of islands and peninsulas that extend south of Brunswick, Bailey Island and Harpswell are accessed by Route 24 and Route 123, respectively. For an especially scenic drive, take Route 24 from Brunswick to Bailey Island, then backtrack to Mountain Road, which links to Route 123, where you can drive south to the end of Harpswell, or return to Brunswick.

BATH

Upstanding and brick lined, this is a city that's launched fleets around the world, from tall ships to modern-day military vessels. Bath still lives and breathes the sea, and the Kennebec River bristles with cranes, but it's the maritime past that's most enchanting for visitors, from the transporting exhibits at the Maine Maritime Museum to Maine's First Ship, a quirky project that's resurrecting a colonial-era pinnace. And beyond the city, it's worth getting sidetracked on your way to some of the Mid-Coast's best beaches and lobster rolls.

Sights

MAINE MARITIME MUSEUM

Wide, deep, and sheltered from the raging sea, the Kennebec River is the perfect place for building and launching ships; indeed, the first oceangoing ship built by English shipwrights in the Americas—the *Virginia of Sagadahoc*—was constructed here, a 30-ton pinnace measuring less than 50 feet from stem to stern. That ship was just the beginning, and in the mid-18th century, shipbuilding was a roaring industry, with a couple-dozen shipyards launching merchant, naval, and pleasure vessels connecting this clattering town in rural Maine with every corner of the globe.

One of those shipyards, Percy & Small, has been transformed into the wonderful **Maine Maritime Museum** (243 Washington St., 207/443-1316, www.mainemaritimemuseum.org, 9:30am-5pm daily, $16 adults, $14.50 seniors, $10 youth 6-12, children under 6 free),

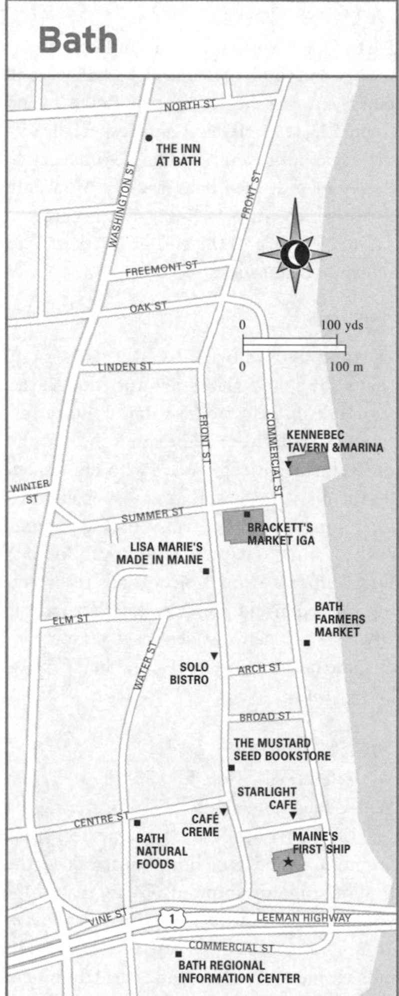

a sprawling 20-acre site with exhibits on the state's seafaring traditions.

The yard is dominated by a soaring metal skeleton that evokes the Percy & Small-built *Wyoming*, the largest schooner ever made. (Most of the sculpture's proportions are true to size, but the masts stop short of *Wyoming*'s 177 feet, as the full-sized version would require warning lights for passing aircraft.) Other highlights include reproductions of a shipyard's various workstations, in-depth explorations of lobstering on the Maine coast, and exhibits illustrating the many sides of New England's maritime traditions. Tickets are good for a second visit within a seven-day period, and admission is free if you join one of the museum's scenic cruises.

MAINE'S FIRST SHIP

In a tiny shipyard in downtown Bath, a quixotic, creative group of volunteers is reconstructing the *Virginia of Sagadahoc* based on the (very) sketchy descriptions that have survived from colonial times. In keeping with the lighthearted, ad hoc attitude of the group, some building materials are recycled, and bits of the ship's framework retain printing from former lives. But the wooden-pegged skeleton is smart as can be, and it's a treat to stop by during construction. Meet the building crew of **Maine's First Ship** (1 Front St., 207/433-4242, www.mfship.org, 11am-3pm Fri.-Sun. June-early July, 10am-3pm Tues.-Sat., 11am-3pm Sun. early July-early Sept., 11am-3pm Fri.-Sun. early Sept.-early Oct.) on open-build days, or visit any time to peek through the fence as the pinnace takes shape.

Entertainment and Events

Most of the year, **Bath Iron Works** (700 Washington St., 207/443-3311, www.gdbiw.com) is off-limits to the public. That changes during one of its infrequent but spectacular ship launchings. Then the whole town comes out for the celebration, and flags, food, and local dignitaries fill the waterfront to break champagne on the hull.

Sports and Recreation

★ POPHAM BEACH STATE PARK

With a broad swath of soft sand, **Popham Beach State Park** (10 Perkins Farm Ln., Phippsburg, 207/389-1335, $8 adults, $2 seniors, $1 children 5-11, children under 5 free), is more Miami than Mid-Coast, one of the most beloved beaches in Maine. It's hemmed in by a pair of rivers—the Kennebec and Morse Rivers reach the ocean here—and when the tide goes out, you can walk to tiny

Fox Island that's just off the beach (beware of getting stranded).

Popham's charms mean it can be jam-packed on busy days, so plan to arrive early, or head to the nearby **Reid State Park** (375 Seguinland Rd., Georgetown, 207/371-2303, 9am-sunset daily, $8 adults, $2 seniors, $1 children 5-11, children under 5 free), where you'll find two sandy beaches framed by rocky outcroppings, a headland with great views to Seguin Island lighthouse, and breaking waves for some of the best surfing in Maine.

BOATING

Get an up close look at the hulking naval ships in Bath's floating dry docks on one of Maine Maritime Museum's hour-long **Shipyards & Lighthouses Cruises** (243 Washington St., 207/443-1316, www.mainemaritimemuseum.org, noon and 2pm daily mid-June-early Sept., $34 adults, $18.50 youth 6-12, $5 children under 6, ticket prices include museum admission), which also passes by the Doubling Point Lighthouse and Kennebec Range Lights. Check the website for longer tours that go farther afield, which are available more sporadically.

Another wonderful way to explore the coastline is by hopping a boat to **Seguin Island** (207/443-4808, www.seguinisland.org), where Maine's tallest lighthouse sends beams over 20 miles to sea from a first-order Fresnel lens that's been used since 1857. Make the 30-minute trip on the passenger-only **Seguin Island Ferry** (Popham Beach, 207/841-7977, www.fishntripsmaine.com, 11am departure, 2:30pm return Sun.-Tues. and Thurs.-Fri. July-Aug., some trips available June and Sept., round-trip $30 adults, $25 children 12 and under, $40 overnights), and spend a few hours exploring beaches, trails, and the lighthouse itself.

Food

BATH

While the menu of pub classics and seafood is pretty ordinary (and reportedly inconsistent), that's not really the point at **Kennebec Tavern & Marina** (119 Commercial St., 207/442-9636, www.kennebectavern.com, 11am-9pm Sun.-Thurs., 11am-10pm Fri.-Sat., $9-30), which boasts a fabulous outdoor seating area that juts out into the current of the Kennebec River, offering great views of passing boats. On cool days, there's not much to tempt diners into the bland dining room, but summer afternoons are the perfect time to

reconstructing Maine's "first ship" in Bath

relax in the shade with a cold beer and a pile of fried scallops.

Tucked belowground on a sloping side street, **Starlight Cafe** (15 Lambard St., 207/443-3005, 7am-2pm Tues.-Fri., 8am-2pm Sat., $6-13) has a quirky dining room filled with hand-painted chairs and vintage Trivial Pursuit cards so diners can pass the time while waiting for hearty breakfasts and comforting lunch plates. Enormous raspberry pancakes, the turkey-stuffed Thanksgiving Sandwich, and haddock chowder are all favorites, and the friendly staff is pure local charm.

As the name suggests, stepping into **The Cabin** (552 Washington St., 207/443-6224, www.cabinpizza.com, 10am-10pm daily, $8-14) feels like ducking below the deck of an old ship. Nautical bric-a-brac and dark wood complete the effect, and while the pizza might not live up to its claims of "Best in Maine," it's pretty darn good all the same. Chewy crusts, generous toppings, and addictive, bready garlic knots keep this a favorite with locals and visitors. No credit cards.

With views of the action in the heart of historic Bath, **Café Crème** (56 Front St., 207/443-6454, 7:30am-5:30pm Mon.-Sat., 8:30am-5:30pm Sun., $2-8) is the place to watch the town drift by with a cup of chai or cappuccino. This little coffee shop has wireless Internet, plenty of tables, and sweet and savory treats made by a local baker.

Pick up organic produce and bulk items at **Bath Natural Market** (36 Centre St., www.bathnaturalmarket.com, 9am-6pm Mon.-Fri., 9am-5pm Sat., noon-4pm Sun.), or visit **Brackett's Market IGA** (185 Front St., 207/443-2012, 7am-8pm daily), a small, locally owned grocery store by the waterfront. Local farmers and producers operate the thriving, year-round **Bath Farmers Market** (Waterfront Park, Commercial St., 8:30am-noon Sat.May-Oct.; Bath Freight Shed, 27 Commercial St., 9am-noon Sat. Nov.-Apr., www.bathfarmersmarket.com).

SOUTH OF BATH

South of Bath in Georgetown, ★ **Five Islands Lobster Co.** (1447 Five Islands Rd., Georgetown, 207/371-2990, www.fiveislandslobster.com, check website or call for hours before visiting, $8-18) regularly makes "best of" lists for lobster rolls, steamers, and fried oysters, and it's right on the way to Reid State Park. This is a classic waterside joint with picnic tables and views of a picture-perfect bay dotted with tiny forested islands.

Cheerfully quirky and fresh as can be, **North Creek Farm** (24 Sebasco Rd., Phippsburg, 207/389-1341, www.northcreekfarm.org, 9am-6:30pm daily, café 11:30am-3:30pm Mon.-Sat., 9am-2pm Sun., $3-12) is a little bit flower nursery, a little bit country store, and a little bit café. Order a Reuben sandwich with kimchi and it comes decked in blossoms, and the homemade baked goods and fruit pies are a special treat. A Sunday morning brunch menu includes sweet and savory treats and farm eggs every way. With just a couple of small tables in the café, ordering food to-go is a good option.

Ten minutes south of downtown Bath, the **Winnegance Restaurant and Bakery** (36 High St., 207/443-3300, 6am-4pm daily, $4-11) is a popular stopover for day-trippers on their way to Popham Beach. Scones and muffins are baked fresh in the back of the old-fashioned shop, and a few small tables are available for enjoying breakfasts of pancakes or eggs and bacon, or homemade soup and sandwiches.

Accommodations and Camping

Many bed-and-breakfasts in the area are members of **Mid-Coast Maine Inns** (www.midcoastmaineinns.com), which posts a helpful spreadsheet of available rooms in the area that is usually up to date. While staying in Bath is most convenient, a few wonderful campgrounds and a historic inn are tucked down the peninsula by the water, away from the bustle of Route 1.

UNDER $100

Simple, sweet, and neat as a pin, **New Meadows River Cottages** (4 Armstrong Way, West Bath, 207/442-9299, www.newmeadowsrivercottages.com, $89-109) are nothing fancy, but the stand-alone rooms have a double bed or double and single as well as air-conditioning, coffeemakers, fridges, and little sitting areas; higher rates are for cottages with kitchenettes.

$150-200

Gardens surrounding **The Inn at Bath** (969 Washington St., Bath, 207/808-7904, www.innatbath.com, $150-190) are overflowing with blooming rhododendrons and wild mountain laurel, and the interior of the Greek Revival-style building is full of art and unfussy antiques. The quiet neighborhood is about a 15-minute walk from downtown Bath, and breakfasts are an appealing spread of fresh fruit, granola, and one hot option. All rooms have private baths and air-conditioning, but they differ widely in style and decor, and one room opens onto the kitchen.

$200-250

Historic and beautiful, the ★ **1774 Inn** (44 Parker Head Rd., Phippsburg, 207/389-1774, www.1774inn.com, $180-260) is among the most romantic places to stay along the coast, with chairs tucked around its sprawling grounds that abut the Kennebec River. Though the inn is just 7.5 miles south of Bath, the experience is serene and secluded. Many of the rooms, which vary widely in style, are exquisite, and guests rave about the thoughtful breakfasts. For an ultra-private experience, book the more rustic Woodshed Room, a self-contained suite near the river with a private veranda and stunning views.

CAMPING

Splash out for an oceanfront spot at ★ **Hermit Island Campground** (6 Hermit Island Rd., Phippsburg, 207/443-2101, www.hermitisland.com, $39-63) and you'll get prime views of sandy beaches and coastline. This is a 25-minute drive from Bath, and snagging one means planning ahead (the by-mail reservation system is byzantine), but even the "value" sites are within easy strolling distance of the shore. No credit cards.

A little bit closer to Route 1, **Meadowbrook Camping Area** (33 Meadowbrook Rd., Phippsburg, 207/443-4967, www.meadowbrookme.com, tents $31-33, hookups $35-43) has smallish sites that are a tad too closely set in woods and an open meadow, with many campers who come for the whole season, but you can sign up for daily lobster dinners and have a feast at your site or the communal outdoor seating area.

Camping is permitted on **Seguin Island,** accessible by ferry from Phippsburg's Popham Beach, mid-May-early October (207/443-4808, www.seguinisland.org, minimum $50 donation). There's no running water, but composting toilet facilities are provided. Reservations are required.

Information

The **Bath Regional Information Center** (15 Commercial St., 207/442-7291, www.visitbath.com, 9am-7pm daily mid-Apr.-Dec., 9am-7pm Mon.-Fri. Jan.-mid-Apr.) has great resources and advice for the entire Mid-Coast area, and its website is frequently updated with tours and events in town.

Getting There and Around

Bath is located on Route 1 on the banks of the Kennebec River, a 35-minute drive from Portland. South of Bath, the highway gives way to small, winding roads: follow Route 209 to Phippsburg, or Route 127 to Georgetown. Bus service to Bath is available from **Greyhound** (214/849-8966, www.greyhound.com). **Concord Coach Lines** (100 Thompson's Point Rd., Portland, 800/639-3317, www.concordcoachlines.com) operates buses from Boston and New York City that connect to Portland, where you can transfer to Brunswick.

Parking in Bath is free for up to two hours on the street or in municipal lots on

Commercial, School, and Water Streets. The **town website** (www.cityofbath.com) has maps for both "Parking" and "Secret Parking." A convenient way to see Bath car-free is the **Bath Trolley** (207/443-8363, www.cityofbath.com, $1), which runs every 30 minutes on a fixed loop that connects the Winnegance General Store with the Maine Maritime Museum and downtown.

WISCASSET

Wiscasset's self-branding as the "prettiest village in Maine" might not convince passing visitors, who often remember the map-dot town more for its notorious bottleneck traffic. Get away from the backup, though, and the old-fashioned community is perfectly charming, with much of its downtown listed on the National Register of Historic Places.

Sights

The town's **self-guided walking tour** offers a perfect ramble through old captain's homes and federal-style mansions, with informative plaques along the way. Start the tour at the large plaque adjacent to **Sarah's Café** (45 Water St.), and pick up a brochure that traces the picturesque route. Most of the stops are great for just wandering by, but it's worth popping inside **Castle Tucker** (2 Lee St., 207/882-7169, 11am-4pm Wed.-Sun. June-mid-Oct., tours every 30 minutes, $8 adults, $7 seniors, $4 students), an 1807 captain's home overlooking the river with Victorian furnishings and a stunning spiral staircase.

Shopping

Unsurprisingly, Wiscasset is a major center for antiquing, with more than two dozen shops filled with everything distressed, restored, and charmingly shabby. A sprawling collection of pieces from many dealers can be found at **Wiscasset Village Antiques** (536 Rte. 1, 207/882-4029, www.wiscassetvillageantiques.com, 9am-7pm daily); find a more curated collection of European textiles and furnishings at **The Marston House** (101 Main St., 207/882-6010, www.marstonhouse.

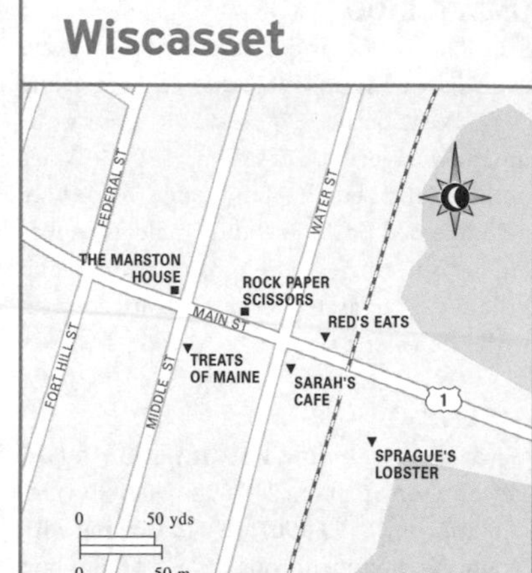

com, noon-5pm Thurs.-Sun., or by appointment), which specializes in homespun pieces from the 18th-19th centuries. Pick up treasures with a more contemporary aesthetic at **Rock Paper Scissors** (68 Main St., 207/882-9930, 10am-5pm Mon.-Sat., noon-5pm Sun.), a pretty gift shop stocked with quirky stationery and dreamy gifts.

Food

Yet another top contender on annual "best lobster roll" lists, **Red's Eats** (41 Water St., 207/882-6128, 11:30am-10pm daily, $7-25, cash only) is a James Beard Award-winning shack that fills its buns with a pound of drawn (not chopped) meat, served with a little cup of clarified butter on the side. Picnic tables and umbrellas with views of the water are available on-site, but note two drawbacks to eating at Red's: The line can stretch upwards of an hour at busy times, and it's located right beside the idling cars stuck in Wiscasset traffic. Just across the street is **Sprague's Lobster** (22 Main St., 207/882-1236, 11am-8pm daily, $7-20); it hasn't racked up the same list of awards as Red's, but sells similar lobster rolls at a lower price (albeit with somewhat less meat).

Half country bakery, half gourmet store, **Treats of Maine** (80 Main St., 207/882-6192, www.treatsofmaine.com, 7:30am-5:30pm Mon.-Sat., 10am-4pm Sun., $3-7) serves pastries ranging from down-home to gourmet, with hefty chocolate babkas, fruit scones, muffins, and layered French confections. The long counter is a welcome place to enjoy a sweet and cup of coffee, but this place excels at takeout feasts of quiche, wine, cheese, and dessert.

A nondescript exterior hides the tasteful dining room at **Little Village Bistro** (65 Gardiner Rd., 207/687-8232, www.littlevillagebistro.com, 4:30pm-9pm Tues.-Sat., $11-20), which turns out to be a sweet haven with well-prepared, classic cuisine. Regulars love the crab cake appetizers and wild mushroom pizza, and the menu of simple pastas, braised Italian-style meats, and fresh seafood is full of flavor and thoughtful touches. Reservations are recommended.

Accommodations

Walking distance from Wiscasset's historic downtown, the **Snow Squall Inn** (5 Bradford Rd., 207/882-6892, www.snowsquallinn.com, $95-180) is all comfort and relaxation. Rooms are bright and uncluttered, with soft linens and simple furnishings, and the well-traveled, gracious owners prepare a fabulous breakfast each morning, with hot and cold options. The property includes a barn that's been converted into an airy yoga studio, and classes are offered throughout the day (www.wickedgoodyoga.com, $14).

With a convenient location on Route 1, the pet-friendly **Wiscasset Woods Lodge** (596 Rte. 1, 207/882-7137, www.wiscassetwoods.com, $90-200) runs right up against the forest, where there's a short hiking trail, a bocce court, and a fire pit for guest use (complete with s'more-making supplies). The feel is more woodsy motel than lodge, but the friendly owners serve a hearty hot breakfast that sets it apart from the other options along the highway.

Getting There

Wiscasset, and the town's famously backed-up bridge, is located on Route 1, roughly 50 minutes from Portland. Bus service to Wiscasset is available from **Greyhound** (214/849-8966, www.greyhound.com) and **Concord Coach Lines** (100 Thompson's Point Rd., Portland, 800/639-3317, www.concordcoachlines.com).

BOOTHBAY

Ask a native Mainer for directions on the Mid-Coast, and you're likely to hear the classic refrain: "You can't get there from here!" The Boothbay and Pemaquid Peninsulas, accessible from Route 1 via Wiscasset and Damariscotta, respectively, are separated by a river that opens onto jagged bays, which means the lobster shacks, gardens, and lighthouses that rim the sea are much farther apart than they appear on a map. These two peninsulas are also the primary access points for boat tours to Eastern Egg Rock, a seven-acre island whose granite shoreline offers a unique habitat for puffins, guillemots, and dozens of other nesting and migratory birds. It's the first of its kind, a restored colony, the success of which inspired dozens of imitators worldwide, as scientists work to protect the dwindling seabird population.

Boothbay is a scenic stretch of bays that culminates in the town of Boothbay Harbor, the pinnacle of Maine's fudge and T-shirt shop kitsch. It's beyond hectic during school vacation months, but with dozens of ways to get out on the water, it's easy to see why the spot is so beloved.

Sights

COASTAL MAINE BOTANICAL GARDENS

Pathways overflowing with native species, shady groves of rhododendrons, and 125 acres of carefully tended plants roll right to the water's edge at **Coastal Maine Botanical Gardens** (132 Botanical Gardens Dr., 207/633-8000, www.mainegardens.org, 9am-5pm daily mid-Apr.-Oct., $16 adults, $14 seniors, $8 children 3-18, children under 3 free), one the finest in New England. Free tours of the highlights are scheduled at 11am daily, with additional tours of native plants and rare specimens offered once a week. The

Upper Mid-Coast

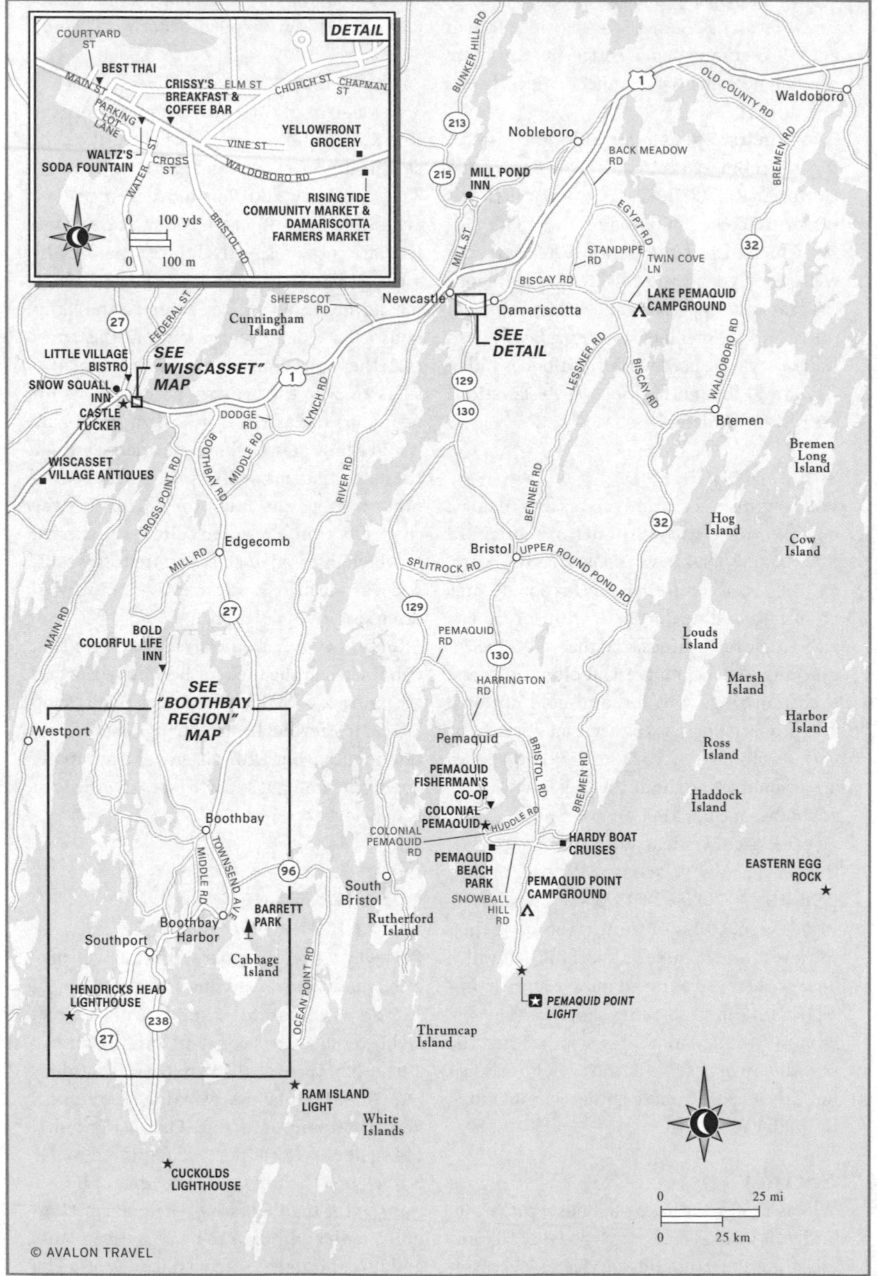
DETAIL
COURTYARD ST
BEST THAI
MAIN ST
CRISSY'S BREAKFAST & COFFEE BAR
ELM ST
CHURCH ST
CHAPMAN ST
PARKING LOT LANE
YELLOWFRONT GROCERY
VINE ST
WALTZ'S SODA FOUNTAIN
CROSS ST
WATER ST
WALDOBORO RD
BRISTOL RD
RISING TIDE COMMUNITY MARKET & DAMARISCOTTA FARMERS MARKET
0 100 yds
0 100 m
BUNKER HILL RD
OLD COUNTY RD
Waldoboro
Nobleboro
BACK MEADOW RD
BREMEN RD
MILL POND INN
EGYPT RD
MILL ST
STANDPIPE RD
TWIN COVE LN
BISCAY RD
LAKE PEMAQUID CAMPGROUND
SHEEPSCOT RD
Newcastle
Damariscotta
SEE DETAIL
Cunningham Island
FEDERAL ST
LITTLE VILLAGE BISTRO
SEE "WISCASSET" MAP
SNOW SQUALL INN
CASTLE TUCKER
DODGE RD
LYNCH RD
LESSNER RD
WALDOBORO RD
Bremen
WISCASSET VILLAGE ANTIQUES
BOOTHBAY RD
MIDDLE RD
CROSS POINT RD
RIVER RD
BENNER RD
Bremen Long Island
Hog Island
Cow Island
Edgecomb
MILL RD
Bristol
UPPER ROUND POND RD
SPLITROCK RD
MAIN RD
BOLD COLORFUL LIFE INN
PEMAQUID RD
Louds Island
HARRINGTON RD
Marsh Island
SEE "BOOTHBAY REGION" MAP
Westport
Pemaquid
Harbor Island
Ross Island
BRISTOL RD
BREMEN RD
PEMAQUID FISHERMAN'S CO-OP
Haddock Island
COLONIAL PEMAQUID
HUDDLE RD
Boothbay
COLONIAL PEMAQUID RD
HARDY BOAT CRUISES
PEMAQUID BEACH PARK
TOWNSEND AVE
EASTERN EGG ROCK
South Bristol
PEMAQUID POINT CAMPGROUND
SNOWBALL HILL RD
BARRETT PARK
Rutherford Island
Boothbay Harbor
Southport
Cabbage Island
OCEAN POINT RD
PEMAQUID POINT LIGHT
HENDRICKS HEAD LIGHTHOUSE
Thrumcap Island
RAM ISLAND LIGHT
White Islands
CUCKOLDS LIGHTHOUSE
0 25 mi
0 25 km
© AVALON TRAVEL

garden also organizes one-hour tours up the Back River on ***The Beagle,*** a small, blessedly quiet electric boat; when bundled with garden admission, the boat tour costs approximately $20 per person, making it an affordable way to enjoy the coast.

BOOTHBAY RAILWAY VILLAGE

Halfway down the Boothbay Peninsula, the **Boothbay Railway Village** (586 Wiscasset Rd., 207/633-4727, www.railwayvillage.org, 10am-5pm daily late May-mid-Oct., $12 adults, $10 seniors, $6 children 3-18, children under 3 free) is a highlight for many families with children. The narrow-gauge steam train that circles the village might be the star attraction, but trains are just the beginning of this 10-acre village. Old-fashioned filling stations and homes are interspersed with displays of antique cars and firefighting equipment, blacksmithing demonstrations, baby goats, and model trains.

LIGHTHOUSES

At the tip of the Boothbay Peninsula are five **lighthouses,** of which four can be spotted by driving around Routes 96, 27, and 238. At the very tip of Route 96, the little **Ram Island Light** is visible from Ocean Point. Make a counterclockwise loop of the more westerly Southport Island to see **Hendricks Head Light** off Beach Road in West Southport; the offshore **Cuckolds Lighthouse,** visible from the tip of Town Landing Road at the southern extreme of the island; and **Burnt Island Light,** best seen from Capitol Island Road. Get a taste of what life was like on an island lighthouse station by joining a fascinating boat tour to **Burnt Island** (Pier 8, Boothbay Harbor, 207/633-2284, www.balmydayscruises.com, 1:45pm Mon. and Thurs. July-Aug., $25 adults, $15 children, children under 3 free), where actors portray the family of an early 20th-century lighthouse keeper. It's common to spot seals and porpoises during the 15-minute boat ride to the island, and the 2.5-hour island portion includes a nature walk and time to explore the scenic trails.

Entertainment and Events

Boothbay Harbor's pretty waterfront is bright with sails and flying colors as the town kicks off summer with **Windjammer Days** (www.windjammerdays.org, late June), which includes the annual Blessing of the Fleet.

Sports and Recreation

BEACHES

The Boothbay Peninsula doesn't have much sand to break up its rocky headlands, but **Barrett Park** (Lobster Cove Rd., Boothbay Harbor) is a nice place to enjoy the water views. Two rock beaches make for good tidepooling at low tide and have shady picnic tables, swings, and bathroom facilities.

BOATING

A seven-acre sprawl of granite boulders and low-lying vegetation, **Eastern Egg Rock** doesn't look like a very cozy nesting ground, but the wildlife sanctuary was the first restored seabird colony in the world. Nesting seabird populations have been hard-hit by hunters, egg collectors, fishing practices, and pollution, and until the restoration process began, puffins hadn't shacked up here since 1885. **Puffins** are now on the island mid-June-August.

From Boothbay Harbor, book a trip with **Cap'n Fish's** (42 Commercial St., Boothbay Harbor, 207/633-3244, www.mainepuffin.com, 2.5-hour puffin tour $35 adults, $20 children 12 and under, $15 dogs; 4-hour puffin and whale tour $75 adults, $45 youth 6-14, $30 children under 6, $15 dogs), whose puffin cruises, accompanied by an Audubon naturalist, pass three lighthouses and scattered islands on the way out to Eastern Egg Rock. The company's combination puffin and whale cruises commonly spot finback and minke whales, as well as the humpback whales that arrive on the coast in July.

Food

With a mid-peninsula location just past the Boothbay botanical gardens, **Trevett Country Store** (381 W. Barter's Island Rd.,

Boothbay Region

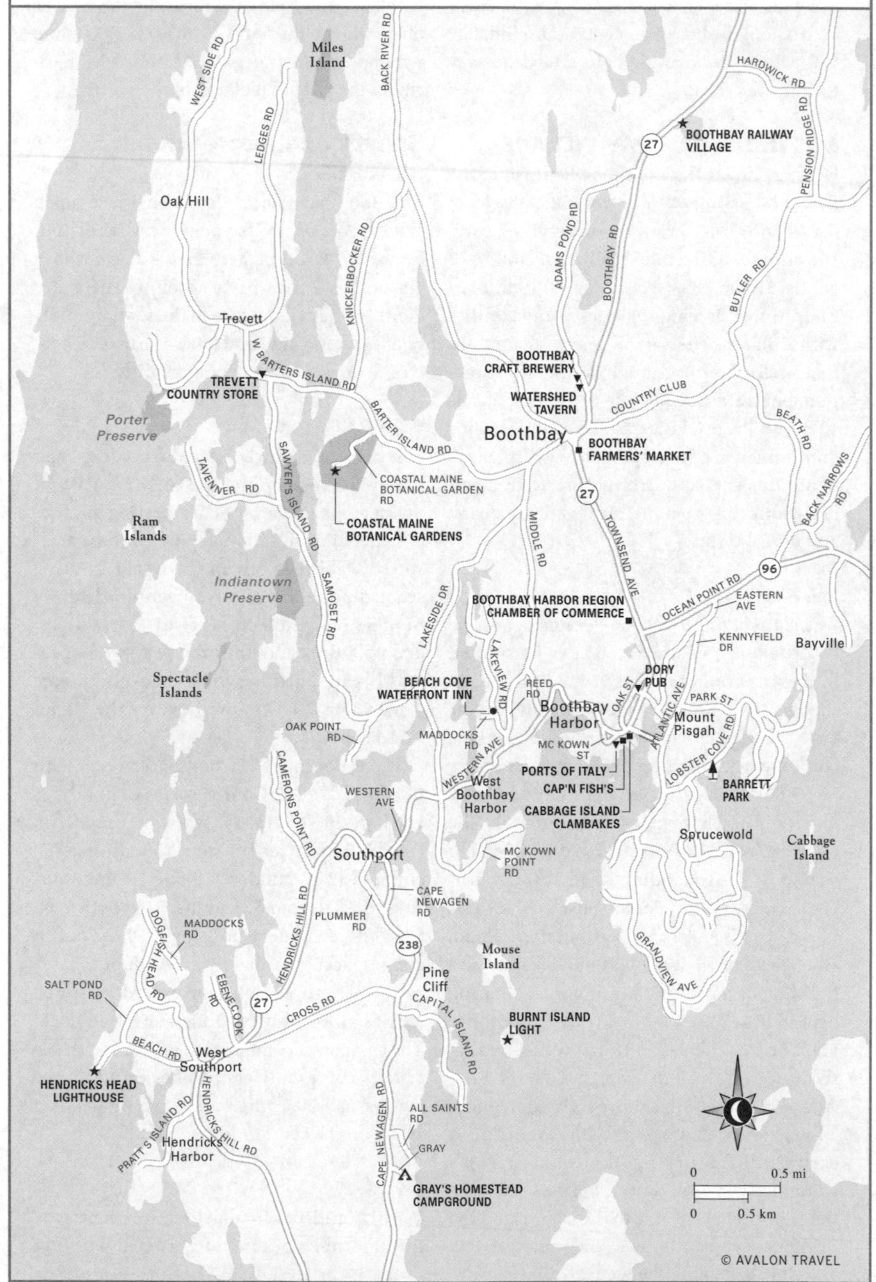
Miles Island
BACK RIVER RD
WEST SIDE RD
LEDGES RD
HARDWICK RD
BOOTHBAY RAILWAY VILLAGE
27
PENSION RIDGE RD
Oak Hill
ADAMS POND RD
BOOTHBAY RD
KNICKERBOCKER RD
BUTLER RD
Trevett
W BARTERS ISLAND RD
BOOTHBAY CRAFT BREWERY
TREVETT COUNTRY STORE
WATERSHED TAVERN
COUNTRY CLUB
Porter Preserve
BARTER ISLAND RD
BEATH RD
Boothbay
BOOTHBAY FARMERS' MARKET
SAWYER'S ISLAND RD
TAVENNER RD
COASTAL MAINE BOTANICAL GARDEN RD
COASTAL MAINE BOTANICAL GARDENS
BACK NARROWS RD
Ram Islands
MIDDLE RD
TOWNSEND AVE
96
Indiantown Preserve
SAMOSET RD
LAKESIDE DR
OCEAN POINT RD
EASTERN AVE
BOOTHBAY HARBOR REGION CHAMBER OF COMMERCE
KENNYFIELD DR
Bayville
LAKEVIEW RD
Spectacle Islands
BEACH COVE WATERFRONT INN
REED RD
OAK ST
DORY PUB
Boothbay Harbor
PARK ST
ATLANTIC AVE
Mount Pisgah
OAK POINT RD
MADDOCKS RD
MC KOWN ST
LOBSTER COVE RD
CAMERONS POINT RD
WESTERN AVE
PORTS OF ITALY
West Boothbay Harbor
CAP'N FISH'S
BARRETT PARK
WESTERN AVE
CABBAGE ISLAND CLAMBAKES
Sprucewold
Cabbage Island
Southport
MC KOWN POINT RD
CAPE NEWAGEN RD
HENDRICKS HILL RD
PLUMMER RD
DOGFISH HEAD RD
MADDOCKS RD
238
Mouse Island
GRANDVIEW AVE
SALT POND RD
EBENECOOK RD
Pine Cliff
27
CROSS RD
CAPITAL ISLAND RD
BURNT ISLAND LIGHT
BEACH RD
West Southport
HENDRICKS HEAD LIGHTHOUSE
PRATT'S ISLAND RD
HENDRICKS HILL RD
CAPE NEWAGEN RD
ALL SAINTS RD
Hendricks Harbor
GRAY
GRAY'S HOMESTEAD CAMPGROUND
0
0.5 mi
0
0.5 km
© AVALON TRAVEL

Trevett, 207/633-1140, 7am-8pm daily, $5-20) might seem like a back-road convenience store, but it's a local favorite for sandwiches, simple breakfasts, and fresh seafood. In warm months, the outdoor sundeck is a charming place to eat, with water views and a cool breeze.

All cedar shake and dark wood, the **Watershed Tavern** (301 Adams Pond Rd., 207/633-3411, www.boothbaycraftbrewery.com, 4:30pm-8pm Wed.-Sat., $12-29) has the kind of cave-like interior best enjoyed when the weather turns blustery. The food includes a fairly standard pub lineup of burgers, salads, and pizzas, but with some meat from local farms and appealing house-made additions. This is the brewpub side of **Boothbay Craft Brewery** (207/633-3411, www.boothbaycraftbrewery.com, tours $5), which runs 30-minute tours at 3pm daily, followed by a beer tasting. Naturally, those beers are on tap at the tavern: Brews range from super-drinkable session ales to imperial stouts and red IPAs.

A destination for sophisticated, traditional food, ★ **Ports of Italy** (47 Commercial St., 207/633-1011, www.portsofitaly.com, 4:30pm-9pm daily May-Dec., $18-34) stands head and shoulders above the crowded Boothbay Harbor restaurant scene. Thoughtful service and consistently high-quality food, an excellent wine list, and pleasant seating on an outdoor patio make this a good choice for a romantic evening or celebration. Reservations are essential.

Casual cousin to the attached Thistle Inn, the **Dory Pub** (55 Oak St., Boothbay Harbor, 877/633-3541, www.thethistleinn.com, 5pm-close Tues.-Sat., $10-16) serves a simpler, solid menu in a fun space. Cozy up to the bar—made from an actual dory boat—for burgers, crab cakes, or piles of Maine mussels steamed in white wine. Great cocktails and an extensive beer and wine list make this a nice first stop of the evening for drinks and snacks.

Vendors from around the region set up stalls at **Boothbay Farmers' Market** (1 Common Dr., www.boothbayfarmersmarket.com, 9am-noon Thurs. mid-May-early Oct.).

★ LOBSTER FEAST

Like a Polynesian *imu* or Maya *p'ib*, the classic method of cooking up a New England lobster is using a pit oven lined with rocks and heated with a blazing fire. The pit is then filled with seaweed, lobsters, clams, and corn on the cob, covered with more seaweed (along with some sand or tarps), and left to cook for hours, infusing everything inside with a briny tang. Aside from swapping out the sand pit for some giant, wood-fired steamers, **Cabbage Island Clambakes** (Pier 6, Boothbay Harbor, 207/633-7200, www.cabbageislandclambakes.com, mid-June-mid-Oct., 4-hour boat tour and clambake $63) does them in classic Maine style. The family-run operation takes a slow cruise to **Cabbage Island,** where you'll sit down to two steamed lobsters, white clams, fish chowder, new potatoes, and corn, followed by blueberry cake and coffee. The experience is simply one of the finest ways to get a taste of this traditional feast in Maine.

Accommodations and Camping

$100-150

By a quiet lake between the botanical gardens and downtown Boothbay Harbor, the motel-like ★ **Beach Cove Waterfront Inn** (48 Lakeview Rd., Boothbay Harbor, 207/633-0353, www.beachcovehotel.com, $99-215) is a great budget option. All rooms have views of the water and come stocked with a fridge, microwave, and coffeemaker, and a small continental breakfast is served in the lobby. Decor is simple and a bit dated, and some visitors find the walls overly thin, but staying at the inn gets you free access to a fleet of canoes and rowboats to enjoy on the lake.

$150-250

With a great location on the quieter, southeastern side of the harbor, **Brown's Wharf Inn** (121 Atlantic Ave., Boothbay Harbor, 207/633-5440, www.brownswharfinn.com, $175-225) is a 15-minute walk to downtown shops and restaurants. Balconies in the water-facing rooms have great views across

TOP EXPERIENCE

Lobster Feasts

Dripping butter, cracking lobster shells, steaming corn on the cob...Maine's lobster may be famously sweet and tender, but enjoying the state's favorite food is about more than flavor. Settling into a lobster feast is a quintessential—and often messy—Maine experience that's been a beloved tradition for generations.

And while dining on lobster isn't cheap, the Maine lobster experience isn't haute cuisine by any stretch. In fact, the most iconic way to enjoy the crustaceans at one of the state's many venues with "lobster in the rough," where traditional dinners are served out-of-doors, often at a picnic table. This is the time to roll up your sleeves, tie on a lobster bib, and go local, using a lobster cracker and pick to extract every bit of juicy flesh.

When served "in the rough," lobster is sold by weight, so you can choose the size of your dinner—small ones are about a pound, and the biggest critters can be as large as four pounds. You may also have the option to choose a hard shell or soft shell lobster: soft shell lobsters have recently molted, or shed their shell, and tend to have slightly more tender flesh that's often preferred by Mainers. Hard shell lobsters are firmer, and cost more per pound, as there tends to be more lobster flesh packed inside the shell.

The classic accompaniments to a lobster dinner include coleslaw, corn on the cob, dinner rolls, and drawn, or clarified, butter for dunking the meat. There are lobster joints all up and down the coast, from Quoddy Head to Kittery, and while menus don't vary much, locals remain fiercely loyal to their lobster shack of choice. After rigorous sampling, here are our favorites:

- **Thurston's Lobster Pound, Acadia National Park** (9 Thurston Rd., Bernard, 207/244-7600, www.thurstonforlobster.com, daily 11am-9pm, $7-30). There are usually lines out the door of this longtime Mount Desert Island institution, but that means you'll have time to watch the fascinating seafood ballet that unfolds on the porch: servers drop net bags of clams, lobsters, and mussels into a giant steamer, setting individual timers with your order number. Meals emerge, get plated with all the fixings and a hefty chunk of blueberry cake, and are served to diners on decks that jut into lovely Bass Harbor.
- **Cabbage Island Clambakes, Boothbay Harbor** (Pier 6, Boothbay Harbor, 207/633-7200, www.cabbageislandclambakes.com, mid-June-mid-Oct., four-hr boat tour and clambake $63) serves lobster as part of their clambakes after ferrying guests to Cabbage Island. Once you arrive, sit down to two steamed lobsters, white clams, fish chowder, new potatoes and corn, followed by blueberry cake and coffee. The experience is simply one of the finest ways to get a taste of this traditional feast in Maine.
- **Chauncey Creek Lobster Pier, Kittery** (16 Chauncey Creek Rd., Kittery Point, 207/ 439-1030, www.chaunceycreek.com, 11am-8pm daily, $8-35) is an "in-the-rough" spot with bright picnic tables at the edge of a peaceful river. Make like the locals and bring your own beer, wine, and side dishes, then pick a lobster from the tank.
- **Five Islands Lobster Co., Georgetown** (1447 Five Islands Rd., Georgetown, 207/371-2990, www.fiveislandslobster.com, check website or call for hours before visiting, $8-18). A classic waterside joint with picnic tables and views of a picture-perfect-bay, this seasonal shack is worth the detour, and is also beloved for their wonderful lobster rolls. BYO beer and wine to go with lobster dinners that arrive on metal trays.

If it's hard to swallow a $30 meal served with paper napkins, get this: lobster was long considered "poverty food" in New England. Native Americans used lobsters as fishing bait and fertilizer, and early colonists dished up lobster dinners to prisoners and indentured servants. Lobster only got classy with the advent of widespread rail travel—according to lobster lore, chefs in dining cars began serving the crustaceans to inland passengers who didn't know it wasn't "fancy" food. Times, and prices, have changed.

the harbor, and while the bathrooms are a bit cramped, rooms have plenty of space to spread out.

Gorgeous lawns roll from a rambling farmhouse to the water's edge at the **Bold Colorful Life Inn** (802 Back River Rd., 207/633-6566, www.boldcolorlifeinn.com, $129-209), a laid-back estate that's halfway down the Boothbay Peninsula. Enjoy the quiet spot in a hammock, or wander the trails and gardens. Common spaces include a great room with a piano and bookshelves, and the unsurprisingly bright and colorful rooms have private baths. The inn is run by a welcoming psychotherapist and life coach.

OVER $250

Isolated and luxurious, ★ **The Inn at Cuckolds Lighthouse** (40 Town Landing Rd., Southport, 855/212-5252, www.innatcuckoldslighthouse.com, $350-600) is on a small island south of Boothbay and among the most romantic places to stay in Maine. The 1892 lighthouse has just two suites—book the whole darn island if you want a *really* private experience—and high-end amenities. Boat transportation to the island, afternoon tea and cocktails, and views of crashing waves make this a place apart, and all transportation and treats are included in the price of a night's stay.

CAMPING

Drift off to the sound of crashing waves at **Gray's Homestead Campground** (21 Homestead Rd., Southport, 207/633-4612, www.graysoceancamping.com, sites $48-53), an old-fashioned and friendly spot four miles south of Boothbay Harbor. Fire rings and a swimming beach give the campground a holiday atmosphere, and it also has laundry facilities, hot showers, and a dump station.

Information

The **Boothbay Harbor Region Chamber of Commerce** (192 Townsend Ave., Boothbay Harbor, 207/633-2353, www.boothbayharbor.com, 8am-5pm Mon.-Fri., 10am-4pm Sat.-Sun. mid-May-early Oct., 8am-5pm Mon.-Fri. early Oct.-mid-May) runs a visitors center at its office.

Getting There and Around

Boothbay Harbor is located at the southern end of the Boothbay Peninsula, accessed by Route 27, a spur that leaves Route 1 at Wiscasset (13 mi, 20 min.). There is currently no public transport to Boothbay Harbor.

The only place in this region where parking is an issue is in Boothbay Harbor, where it's worth leaving your car in one of the town's metered lots; the largest is adjacent to the **town office** (11 Harbor St., Boothbay Harbor, $1 per hour, $7 full day). That town also has the only noteworthy in-town transit, the **Rocktide Trolley,** a free sightseeing trolley that makes a limited loop through downtown starting from the **Rocktide Inn** (35 Atlantic Ave., Boothbay Harbor, 207/633-4455, www.rocktideinn.com).

PEMAQUID REGION

Across the Damariscotta River from the Boothbay Peninsula, the Pemaquid Peninsula is just as scenic, and blissfully uncrowded. The main reason travelers venture down Route 129 toward Pemaquid Point is the Pemaquid Point Light, a lonely tower that looks out at a gorgeous sweep of coastline, but it's worth lingering for a day on the beach or a wildlife-spotting trip to Eastern Egg Rock, a barren islet that's paradise for nesting puffins. At the head of the peninsula, Damariscotta is full of small-town charm and historic homes, an easy place to while away an afternoon or a weekend.

Sights

★ PEMAQUID POINT LIGHT

Crashing waves and jagged rocks are the perfect setting for **Pemaquid Point Light** (3115 Bristol Rd., New Harbor, 207/677-2492, www.visitmaine.com, 9am-5pm daily early May-late Oct., $3). Classic calendar material, it was commissioned by John Quincy Adams and is considered by many the loveliest of New England's lights—by popular vote, its image landed on the Maine state quarter. Climb a wrought-iron spiral staircase to the top of the tower for a seagull's-eye view of the craggy headland, and get an up close look at the fourth-order Fresnel lens, one of just six in the state. After exploring the tower and clambering around the rocks, it's worth stopping in to the adjoining keeper's house, where the **Fisherman's Museum** (207/677-2494, 10:30am-5pm daily mid-May-mid-Oct., free) displays mementos of the lobstering life. Also on-site is the **Pemaquid Art Gallery** (207/677-2752, 10am-5pm daily early June-late Oct.), which displays juried work from local artists.

COLONIAL PEMAQUID

Three forts were raised and destroyed at the gaping mouth of the Pemaquid River as fur traders, pirates, the English, Native Americans, the French, and early settlers scrapped for control of the strategic stronghold. **Colonial Pemaquid State Historic Site** (2 Colonial Pemaquid Dr., New Harbor, 207/677-2423, www.friendsofcolonialpemaquid.org, 9am-5pm daily late May-late Aug., $4 adults, $1 seniors, children under 12 free) offers a look at those tumultuous times, with historical reenactments, demonstrations, and nicely preserved structures. **Fort William Henry** is the centerpiece of the site (and a reconstruction of the second fort built here), where a trio of flags fly above a stone tower; the fort's permanent exhibit explores the intersection of fur trading and politics in the early years of European settlement. The sprawling grounds offer plenty to explore, including a visitors center museum, an 18th-century cemetery, and an herb garden stocked with plants that 17th-century settlers used for food and medicine, and the seaside site is a pleasant place to bring a picnic.

Entertainment and Events

During the warming days of May and early June, hundreds of thousands of **alewives** make the trip to Damariscotta Lake, traveling over a fish ladder that was first built in 1807, then restored in 2010. A few hundred years ago, these fish, a kind of herring, would have been ubiquitous in Maine's streams, but these days they're far less common. To catch the alewife run, with fish squirming between rocks as they travel upriver, head to the **Damariscotta Mills Fish Ladder** (www.damariscottamills.org); from the intersection of Route 215 and Route 1, take Route 215 north for 1.6 miles, where you'll see a small parking area on your left. In season, the website is updated with the latest whereabouts of the alewives.

Sports and Recreation

BEACHES

Just south of Colonial Pemaquid is the appealing **Pemaquid Beach Park** (Snowball Hill Rd., Bristol, 207/677-2754, 8am-5pm daily, $4 adults, children under 12 free), a 0.25 mile of pristine white sands with a concession stand, boogie board, umbrella, and beach chair rentals, and nice views along the coast.

BOATING

Just five miles from Eastern Egg Rock, **Hardy Boat Cruises** (132 Rte. 32, New Harbor, 207/677-2026, www.hardyboat.com, 1.5-hour puffin tour $32 adults, $12 children 2-11, children under 2 free) is just five miles from Eastern Egg Rock and runs early evening trips with an Audubon naturalist aboard—it's a good chance to catch the puffins rafting together in the water and lounging on the rocks. Hardy operates a somewhat smaller boat than the tours that operate from Boothbay Harbor, meaning fewer crowds and a slightly rougher ride when waves are choppy.

Food

The old-timey treats at **Waltz's Soda Fountain** (167 Main St., Damariscotta, 207/563-7632, 7am-4pm Mon.-Sat., $2-9) are right at home in Damariscotta's brick-and-window glass downtown. Twirl on the red leather stools, sip an egg cream or ice cream soda, or go all-out with a sundae under gobs of hot fudge sauce. A simple menu of sandwiches and snacks is also available, albeit overshadowed by the creamier options.

An outlier among Mid-Coast lobster shacks and bistros, **Best Thai** (74 Main St., Damariscotta, 207/5633-1440, www.bestthaimaine.com, noon-3pm and 4pm-8:30pm Tues.-Sat., lunch $8-11, dinner $12-17) really does serve the best Thai food in the region (until you hit its sister restaurant in Bath). Panang curry and noodle dishes are consistently good, and the *tom kha* (chicken soup) gets rave reviews.

Find sweet treats and the best breakfasts in town at **Crissy's Breakfast & Coffee Bar** (212 Main St., Damariscotta, 207/563-6400, www.cbandcb.com, 8am-2pm daily, $3-11). Gluten-free rice bowls are piled with meat, eggs, and veggies, while breakfast sandwiches are generous and served alongside crispy home fries. The lunch menu is also served all day, a savory mix of sandwiches, burritos, and salads.

Pemaquid's take on lobster "in the rough," the ★ **Pemaquid Fisherman's Co-Op** (32 Co-op Rd., Pemaquid, 207/677-2642, noon-7:30pm daily, $7-25) has the seafood, and you can bring the fixings. Bring beer or wine—some regulars even bring their own side salads—to go with whole lobsters swabbed in melted butter, steamers, and crabs. Outside seating offers great views of the Pemaquid River.

Find all the basics at **Yellowfront Grocery** (5 Coastal Market Dr., Damariscotta, 207/563-3507, 7am-8pm Mon.-Sat., 8am-7pm Sun.), or visit **Rising Tide Community Market** (323 Main St., Damariscotta, 207/563-5556, www.risingtide.coop, 8am-8pm daily), a cooperatively owned natural food store that also has a deli and café.

The **Damariscotta Farmers Market** (www.damariscottafarmersmarket.org) has two locations for its Monday and Friday markets. On Monday early June-late September, find the vendors at the **Rising Tide Community Market** (323 Main St., 3pm-6pm Mon.), and on Friday mid-May-late October, farmers set up at **Round Top Farm** (3 Round Top Rd., 9am-noon Fri.).

Accommodations and Camping

You'll have your own sweet little place on the beach at **Ye Olde Forte Cabins** (18 Old Fort Road, Pemaquid Beach, 207/677-2261, www.yeoldefortecabins.com, $125-260), a simple, homey resort by John's Bay. The accommodations are rustic, with a shared cookhouse and showers, and the cabins are tightly packed on the green lawn, but it's full of old-fashioned New England charm. Book well in advance, as longtime regular can fill these up in summer months.

Leave the crowds (and any hope of cell service) behind at ★ **Mill Pond Inn** (50 Main St., Nobleboro, 207/352-4044, www.millpondinn.com, $150-180), which has five guest rooms on the shore of Damariscotta Lake. Fresh flowers in each room and a wonderfully peaceful setting make this feel like a retreat from the world. The full country-style breakfast often includes blueberry pancakes or French toast, bacon, and eggs, and the friendly innkeepers have a great collection of books, games, and music to enjoy during your stay. The house was built in 1780, and retains a wonderfully historical feel.

Quiet and filled with shade trees, **Pemaquid Point Campground** (9 Pemaquid Point Campground Rd., New Harbor, 207/677-2267, www.pemaquidpointcampground.com, tent sites $27, RV sites $37, no credit cards) has hot showers, a playground, horseshoe pits, and easy access to the beach, Colonial Pemaquid, and the lighthouse, so you can beat the crowds coming from Boothbay. If you're just passing through and don't want to make the 20-minute trek down the peninsula, book a site at **Lake Pemaquid Campground** (100

Twin Cove Rd., Damariscotta, 207/563-5202, www.lakepemaquid.com, $36-48), whose 200 sites surround a pleasant, freshwater lake.

Information

Information on the area is available through the **Damariscotta Region Chamber of Commerce** (15 Courtyard St., Damariscotta, 207/563-8340, www.damariscottaregion.com, 8:30am-4:30pm Mon.-Fri.).

Getting There

Damariscotta is located on Route 1, an hour from Portland, and the Pemaquid Peninsula extends south from town, accessed by Route 129 and Route 130. **Concord Coach Lines** (100 Thompson's Point Rd., Portland, 800/639-3317, www.concordcoachlines.com) has bus service to Damariscotta from Portland, stopping in front of **Waltz Pharmacy** (167 Main St.).

Penobscot Bay

Down East begins where the Penobscot River opens onto a scenic bay filled with low-lying rocky islands. This is classic sailing territory, though submerged shoals and the maze-like geography make navigation difficult. Lobster boat captains work hundreds of traplines passed down through generations. Much of the bay's edge is thoroughly rural, with forest broken only by the occasional village, but at the southern end is a trio of beautiful communities—Rockland, Rockport, and Camden—each with a scenic harbor and plenty to explore.

ROCKLAND

A thriving commercial fishing fleet has long been the heart of this working harbor, and at first glance the sturdy brick Main Street has a staid, old-fashioned look. It's got a deep history with the sea: The Abenaki name for the harbor is Catawamtek, "great landing place," and in the 19th century, the waterfront was alive with shipbuilding and lime production as fishing boats arrived laden with cod and lobster.

Rockland's charms have long been overshadowed by picture-perfect Camden and Rockport, but in recent years the storefronts have filled up with destination restaurants and cozy bistros, and it has begun to feel unexpectedly chic. It's a good home base for exploring Penobscot Bay, and remains fairly low-key. Even if you're making tracks for Acadia or other parts of Down East Maine, it's worth stopping to see the fabulous collection of Andrew Wyeth paintings at the Farnsworth Art Museum and walk the breakwater to the harbor lighthouse.

Sights

★ FARNSWORTH ART MUSEUM

The main draw may be the unparalleled collection of works by the artists of the Wyeth family, but the wonderful **Farnsworth Art Museum** (16 Museum St., 207/596-6457, www.farsworthmuseum.org, 10am-5pm Tues.-Sun. Nov.-Dec. and Apr.-May, 10am-5pm Wed.-Sun. Jan.-Mar., 10am-5pm daily July-Oct., $15 adults, $13 seniors, $10 students 17 and older, children under 17 free) encompasses far more. Explore beautifully curated works depicting Maine's landscape and people, including pieces by Robert Bellows, Eastman Johnson, Winslow Homer, and George Inness.

The **Wyeth Center at the Farnsworth Art Museum** highlights the very different works of Andrew Wyeth's father, N. C., and his son Jamie. Andrew Wyeth's best-known work, *Christina's World*, isn't here (it's at MoMA in New York City), but the next best thing is—the house that inspired the arresting and melancholy character study. Docents can give you directions to the museum-operated **Olson House** (Hathorn Point Rd., Cushing, $5), a half-hour drive away; it was once home

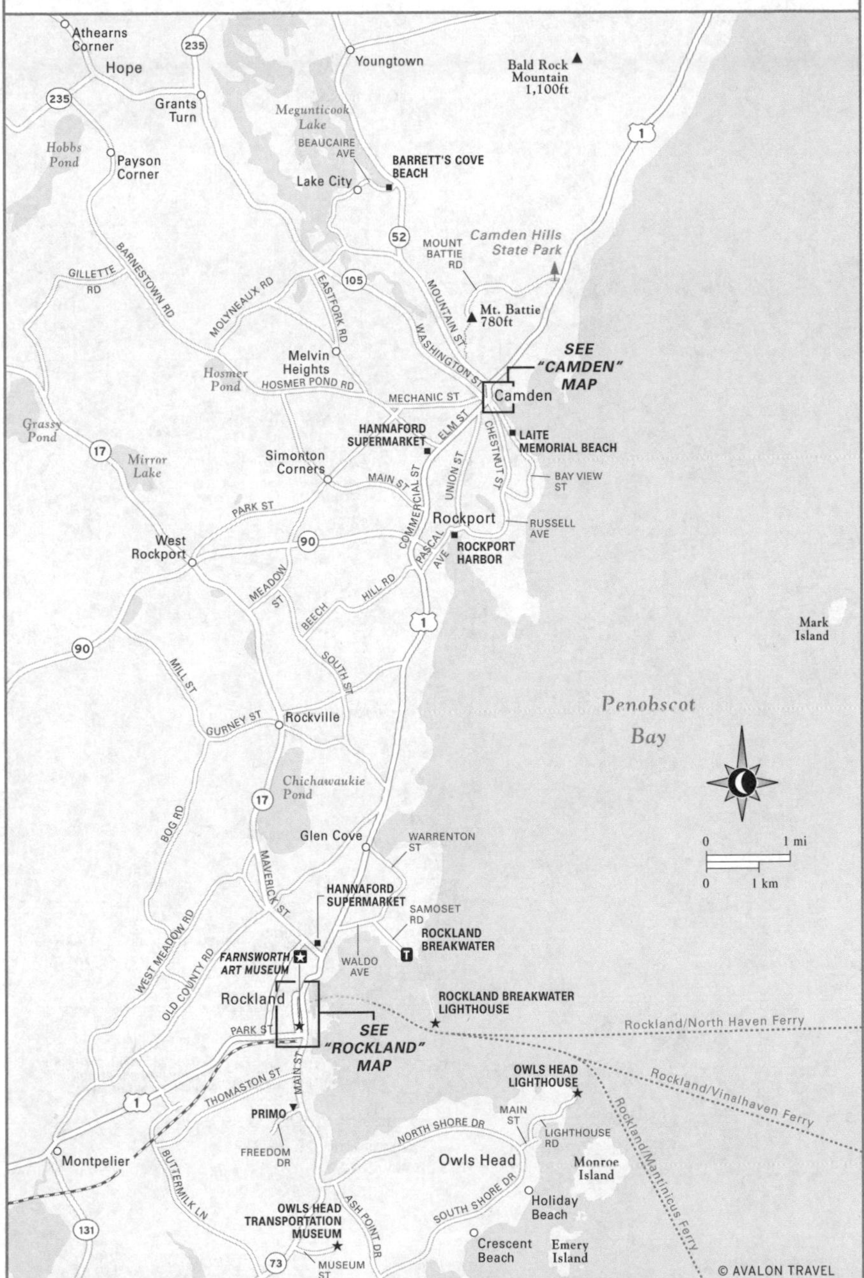
Penobscot Bay
Athearns Corner
Hope
235
Youngtown
Bald Rock Mountain 1,100ft
Grants Turn
Megunticook Lake
1
Hobbs Pond
Payson Corner
BEAUCAIRE AVE
BARRETT'S COVE BEACH
Lake City
52
MOUNT BATTIE RD
Camden Hills State Park
BARNESTOWN RD
GILLETTE RD
MOLYNEAUX RD
EASTFORK RD
105
MOUNTAIN ST
Mt. Battie 780ft
WASHINGTON ST
Melvin Heights
SEE "CAMDEN" MAP
Hosmer Pond
HOSMER POND RD
MECHANIC ST
Camden
Grassy Pond
HANNAFORD SUPERMARKET
ELM ST
CHESTNUT ST
LAITE MEMORIAL BEACH
17
Mirror Lake
Simonton Corners
MAIN ST
COMMERCIAL ST
UNION ST
BAY VIEW ST
PARK ST
Rockport
RUSSELL AVE
West Rockport
90
PASCAL AVE
ROCKPORT HARBOR
MEADOW ST
HILL RD
BEECH
Mark Island
MILL ST
SOUTH ST
Penobscot Bay
GURNEY ST
Rockville
Chichawaukie Pond
BOG RD
Glen Cove
WARRENTON ST
0 1 mi
0 1 km
MAVERICK ST
HANNAFORD SUPERMARKET
SAMOSET RD
ROCKLAND BREAKWATER
WEST MEADOW RD
OLD COUNTY RD
FARNSWORTH ART MUSEUM
WALDO AVE
Rockland
ROCKLAND BREAKWATER LIGHTHOUSE
Rockland/North Haven Ferry
PARK ST
SEE "ROCKLAND" MAP
OWLS HEAD LIGHTHOUSE
Rockland/Vinalhaven Ferry
THOMASTON ST
MAIN ST
PRIMO
MAIN ST
LIGHTHOUSE RD
NORTH SHORE DR
Rockland/Matinicus Ferry
Montpelier
BUTTERMILK LN
FREEDOM DR
Owls Head
Monroe Island
SOUTH SHORE DR
Holiday Beach
ASH POINT DR
OWLS HEAD TRANSPORTATION MUSEUM
131
Crescent Beach
Emery Island
73
MUSEUM ST
© AVALON TRAVEL

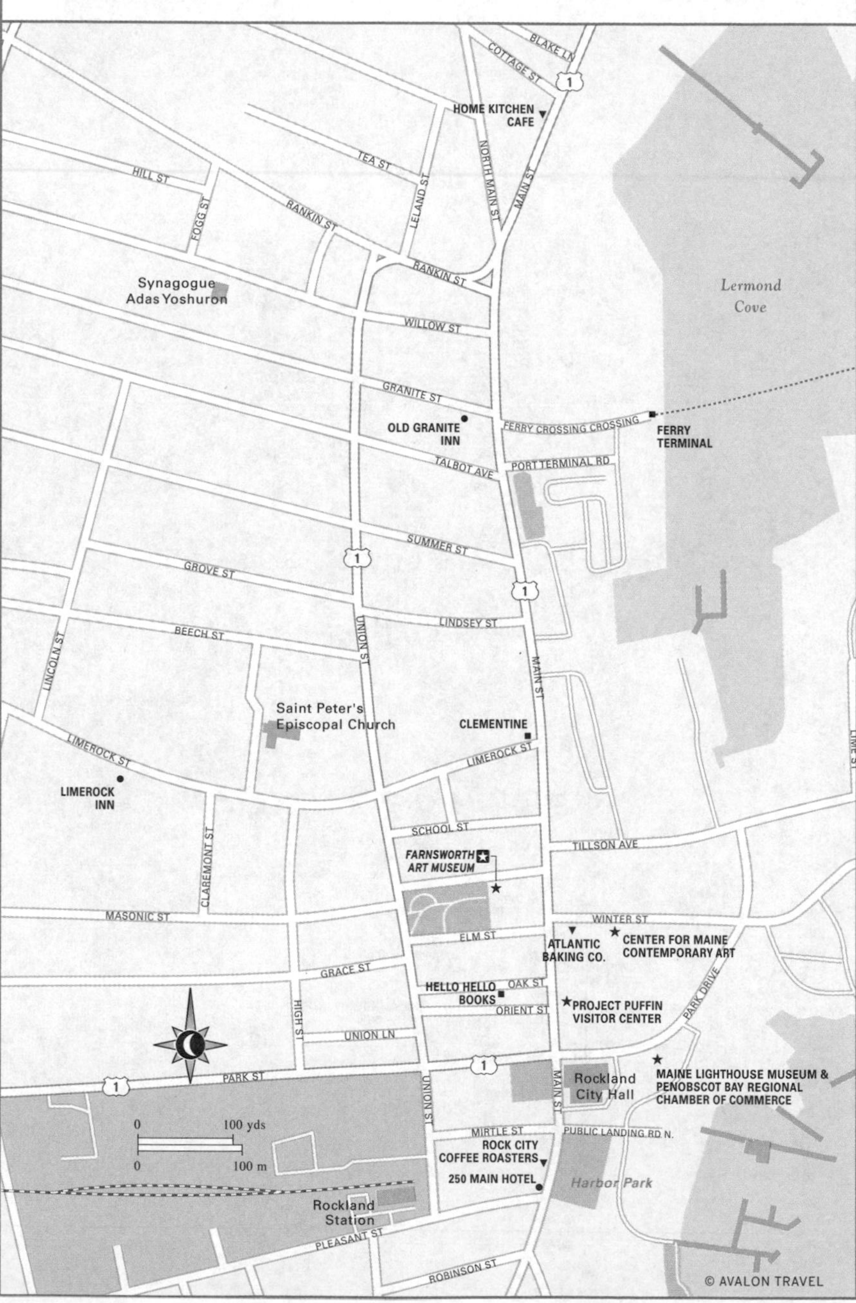
Rockland
BLAKE LN
COTTAGE ST
HOME KITCHEN CAFE
TEA ST
HILL ST
NORTH MAIN ST
MAIN ST
LELAND ST
FOGG ST
RANKIN ST
Synagogue Adas Yoshuron
Lermond Cove
WILLOW ST
GRANITE ST
OLD GRANITE INN
FERRY CROSSING CROSSING
FERRY TERMINAL
TALBOT AVE
PORT TERMINAL RD
SUMMER ST
GROVE ST
LINDSEY ST
BEECH ST
UNION ST
LINCOLN ST
Saint Peter's Episcopal Church
CLEMENTINE
LIMEROCK ST
LIMEROCK INN
LIME ST
SCHOOL ST
TILLSON AVE
FARNSWORTH ART MUSEUM
CLAREMONT ST
MASONIC ST
WINTER ST
ELM ST
ATLANTIC BAKING CO.
CENTER FOR MAINE CONTEMPORARY ART
GRACE ST
HELLO HELLO BOOKS
OAK ST
ORIENT ST
PROJECT PUFFIN VISITOR CENTER
PARK DRIVE
HIGH ST
UNION LN
PARK ST
Rockland City Hall
MAINE LIGHTHOUSE MUSEUM & PENOBSCOT BAY REGIONAL CHAMBER OF COMMERCE
0
100 yds
0
100 m
MIRTLE ST
PUBLIC LANDING RD N.
ROCK CITY COFFEE ROASTERS
250 MAIN HOTEL
Harbor Park
Rockland Station
PLEASANT ST
ROBINSON ST
© AVALON TRAVEL

Life Aboard Maine's Oldest Schooner

When Captain Garth Wells and Jenny Tobin purchased the *Lewis R. French* in 2004, Wells had worked on the historic schooner for five years, long enough to know the joys—and staggering work—of sailing and maintaining a traditional ship in Maine. First launched in Christmas Cove, Maine, in 1871, the *Lewis R. French* is the oldest Maine-built schooner still afloat, and Wells and Tobin believe that she's the oldest commercial schooner that's sailing in the United States. We spoke with co-owner Jenny Tobin, who's sailed the coasts of both North and South America, and served as mate, cook, and messmate aboard the *French*.

WHAT'S A WINDJAMMER?

A windjammer is a traditionally rigged sailboat that takes passengers on overnight cruises—it's also a schooner, which is the technical term for the rig of the boat, meaning it has two or more masts, with the main mast in the back.

WHAT DO YOU LIKE ABOUT SAILING A HISTORIC VESSEL?

I like being able to keep a historic vessel alive. It has had many owners, and we want to keep her in top shape. We like being part of the history of the boat. We like that it's such a different experience for people; you can totally escape for this unplugged vacation.

HOW DO YOU KEEP THE *LEWIS R. FRENCH* IN SAILING SHAPE?

We do a lot of things. Every year we haul it out of the water in Rockland to repaint the bottom, and every 18 months the Coast Guard comes to inspect it. Two months before the sailing season, the crew arrives to sand and paint everything, and in the winter we do basic maintenance, fixing things in the rig, the blocks. And a lot of times the captains here have to make things themselves, like the booms and the gaffs, but there are a couple of traditional riggers in the country where you can still buy an old block—there's an amazing traditional sailmaker in Boothbay where we get all of our sails.

DO YOU HAVE A FAVORITE TIME OF YEAR TO SAIL IN MAINE?

I like them all! The summer is gorgeous, and the winds pick up in the fall, with really crisp, beautiful days that we get to do really great sailing. In the fall, people are amazed that they're on a historic vessel, just flying across the coast of Maine on an old boat. There are so many protected anchorages, so many islands to explore, you never run out of places to go.

to Christina Olson, disabled by illness, and her eccentric brother Alvaro. On-site guides tell the story of the painting, which was based on an actual event when Wyeth came across Christina crawling home from her parents' graves. June-September, admission to Farnsworth Art Museum is free 5pm-8pm on Wednesday.

OWLS HEAD TRANSPORTATION MUSEUM

The little town of Owls Head, a 10-minute drive south from Rockland, seems an unlikely place for the sprawling **Owls Head Transportation Museum** (117 Museum St., Owls Head, 207/594-4418, http://owlshead.org, 10am-5pm daily, $14 adults, $10 seniors, youth under 18 free), whose remarkable collection of pre-1940s vehicles celebrates everything that whirs, sputters, rolls, and glides. Aircraft, automobiles, and motorcycles are all fully functional, and the bicycle exhibit covers everything from an 1868 velocipede "boneshaker" to a turn-of-the-20th-century dual propulsion tricycle. Ask upon arrival about riding in a Ford Model T; if a staff member is available, he or she will take you for a turn around the grounds. Aircraft—including 19th-century gliders, a Wright flyer, biplanes, and a "Red Baron"-style triplane—get off the ground during outdoor events that take place frequently during the summer months.

OTHER SIGHTS

Almost 700,000 tons of granite were sunk off Jameson Point to create the **Rockland Breakwater** (207/785-4609, www.rocklandharborlights.org), a 4,346-foot pile of rocks with a pretty brick lighthouse at the end. The scale of the building project, which was completed in 1900, is staggering, and the bulk of the structure is underwater—a cross section of the breakwater would be trapezoidal, with the base measuring 175 feet across. Walking the breakwater is an experience in itself, as sailboats, seabirds, and seals add to the scenery, and the **Rockland Breakwater Lighthouse** is fun to visit when open (if the flag is flying, the lighthouse is open—sharp-eyed visitors can spot the flag from Jameson Point, or check out the oddly hypnotizing live webcam feed on the breakwater website). Don't set out down the breakwater during storms, though, as heavy waves can wash over the rocks.

Short and pert, the **Owls Head Lighthouse** (Lighthouse Rd., Owl's Head, free) commands beautiful views of the rocky coastline, and is accessible via a short, gentle walk through coastal forest. Over the years, the lighthouse has collected a remarkable list of legends and ghost stories. The light is said to be haunted by two ghosts (one helpful spirit left one-way tracks in the snow when he visited to polish the brass and clean the lens), and the lighthouse has been the site of some remarkable rescues. In a December 1850 storm, a small schooner smashed up on the rocks near Owls Head, and two survivors huddled on the rocks while a third sought help. By the time a search party arrived, the two are said to have been fully encased in a block of frozen sea spray; the rescuers chipped off the ice and dunked the victims in cold water to revive them. According to legend, the two survivors later married and had four children.

While it might not thrill the casual visitor, lighthouse aficionados shouldn't miss the **Maine Lighthouse Museum** (1 Park Dr., 207/594-3301, www.mainelighthousemuseum.com, 10am-5pm Mon.-Fri., 10am-4pm Sat.-Sun., $8 adults, $6 seniors, children under 12 free), which bills itself as the country's most significant collection of lenses and artifacts. The attached chamber of commerce has brochures and maps for lighthouse hopping up the coast. If puffins are more your thing, stop by the **Project Puffin Visitor Center** (311 Main St., 207/596-5566, www.projectpuffin.

walking the Rockland Breakwater

Wildlife-Watching

puffin

Lobsters might be Maine's headlining animal attraction—and the crustaceans are well worth a trip unto themselves—but the state's wildlife is far wilder than many visitors imagine. The deep inland forests are home to some 65,000 **moose,** the largest species of deer in the world: Adult males can stand almost seven feet high at the shoulder, with antlers that span six feet. It's common to see **humpback, finback,** and **minke whales** along the coast, and the luckiest sea watchers might spot a North Atlantic **right whale** on its annual migration from the Labrador Sea to warmer waters on the coastline of Georgia and Florida. An expansive coast means lots of room for birds, and Maine is home to the first restored seabird colony in the world, **Eastern Egg Rock,** where **puffins** and **terns** are making a comeback—a remarkable achievement, given that in 1901 there was just one nesting pair of Atlantic puffins in the entire United States. Here are some of the best ways to explore Maine's wild side:

Spot a whale in Kennebunk: Catch a ride on ***Nick's Chance*** (4 Western Ave., Kennebunk, 207/967-5507, www.firstchancewhalewatch.com, 4.5-hour trip $48 adults, $28 children 3-12) to the offshore banks, where whales fill their giant maws with teeny, tiny creatures of the sea.

Cuddle a crustacean at Acadia National Park: Among the best activities for kids in the state, the **Dive-In Theater Boat Cruise** (105 Eden St., Bar Harbor, 207/288-3483, www.divered.com, $42 adults, $37 seniors, $32 children 5-11, $16 children under 5) is all about getting personal with the creatures of the deep—"Diver Ed" brings everything from anemones to lobsters from the seafloor, then offers guests a chance to shake their clammy claws.

Spy on the puffins at Eastern Egg Rock: Boats depart for the rocky island from locations in Boothbay and on the Pemaquid Peninsula, both with expert naturalists aboard: **Cap'n Fish's** (42 Commercial St., Boothbay Harbor, 207/633-3244, www.mainepuffin.com, 2.5-hour puffin tour $35 adults, $20 children 12 and under, $15 dogs; 4-hour puffin and whale tour $75 adults, $45 youth 6-14, $30 children under 6, $15 dogs) has a bigger boat for a smoother ride, but **Hardy Boat Cruises** (132 Rte. 32, New Harbor, 207/677-2026, www.hardyboat.com, 1.5-hour puffin tour $32 adults, $12 children 2-11, children under 2 free) is adventurous and fun, away from the crowds of Boothbay Harbor.

audubon.org, 10am-5pm Wed.-Sun. May, 10am-5pm daily June-Oct., free), which has a small but interesting exhibit on the birds and their habitat on Eastern Egg Rock.

Entertainment and Events

Lobster lovers arrive from all over for the five days of cook-offs and contests at the **Maine Lobster Festival** (800/596-0376, www.mainelobsterfestival.com, early Aug.), which has been held in Rockland since 1947. The event doesn't really get going until King Neptune crowns the Maine Sea Goddess on Wednesday night, and then it's a frenzy of pancake breakfasts, music, and 20,000 pounds of lobster that go straight from the boats into the world's largest lobster pot. It ends on Sunday with the International Great Crate Race, where fleet-footed contestants run across lobster crates suspended in the harbor, overseen—and sometimes fished out—by umpires in rowboats.

Sports and Recreation

Unlike more cumbersome square-rigged ships, Maine's "windjammer" schooners can sail close-hauled to the wind, making them remarkably nimble and fast for their size. Five of the nine ships that make up the **Maine Windjammer Association** (207/374-2993, www.sailmainecoast.com) are National Historic Landmarks, and they're overhauled each spring with fresh paint, polished brass, and gleaming wood. Without a steady stream of tourists, it's hard to imagine these ships staying afloat; even a small wooden sailboat is a labor of love, and a grand, historic schooner even more so.

Cruises range 3-6 days in length, poking around rocky islands, sailing into coves in search of seals, and providing evening deck views under brilliant stars. Accommodations are cramped, but increasingly the schooners are creating a more luxurious experience, with wine tastings and thoughtfully prepared food. Guests can lend a hand in hoisting sails and anchors, or just lie back and watch the show.

The ***J. & E. Riggin*** (207/594-1875, www.mainewindjammer.com, 3-day trips from $596) leaves from Rockland and is known for the best schooner food on the coast, and the 1922 ***Ladona*** (207/594-4723, www.schoonerladona.com, 3-day trips from $968) has cornered the upper end of the market after a recent overhaul, with wonderfully pristine deck chairs, luxurious beds, and elegant tiled showers.

Food

Powered by beans from the nearby Rock City Coffee Roasters, the **Rock City Cafe** (316 Main St., 207/594-4123, www.rockcitycoffee.com, 6am-7pm Mon.-Thurs., 6am-9pm Fri.-Sat., 7am-6pm Sun., $2-6) has excellent brews alongside a menu of light meals and fresh pastries.

A huge menu of hearty breakfasts and lunch plates is the draw at **Home Kitchen Café** (650 Main St., 207/596-2449, www.homekitchencafe.com, 7am-3pm Mon. and Wed.-Sat., 8am-3pm Sun., $7-13), a bright, friendly spot with a sunny rooftop patio. The recurring lobster tacos special is legendary, but the café's homemade sticky buns and corned beef hash also have passionate fans.

The busy bakers at **Atlantic Baking Co.** (351 Main St., 207/596-0505, www.atlanticbakingco.com, 7am-6pm Tues.-Sat., $3-11) turn out an impressive display of sweets, breads, and savory pastries. This centrally located spot is a favorite for quick, simple lunches of soups, salads, or sandwiches on house-made bread, and is also good for picnic supplies if you're headed out to Owls Head Lighthouse or the Rockland Breakwater.

Superb farm-to-table cuisine is beautifully presented at ★ **Primo** (2 S. Main St., 207/596-0770, www.primorestaurant.com, 5pm-10:30pm Wed.-Mon., $32-40), an Italian restaurant on a four-acre farm. James Beard Award-winning chef Melissa Kelly creates a menu that changes with the season, and plates are a heady blend of classic flavors and Maine ingredients, like seared scallops with morel mushrooms and fiddleheads, or a branzino fillet with local whelks, shrimp, and clams. Reservations are recommended: Book the downstairs dining room for a romantic, more formal feel, or dine in the upstairs lounge, full of colorful nooks, bar seating, and a convivial atmosphere. Cocktails are as garden-fresh as the food.

On the north end of town is a **Hannaford Supermarket** (75 Maverick St., 207/594-2173, 6am-11pm Mon.-Sat., 7am-9pm Sun.), and the tiny **Good Tern Natural Foods Co-Op and Café** (750 Main St., 207/594-8822, www.goodtern.com, 8am-7pm Mon.-Sat., 9am-5pm Sun.) has a good selection of organic, GMO-free foods, a deli, and a small café with a sitting area.

Accommodations

Rockland has few accommodations compared to Rockport and Camden, making Airbnb a good option here.

The Lobstering Life

Leah and Leslie Ranquist got their first taste of lobstering as children when their grandfather took them out in his skiff to bait traps and band lobsters. After completing a strenuous apprentice program, the two sisters, who both prefer the traditional term "lobsterman," began carrying on the family tradition from their home on Swan's Island, where each captains a lobster boat. Following a long day of hauling some of her 600 traps, Leah shared a bit about the lobstering life:

WHAT'S A TYPICAL DAY LIKE FOR YOU?

It's pretty repetitive—at 5 or 5:30 I'll head out and haul through 180-250 traps, depending on the day, then I head back in. My sternman is there to bait the pockets and band the lobsters, and I fish singles, pairs, and triples. A triple is three traps on one buoy, so when that first trap comes up, I'll have him grab the first trap, and I'll grab the second trap.

WHAT DO YOU LIKE ABOUT LOBSTERING?

I like a lot about lobstering! I mostly like that I'm my own boss, and I can make my own schedule. It's pretty relaxed, and I like being out on the water. The beautiful days are really worth the not-so-good ones. I'll be fishing five or six days a week for six months a year, then I haul my traps out in November, and I pick away at them and fix them through the winter. I do have to work in the winter, but that's my version of taking a break.

WHAT ARE SOME CHALLENGING THINGS FACING THE MAINE LOBSTER INDUSTRY IN COMING YEARS?

We're trying to prepare for uncertainty. Lobsters have been doing very good the last few years, and not knowing if it's going to keep up, or if they'll disappear like other fisheries have, we have to plan for disaster just to keep in mind that it might not be there forever.

WHAT'S YOUR FAVORITE WAY TO EAT A LOBSTER?

Steam it in a pot, then eat it hot with hot butter! I also enjoy a lobster roll here and there.

$150-200

Modern touches and eclectic, original art keep the ★ **Old Granite Inn** (546 Main St., 207/594-9036, www.oldgraniteinn.com, $150-215) from feeling fusty, but the common spaces of the granite colonial house retain a historical feel. Rooms range from a compact queen with detached private bath to four-person suites that are an excellent value for families; some have electric fireplaces and whirlpool tubs, while two rooms on the 2nd floor boast views of the Rockland Harbor Lighthouse. The hearty breakfasts served in the communal dining room get raves from guests.

$200-250

The elegant Queen Anne architecture of **LimeRock Inn** (96 Limerock St., 800/546-3762, www.limerockinn.com, $169-249) is brightened up with an eye-popping coat of teal paint and garden full of blooming plants. Welcoming owners and a location that's walking distance from downtown restaurants and the Farnsworth Art Museum make this a good choice for exploring Rockland, but the gracious wraparound porch, living room, and comfortable rooms are tempting reasons to stay in as well. All rooms have a private bath and fun, varied decor that ranges from a somewhat princessly pink suite to staid Yankee plaid.

OVER $250

Luxurious and ultramodern, **250 Main Hotel** (250 Main St., 207/594-5994, www.250mainhotel.com, $279-400) offers stunning views of the harbor from many rooms, some of which feature floor-to-ceiling glass. Clever nautical touches and original art are everywhere in the hotel's 26 rooms and common spaces. Don't miss the wonderful rooftop patio.

Information

The **Penobscot Bay Regional Chamber of Commerce** (1 Park Dr., 207/596-0376, www.therealmaine.com) runs a large and well-stocked information center in a new building by the harbor.

Getting There

Rockland is located on Route 1, 1.75 hours from Portland. Daily bus service to Rockland is available from **Concord Coach Lines** (100 Thompson's Point Rd., Portland, 800/639-3317, www.concordcoachlines.com), which stops at the **Maine State Ferry Terminal** (517A Main St.). There's free, two-hour parking on Main Street, and a larger lot at **Oceanside High School** (400 Broadway, July and Aug. only).

CAMDEN AND ROCKPORT

Forested, sloping hills running straight to the water are the perfect frame for Camden's sheltered harbor and picturesque downtown; the elegant little community is one of New England's most beautiful. Schooners and sleek yachts stand at attention on mooring buoys and floating docks, and on quiet mornings you can hear spanking lines and outboard motors from all over town. There's no finer place on the coast to see Maine's windjammer fleet, breathtaking wooden vessels crowned with acres of flying sails and trim lines.

All that beauty has made Camden a tourist destination since the mid-19th century, and downtown can be a madhouse in the heat of summer. When the ice cream shop has a line out the door and there's nowhere to park within a mile of the water, it's worth taking in your harbor views from the relative quiet of Camden Hills State Park, where Mount Megunticook and Mount Battie look out on Penobscot Bay.

Just down the coast, tiny Rockport feels like Camden in dollhouse scale: Turn away at the wrong moment, and you'd totally miss the perfect little harbor and downtown. There are just a few restaurants on the little Main Street, and no sights to speak of, but the waterfront park is ideal for watching lobster boats and sailors.

Sights

Starting in the 18th century, Mainers produced lime by burning locally quarried limestone in wood- and coal-fired kilns. At the time, lime was an essential part of almost any construction project, and, at the industry's peak in 1892, millions of casks of lime left the Maine coast. Keep an eye out and you'll see traces of the lime business everywhere, including a ruined **lime kiln** by the river in the Rockport Harbor. Featuring Maine's best artists, the **Center for Maine Contemporary Art** (21 Winter St., Rockport, 207/236-2875, www.cmcanow.org, 10am-5pm Mon.-Sat., noon-5pm Sun. late May-Oct., 10am-5pm Wed.-Sat., noon-5pm Sun. Nov.-late May, $8 adults, $6 seniors, youth 18 and under and students with ID free) is worth a look for its dozens of summer art shows held in a converted firehouse.

While it's not quite as extensive as the maritime museum in Bath, the collection of nautical treasures, art, and artifacts at the **Penobscot Marine Museum** (5 Church St., Searsport, 207/548-0334, www.penobscotmarinemuseum.org, 10am-5pm Mon.-Sat., noon-5pm Sun. late May-mid-Oct., $15 adults, $12 seniors and students, $10 children 8-15, children under 8 free) is fascinating. You'll find a trove of model ships and scrimshaw here, along with practical tools and navigation equipment. The museum is about 30 minutes up the coast from Camden, in Searsport, so make a stop on the way to Acadia National Park.

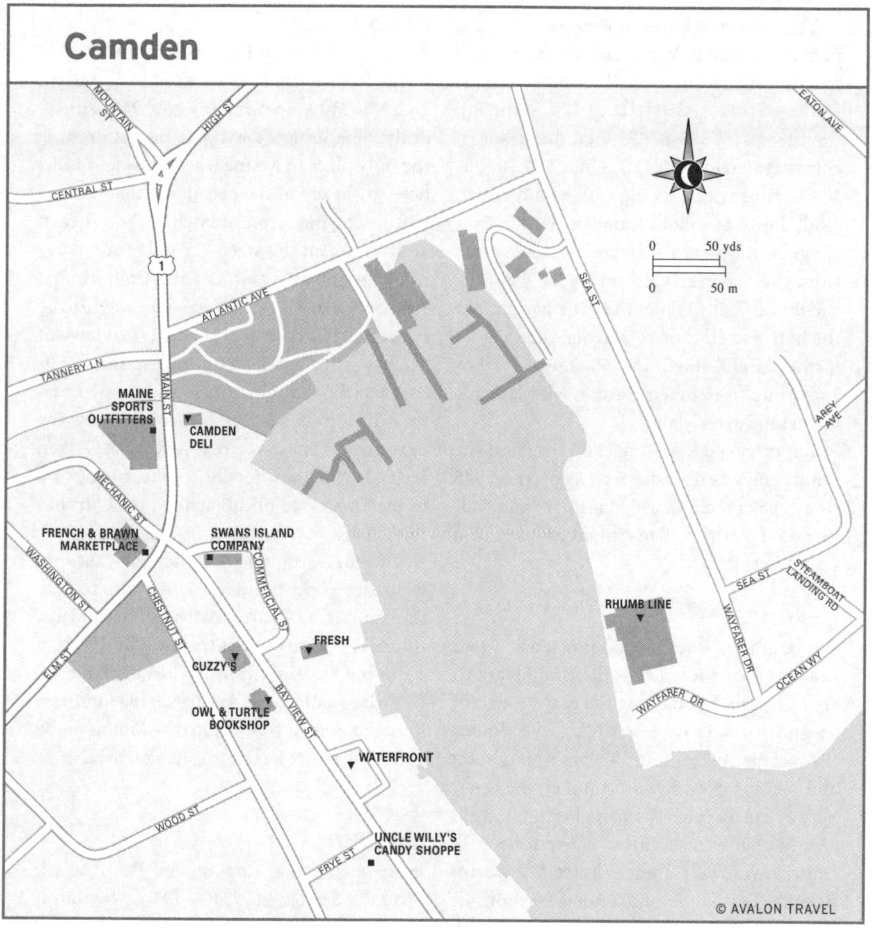

Camden

Entertainment and Events

Like the other tourist towns on the coast, Camden's summer is a whirl of themed weekends and small festivals. The real centerpiece of the season, though, is the **Camden Windjammer Festival** (207/236-4404, www.camdenwindjammerfrestival.org, early Sept.), when the harbor fills with two dozen magnificent schooners. Boat parades, fireworks, and a lobster-trap race make this a fun time to visit, but book accommodations far in advance.

Sports and Recreation

PADDLING PENOBSCOT BAY

As beautiful as Rockport and Camden are, getting out on a boat is the only way to really take in Penobscot Bay. Tiny forested isles and town-sized islands are dreamlike on sunny days, when the sparkling water lights up the coast. But the bay is a sprawl of rocky shoals and hazards, and a thick layer of fog can turn even familiar harbors into a dangerous maze. Would-be adventurers shouldn't be deterred—local captains and kayak guides are well versed in keeping people safe.

The lacy, rock edges of Penobscot Bay are perfectly suited to kayaks, which can nose in and out of coves too small for bigger boats. **Maine Sports Outfitters** (24 Main St., Camden, 207/236-8797, www.mainesport.com, kayak trips $40-125 adults, $35-75 kids 10-15) runs trips ranging from two hours to a full day. A two-hour Camden Harbor Tour is a good way to see the schooners and yachts from the water as you work your way to a small island at the mouth of the harbor, but the half-day Harbor-to-Harbor paddle goes farther afield, starting in Rockport Harbor and going to Camden Harbor, with a picnic lunch on Curtis Island.

Experienced kayakers can rent from the same company (full-day sea kayak rental $45 single, $55 tandem), which is full of good advice on day trips and overnight paddles from Camden Harbor.

BEACHES

The Camden area isn't known for great beaches, but there are some fine places to cool off on a hot day: At the eastern end of Megunticook Lake, **Barrett's Cove Beach** (Beauclaire Ave., off Rte. 52) has a bit of sand and picnic tables. By midsummer, the water here is far warmer than the bay, making it a good choice for families. A one-mile walk from downtown Camden, **Laite Memorial Beach** (south side of Camden Harbor, off Bay View St.) is a pleasant, grassy park with a sandy beach that narrows to a sliver at high tide.

BOATING

Sailing out of Camden, the 1871 ***Lewis R. French*** (270/230-8320, www.schoonerfrench.com, 3-night trips from $625) is the oldest windjammer in the United States, and still has no inboard engine; with all sails set, she flies a remarkable 3,000 square feet of canvas. Another Camden favorite is the ***Angelique*** (800/282-9989, www.sailangelique.com, 3-night trips from $595), a modern vessel that's particularly dramatic under deep-red, gaff-rigged sails.

HIKING

Aside from Mount Desert Island, **Camden Hills State Park** (280 Rte. 1, Camden, 207/236-3109, www.maine.gov, 9am-sunset daily, $6 adults, $2 seniors and children) is the only place in Maine where the mountains hew so closely to the coast, and the views of Penobscot Bay are unmatched. You'll earn your views on the steep 2.6-mile round-trip **Megunticook Trail** as you climb almost 1,000 feet in elevation on your way to the summit. Another good choice for views of the bay is the 3-mile loop trail up the 1,200-foot **Bald Rock Mountain,** where two rustic Adirondack shelters are set just below the bare crest. Unless you're a very brisk walker, set aside two hours for either hike, and be sure to pick up a free hiking map at the entrance to the park.

Of course, you also don't have to walk anywhere for views in this park. An auto road to the summit of **Mount Battie** climbs from just inside the state park entrance. The 19-year-old Edna St. Vincent Millay, a Rockland native who would go on to win the 1923 Pulitzer Prize for poetry, was inspired by Mount Battie when she wrote her poem "Renascence."

Food

CAMDEN

Even when you are looking for ★ **Rhumb Line** (59 Sea St., 207/230-8495, www.rhumblinecamden.com, 4:30pm-9:30pm Mon. and Wed.-Fri., 11:30am-9:30pm Sat.-Sun., $7-25), it's easy to miss, tucked between the waterfront and a cavernous working boatyard. The small seafood restaurant is across the harbor from the core of downtown, and it's a pleasure to enjoy the alternative vantage point from the outdoor bar and patio seating. Opened in 2016, the restaurant generated buzz with creative cocktails and fresh boat-to-table seafood. The menu includes the usual fried fare, along with offbeat sashimi and ceviche, and the rustic-chic interior is right at home on the water's edge.

Find great coffee and something to read at **Owl & Turtle Bookshop** (33 Bay View St.,

Walking from Rockport to Camden

One of the area's most splendid walks is the two-mile **stroll from Rockport to Camden,** following a two-lane road past great water views and fine New England architecture. Make the first stop on the walk in Rockport, where you'll find a statue of **Andre the Seal** at the **Rockport Marine Park** (Harbor View Dr., free parking). The harbor seal, who died in 1986, was the honorary harbor master here after being raised by a local family. When he was old enough to fend for himself, Andre was released into the wild, but the seal came back to spend every summer at Rockport Harbor.

From the statue, continue across the bridge to **Russell Avenue,** which wraps through the village and into a series of fields that overflow with wildflowers in the spring. Watch for **Aldermere Farms** (70 Russell Ave., Rockport, www.aldermere.org), on the right-hand side, where Belted Galloway cows munch grass in pastures overlooking Penobscot Bay.

As you enter Camden, Russell Avenue turns into Chestnut Street and runs right into the heart of town. For a side trip to **Laite Memorial Beach** (Bay View St., Camden), turn right onto Cedar Street, which leads toward the water. There's no local bus service to loop back to Rockport, so you can make the walk a four-mile round-trip, or get a cab from **Schooner Bay Taxi** (207/594-5000, one-way trip from Camden to Rockport $9).

207/230-7335, www.owlandturtle.com, 8am-6pm Tues.-Sat., $2-5), which also has a small selection of fresh pastries. Friendly staff and a good crowd of locals make this a nice place to linger with a crossword puzzle.

No one goes to **Cuzzy's** (21 Bay View St., 207/236-3272, www.cuzzysrestaurant.com, 11am-1am daily, $5-20) for a gourmet meal, but that's somewhat beside the point. There's a huge menu of affordable pub food, very decent chowder, and all kinds of fried seafood to eat at the bar, where fishers and schooner crews come to relax in a cave-like interior or on the sunny back patio. Happy hour specials on cheap beer and pizza are available 3pm-6pm daily.

With a solid menu of seafood standards and patio seating that juts over the harbor, **Waterfront** (40 Bay View St., 207/236-3747, www.waterfrontcamden.com, 11:30am-9pm daily, $9-30) is a perennial favorite. No individual dish seems to blow anyone away, but watching the boats roll in and out of the harbor over a glass of local beer and plate of oysters is a true Camden experience. On busy nights, waits can get very long, and since the interior seating is a bit lackluster, it's often worth going elsewhere.

Reasonably priced sandwiches, soups, and salads at **Camden Deli** (37 Main St., 207/236-8343, www.camdendeli.com, 7am-9pm daily, $7-10) are a simple option right downtown. Limited seating is available inside (window seats have great views of the harbor), but this is a nice place to pick up sandwiches to take around the corner to the small park where paths and benches face the water.

In a cheerfully decorated, historic brick building, **Fresh & Co.** (1 Bay View Landing, 207/236-7005, www.freshcamden.com, 5pm-8:30pm daily, $21-28) is just that, with an eye-opening menu of international food that skews Asian. The huge, homemade lobster ravioli with wonton wrappers is a favorite here, as is the "deconstructed" lamb moussaka as well as tiger shrimp with black rice and ginger barbecue sauce. Despite the upscale food (and prices), this restaurant has a casual atmosphere, with outdoor seating and the occasional live act.

Find high-quality baked goods, meat, cheese, and drinks at **French & Brawn Marketplace** (1 Elm St., 207/236-3361, www.frenchandbrawn.com, 6am-8pm daily), which is the only market in downtown Camden. More basic goods are available from **Hannaford Supermarket** (145 Elm

St., 207/236-8577, 7am-10pm Mon.-Sat., 7am-9pm Sun.), on the main road south of town. Small but vibrant, the **Camden Farmers Market** (Knox Mill between Washington and Knowlton, Sat. market 9am-1pm May-Nov., Wed. market 3:30pm-6pm mid-June-Nov.) has local breads, cheeses, vegetables, and fruit.

Rockport

Tiny Rockport doesn't have much of a dining scene, but ★ **Nina June** (24 Central St., 207/236-8880, www.ninajunerestaurant.com, 5:30pm-9:30pm Tues.-Fri., 10am-2pm and 5:30pm-9:30pm Sat., 11:30am-2pm Sun., brunch $6-18, lunch/dinner $20-30) is a noteworthy exception. A deck overlooking the Rockport Harbor makes a sublime setting for a Mediterranean menu that changes with the season. A typical fall menu might include bucatini with lamb neck ragu and grilled swordfish beside a pile of shaved cucumber and cherry tomatoes. Saturday lunch means a hearty menu of Italian specialties, while Sunday brunch ranges from traditional breakfasts like strata or pancakes to white-almond gazpacho and other savory entrées.

Accommodations and Camping

UNDER $100

The trim little cottages at ★ **Oakland Seashore Cabins** (112 Dearborn Ln., Rockport, 207/594-8104, www.oaklandseashorecabins.com, $75-150) are rustic and a bit of a tight squeeze, but they're set right on the edge of a private pebble beach between Rockland and Rockport, making them a fabulous value and wonderfully peaceful place to stay. This property also includes motel rooms at a similar price, and while they're a decent option, the cabins are the clear winner. The cabins with kitchenettes are stocked with very basic cooking equipment, and the largest sleep up to five people. No televisions, telephones, or coffeepots here (and the wireless access is hit or miss).

$100-150

A quiet, 15-minute walk from Rockport's gem of a harbor, **Schooner Bay Motor Inn** (337 Commercial St., Rockport, 888/308-8855, www.sbaymotorinn.com, $90-179) has trim furnishings and a thoughtful, local character that sets it apart from the other motels along Route 1. Light sleepers should request a room at the forested back of the property, where there's a small, shady creek. A breakfast of fresh pastries, fruit, and homemade quiche is served May-December.

If you're looking for a lower-budget place to stay in downtown Camden, **The Towne Motel** (68 Elm St., Camden, 207/236-3377, www.camdenmotel.com, $124-150) is hard to beat. The superclean, motel-style rooms are nothing fancy, but the friendly owners are gradually overhauling them; updated rooms are the same price as the older ones, but with smart, fresh colors and little artistic flourishes. All rooms have coffeemakers, cable televisions, air-conditioning, wireless Internet, and small fridges, and an appealing breakfast is served during summer months; in the off-season, the owners deliver a little breakfast packet to each room that includes their killer homemade granola.

$150-250

Find Maine country style with a few nautical touches at the **Blue Harbor House Inn** (67 Elm St., Camden, 207/236-3196, www.blueharborhouse.com, $155-199), a homey spot that's a short walk from downtown. Rooms are stocked with coffeemakers and comfortable beds, and afternoon tea and the innkeeper's two-course breakfast are served in a welcoming common room. All rooms have en suite bathrooms, and more expensive options have steam showers or claw-foot soaking tubs.

An expansive lawn rolls all the way to a private beach, a wonderful perk that makes the **High Tide Inn** (505 Rte. 1, Camden, 207/236-3724, www.hightideinn.com, $175-195, deck house $170-260) feel like a retreat just a few minutes' drive from downtown Camden. A handful of options are available on this property: the somewhat lackluster Oceanview Motel (where you can just spy a bit of blue); the sweet, compact rooms in the old-fashioned inn; a collection of oceanfront rooms a stone's throw from the water; and six little cottages, nostalgic and rustic. A homemade continental breakfast is served on a glass-enclosed porch with views to the water.

OVER $250

Find all the top-end perks at ★ **16 Bay View** (16 Bay View St., Camden, 207/706-7990, www.16bayview.com, $250-500), a 21-room boutique hotel with perfect views of the harbor from oceanside rooms and the rooftop bar. Great piles of silky pillows, gas fireplaces, spa bathrooms, and balconies are luxurious, and the hotel, which opened in early 2016, is beautifully decorated. A continental breakfast is served in the Prohibition-themed Vintage Room.

CAMPING

Set in the rolling forest along the coast, ★ **Camden Hills State Park** (280 Rte. 1, 207/236-3109, www.maine.gov, $38-49) has amazing views of Penobscot Bay, trails to explore, and level campsites that range from simple tent pads to extra-large options, with water, electric, and space for a 35-foot camper. The campground is divided into reservable sites that must be booked 48 hours in advance (though it's worth planning ahead for peak season), and a smaller number of sites set aside on a first-come, first-served basis.

Information

The **Camden-Rockport-Lincolnville Chamber of Commerce** (Public Landing, 207/236-4404 or 800/223-5459, www.visitcamden.com, 9am-4pm Mon.-Sat.) runs a helpful information center on the Camden waterfront.

Getting There and Around

Camden is located on Route 1, 1.75 hours from Portland, and two hours from Bar Harbor. Daily bus service to Rockport from Portland is available from **Concord Coach Lines** (100 Thompson's Point Rd., Portland, 800/639-3317, www.concordcoachlines.com), which stops at Maritime Farms (20 Commercial St., Rockport).

No real in-town public transit is available in any of the Penobscot Bay locales, but they're small enough to explore on foot. In Camden, free parking is available at two public lots (Washington Street, turn north when Route 1 passes the Camden Village Green).

BANGOR

The third-largest city in Maine, industrial Bangor is invigorated by students at the University of Maine, who infuse young energy into an otherwise stolid and sleepy place. If you've read anything written by resident celebrity Stephen King, however, you'll know that sleepy northern towns aren't always what they seem—a towering statue of the folk forester Paul Bunyan points to the city's past as a buzzing lumber port, and there's a remarkably good art museum on the university campus.

Stephen King Tour

Born in Portland, Stephen King came to Orono to attend college and has remained in the area ever since. The first stop on most horror-lovers' itineraries is the author's house, a **creepy Victorian** (47 W. Broadway) whose wrought-iron gate is adorned with spiders, bats, and a mythical-looking snake. For the full SK immersion, join an outing with **SK Tours of Maine** (207/947-7193, www.sk-tours.com, 3-hour tours $45 adults, children under 13 free), led by a fanatically knowledgeable guide. In addition to the author's own haunts, the tours visit places that King has woven into novels like *It* and *Pet Sematery.*

Other Sights

According to Bangor boosters, the town's **Paul Bunyan Statue** (519 Main St.) is the largest in the world—but who's counting? Built in 1959, it towers 31 feet above Main Street—and it came to life as "Giant" in the pages of Stephen King's book *It*.

A first-rate collection of contemporary work is housed at the **University of Maine Museum of Art** (Norumbega Hall, 40 Harlow St., 207/561-3350, www.umma.umaine.edu, 10am-5pm Tues.-Sat., free), which features the art of Roy Lichtenstein, Richard Estes, and David Hockney.

Food

Run by a group of Franciscan friars, the ★ **Friars' Bakehouse** (21 Central St., 207/947-3770, 8:30am-2pm Tues.-Thurs., 8:30am-1:30pm Fri., $5-20) serves a homey menu of soups and sandwiches on its house-made bread, with a pastry case full of sticky buns and oversized cookies. The lobster roll is one of the few around that's not based on store-bought white rolls, and it's stuffed with an impressive pile of meat in generous pieces.

A sign of changed times in Bangor, the stylish **Timber Kitchen & Bar** (22 Bass Park Blvd., 207/433-0844, www.timberkitchenandbar.com, 11am-11pm Mon.-Thurs., 11am-midnight Fri.-Sat., 11am-10pm Sun., $12-33) is convivial and fun, with places to gather indoors and by an outside fire. Flatbreads, burgers, and house-made pasta are the heart of the menu, but the seafood stew is outstanding. The restaurant's happy hour (4pm-6pm Mon.-Fri.) is popular, with discounted drinks and bar snacks.

With a roadhouse feel and a perpetual lineup of big-rig trucks, **Dysart's Restaurant & Truck Stop** (530 Coldbrook Rd., 207/942-4878, www.dysarts.com, 24 hours daily, $7-16) is something of a legend in these parts, the kind of place that would merit its own country song if Mainers went in for that sort of thing. Enormous sandwiches, big slices of blueberry pie, whoopie pies, cinnamon rolls the size of a (small) head, and house-made hash bring in crowds to the cavernous dining room. Breakfasts are an old-fashioned feast.

Accommodations

Aside from a cluster of chain hotels by the highway exit, Bangor's main accommodation is a clanging downtown casino, so it's often best to stick to the interstate. The best value among the roadside motels may be the **Bangor Inn & Suites** (701 Hogan Rd., 207/947-0357, www.bangorinnandsuites.com, $90-130), a basic spot with clean, if dated, rooms and an unusually good breakfast of homemade muffins, eggs cooked to order, and sides.

More spiffed up and spacious, Marriott's

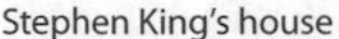

Stephen King's house

TownePlace Suites Bangor (240 Sylvan Rd., 844/631-0595, www.marriott.com, $150-300) has a reasonable self-serve breakfast in the downstairs dining area, with a gym and a pool on-site. While mostly geared toward extended stays, there are suites equipped with kitchenettes and small living rooms.

Getting There

Bangor is located on I-95, 2 hours from Portland and 1.25 hours from Bar Harbor and Acadia National Park. Daily bus service to Bangor from Portland and Boston is available from **Concord Coach Lines** (100 Thompson's Point Rd., Portland, 800/639-3317, www.concordcoachlines.com), which stops at the **Bangor Transportation Center** (1039 Union St.). **Greyhound** (214/849-8966, www.greyhound.com) also stops in town, with service around the northeast.

Blue Hill Peninsula

Another gorgeous web of bays and narrow harbors, Blue Hill Peninsula is an escape from the crowds in Bar Harbor and Camden. No one sight anchors the region's many charms, but it's an appealing place for a slow drive or lunch by the water. The far-flung seaside town of Castine has a historic center and a marine that fills with yachts and runabouts, while the community of Blue Hill remains a haven for artists and eccentrics drawn to the beauty of the coast.

SIGHTS

Castine

You can take in the heart of historic Castine on foot, and the **Castine Historical Society** (13 and 17 School St., 207/326-4118, www.castinehistoricalsociety.org) issues a free map that outlines a self-guided walking tour—the maps are available at the historical society, as well as at many shops around town.

Highlights of the walk include the astounding collection in the **Wilson Museum** (107 Perkins St., 207/326-9247, www.wilsonmuseum.org, 10am-5pm Mon.-Fri., 2pm-5pm Sat.-Sun. late May-Sept., free), which includes African prehistoric artifacts, Balinese shadow puppets, fire department memorabilia, and old maps and ships' logs.

A short and pleasant walk from downtown is **Dyce Head Lighthouse,** a 19th-century classic tapered white tower. In the summer, midshipmen conduct tours of the *State of Maine*, the 500-foot training vessel owned by the **Maine Maritime Academy** (Pleasant St., Castine, 800/464-6565, www.mainemaritime.edu). Though not available for tours, be sure to notice the academy's other beauty, the schooner *Bowdoin*, which Maine explorer Adm. Donald MacMillan took on his many expeditions to the North Pole. During the summer months, the historical society leads hour-long tours of Castine on selected Saturdays; check the website for an updated schedule.

Blue Hill

If Leonardo da Vinci had lived in Maine at the turn of the 19th century, he would have been fast friends with Jonathan Fisher, a preacher who dabbled in painting, poetry, farming, and literally dozens of other fields. Memorabilia and items made by the man himself are on view at the **Jonathan Fisher House** (44 Mines Rd., 207/374-2459, www.jonathanfisherhouse.org, hours vary, May-Sept., $5).

The gardens and hand-built home of Helen and Scott Nearing, intellectuals, writers, and farmers who helped lead the first wave of back-to-the-landers in New England, are carefully preserved at the **Good Life Center** (372 Harborside Rd., Harborside, 207/326-8211, www.goodlife.org, 1pm-4pm Thurs.-Mon. late June-early Sept., $10 suggested donation), which explores their legacy and ideals.

ENTERTAINMENT

Three dozen members strong, the **Flash! In the Pans** (207/374-2140, www.peninsulapan.org) community steel band brings a taste of the Caribbean to Maine with outdoor steel-band concerts around the peninsula all summer long. On alternate Mondays they instigate a street party in the small town of Brooksville.

FOOD

When thoughts of midday snacks start hitting, set your sights on **Markel's Bakehouse** (26 Water St., Castine, 207/326-9510, www.markelsbakehouse.com, 7am-3pm daily summer, closed Sun.-Mon. in off-season, $2-9), where the cases are filled with strawberry and cream croissants, snickerdoodle cookies, and giant honey shortbreads. The menu also includes hearty breakfasts and lunches of soups, sandwiches, and salads.

The dining room of the **Pentagöet Inn** (26 Main St., 207/326-8616, www.pentagoet.com, 8am-10pm daily mid-May-Sept., $17-26) has a refined colonial ambience that somehow strangely sympathizes with Ella Fitzgerald and Louis Armstrong crooning in the background. The menu is an impeccable mix of New England seafood and homemade pastas, highlighted by haute cuisine accents like white truffle oil, goat cheese cream, and tarragon bourride.

Easily worth a bit of a side trip from Castine or Blue Hill, ★ **Buck's Restaurant** (6 Cornfield Hill Rd., Brooksville, 207/326-8688, www.bucksrestaurant.weebly.com, 5:30pm-8pm Tues.-Sat., $19-28) serves New American dishes with lots of heart: think smoked mackerel pâté, baked pollock, and Acadian jambalaya. It's a great meal, but unfussy—you could arrive in heels or boat shoes.

ACCOMMODATIONS

A quick walk from the beach and with blissful views, the rustic **Castine Cottages** (33 Snapp's Way, Castine, 207/326-8003, www.castinecottages.com, $90-200) are two-bedroom stand-alones with full kitchens, outdoor grills, and very cute decor.

With smart New England decor and wonderfully hospitable owners, the **Blue Hill Inn** (40 Union St., Blue Hill, 207/374-2844, www.bluehillinn.com, $115-220) is beloved for blueberry pancakes and thoughtful amenities. Wine and snacks are served each evening, and some of the rooms have their own romantic little sitting areas, complete with personal fireplace.

Maine Island style gets a dose of sophistication at **The Castine Inn** (33 Main St., Castine, 207/326-4365, www.castineinn.com, $120-200). Rooms are sunny and decorated in soothing tones, queen beds, and delicate window treatments (many of which frame views of the surrounding gardens and nearby harbor). Breakfast is included and delicious—especially if the apple bread French toast is on offer.

GETTING THERE

The Blue Hill Peninsula extends south from Route 1, between Penobscot Bay and Blue Hill Bay, and is accessible on Route 175 and Route 172. No public transportation options to the area are currently available.

Acadia National Park

Look for ★ to find recommended sights, activities, dining, and lodging.

Highlights

★ **Cadillac Mountain:** The tip of this granite-topped mountain catches America's first sunrise for part of the year, and dawn gatherings on the summit are a New England rite of passage (page 207).

★ **Carriage Roads:** Bike this extraordinary network of car-free roads—or hop a horse-drawn carriage to a rocky summit (page 208).

★ **Thuya Garden and Asticou Azalea Garden:** Climb the monumental granite path to Thuya Garden, then walk paths lined with armfuls of blossoms spring-fall (page 210).

★ **Bar Island Trail:** Walk from Bar Harbor to a rocky little island on a pathway that is only exposed at low tide, watching for stranded sea creatures along the way (page 217).

★ **West Quoddy Head Light:** Make the long drive to the easternmost point in the continental United States, and you'll be rewarded with big tides and bigger views (page 221).

★ **Hiking Mount Katahdin:** The northern terminus of the 2,200-mile Appalachian Trail is one of New England's most dramatic peaks, with vertigo-inducing ridges, wild weather, and a maze of gorgeous footpaths (page 223).

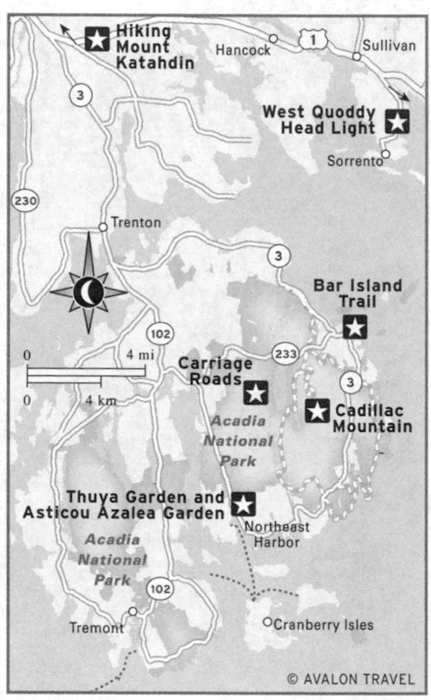

Maine's scenic drama comes to a head in Acadia National Park, a 47,000-acre preserve that spills across Mount Desert Island to the surrounding islets and shoreline.

Twenty-four mountain peaks describe the island's dramatic history in sparkling granite: 450 million years ago, mini continent Avalonia rammed into the hulking North American plate, forming a platform that would be buried under sand, silt, volcanic lava, and ash, then raked by a series of massive glaciers. Geologic clues are everywhere here, from odd-looking rocks left perched on mountaintops to ice-carved, U-shaped valleys and deep gouges in bare granite. A deep, fjord-like bay nearly splits the island in two. For ocean-view hiking, rocky trail exploration, and tide pooling, New England's only national park is incomparable.

The Wabanaki people have inhabited this stretch of coast for thousands of years, hunting and fishing in year-round settlements and trading widely with other regional groups. In 1604, French explorer Samuel de Champlain stopped by long enough to record a name—*Isles des Monts Déserts*, or Islands of Bare Peaks—and was followed by waves of Jesuit missionaries, French and British soldiers, and city people seeking simpler country pleasures.

It remains an extraordinary place, with rugged mountains, beaches, and headlands so tightly packed they can be explored in a single day. Acadia is glorious in the summer sunshine, but it's equally entrancing when thick fog creeps across the water, isolating the island into a world of its own. One vibrant town and a handful of scattered communities are interwoven with the park land, so your experience in Acadia can be as luxurious, or remote, as you choose.

Continue past Acadia National Park, and the long coast leads to the easternmost point in the continental United States, the far-flung outpost of Lubec, whose West Quoddy Head Light is a candy-striped beacon that marks the end of America.

Head far inland to Baxter State Park, where Maine's highest mountain marks the northern terminus of the 2,200-mile Appalachian Trail. It's a peak that has drawn spiritual seekers and adventurers for centuries, and

Previous: a carriage road bridge in Acadia National Park; Lubec's West Quoddy Head Light. **Above:** hiking on Cadillac Mountain.

to many mountain lovers, Katahdin's rocky ridges and moods outshine the more developed alpine landscape of New Hampshire's Mount Washington.

PLANNING YOUR TIME

Mount Desert Island is 108 square miles, and accounting for winding roads and slow-moving traffic, it can take quite a while to drive from one side to the other. When visiting, then, it's worth choosing one of the two sides as a home base: Opt for Bar Harbor for great access to kid-friendly activities, shops, and restaurants, or sleep on the western "quiet side" to escape the crowds. Spring-fall, the free Island Explorer shuttle makes frequent loops of the island following eight different routes; if you'd like to explore car-free (highly recommended), choose accommodations on a shuttle route. As in other destinations on coastal Maine, the true high season is during the school vacation months of July and August. Many prices drop substantially in June and September, whose mild weather and sunshine also make them some of the prettiest months on the island. The leaves begin to change color toward the end of September, reaching a brilliant peak in mid-October. While the Park Loop Road is open year-round, many restaurants and hotels close their doors between November and May.

ORIENTATION

For many people, Acadia National Park and Mount Desert Island are synonymous, but the national park is a patchwork that covers much of the island and a bit of mainland coast. The bulk of the park territory is on the eastern side of Mount Desert Island, where the Park Loop Road circles some of the most dramatic scenery and best-known hiking trails. On the other side of Somes Sound is the "quiet side," good for less frequented hikes. The remaining parkland is on the harder-to-reach Isle au Haut, and the Schoodic Peninsula, which is linked by passenger ferry to Bar Harbor.

Acadia National Park

TOP EXPERIENCE

VISITING THE PARK

Entrances

Because of the patchwork way Acadia National Park was stitched together, driving around Mount Desert Island means passing in and out of park territory, often without notice. The only real gateways to the park are the kiosks at the on-ramps to Park Loop Road, where you'll be asked to present your pass; otherwise, leave it displayed in your car (park rangers suggest that cyclists and motorcyclists carry their pass with them on hikes).

Park Passes and Fees

May-October, the entrance fee for a private vehicle seating 15 people or fewer is $25. Motorcycles with one or two passengers pay $20, cyclists and pedestrians pay $12 each, and individuals 15 years old and younger are admitted free of charge. Most passes are valid for seven days; annual passes to Acadia National Park are $50, while an Interagency Annual Pass is $80 and covers all National Park Service and Forest Service entrance fees. Active military, people with disabilities, and U.S. fourth-grade students are eligible for a free Interagency Annual Pass; a lifetime interagency pass is available to seniors for $80. Passes are sold at all park visitors centers, campgrounds, and information booths, but for trips during peak season, it's worth purchasing online to avoid lines (www.yourpassnow.com).

Visitors Centers

As Route 3 crosses the Mount Desert Narrows, the small **Thompson Island Information Center** (8:30am-5:30pm daily

Acadia National Park

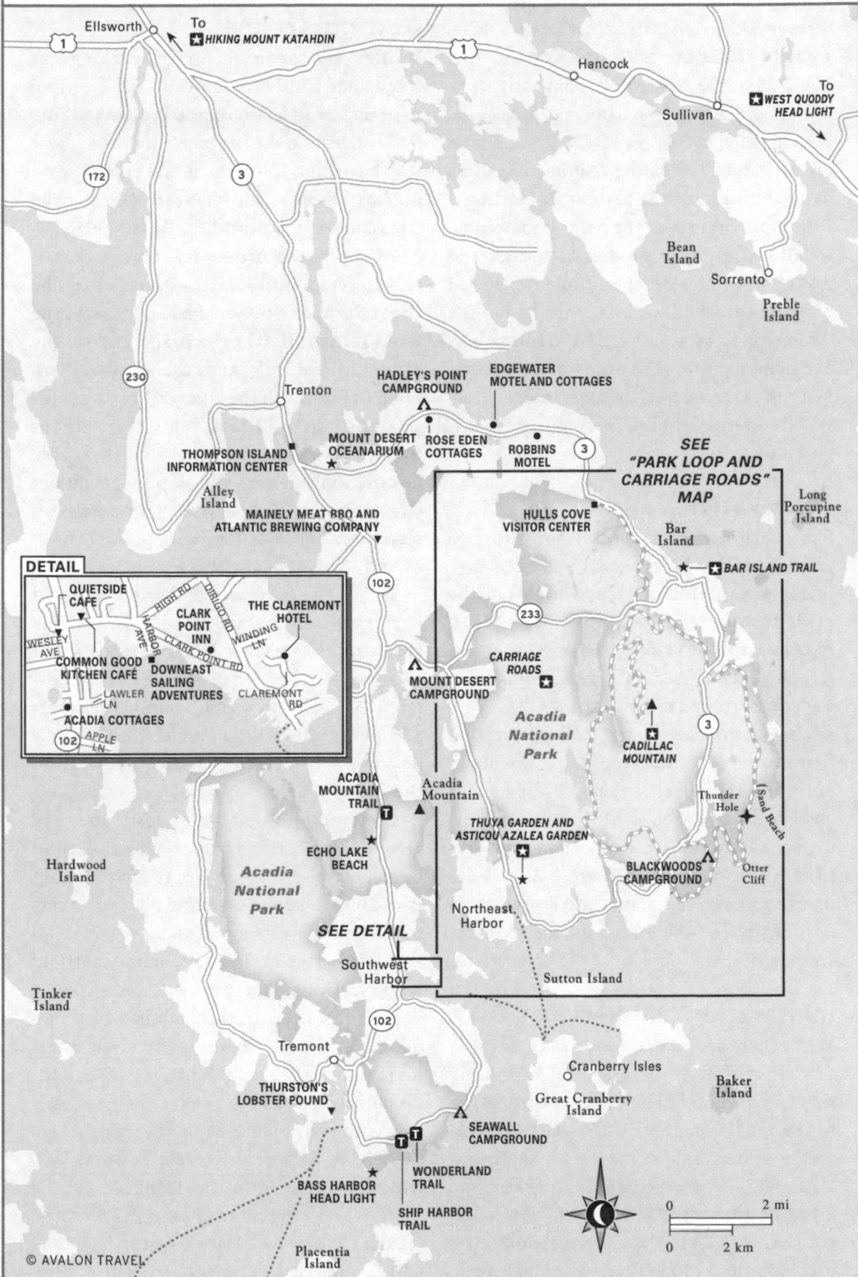

mid-May-mid-Oct.) is on the right, and it's a useful stop for passes and maps if you're making a beeline to a trail or campground on the west side of the island. Otherwise, keep going to **Hulls Cove Visitor Center** (Rte. 3, 207/288-3338, 8:30am-4:30pm daily Apr.-mid-June, 8:30am-6pm daily mid-June-Aug., 8:30am-4:30pm daily Sept.-Oct.), which has several exhibits orienting visitors to Acadia's natural and cultural history, including a 15-minute film about the park. It's also possible to sign up for guided naturalist and history programs here; multiple ranger-led programs are held each day throughout the summer in Acadia National Park, from walks and demonstrations to outdoor art lessons. Many of these are free; for more information, visit the events webpage (www.nps.gov/acad/planyourvisit).

Reservations

Reservations are essential for the two campgrounds—Blackwoods and Seawall—inside the national park, which can be made through the **National Recreation Reservation Service** (877/444-8777, www.recreation.gov). A small number of sites in each campground are set aside for day-of arrivals with no reservations; call each location first thing in the morning to inquire about openings, though sites don't become available every day. When visiting the island during school vacations, it's important to reserve in advance almost everywhere, but there are many rooms on the island, and it's generally possible to find something during shoulder seasons.

Information and Services

While there are no markets, banks, or other services within Acadia National Park itself, they can be found in nearby **Bar Harbor,** or in the much smaller **Southwest Harbor** on the western side of the island. Southwest Harbor has two **banks,** a small **market,** and a **public library** (338 Main St., Southwest Harbor, 207/244-7065, www.swhplibary.org, 9am-5pm Mon.-Tues. and Thurs.-Fri., 9am-8pm Wed., 9am-1pm Sat) with free **Internet access.**

Getting Around

While a car is convenient for reaching less frequented trailheads, and for early morning trips up Cadillac Mountain, limited parking and congestion during busy months make it worth parking your vehicle and exploring on public transport. Late June-early October, the free, convenient **Island Explorer** (207/667-5796, www.exploreacadia.com) makes it easy to get around Acadia without a car. The fleet of propane-powered buses follows nine fixed routes all over the island and on the Schoodic Peninsula, and covers most of Park Loop Road and all the villages, hotels, campgrounds, and trailheads. While there are automatic stops at many of the most notable destinations, drivers will stop to let you out whenever it's safe. Likewise, many hotels can recommend spots to flag down passing buses, even if there's not an official stop nearby.

To see the only part of Acadia National Park that's on the mainland, take the **Bar Harbor Ferry** (Bar Harbor Inn Pier, 7 Newport Dr., 207/288-2984, www.barharborferry.com, late June-Sept., round-trip tickets $26 adults, $16 children under 12, $75 families) to the tiny town of **Winter Harbor** on the **Schoodic Peninsula.**

Even more so than other destinations in New England, this is an excellent place to have a bicycle, as the slow-moving traffic on Park Loop Road and extensive network of car-free carriage roads are ideal for riders of all skill levels. If you'd like to combine shuttling with bicycling, note that the Island Explorer buses have racks that accommodate up to 6 bikes, but popular routes (particularly afternoon return trips from Jordan Pond) can fill up quickly. For a better chance of catching a ride with your bike, look up the schedule for the **Island Explorer Bicycle Express** bus, which has a trailer that fits 12 bikes.

To take in the main sites in 2.5-3 hours, **Acadia National Park Tours** (207/288-0300, www.acadiatours.com, $30 adults,

$17.50 children 12 and under) runs a bus contracted with the NPS to give sightseeing tours of Park Loop Road. The 2.5-hour narrated trip includes three 15-minute stops to stretch your legs and snap photos, and tickets can be purchased from **Testa's Restaurant** (53 Main St., Bar Harbor, 207/288-3327, 8am-9pm daily).

SIGHTS

★ Cadillac Mountain

At 1,528 feet, this rounded granite mountain is the highest point on the Atlantic Seaboard. The summit is gouged with deep, north-south scratches left by retreating glaciers, and leathery, subalpine plants sprout from the rocky crevices. Even on a summer day, it's easy to imagine the icy winds that howl across the mountain in the winter, stunting spruce and pitch pine trees into gnarled miniatures. In the booming tourist years of the late 19th century, a narrow-gauge cog railway was built to the top of the mountain, much like the railway up Mount Washington, but those tracks are long gone. These days, visitors hike or drive to the summit, where there's a gentle, scenic trail and views across Penobscot Bay.

Watching the sun come up from the peak of Cadillac Mountain is an iconic part of the Acadia National Park experience. In the fall and winter months, it's the first place in the United States to see the sunrise.

The 3.5-mile **Cadillac Mountain Road,** off the Park Loop Road, winds up the mountain, which is how most visitors arrive in the early morning hours, though there are also several walking trails to the summit. The most scenic of these is the **South Ridge Trail,** a 7-mile round-trip hike that starts near Blackwoods Campground and climbs 1,350 feet at a steady, moderate pace. If you're hoping to catch the sunrise after hiking the trail, plan to bring lights and warm clothing, and allow 2-4 hours each way, depending on your hiking speed.

Although it is often crowded, it's possible—especially outside of high season—to find yourself alone on the summit as dawn breaks over Penobscot Bay, lighting up islands and deep forests. A more likely scenario involves clusters of chatting families and several sleepy hikers who started up the peak in the middle of the night. Inevitably, though, the crowd begins to thin as soon as the sky lights up, and one of the nicest times to enjoy the short 0.3-mile **Summit Loop** is when everyone else heads to Bar Harbor for breakfast.

view from Cadillac Mountain

Park Loop Road

Passing headlands, trailheads, beaches, and stunning views of Penobscot Bay, the 27-mile Park Loop Road winds through some of Acadia's finest scenery. Traffic moves one way—clockwise—from the main entrance near Hulls Cove Visitor Center to Jordan Pond, then two-way traffic completes the loop and heads all the way up to the summit of Cadillac Mountain. Alternate entrances, where passes are also checked, are at Sieur de Monts, south of Bar Harbor; Sand Beach; Stanley Brook, by Seal Harbor; and off Route 233, just north of Cadillac Mountain Road. For much of the one-way section, parking is allowed in the right-hand lane, which makes it easy to spot a view and pull over for a closer look. It also means the road is often full of unexpected parked cars, pedestrians, and cyclists (along with the occasional moose), so it's important to take the Park Loop Road at a careful pace. There are also several low bridges that may be a problem for some RVs—the lowest of these is the 10-foot, 4-inch span across the Stanley Brook Entrance.

biking the carriage roads of Acadia National Park

Driving the Park Loop Road

Driving the whole road at once is a nice way to get an overview of the park, but allow plenty of time to stop for picture-taking, tide pooling, walking, and otherwise exploring. From the main entrance at Hulls Cove, the road rises steeply to **Sieur de Monts,** where the small **Wild Gardens of Acadia** re-creates typical habitats found on Mount Desert Island, from heath to coniferous forest, with over 400 species of indigenous plants.

One of the finest places to swim on the whole island is **Sand Beach,** where a parking lot and short walking trail lead to a pleasant stretch of beach and **Great Head.** Along the rocky coast that follows, be sure to stop at **Thunder Hole,** a deep inlet with a submerged cavern that can roar and send water 40 feet into the air when waves hit just right; for the best show, try to visit two hours before high tide.

The horizon opens back up at **Otter Cliff,** a 110-foot granite wall that's one of the tallest coastal headlands this side of Rio de Janeiro. After the turn back inland, the **Jordan Pond House** is a traditional stopping-off point for afternoon tea and hot popovers, with a view of a glacial tarn and distant mountains. Finally, a side road rises through a series of switchbacks to the park's grand attraction, the road to the top of **Cadillac Mountain.**

★ Carriage Roads

Concerned that Mount Desert Island would be destroyed with the introduction of automobiles, John D. Rockefeller Jr. started building a vast network of roads in 1913, determined they would remain closed to motorized traffic. Today, the 47 miles of crushed-stone roads are perfect for walking and biking as well as a favorite destination of cross-country skiers in the winter. The roads curve gently through a forest of birch, beech, and maple trees, over beautifully crafted granite bridges, and through tunnels and arches, perfect for exploration by bicycle. Numbered wooden

Park Loop and Carriage Roads

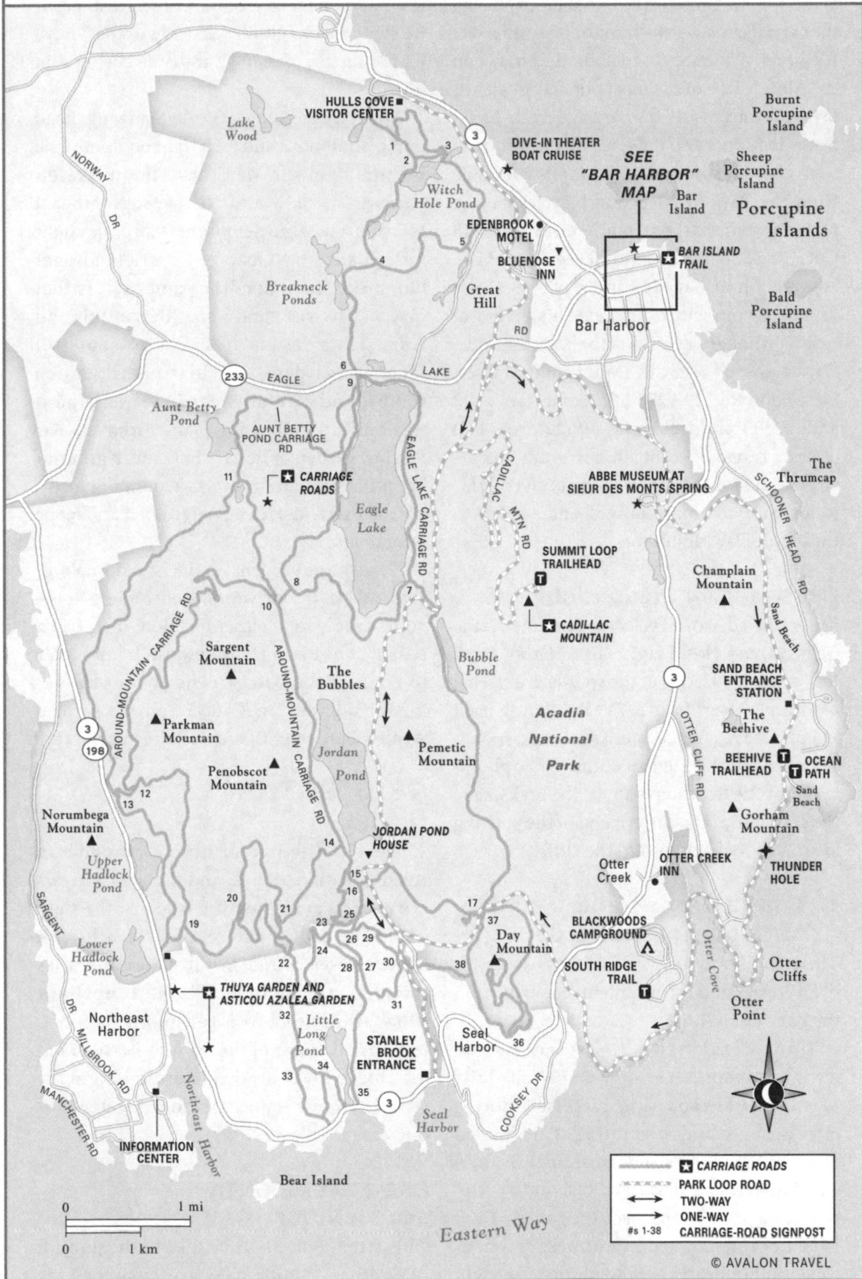

signposts at each intersection make it easy to find your way around. A park map, available at the visitors center, is essential for exploring the carriage roads, which continually intersect with the Park Loop Road and other roads on the island. Two of the most popular **parking areas** for accessing the carriage roads are at Sieur de Monts and the Jordan Pond House.

A *Carriage Road User's Map* is available from the Park Service, and bicycles can be rented in Bar Harbor from **Acadia Bike** (48 Cottage St., 800/526-8615, www.acadiabike.com, $18 half day, $23 full day). To really immerse yourself in Rockefeller's vision of Acadia, though, take an actual carriage ride. **Carriages of Acadia** (Wildwood Stables, Park Loop Rd., 207/276-3622, tours from $22 adults, $14 children 6-12, $9 children 4-5) offers a range of jaunts in horse-drawn carriages, including tours of stone bridges, trips to Jordan Pond for popovers, and a climb to the top of Day Mountain.

Bass Harbor Head Light

Set on the edge of a rocky sea cliff, the scenic **Bass Harbor Head Light** (Bass Harbor Head Rd., off Rte. 102A) is at the southern extreme of Mount Desert Island. The lighthouse itself is a private residence, but it's a scenic spot to catch the morning light. For the classic photograph of the lighthouse above the rocks, take the staircase at the eastern end of the parking lot and shoot back toward the cliffs.

★ Thuya Garden and Asticou Azalea Garden

This pair of tranquil gardens is a must-see for plant lovers and a convenient side trip from the Park Loop Road.

Thuya Garden (Rte. 3, Northeast Harbor, www.gardenpreserve.org, 7am-7pm daily May-Oct., trails and garden accessible during off-season weather permitting, $5 requested donation) is in the semiformal English style, with butterfly gardens, pavilions, and a pretty reflecting pool. To approach the gardens from Park Loop Road, head southwest and continue on Stanley Brook Road, turning right onto Route 3. A sign on the harbor side of Route 3 marks a small parking area opposite the Asticou Terrace Trail, whose great, granite switchbacks climb 0.25 mile to the Thuya Garden gates, passing a trailside shelter and lookout.

For Asticou Azalea Garden parking, head north on Route 3 and turn right on Route 198. Beginning in late May, the **Asticou Azalea Garden** (Rte. 3 and Rte. 198, Northeast Harbor, www.gardenpreserve.org, daylight hours daily May-Oct., free) is a riot of bright blooming rhododendrons and azaleas that give way to irises and water lilies in July and August. Its design celebrates attributes of Japanese gardens—circular paths, garden rooms, and carefully tended views—and it was built in 1956 using plants from the Bar Harbor garden of Beatrix Farrand, a groundbreaking gardener who was a founding member of the American Society of Landscape Architects.

To visit the gardens on the Island Explorer shuttle, ask the driver on Route #5 or Route #6 to drop you at either location, then flag a passing bus to continue onward. It is possible to connect the two gardens on foot by taking the sidewalk on Route 3 from the Asticou Azalea Garden to the Asticou Terrace Trail.

RECREATION

Hiking

There is a lifetime of hiking available in Acadia National Park, and the park rangers are experts at helping you find just the right trail. The following are a few favorites on Mount Desert Island; for all of these hikes, it's essential to bring an **Acadia National Park map** (available for free at all information centers). While most of the trails are easy to follow, the many trails that intersect within the park would be impossible to navigate without a map.

CADILLAC MOUNTAIN SOUTH RIDGE TRAIL

This strenuous, 3.5-mile hike to the summit of Cadillac Mountain departs from the Park

Loop Road near Blackwoods Campground, passing through thick forest, then emerging onto pink granite with gorgeous views of the surrounding mountains. Hike the **South Ridge Trail** as an out-an-back, or continue down the other side, following the 2.2-mile **North Ridge Trail** to a trailhead on the one-way section of the Park Loop Road, where you can flag down an Island Explorer shuttle.

ACADIA MOUNTAIN

For fabulous views to Somes Sound and the ocean, the 1.8-mile round-trip walk up **Acadia Mountain** is a favorite; with 500 feet of elevation gain, it's an easier peak to hike than Cadillac Mountain. The clearly marked parking lot for the Acadia Mountain Trail is on Route 102, 3.1 miles north of Southwest Harbor.

WONDERLAND TRAIL AND SHIP HARBOR TRAIL

The "quiet side" of Mount Desert Island has plenty of hikes as well, and these are often less busy than the eastern trails. On the southern edge of the island, the 1.3-mile round-trip **Ship Harbor Trail** is a good place to walk through scenic coastal forest offering views along a deep inlet, and the 1.5-mile round-trip **Wonderland Trail** is just up the road, with great tide pools on a rocky beach, and a jumble of granite boulders. For the trailheads, drive south from Southwest Harbor and turn left onto Route 102A to follow the coast. The clearly marked Wonderland Trailhead is 4.1 miles past the turnoff onto Route 102A, and the Ship Harbor Trailhead is a short distance farther. Both have parking lots.

BEEHIVE TRAIL

Sure-footed hikers can head up one of the island's "iron rung" trails, where the paths are supplemented by metal bars set directly in the granite. The strenuous **Beehive Trail** is one of these, with exposed, stony sections along the south face of the 520-foot Beehive peak that make the hike seem longer than its 1.6 miles round-trip. To reach the trailhead, leave your car in the Sand Beach parking lot (which is also a stop on the Island Explorer shuttle bus) and cross the Park Loop Road.

Tidepools

Fluctuating water levels strand sea creatures in rocky pools all along the Mount Desert Island coast, but finding them involves careful planning. Pick up a copy of the *Acadia Weekly* or stop by any of the ranger stations for information on the tides, which range between 10 and 15 feet around the island. The best time to spot wildlife is 1.5 hours before and after extreme low tide.

When searching for tidepools, bring a pair of shoes with good traction that you don't mind getting wet and sandy, and pay close attention to water levels, as some rocky outcroppings can be stranded by rising water.

One favorite way to explore is by walking to **Bar Island** from downtown Bar Harbor (follow Bridge St.); for 1.5 hours before and after low tide, a 0.8-mile gravel bar that leads from the end of Bridge Street is exposed. There are walking trails on the tiny island, and the outgoing tide usually leaves some sea stars and crabs in sandy tidepools along the bar.

On the southwest side of the island, **Ship Harbor** and **Wonderland Trails** are also good choices, with plenty of nooks and crannies to trap interesting things in the intertidal zone. **Ranger-led tidepool programs** (www.nps.gov/acad/planyourvisit/calendar.htm) are held at Ship Harbor and Sand Beach in July and August. Drive south from Southwest Harbor and turn left onto Route 102A to find the well-marked Wonderland Trailhead 4.1 miles past the turnoff onto Route 102A, and the Ship Harbor Trailhead a short distance farther. Both have parking lots.

Paddling

Get a harbor seal's view of the island's rugged coast by touring in a sea kayak. A handful of well-regarded operators lead trips open to paddlers of all skill levels. Visit the remoter western side of the island with **National Park Sea Kayak Tours** (39 Cottage St., Bar Harbor, 800/347-0940, www.acadiakayak.com, $48-52), which plans its trips through Western Bay and Blue Hill Bay so you head downwind. Tours last 2.5-3 hours. **Acadia Park Kayak Tours** (Bar Harbor, 207/266-1689, www.acadiaparkkayak.com, $45-60) launches right in downtown Bar Harbor and schedules exciting nighttime stargazing tours. Tours run 3.5-4 hours.

Swimming

There are two beaches in Acadia with summer lifeguards. The water at **Sand Beach,** just off the Park Loop Road, stays in the high 50s throughout the summer, but that's warm enough for plenty of visitors; come here for saltwater, views, and a beach vacation atmosphere. Find (somewhat) warmer water at **Echo Lake Beach,** on the west side of Route 102 between Somesville and Southwest Harbor. The lake floor drops gradually from the shoreline, making this a good choice for families with children.

Boating

If Maine's lobstermen had a celebrity spokesperson, it would have to be Captain John Nicolai of ***Lulu* Lobster Boat Ride** (55 West St., Bar Harbor, 207/963-2341, www.lululobsterboat.com, 2-hour tour $35 adults, $32 seniors and U.S. military, $20 children 6-12), who keeps up a great running patter about the lobstering life (and the life of a lobster). Come April-early June to spot adorable baby seals lolling around near Egg Rock Lighthouse.

By far one of the best things to do on the island with nature-loving kids is head out on a **Dive-In Theater Boat Cruise** (105 Eden St., Bar Harbor, 207/288-3483, www.divered.com, $42 adults, $37 seniors, $32 children 5-11, $16 children under 5) with "Diver Ed." Ed (and his sidekick "mini Ed") suit up in scuba gear equipped with underwater microphones and cameras. The crowd on decks can follow along, then Ed reappears with underwater creatures that kids can touch before sending them back to the ocean floor. The boat departs from the College of the Atlantic, where you can park for free in the North Lot.

A classic style of sailboat along the East Coast is the Friendship sloop, a graceful, gaff-rigged boat that originated in Friendship, Maine, in the late 19th century. Friendship sloop *Surprise*, operated by **Downeast Sailing Adventures** (Cranberry Island Dock, Southwest Harbor, 207/288-2216, www.downeastsail.com, 2-hour sail $50 pp, private sail $125 per hour for up to 6 people), has been sailing the Maine coast since 1964 and offers an intimate, beautiful way to experience it.

FOOD

The Jordan Pond House is the only restaurant in the park proper, but there are places to eat scattered around the island, and some make great destinations unto themselves.

Enjoying popovers and tea on the lawn at ★ **Jordan Pond House** (2928 Park Loop Rd., Seal Harbor, 207/276-3316, www.acadiajordanpondhouse.com, 11am-9pm daily, $7-25) is a classic Acadia experience: The warm, oversized pastries are perfect with melting butter and house-made strawberry jam, and the restaurant has stunning views of the glacial tarn with the granite "bubbles" in the background. The restaurant itself was rebuilt in 1979 and the interior is fairly charmless, but the afternoon tea experience is delightful and should not be missed.

Jordan Pond House doesn't completely own the popover world on Mount Desert Island. While it has no views to speak of, everyone agrees ★ **Common Good Kitchen Café** (19 Clark Point Rd., Southwest Harbor, 207/266-2733, www.commongoodsoupkitchen.org, 7:30am-11am daily May-Oct., by donation) would win hands down in a popover-to-popover showdown. A simple menu of oatmeal, coffee, and popovers is served by volunteers on a sunny patio, with all proceeds going to a meal delivery service for disadvantaged islanders during the winter months.

With a location between Route 102 and Route 3, **Mainely Meat BBQ** (15 Knox Rd., Bar Harbor, 207/288-9200, www.atlanticbrewing.com, 11:30am-8pm daily May-Oct., $11-19) is the convenient and casual on-site restaurant of **Atlantic Brewing Company** (10am-6pm daily May.-Oct., free tastings). Large portions of barbecue basics come with coleslaw, potato salad, and baked beans; ribs are a favorite for many visitors. Tours of the brewery are at 2pm, 3pm, and 4pm daily during peak season, and are capped at 25 people.

A menu of sandwiches, seafood, and pizza served in a family-run diner setting makes the **Quietside Café** (360 Main St., Southwest Harbor, 207/244-9444, 11am-10pm Mon.-Sat., 11am-9pm Sun., hours vary in off-season, $6-12) a mainstay for laid-back lunches, dinners, and ice cream. The butter lobster stew is a favorite, and the blueberry pie à la mode also gets rave reviews.

If this lobster-loving author had to choose just one of the many lobster places to eat in Maine, it would be ★ **Thurston's Lobster Pound** (9 Thurston Rd., Bernard, 207/244-7600, www.thurstonforlobster.com, 11am-9pm daily, $7-30), just outside the park off Route 102 in Bernard. Consider arriving early or late to avoid the line, which can stretch far out the door, but it's worth making an evening trip to the "quiet side" for a traditional lobster dinner or an overstuffed lobster roll (perhaps followed by sunset at the Bass Harbor Head Light). The restaurant has two sides: Line up on the right to order a whole lobster dinner or sit in the main dining area, or head to the left to sit in the bar, where the rest of the menu is available. You can also sit in the bar with a lobster dinner—it just needs to be ordered in that long line. It's not an unpleasant wait, though, as it's fascinating to watch the servers run in and out with great bags of clams and lobsters to drop in the industrial-sized boiler outside. A casual atmosphere, local beers on tap, and views of the pretty harbor make this a true gem.

ACCOMMODATIONS AND CAMPING

A couple of campgrounds are within Acadia National Park's boundaries, but there are no hotels or inns within the park itself; lodging listings here cover places to stay on the "quiet side" that are still convenient to park activities and sights.

$100-150

Completely surrounded by national park land, the **Otter Creek Inn** (47 Otter Creek Dr., 207/288-5151, www.ottercreekmaine.com, May-Oct., $115-180) is a perfect place (almost) for non-campers to stay in Acadia. The rooms and cabins are simple but sufficient, and a continental breakfast is served in the attached market. Some guests have noted the rooms' thin walls, but the price, which drops below $100 outside of peak season, is hard to beat.

$150-250

The self-contained units at ★ **Acadia Cottages** (410 Main St., Southwest Harbor, 207/244-5388, www.acadia-cottages.com, $140-170) are simple and old-fashioned, but well-appointed kitchens, outdoor fire pits, and comfortable mattresses are a cut above other cabins on the island. Wooded grounds make these feel relatively private, and the cottages are walking distance from Southwest Harbor.

Views of Southwest Harbor and a friendly, hospitable atmosphere are the draws at **Clark Point Inn** (109 Clark Point Rd., Southwest Harbor, 207/244-9828, www.clarkpointinn.com, $169-239), which has five guest rooms cheerfully decorated in country style. Three-course breakfasts, afternoon cookies and snacks, and welcoming common spaces make this a favorite with adults-only guests.

Over $250

Perched on the end of Somes Sound, **The Claremont Hotel** (22 Claremont Rd., Southwest Harbor, 207/244-5036, www.theclaremonthotel.com, inn $220-342, cottages $318-444) is an 1884 grande dame that rambles across a six-acre, waterfront property. The 24 rooms in the main house have been recently renovated, but are full of historical charm, their old-fashioned quirks left intact (which is not necessarily to everyone's taste). This feels like a glimpse of old Maine, and for afternoons on the porch, games of croquet on the perfectly trimmed lawn, and sunset drinks at a dockside bar, it remains a wonderful destination.

Camping

Only two of the campgrounds on Mount Desert Island are inside the park proper, set on the southernmost part of Mount Desert Island on opposite sides of Somes Sound. It's worth reserving either of these far in advance for busy times, but each sets aside a small number of non-reservable sites. Call first thing in the morning to check availability. **Blackwoods Campground** is right on Park Loop Road (Rte. 3, 207/288-3274, www.nps.gov/acad, May-Oct. $30, Apr. and Nov. $15, free primitive sites available Dec.-Mar.), adjacent to an Island Explorer shuttle stop and convenient to Bar Harbor and Cadillac Mountain. The 306 forested sites often fill up; the campground can feel busy and noisy during peak season. There's no hookups or showers, but free firewood is provided, and a spot just outside the entrance offers hot, coin-operated showers. Or set up your tent on the "quiet side" at **Seawall Campground** (Rte. 102A, 207/244-3600, www.nps.gov/acad, late May-early Sept., $22-30), 18 miles from Bar Harbor, and a prime location for beautiful sunsets on the shore as well as access to less trafficked hikes and Bass Harbor Head Light. Like Blackwoods, Seawall has no hookups or showers, but it offers coin-operated showers and a general store five minutes away. Many cell phones get no reception on this side of the island.

The privately owned ★ **Mount Desert Campground** (516 Sound Dr., off Rte. 2, 207/244-3710, www.mountdesertcampground.com, late May-early Oct., $39-69) splits the difference, with a superb location at the head of Somes Sound that's the perfect jumping-off point for exploring all of the island. Tent sites roll right up to the water (pricing varies depending on the season and proximity of the site to the water), hookups are available, and the campground rents all kinds of boards and boats for getting in the sound, as well as a launching ramp for private boats. Bathhouses have free hot showers, and the small, convivial "gathering place" offers wireless Internet, snacks, coffee, and ice cream.

There's a summer camp atmosphere at **Hadley's Point Campground** (33 Hadley Point Rd., off Rte. 3, 207/288-4808, www.hadleyspoint.com, mid-May-mid-Oct., tents $27-30, hookups $37-48, cabins $60-80), making it a good choice for families, though tent sites are set close together and don't provide much privacy. A heated swimming pool, coin-operated showers, laundry facilities, a playground, and wireless Internet are available. The campground is on the Island Explorer shuttle bus route for easy access to Bar Harbor, and there's a public beach within easy walking distance. The rustic, tidy cabins have private bathrooms, three beds, and a fire pit (bring your own linens).

SCHOODIC PENINSULA

Facing the eastern side of Mount Desert Island, on the mainland Schoodic Peninsula, this quiet section of Acadia National Park is perfect for exploring when the main site starts getting overcrowded. You can reach the Schoodic Peninsula from the mainland, or hop a ferry from Bar Harbor, then get around by car, bike, or on the Island Explorer.

Schoodic Loop Road

This scenic, 6-mile loop road passes through some of the most spectacular scenery on the Schoodic Peninsula, with a turnout to **Schoodic Point,** the jutting tip of the peninsula, which commands great views of the Atlantic Ocean and Mount Desert Island.

Much of the road is one-way, traveling from Winter Harbor, then looping counter-clockwise toward Birch Harbor, with a series of picnic spots and pullouts, often with short walking trails. RVs are not allowed past Schoodic Woods Campground.

Sports and Recreation

Far less trafficked than the Mount Desert Island section of the park, the **Schoodic Peninsula** is great for **bicycles.** The highlight is the Schoodic Loop Road, but it's possible to explore all day by linking the paved road to the 8.3 miles of **off-road bike trails** that loop through the interior of the peninsula. For a complete circuit, start riding the Schoodic Loop Road at the Schoodic Woods Campground, then return to the starting point on the trails, cutting back west just before the one-way section of the road ends at Bunker Harbor.

Camping

The newest campground in the Acadia National Park network, **Schoodic Woods Campground** (54 Far View Dr., Winter Harbor, 207/288-3338, www.recreation.gov, tents $22-30, RVs $30) has 93 sites, including a section of walk-in-only spots that's great for a secluded night in the woods. There are campfire rings and a dump station, but no showers, and the closest supplies are two miles away in Winter Harbor. The campground is located on the Schoodic Peninsula Island Express loop.

Information

Maps and information are available at the Schoodic Woods Campground **nature center** (54 Far View Dr., Winter Harbor, 207/288-3338, www.recreation.gov, 8am-10pm daily, off-season hours may vary), which is a good first stop for maps and information.

Getting There and Around

The Schoodic Peninsula is south of Route 1, linked to the highway by Route 186, which passes through the community of Winter Harbor.

To reach the Schoodic Peninsula from Mount Desert Island, take the **Bar Harbor Ferry** (Bar Harbor Inn Pier, 7 Newport Dr., 207/288-2984, www.barharborferry.com, late June-Sept., round-trip tickets $26 adults, $16 children under 12, $75 families) to the tiny town of **Winter Harbor** on the **Schoodic Peninsula.**

It's possible to reach all the key sites on the Schoodic Peninsula on the #8 loop of the **Island Explorer** (207/667-5796, www.exploreacadia.com), which connects with the ferry terminal in Winter Harbor.

Bar Harbor

Times have changed since the first 19th-century "rusticators" came to Bar Harbor for society parties with wilderness views. The stunning landscape of forested islands is still there, but the town itself can feel overstuffed and kitschy, an ice cream-fueled frenzy of T-shirt shops and lobster souvenirs. Still, Bar Harbor is the "town" for Mount Desert Island, with restaurants, museums, services, and loads of places to stay. This is the jumping-off point for many boat cruises and activities, and a perfect foil to the quiet trails and mountaintops inside Acadia National Park.

SIGHTS

Step into the world of Mount Desert Island's earliest locals at the **Abbe Museum,** which has two campuses focusing on modern-day and bygone Wabanaki lives. Visit the **Abbe Museum downtown location** (26 Mount Desert St., 207/388-2519, www.abbemuseum.org, 10am-5pm daily May-Oct., call for off-season hours, $8 adults, $4 children 11-17, children under 11 and Native Americans free) for a stronger focus on today's Wabanaki, along with stories from the past and a few artifacts. Located inside Acadia National Park, the **Abbe Museum at Sieur de Monts**

Bar Harbor

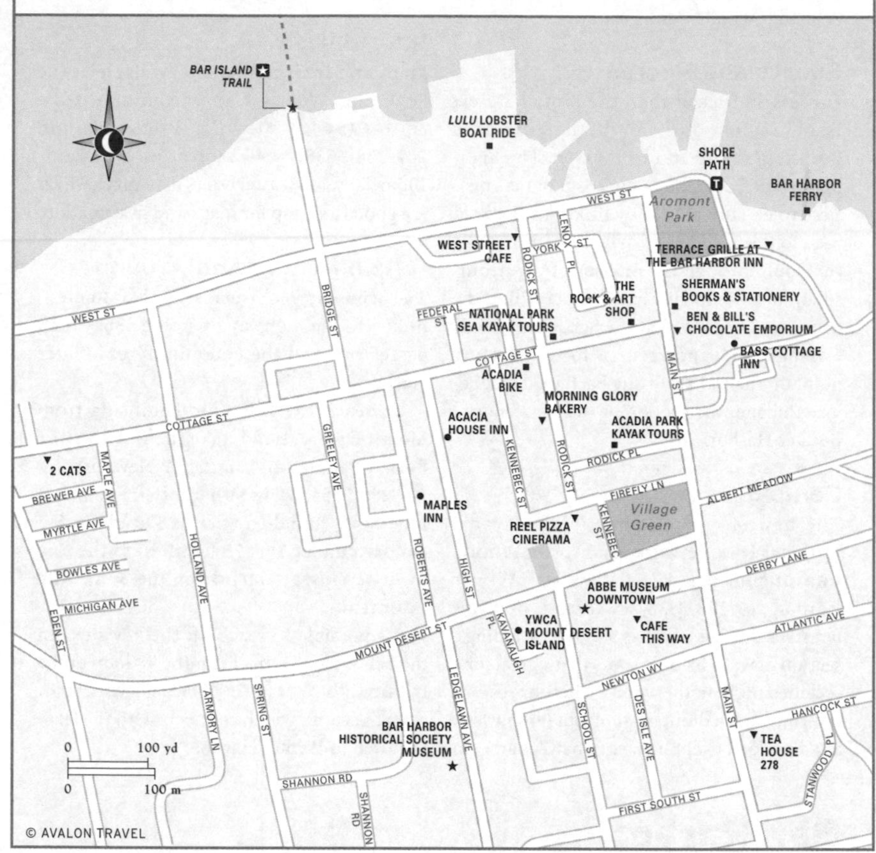

Spring (Sieur de Monts, Park Loop Rd. and Rte. 3, 10am-5pm daily late May-mid-Oct., $3 adults, $1 children 11-17, children under 11 and Native Americans free) is much smaller, but has fascinating artifacts and depictions of archaeological digs in the area. A ticket to Abbe Downtown also includes admission to the Sieur de Monts Spring venue, and the cost of the Abbe Museum at Sieur de Monts Spring ticket is deducted from the admission price if you visit the downtown location as well.

Small but interesting, the **Bar Harbor Historical Society Museum** (33 Ledgelawn Ave., 207/288-3807, www.barharborhistorical.org, 1pm-4pm Mon.-Fri. June-Oct., by appointment in winter, free) has a remarkable collection of images from the town's Gilded Age heyday—think lots of full-length tennis skirts and boating parties. The 1916 building in which it's housed is as intriguing as the contents. It was built by Colonel and Louise Drexel Morell (who appear in stained-glass windows on the 2nd floor). Louise was sister to Saint Katherine Drexel, who gave up her share of the family's considerable fortune to become a missionary in the American Southwest. She was a strong advocate for Native American and African American rights and was canonized in 2000.

Follow the life of a lobster from itsy-bitsy

hatchling to full-grown, claw-snapping adult at **Mount Desert Oceanarium** (1351 Rte. 3, 207/288-5005, www.theoceanarium.com, 9am-5pm Mon.-Sat. mid-May-late Oct., $15 adults, $10 children), a bayside nature center with a lobster hatchery, live seals, and marsh trails. The museum tour, a series of three 30-minute presentations, is a bit long and stationary for active kids, but Audrey and David Mills have been talking lobsters for years and are a great source of info about Maine's marine ecology.

★ Bar Island Trail

There's a 0.8-mile gravel bar leading from downtown to **Bar Island,** a path that's only exposed for 1.5 hours before and after low tide. To reach the **Bar Island Trail,** follow Bridge Street to the end, then keep walking across the sand, watching for the many tide pools that are exposed by the retreating tide. Once you're at the island, a small footpath winds through the trees, to an overlook with great views back toward Bar Harbor.

Or you can catch the ships come in and out of the harbor from Bar Harbor's gentle **Shore Path,** a paved walking trail that stretches 0.75 mile from the town pier to Wayman Lane. It's especially nice as a morning walk, when the harbor begins to flood with early sunshine.

ENTERTAINMENT AND EVENTS

After a day of hiking peaks and ocean swimming, **Reel Pizza Cinerama** (33 Kennebec Pl., 207/288-3811, www.reelpizza.net, pizzas $14-23) beckons; the single-screen theater is stocked with comfy, mismatched couches and counter seats for settling in with pizza and beer. End of June-mid-August, the **Bar Harbor Town Band** (www.barharborband.org) plays hour-long concerts on the Village Green; shows are at 8pm on Monday and Thursday. Another summer tradition is heading to the **Great Room** lounge at the **Bluenose Inn** (90 Eden St., 800/445-4077, www.barharborhotel.com), where pianist Bill Trowell plays laid-back favorites every night at 7pm late May-October.

SHOPPING

Many of the shops in Bar Harbor sell variations on a theme—lobster and moose stuffed animals, T-shirts, Christmas ornaments. Find these along Main Street. Before you go on a wildlife expedition, stop by **Sherman's Books & Stationery** (56 Main

Bar Harbor

St., 207/288-3161, www.shermans.com, 9am-10:30pm daily), which carries an exceptional selection of bird-watching and wildlife guides and trail maps in addition to a full stock of books and cards. Another fun stop is **The Rock & Art Shop** (13 Cottage St., 207/288-4800, www.therockandartshop.com, 9am-8pm daily, hours vary seasonally), which does have both rocks and art, but also stuffed fish, skulls, and other fascinating, odd treasures.

FOOD

In a bright, rambling home on the edge of downtown, ★ **2 Cats** (130 Cottage St., 207/288-2808, www.twocatsbarharbor.com, 7am-1pm daily, $4-9) is a funky gem and the best place for breakfast on the island. Simple breakfast classics like eggs Benedict and blueberry pancakes are done nicely, and the café's fresh, flaky biscuits come with a dreamy side of homemade strawberry butter. Come early to snag a spot on the deep wraparound porch.

For fresh pastries, espresso, and sandwiches on bagels and house-made bread, **Morning Glory Bakery** (39 Rodick St., 207/288-3041, 7am-5pm Mon.-Fri., 8am-5pm Sat.-Sun., $3-12) is a longtime favorite. You'll find a few tables inside (and wireless Internet) at this casual, counter-service spot, but don't miss the back patio on sunny days, where comfy Adirondack chairs and a little garden await.

A menu of classic seafood options, salads, and pasta is surprisingly reasonable at this waterside spot, given that the ★ **Terrace Grille at the Bar Harbor Inn** (7 Newport Dr., 207/288-3351, www.barharborhinn.com, 11:30am-dark daily, $12-30) has the best outdoor seating in town. Tables on the lawn and patio overlook the harbor and Bar Island, making this a great place to catch a sunset over a bowl of chowder or lobster stew. At $39, the lobster bake—a boiled lobster with chowder, clams, mussels, sides, and blueberry pie—is an excellent deal for downtown Bar Harbor.

A quiet atmosphere, simple decor, and a pretty garden make **Tea House 278** (278 Main St., 207/288-2781, www.teahouse278.com, 11am-7pm Wed.-Sat., 11am-5pm Sun. mid-May-early Oct., $3-13) a respite from bustling Bar Harbor, and servers are trained in the traditional preparation of Chinese teas. A small menu of snack food includes tea eggs, sweets, nuts, and egg rolls.

Simple, sunny, and laid-back, **West Street Cafe** (76 West St., 207/288-5242, www.weststreetcafe.com, 11am-9pm daily, $14-30) has a big menu of beef and chicken dinners, pastas, and seafood. The lunch menu of "Earlybird Specials" is served until 6pm, and is an excellent value for an early dinner, especially the $20 lobster plate and $25 lobster dinner with chowder and blueberry pie.

It would be easy to miss **Cafe This Way** (14 Mt. Desert St., 207/288-4483, www.cafethisway.com, 7am-11:30am and 5:30pm-9pm Tues.-Sat., 8am-1pm and 5:30pm-9pm Sun., breakfast $6-12, dinner $19-28), a restaurant with art nouveau flair that's tucked down an alley between School and Main Streets. Breakfast omelets, burritos, and blueberry pancakes get raves, and a menu of grilled seafood and salads is full of fresh flavors. While most Bar Harbor kids' menus are identical lists of fried food and cheesy pasta, Cafe This Way stands out with small plates of grilled meat and seafood served with mashed potatoes and corn on the cob.

Farmers and artisans from around Penobscot Bay attend the **Eden Farmers Market** (YMCA, 21 Park St., 9am-noon Sun. mid-May-Oct.), which is a great place to find farm-fresh Maine blueberries in season.

There are two ice cream greats in downtown Bar Harbor: The granddaddy is **Ben & Bill's Chocolate Emporium** (66 Main St., 207/288-3281, www.benandbills.com, 8:30am-10pm Mon.-Sat., 10am-10pm Sun., $3-7), a candy store with a zillion flavors (including Maine lobster), big servings, and a landmark lobster sculpture out front that's a classic Bar Harbor selfie spot. The scoop-wielding young Turks of the waffle cone scene are at **Mount Desert Ice Cream** (7 Firefly Ln., 207/801-4001, www.mdiic.com, 11am-11:30pm daily June-early Sept., hours vary during shoulder season, $3-7), where flavors range from Maine Sea Salt Caramel to Blueberry Sour Cream and Chocolate Wasabi. Not all the flavors are quite so offbeat—President Barack Obama ordered a scoop of plain ol' coconut while visiting with his family in 2010.

ACCOMMODATIONS

Under $100

Seriously no frills, **Robbins Motel** (Rte. 3, 207/288-4659, www.robbinsmotel.com, May-mid-Oct., $39-69) features the rates of yesteryear and rooms to match. Amenities include cable TV, a pool, and wireless Internet, but the overall experience is pretty bare bones.

Right in the heart of Bar Harbor, the **YWCA Mount Desert Island** (3 Mt. Desert St., 207/288-5008, www.ywcamdi.org, $44, discounts for longer stays) has dorm-like housing for women only, with a large communal kitchen and shared baths. It's generally important to book well in advance to stay here, but worth asking about last-minute availability.

$100-150

The smallest cottages at **Rose Eden Cottages** (864 Rte. 3, 207/288-3038, www.roseeden.com, $55-178) are like nautical dollhouses, with just enough room for a double bed, coffeemaker, and compact bathroom. Each of the 11 cottages is different, some with kitchenettes, second bedrooms, and sitting areas; the largest has a full kitchen. A location on the main road 7.5 miles outside of Bar Harbor means that the sounds of traffic are an issue for some guests, but the owners provide white noise machines, and some units are set farther back on the grassy property, which has a gas grill and laundry facilities for guests. The friendly owners also prepare good-value lobster dinners to go.

One of the best values among the generic digs that line Route 3 is **Edenbrook Motel** (96 Rte. 3, 800/323-7819, www.edenbrookmotelbh.com, $85-130), which is adjacent to the College of the Atlantic and 1.5 miles outside of Bar Harbor. The simple, superclean rooms have air-conditioning, television and coffeemakers, and the Island Explorer shuttle stops right in front, making it a breeze to head into town or the park.

Smart, whitewashed cottages and tidy motel-style rooms look out on Frenchman's Bay at ★ **Edgewater Motel and Cottages** (137 Old Bar Harbor Rd., 207/288-3941, www.edgewaterbarharbor.com, cottages $82-170, motel $86-145), where a broad lawn dotted with Adirondack chairs gives a resort feel to this five-acre property that's 6.5 miles from Bar Harbor. The cottage kitchens are stocked with cooking equipment and coffeemakers, and you can spot harbor seals and porpoises from the outdoor decks.

$150-250

With a location right in downtown Bar Harbor, the ★ **Acacia House Inn** (6 High St., 800/551-5399, www.acaciahouseinn.com, $80-195) is a wonderful value, with sweet, simple decor and great breakfasts cooked with lots of local and organic ingredients, including eggs from the friendly innkeepers' own chickens. All rooms have private bathrooms, organic cotton sheets, and cable TV. The quiet side street the inn sits on lends a surprisingly laid-back atmosphere given the downtown location.

Another downtown gem is the **Maples Inn** (16 Roberts Ave., 207/618-6823, www.maplesinn.com, $119-219), a charming Victorian bed-and-breakfast with seven well-appointed rooms (one has a detached private bath, while others have private in-room baths). One of the owners is a professional chef who prepares personalized menus and afternoon cookies for guests, and the rocking chairs on the shady front porch are an idyllic place to relax after a day of exploring.

Over $250

Stylish and luxurious, the **Bass Cottage Inn** (14 The Field, 207/288-1234, www.basscottage.com, $260-400) strikes a balance between the personal experience of a bed-and-breakfast and the thoughtful service of a top-end hotel. The inn is tucked down a private lane a few minutes' walk from the waterfront, so it feels like a retreat in downtown Bar Harbor. The 1885 building has been carefully restored with a clean, airy design and comfortable common spaces. Breakfast is prepared to order, and evening wine and snacks create a convivial atmosphere.

INFORMATION AND SERVICES

The **city's informative website** (www.barharborinfo.com) has useful walking maps of the town, and there's a **visitors center** (19 Firefly Ln., 207/288-3338, 8am-5pm daily June-Oct.) on the Bar Harbor Green. There are several **banks** and **ATMs** located along Main Street and Cottage Street in downtown, and free wireless Internet is available at **Jesup Public Library** (34 Mt. Desert St., 207/288-4245, www.jesuplibrary.org, 10am-8pm Wed.-Thurs., 10am-5pm Fri.-Sat. and Tues.).

GETTING THERE

Air

It's relatively easy to reach Bar Harbor without wheels of your own. **Cape Air** (a JetBlue affiliate) and **Pen Air** offer direct flights from Boston to **Bar Harbor-Hancock County Airport** (www.bhbairport.com); during its months of operation between June and mid-October, the **Island Explorer** (207/667-5796, www.exploreacadia.com) shuttle has free service from the airport to Bar Harbor. Hertz and Enterprise both offer car rentals at the airport.

Train

The Amtrak **Downeaster** (800/872-7245, www.amtrakdowneaster.com) runs from Boston along the coast as far as Brunswick, where it's possible to rent a car or connect with a twice-daily bus service to Bangor on **Concord Coach Lines** (800/639-3317, www.concordcoachlines.com).

Bus

Greyhound (800/231-2222, www.greyhound.com) offers bus service to Bangor from Brunswick and Portland, as does **Concord Coach Lines** (800/639-3317, www.concordcoachlines.com). From Bangor, **Downeast Transportation** (207/667-5796, www.downeasttrans.org) operates an afternoon bus to Bar Harbor on Monday and Friday from the Concord Coach station. You can also take the **Bar Harbor-Bangor Shuttle** van service (207/479-5911, www.barharborshuttle.com, $45, advance reservation required).

GETTING AROUND

As in the national park, the **Island Explorer** (207/667-5796, www.exploreacadia.com) is the best way to get around Bar Harbor. The **Eden Street route** connects major hotels along Route 3 with the Bar Harbor Green. For the most part, though, the town is easy to walk on foot. Metered parking is available throughout downtown, but the only RV parking is on Main Street south of Park Street on the way out of town.

Down East Maine

A remote stretch of coast with a head-scratcher of a name, "Down East" is the northernmost part of the shore, stretching off toward the wilds of New Brunswick and Nova Scotia. While driving toward the Canadian border might look like "up" to the average landlubber, sailors have a downwind run as they catch the prevailing winds that blow toward Lubec, the easternmost point in the mainland United States—hence the name.

Once you get past Mount Desert Island, the crowds will disappear in your rearview mirror, giving way to long stretches of thick forest and the occasional gas station stocked with hunting and fishing gear. What's the draw? Big tides, big trees, and big country, mostly, or the charm of following Route 1 (U.S. Highway 1), which begins in Key West, Florida, all the way to the edge of the country, and to catch a sunrise from Lubec's candy-striped lighthouse.

LUBEC

★ West Quoddy Head Light

Poking into the Quoddy Narrows that divides Maine and Campobello Island, **Quoddy Head State Park** (973 S. Lubec Rd., 207/733-0911, www.maine.gov/quoddyhead, 9am-sunset daily, visitors center 10am-4pm daily mid-May-mid-Oct., $4 adults, $1 seniors) is the easternmost point of the mainland United States.

Right at the end is one of the most distinctive lighthouses in Maine, **West Quoddy Head Light,** a tower whose bold stripes grace just about every Maine lighthouse calendar that goes to print. In point of fact, the 49-foot-high tower is one of only two in the country painted with red and white stripes—a common practice in Canada as it helps them stand out against the snow. While the tower is not open to the public, the keeper's house has a small museum, and the cliffs are prime viewing for seals, bald eagles, and sometimes even whales.

Setting out from West Quoddy Head Light, **The Coastal Trail** (4-mile round-trip), wraps around the coast, passing **Gulliver's Hole,** a dramatic vertical chasm that drops away through the volcanic rock, and ending at **Carrying Place Cove,** which is ringed by an attractive sandy beach.

Another great walk is the **Bog Trail,** a 0.5-mile spur that passes through swampy terrain that's ideal for pitcher plants, Labrador tea, and baked appleberry, common in the wetlands of northern Canada, but a rarity south of the border.

Other Sights

Smoked fish and salted fish used to be big business on this isolated coast, but when Lubec's local herring processor closed its doors in 1991, it was the last one in the state. Now, the **McCurdy Smokehouse Museum** (50 S. Water St., 207/733-2197, www.lubeclandmarks.org, 10am-4pm daily, free) preserves that fishy history with displays that show how deeply the lives of Mainers has been entwined with the health of fisheries and global fish markets.

Food

The sign at **Frank's Dockside Restaurant** (24 Water St., 207/733-4484, www.franks-dockside.net, 11am-7pm Thurs.-Tues., $11-25)

West Quoddy Head Light

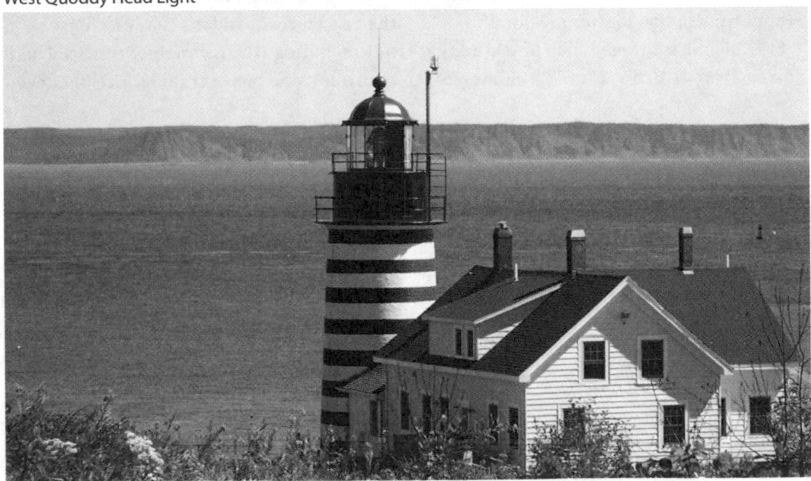

announces that all are welcome, including "suits, clam boots, whackies, khakis, squid snaggers, carpet baggers, deadheads & dreads," and that's about the size of it. Just about everyone in town ends up at Frank's, where classic Maine seafood shares a menu with steaks, burgers, and sandwiches. Prepare to wait, but as the sign suggests, there's some appealing people-watching to do while you're there.

Find locally brewed craft beer and better-than-average pub food at **Lubec Brewing Company** (41 S. Water St., 207/733-4555, 2pm-8:30pm Thurs.-Sun., kitchen opens at 5pm, $7-13), which serves darn-good flatbreads topped with local ingredients like fiddleheads, the crisp green tips of ostrich ferns. On nights with live music, or when the open mic night is happening, this is *the* place to be in Lubec.

Accommodations and Camping

Once a sardine factory, the fishy tang is long gone from ★ **The Inn on the Wharf** (69 Johnson St., 207/733-4400, www.theinnonthewharf.com, $90-180), a motel-style property with tidy apartments and suites. Decks jut out toward the ocean, and there are kitchen and laundry facilities on-site—shared for the suites, with private versions in the apartments. There's an attached restaurant that's an appealing option for fresh seafood.

Full of old-fashioned charm, **Peacock House Bed & Breakfast** (27 Sumer St., 207/733-2403, www.peacockhouse.com, $115-165) is beautifully cared for and welcoming, with plenty of common spaces to relax with a book after a day of exploring. The owners keep the dining room stocked with fresh coffee and homemade cookies, and the breakfasts are outstanding.

With a mix of tent sites and spots for rigs, the main attraction at **Sunset Point RV Park** (37 Sunset Rd., 207/733-2272, www.sunsetpointrvpark.com, $30-40) is the view across Johnson Bay. As the name suggests, sunsets are a specialty, but it's worth rising early to catch the morning sun. If you want to pick up some lobsters or crabs for a boil, the owners have a propane cooker and pots for guest use, and the campground has a small beach for launching kayaks or canoes. The open layout offers little privacy.

Information

A small kiosk on Washington Street is stocked with maps and brochures, and other information is available from Lubec's **Town Hall Office** (40 School St., 207/733-2341, www.townoflubec.com).

Getting There

Lubec is a four-hour drive from Portland, and that's if you take the interstate, following I-95 and I-295 through the interior forest. Opt for the coastal road, and it's closer to five hours, not including (the inevitable) traffic. There is currently no bus or train service to Lubec.

Inland Maine

BAXTER STATE PARK

Mount Katahdin, the 5,267-foot peak at the heart of this thickly forested park, is more than Maine's tallest mountain. It's the northern terminus of the epic, 2,200-mile Appalachian Trail, a summit whose bare, rocky ridges have long inspired adventurers and dreamers alike. In the Abenaki language of the Penobscot people, Katahdin means "The Greatest Mountain," and it looms large in Maine history. After trying (unsuccessfully) to reach the summit in 1846, Henry David Thoreau wrote about Katahdin's terrible beauty, which generations since have often compared to New Hampshire's Mount Washington. While the New Hampshire peak cranes more than 1,000 feet above Katahdin, this is the wilder of the two—no trains or roads to the summit, just a winding, rocky footpath that makes every visitor earn their views.

Visiting the Park

Day-trippers fill up the lots in Baxter State Park, and while it's a wonderful outing, spending a night within the park's boundaries is the best way to experience the silence and scale of the Maine woods. Above all, it's worth planning ahead, as the park is extremely popular. Some forethought means you can book your parking spot in advance and sleep in one of the sought-after campsites with views to the peak. There is no cell phone service in the park.

ENTRANCES AND VISITORS CENTER

There are two entrances to Baxter State Park. If you're traveling from Millinocket, you'll follow Baxter Park Road to the **Togue Pond Gate,** which is by far the most visited, while the northernmost traffic is funneled through **Matagamon Gate** on Grand Lake Road. While information and maps are available at both gates, the only **visitors center** is on the road to Togue Pond Gate—a full 42-mile drive from the other entrance. Hours vary, call the **reservation line** for details (207/723-5140). Admission to the park is $15.

RESERVATIONS

Unless you're feeling lucky, camping reservations are essential, though last-minute arrivals can sometimes be accommodated at the gate. In addition to the **reservation line** (207/723-5140), it's also possible to reserve parking spots in the day-use lot online, ensuring you won't be turned away upon arrival (www.baxterstatepark.org).

Hiking

While Mount Katahdin is the heart of the park, there are 200 miles of trail to explore, including day hikes that are far easier than the strenuous trek to the summit. One favorite is the **Daicey Pond Nature Trail,** beginning at the Daicey Pond Campground. The 1.4-mile loop circles the pond and coincides with the Appalachian Trail. For catching a moose in its favorite hangout, head to **Sandy Stream Pond,** a 0.5 mile hike from **Roaring Brook Campground.** To give the moose the space and quiet they need, access to the pond is limited: Arrive early at Togue Pond Gate for one of the first come, first served **"moose passes"** that are dispensed to hikers.

★ MOUNT KATAHDIN

If you're planning to take on **Mount Katahdin,** it's essential to be prepared—hikers have died on the peak, and many more have been rescued in operations that endanger park staff. The mountain can be summited as a super-strenuous 10.4-mile round-trip day hike from the **Katahdin Stream Campground,** climbing the Hunt Trail to great views of **Katahdin Stream Falls,** across a series of open ledges, and up a final stretch to the summit, which you might share with some celebrating thru-hikers who've just arrived after months on the trail. Plan between 8 and 12 hours for the round-trip hike.

There are a handful of ways on and off the mountain, and one great option is to make an overnight trip by hiking in to the backcountry **Chimney Pond Campground,** spending the night, then rising early for the summit trek. For experienced, strong hikers who don't mind some exposure and scrambling, walking the spectacular **Knife Edge** is surely New England's most dramatic stretch of "trail." The rocky ridge loops southeast from the summit of Katahdin, then curves back north toward Chimney Pond. It's impassible in bad weather, as it's just a walk across the bare rocks, and the tiring descent to Chimney Pond means climbing from one mammoth boulder to the next.

Food

There are no services or restaurants within the park. Approaching from the south, the last services are at the **North Woods Trading Post** (1605 Baxter State Park Rd., Millinocket, 207/723-4326, www.nwoodstradingpost.com, hours vary, call first), which sells gas, camping fuel, and basic groceries. All other restaurants are located in Millinocket, a 30-minute drive from the southern park entrance.

Perfect for a big breakfast before heading into the woods (or a hearty, post-trail lunch), the **Appalachian Trail Café** (210 Penobscot Ave., Millinocket, 207/723-6720, 5am-4pm daily, $4-12) is a favorite for hefty servings and a friendly, small-town atmosphere. This is the land of eggs and fresh hash, juicy burgers, and enormous mounds of fries, but the luxurious bread pudding wins raves.

Blessed with a great location on Millinocket Lake, **River Drivers Restaurant & Pub** (New England Outdoor Center, 30 Twin Pines Rd., Millinocket, 207/723-4528, www.neoc.com, 11am-9pm Mon.-Fri., 7am-9pm Sat.-Sun., $12-34) serves a more grown-up version of post-trail food, from haddock roulade to ribeye steak. Breakfasts are hearty burritos and egg sandwiches, and the Friday fish fry dinner special is a blast (and an excellent deal).

With pizza, beer, and the occasional bonfire out back, **Boatman's Bar & Grill** (10 Medway Rd., Millinocket, 207/723-3200, www.threeriversfun.com, 4pm-11pm daily, reduced hours in spring and fall, call first, $7-18) is run by a local river guiding operation, and if you can catch them while they're serving food, it's a rowdy way to ease back into civilization.

Mount Katahdin trail marker

Accommodations and Camping

Anyone not ready to set up camp can find digs in the town of Millinocket, 30 minutes south of the park's Togue Pond Gate entrance.

With rustic, basic rooms and a friendly, summer camp-like atmosphere, the **Appalachian Trail Lodge** (33 Penobscot Ave., Millinocket, 207/723-4321, www.appalachiantraillodge.com, bunks $25, shared-bath private rooms $35-55, en suite $95-105) is the place to rub shoulders with the thru-hiker set. If you just want to clean up on your way out of the park, the lodge offers showers for $5 a pop, including towels and soap.

In an old-fashioned house downtown, the **Young House Bed and Breakfast** (193 Central St., Millinocket, 207/723-5452, www.theyounghousebnb.com, $115-135) is cozy and friendly, and the big front porch is great for relaxing after a day of exploring. The hosts serve a big and hearty breakfast, and they're able to pack lighter breakfasts to go if you're rising early for a hike.

CAMPING

There are 11 campgrounds within the park, both front-country and backcountry versions. None of the campgrounds has treated water, so visitors must bring their own, or come prepared to treat the natural sources. Toilets are outhouses, and there are no showers. Visitors with a camping reservation must check in at the gate before 8:30pm. To book campgrounds, call the park's **reservation line** (207/723-5140). Campground tent sites are $32, backcountry spots are $21, and rustic cabins are available from $57 (bring your own bedding).

On the northern end of the park, **South Branch Pond Campground** is among the prettiest, with some lean-tos right at the edge of the water. The pond is excellent for swimming, and the campground lends out canoes and kayaks for a nominal $1 fee.

Earn an excellent night's sleep on your way to **Chimney Pond Campground,** a 3.2-mile walk from the Roaring Brook trailhead. Campers have wonderful views across the pond to the Katahdin summit, and it's perfectly placed for hiking the peak.

Information and Services

The **Baxter State Park** website (www.baxterstatepark.com) covers all the basics, with maps and reservation information, but hard copies of maps are available to purchase at the park entrances. There are several banks with ATMs on the main drag in Millinocket, as well as a handful of grocery stores, including **Hannaford Supermarket** (843 Central St., 207/723-8047, 7am-9pm Mon.-Sat., 8am-8pm Sun.).

Getting There

Baxter State Park is accessed by Baxter State Park Road, and the closest town is Millinocket; the park is 1.5 hours from Bangor. There is no public transit to the park.

Background

The Landscape

Covering just over 70,000 square miles, the six states that make up New England could be squeezed into North Dakota. Within that area, however, the region contains a multitude of landforms and habitats. The coastline runs from the sandy beaches then hardens into the granite headlands that splinter the coasts of New Hampshire and Maine. In between, the land rolls through fertile farms, deep pine forests, and mountains covered with old-growth oaks and maples, but the human geography is just as varied, but Maine, Vermont, and New Hampshire among the most rural states in America.

GEOLOGY

New England's weather can seem defined by extremes—steamy summers, freezing winters—but modern-day temperatures have nothing on the fire and ice that first shaped the region. Fire came first, in the form of molten lava that bubbled up violently from the earth's core starting some half a billion years ago. At that time, most of what would become New England was underwater, just off the leading edge of a proto-continent known as Laurentia. As the tectonic plate that held Laurentia moved slowly eastward, it folded under its neighbor and melted, causing an upwelling of magma beneath the surface of the ocean. That upwelling formed a chain of island peaks off the coast of the continent. Eventually, the land mass of Laurentia crashed into these islands during the Ordovician era around 440 million years ago, pushing them up into what is now the Taconic Mountains of far western Massachusetts and southwestern Vermont.

About 100 million years later, in the Devonian era, Laurentia crashed into a subcontinent called Avalonia to the south, rolling over the smaller landmass to create more upwelling of magma. At the same time, the continent collided with its neighboring continent Baltica—the precursor to Europe—causing the ocean floor between them to buckle and fold back over the continent. The combination created the Berkshire Hills, which have backbones of volcanic rock topped with older "basement rock" of gneiss and quartz that once sat on the floor of the sea. The ocean, meanwhile, was squeezed out over Avalonia to create a vast delta of sedimentary rock that now forms the bulk of eastern Connecticut, Rhode Island, and eastern Massachusetts. A bit later, during the Triassic period, a great fault opened up in the middle of the region, creating a 100-mile-long rift valley that would later become the Connecticut River.

At this time, all of the world's continents briefly joined together in a giant landmass called Pangaea. The commingling didn't last long, however. By the Jurassic era, 200 million years ago, the continents were again on the move, and North America and Europe split up to create the Atlantic Ocean. Around the same time, a field of volcanoes opened up in the area of New Hampshire, spewing hot magma in plutons and ring dikes to form the massive granite peaks of the White Mountains. The Whites are the youngest mountains in the region, and the last evidence of volcanic activity, which ended about 130 million years ago. New England's fiery birth was followed by a long period of erosion and settling before fire handed off its job to ice, and the last great ice age began.

Temperatures began to cool gradually about a million years ago. By the Pleistocene

Previous: visiting Acadia National Park at Bar Harbor; the famous Vermont Country Store.

era, some 80,000 years ago (a mere hiccup in geological time), a massive ice sheet began to build up over Canada, more than a mile thick in places. As it did, the sheer weight of the ice caused it to flow southward in a huge glacier, leveling the earth, gouging out valleys, and breaking off mountaintops as it flowed. The farthest glacier reached all the way down to New York City, depositing millions of tons of rocks in a terminal moraine that today forms Long Island, Block Island, Martha's Vineyard, and Nantucket. (Since so much of the earth's water was tied up in ice, sea levels were lower, and all of those islands were once mountains.) A more intense, but less far-reaching, glacier left a second terminal moraine around 20,000 years ago to form the northern spur of Long Island, along with Cape Cod and the Elizabeth Islands.

While the terminal moraines are the most visible result of the glaciers, all of New England was definitively shaped by the ice, which rolled and ebbed across the region for thousands of years. Mountains were pushed over and broken, so that even today in the Whites, the northern slopes offer more gradual ascents for hikers, while the steep southern faces present grueling challenges for rock climbers. Mountaintops and boulders, meanwhile, were picked up by the advancing ice sheet and often deposited miles away from their origins. In some places, these huge glacial boulders, also known as erratics, have become local landmarks, such as the 5,000-ton Madison Boulder in New Hampshire's lake region, the largest erratic in New England.

The glaciers changed the land in other ways as well. As it advanced, the ice sheet pushed away the softer substrate, exposing the harder, immovable granite. In many places, lone mountains called "monadnocks" remain to lord over the surrounding plains. The most famous of these is Mount Monadnock in southern New Hampshire, whose views as far as Boston on a clear day make it an irresistible magnet for hikers.

The last of the glaciers retreated by 15,000 years ago. In their wake, however, the Connecticut River Valley was closed off and filled with meltwater to create a huge inland lake named Lake Hitchcock. For more than 2,000 years, the lake stretched 200 miles from Connecticut to Vermont's Northeast Kingdom. (It was probably quite a sight, colored the striking azure blue of the glacial lakes that now grace Canada and Patagonia.) The layers of silt deposited by the drying lake helped create the rich, loamy soil of Massachusetts's Pioneer Valley—which stands in marked contrast to the rocky, glacial till of the rest of New England. Another glacial lake, Lake Vermont, formed to the west of New England, and drained into modern-day Lake Champlain.

CLIMATE

A location on the dividing line between the cold polar air mass to the north and the warm tropical air currents from the south brings dramatic temperature changes and some climatic surprises. Add a constant supply of moisture from the ocean, and you are guaranteed an unpredictable mix. Despite the regular precipitation, however, New England sees more than its fair share of clear days, when the sky is blue and you can see for miles from the peak of Mount Washington. Moreover, the moderating effect of the warm Gulf Stream ocean currents ensures that New England doesn't see the same extremes of temperature that affect the middle part of the country. Both summers and winters are comparatively mild—though it might not seem that way in the middle of a frigid January cold snap or the sweltering dog days of August.

The coldest part of the year is in January, when the region's temperature averages 21 degrees Fahrenheit, but it can easily sink to 20 below zero for days at a time. That snap of extreme cold is often followed by a period of milder weather known as the January thaw, which sets the stage for February, when the region sees the bulk of its snowfall. The number and severity of winter storms vary with the wind. The hardest hitters come when a zone of low pressure sits off to the east, bringing cold, wet air counterclockwise down from the Maritimes to form a classic nor'easter. Spend much time in the region, and you are bound to hear about the famous Blizzard of '78, a nor'easter that buried areas in up to five feet of snow and caused rises in tides of up to 15 feet.

When winter begins to taper off, the frozen ground melts into a soggy mess, what folks in New Hampshire and Vermont call "mud season." Not that early spring is entirely charmless—this is the time to visit if you want to taste maple syrup fresh from the evaporating pan. The cycle of cold nights and warming days might make for hazardous back road driving, but it's what drives the pump-like action of maple trees, drawing sap into the trunk where it's collected in buckets or tubes.

Following mud season, the world breaks into bloom, with wildflowers poking up from the barren forest floor and lilacs scenting the air. Before you know it, though, summer arrives in all its sweltering glory. Average temperatures only reach 70 degrees, though, so the hottest stretches of 90-degree weather rarely last longer than a few weeks at a time.

Finally, after Labor Day comes many New Englanders' favorite season—fall. The days are crisp but not yet cold, and the air is often dry and pleasantly breezy. As the green chlorophyll leeches out of the tree leaves, it leaves the spectacular reds, oranges, and yellows of New England's star attraction—its famed fall foliage. Not that this season is without its perils, however. While hurricanes aren't as common here as in southern states, every few years in August or September a humdinger speeds over the Gulf Stream and crashes into the coast.

Of course, the foregoing describes a typical year in central New England. Keep in mind that the region stretches 400 miles from the Canadian border to Long Island Sound—the same distance roughly between New York City and Columbia, South Carolina. Correspondingly, temperatures can vary as much as 20 degrees or more from north to south. Adventurer Ranulph Fiennes once noted that "there's no bad weather, only inappropriate clothing"—and that's certainly true in New England.

Plants and Animals

PLANTS

Accustomed to the denuded European landscape, early settlers to New England were bowled over by the deep forests full of timber and game as far as the eye could see. Soaring pines, stretching oaks, and stately chestnuts filled the new land, prompting superlatives in many a Puritan's travel journal. While centuries of lumbering have taken their toll on the woods of the region, much of New England is still appealingly forested. In recent decades, abandoned farms have been reclaimed by the trees, creating even more wooded landscape. And unlike clear-cut land out West, the North Woods of Maine have for centuries been home to sustainable logging practices that have kept the wilderness wild.

Trees

The forests of the region have been divided into zones: a hemlock-white pine-transition hardwood forest in central and western Massachusetts, southern New Hampshire, Vermont, and Maine; and a spruce-northern hardwood forest in northern New Hampshire, Vermont, and Maine. Of course, this greatly simplifies the landscape, but it does provide a good working framework for understanding local fauna.

The forests of southern and eastern New England are abundant with red oak, scarlet oak, hickory, maple, birch, and beech. Along the coast, larger trees give way to hardy pitch pine and scrub oak more suited to salty air and sandy soils.

Central New England has a good mix of broadleaf trees and evergreens. The forest here is dominated by oak and maple—including the famous sugar maple that yields the region's annual crop of maple syrup every spring. The most common tree is the white oak, named for the color of its bark and prized both for its straight timber and wide-spreading canopy. Arguably, this is the best region for leaf-peeping, since maples produce some of the brightest colors, while oaks are slower to turn, extending the season and providing a range of colors at any one time. White pine becomes more common as you travel north, where it can frequently be found growing on reclaimed agricultural land. That tree has smoother bark than its cousin, the red or Norway pine; to tell them apart, count the needles: White pines grow in clusters of five (W-H-I-T-E), while red grow in clusters of three (R-E-D). Other trees growing in this region include hemlock and ash.

In the Great North Woods of northern New England, the deciduous trees eventually give way to endless tracts of boreal forest, consisting of spruce and fir. Unlike pines, whose needles grow in clusters, spruce and fir needles are directly attached to the stem. These coniferous trees are better suited to the short growing season and nutrient-poor soil of Maine, and they've provided an endless source of timber for shipbuilding and fuel. Mixed in with the evergreens is an understory of hardy broadleaf trees, including aspen, beech, and birch. Few New England scenes are more iconic than a stand of white-and-black-striped birch trees in winter, or festooned with canary yellow leaves in fall.

Flowers

The jewel of the New England woodlands is the delicate lady slipper, a member of the orchid family that grows in wetland areas and gets its name from down-curving flowers that resemble women's shoes. The translucent flower, found in pink, white, and yellow varieties, is notoriously difficult to transplant or grow, since it relies on companionable fungi in the soil for its nutrients. If you are lucky enough to see one in the wild, take care not to disturb it, since some species are endangered.

Much more common, if no less beloved by naturalists, is trillium, so called because of its distinctive three-petal flowers. The flower grows in many colors throughout the New England woods, including bright white, deep red, and the particularly beautiful painted trillium, which sports a magenta center tapering off to white edges. One of the first flowers to bloom in April is the bloodroot, which carpets the ground with clusters of white flowers. As the season progresses, other wildflowers visible in the fields and meadows include the fuchsia-colored, anemone-like New England aster; orange clusters of wood poppy; wild bleeding heart; bright-red wild columbine with its distinctive tubelike flowers; and the ghostly sharp-lobed hepatica, which grows in deep woods and swamps and features eight blue-purple petals arranged around an explosion of fine white stamens.

ANIMALS

The best opportunities for seeing wildlife in New England occur along the water. Many animal tours offer chances to see seals and seabirds off the New England coast. Even inland, you are much more apt to stumble upon a moose or black bear from the vantage of a kayak than hiking along a trail. Most of New England's fauna is harmless—the charismatic megafauna of the western states has been mostly hunted to extinction, despite dubious reports of mountain lion sightings that crop up periodically. Even so, use caution when approaching a moose or black bear—especially if its young are in the area. You don't want to get on the receiving end of antlers or claws.

Land Mammals

Up to 6 feet tall, 9 feet long, and with an antler span of 5.5 feet, a bull moose often startles those unprepared for just how *big* it is. It has the air of a gentle giant, but moose can certainly be dangerous, and it's worth giving them a very wide berth, whether you're on foot or in a vehicle. Signs all over New Hampshire and Maine warn drivers about "moose crossings," since countless times each season a car is totaled after hitting one of the 1,500-pound beasts. Take care when driving in those regions at dawn and dusk, especially during the spring and summer months, when the giant animals range widely in search of food. In the autumn, moose retreat to the deep forest, where they are much harder to encounter.

Not quite as imposing are the white-tailed deer that are common in the backwoods. In some places, deer are so plentiful that they have even become a nuisance. The last documented specimen of mountain lion—also called catamount—was taken in Maine in 1938, and the giant cat is generally accepted to be extinct from the region. Every year, however, there are some 100 supposed mountain lion sightings; among the most credible was one in 2009 by a Fish and Game employee outside Concord, New Hampshire. None of the sightings to date, however, have yielded any tracks, fur, or scat that would definitely confirm that mountain lions are back in the region, leaving their fabled existence on par with UFOs or Sasquatch. The smaller bobcat, however, is quite commonly sighted, often mistaken for a small dog. And in far northern New Hampshire and Maine, hikers even occasionally spot the slightly bigger lynx, identifiable by the pointed tufts on its ears.

Not to be confused with the more aggressive grizzlies of western states, the timid black bear is a reclusive tree-inhabiting animal that can sometimes be seen exploring garbage dumps of northern New England at night. Red foxes inhabit both open fields and mixed forest, while the larger gray fox prefers the deep woods of southern New England. Coyotes are more apt to be heard than seen. And gray wolves make only rare visits to northern Maine from their habitat in Canada. No breeding populations currently exist in the region.

The most common mammals, by far, are rodents, which exist in multitudes throughout the six-state area. Gray and red squirrels, chipmunks, and raccoons are familiar sights in both suburban and rural areas. Wilderness locales are home to skunk, marten, mink, ermine, seven types of shrew, three types of mole, mouse, rabbit (including cottontail, jackrabbit, and snowshoe hare), flying squirrel, beaver, vole, otter, and porcupine. One of the lesser-known rodents is the fisher, a large mink-like animal known for its vicious temperament that has become more common in past years. In addition to smaller rodents, it's been known to prey on raccoons, porcupines, and even small deer. Finally, New England is home to nine different species of bat, which roost in abandoned barns and trees, and can often be heard screeching at night in search of insects to eat.

Reptiles and Amphibians

The streams and ponds of New England thrive with frogs, toads, turtles, and other amphibians. Anyone who has camped near standing water in New England is familiar with the deep-throated sound of the bullfrog, which can seem like competing bullhorns at night as the eight-inch-long males puff up their resonant throat sacks in competition for mates. An even more cherished sound in parts of New England is the high-pitched chirping of the spring peeper frogs, which heralds the beginning of warm weather. A dozen different types of turtle inhabit the area; most common is the painted turtle, which sports colorful mosaics of yellow stripes on its neck and shell. More rare is the common snapping turtle, which can live up to its name if provoked. Wetland areas and swamps are also home to many species of salamander, which outdo each other with arresting shades of red, blue, and yellow spots and stripes. The most striking of all is the Day-Glo orange body of the red-spotted newt.

The most typically encountered snake is the common garter snake, a black-and-green-striped snake that is ubiquitous throughout the region, even on offshore islands. Aquatic habitats are inhabited by ribbon snakes and the large northern water snake, which is harmless despite its aggressive demeanor. Woodland habitats are home to the eastern hognose, ringneck, and milk snake, among other species. The venomous timber rattler is rare, existing only in remote, isolated pockets. Thankfully, rattlers tend to shun areas inhabited by humans—and hibernate a full eight months out of the year, from September to April. If hiking in the backcountry, be wary of their distinctive dry rattling sound.

Insects and Arachnids

Ask any New Englander about native insects, and he's apt to immediately identify two: the mosquito and the blackfly. The former find ample breeding ground in the wetlands of the region and feast annually on the blood of hikers and beachgoers. The blackfly is, if anything, even more vicious. Thankfully it is more limited in both range and time period, thriving only in the late spring and early summer in northern New England. The other regional scourge is the gypsy moth, which every 10 years or so appears in the form of thousands of tiny caterpillars that decimate the foliage. Many attempts have been made to curtail the menace, including introduction of a parasitic fly that eats gypsy moth larvae. Unfortunately, the fly also eats larvae of the luna moth, a delicate greenish moth with a wingspan of up to five inches that is New England's most beautiful insect. In recent years, the luna moth has made a comeback, and it is a more common nighttime visitor in the region.

Due to all the variations in habitat, New England is a rich breeding ground for creepy-crawlies, most of which are absolutely harmless. There are more spiders in New York and New England than there are bird species in all of North America. The only poisonous variety, however, is the black widow, which is recognizable by its jet-black body with a broken red hourglass on its abdomen. These spiders are extremely rare, and while their venom is a neurotoxin, only about 1 percent of bites end in death.

Sealife

Early settlers to New England were overwhelmed by its rich fishing stocks. It's also a popular stopover for migratory whale species, including humpback, fin, mike, and North American right whales. Other visitors to New England's oceans include white-sided and bottlenose dolphins, harbor porpoises, leatherback sea turtles, and grey seals, which are especially prevalent on Cape Cod in summer. Despite the filming of *Jaws* on Martha's Vineyard, great white sharks are rare; boaters and divers are more apt to see a harmless basking shark, which likes to feed on surface plankton.

Closer to shore, the most popular animal is the New England clam, of which there are two varieties: the soft-shelled clam or steamer, and the hard-shelled clam or quahog, which is also known as littleneck or cherrystone depending on its size, and is generally found in deeper waters. Tidepoolers are apt to encounter both rock crabs and hermit crabs, along with sea stars, urchins, and periwinkle snails. New England's most famous sea dweller, the lobster, inhabits deep, rocky underwater coves all over the eastern United States. Contrary to popular belief, they are usually brown, blue, or green in color, and only turn red upon cooking. The biggest lobster ever caught was over two feet long and weighed almost 40 pounds.

Birds

New England's location on the Atlantic Flyway from Canada makes the region prime bird-watching country. The region is home to some 200 species of birds that breed, winter, or live year-round in the region. Some common species like the black-and-white chickadee, blue jay, and cardinal are spotted commonly in both rural and urban areas. Others, like the elusive wood thrush, inhabit only the deep forest, where its liquid warblings reward hikers with a mellifluous serenade. Likewise, the ghostly "laughing" of the common loon is a regular sound on lakes in Maine, where the bird also graces the state license plate.

Efforts have been made to preserve the coastal breeding grounds of 30 species of shorebirds, including plovers, sandpipers, and oystercatchers. Seabirds that are commonly seen near land include sea ducks, gulls, terns, and cormorants, while farther out to sea, boaters can spy petrels, puffins, jaegers, and auks. Many of the area's wildlife refuges have active communities of bird-watchers who track recurring species on both land and water.

ENVIRONMENTAL ISSUES

The biggest issue in parts of New England is urban sprawl, caused by the region's increasing population coupled with a lack of developable space.

At the same time, species that were once seen only in the deep woods have been increasingly spotted in the suburbs, where foxes, coyotes, fishers and other animals have posed a threat to family pets. In northern New England, it is not urban sprawl but tourist development that has threatened the wide tracts of open space. With the decline of the timber industry, which generally had a good relationship with outdoorsmen and environmentalists, residents of Maine and New Hampshire have looked for new sources of income from the tourist trade, and struck uneasy bargains to preserve some tracts of land while developing others for roads and resorts.

New England's regulatory economy has ensured that much of the area enjoys clean air and water, even as efforts have been made to clean up the pollution of the mills and factories that boosted the economy in the 20th century. Isolated chemical factories and power plants continue to cause problems in some specific areas. One of the country's first nuclear power plants was commissioned at Seabrook in coastal New Hampshire, which became the site of a protest in the late 1970s that sparked the national movement against nuclear power. Despite that protest and periodic rumblings by environmentalists, Seabrook is still an operating power plant and a tourist destination to boot.

One of the most contentious ongoing issues in the region is the controversy over how to effectively manage the coastal stock of fish and shellfish. Rampant overfishing had decimated the stock of cod, flounder, and other groundfish species by the mid-1980s. At that point, the federal government seized the entire region's fisheries and began a desperate bid to restore populations using quotas and periodic bans. While the effort has been successful at restoring some species, such as haddock and bluefish, others still languish at severely reduced levels—with cod even less plentiful than in the 1980s. And along with the fish stocks, many fishermen have languished as well. Tensions between fishermen and regulators have led to angry protests and outright flouting of quotas, as well as disputes over the numbers used by scientists and environmentalists to justify them. At this point, the two sides are cooperating in an uneasy peace. And while New England's fishing community is nowhere near as vibrant as it once was, it has nevertheless managed to survive.

History

EARLY HISTORY

Native Inhabitants

Hard on the heels of the last glaciers retreating northward, humans began to move into the area now known as New England about 10,000 years ago. By the time European settlers began to poke around the coasts, there were already anywhere from 25,000 to 100,000 Native Americans inhabiting the region. Unlike the Iroquois Confederacy in upstate New York or the mighty Algonquain tribes of Quebec, however, most New England tribes were small and unaffiliated with larger governments, making them both extremely mobile and vulnerable to manipulation and extermination by European settlers.

In southern New England, tribes such as Wampanoags, Narragansetts, and Pequots grew corn, beans, squash, tobacco, and other crops to supplement hunting and fishing. Most extraordinary is the way the groups cultivated the forest itself, burning wide swaths to get rid of the undergrowth and allow parklike land that was ideal for hunting game and harvesting berries—it was said that in the colonial era, it was possible to ride a horse through the forest at a full gallop, as the trees were widely spaced and free of brush. Anyone who's tried to thwack their way up a trail-less mountain knows that times have changed.

North of the Saco River in Maine, tribes such as the Micmacs, Abenakis, Penobscots, and Passamaquoddys were more nomadic by nature, subsisting entirely on hunting, fishing, and gathering. In the spring, they made use of fishing grounds on the coast for shellfish and birds; in the summer, they moved inland to ply the rivers with birch-bark canoes in search of larger game like elk and moose.

Early Visitors

Viking long ships might have sailed the rivers of New England as early as the 11th century; if they did, however, they left no traces to definitively prove it. Instead, legends of Norse visitors from Iceland and Greenland remain just that—legends—supplemented only by highly dubious reports of "discoveries" of Viking rune stones in areas of the Maine and Massachusetts coast. As late as the 1950s, however, historians also doubted that Vikings had colonized Newfoundland—until a settlement was unearthed there in 1960. This settlement was thought by many to be Vinland, a land mentioned in the Viking sagas as founded by Erik the Red west of Greenland. Others, however, have noted that grapes don't grow that far north and instead surmise that the actual location of Vinland is farther south in New England, perhaps on Cape Cod or in the area of Popham Beach, Maine.

The first documented European mariner to spy the New England coast was Giovanni da Verrazano, who sailed up from New York in 1524 and explored Block Island and Narragansett Bay, and rounded Cape Cod to Maine before returning to France. The first settlements in the region, however, didn't come until a half century later, when Bartholomew Gosnold formed a small outpost southeast of Cape Cod (which he named) on what is now Cuttyhunk Island in 1602. That settlement was abandoned, however, when the explorers returned home in the winter.

To the north, French captain Samuel de Champlain sailed along the coast of Maine and New Hampshire, gave his name to Lake Champlain in 1609, and founded several small fur-trading settlements north of New England along the St. Lawrence River in Quebec. Other settlements followed down the coast, mostly small French and English fishing villages on the islands and peninsulas of the Maine coast, which were also abandoned when holds were filled with enough salt cod or beaver pelts to make a profitable crossing back to Europe.

Pilgrims and Puritans

In the end, it was spiritual rather than commercial desires that established a European foothold in New England. After years of fighting between Catholics and Protestants in England, Queen Elizabeth I passed the Act of Uniformity in 1559, making it illegal not to attend official Church of England services. Throughout the next few decades, an increasingly persecuted minority of separatists advocated a break with the official church. After several of their leaders were executed, the separatists fled to Holland in 1608. But the Netherlands alliance with England against Spain meant that persecutions continued there, and the separatists eventually hatched a plan to journey beyond the reach of the Queen by founding a colony in the New World. They received backing from the Virginia Company to set sail aboard the *Mayflower* in 1620.

The Pilgrims, as they would later be called, originally intended to set sail for the nascent colony of Jamestown in Virginia. Blown off course, however, they landed in what is now Plymouth, Massachusetts, outside of the jurisdiction of their backers. Before disembarking, they drafted the Mayflower Compact, a hastily arranged document that established the government of their new Plymouth Bay Colony. The primary author of the document, Rev. William Bradford, became governor. Of the 102 passengers aboard ship, almost half of them were not Pilgrims at all, but adventurers who hitched a ride to the New World, including the capable Captain Myles Standish, hired to be military commander for the colony. His skills were not initially needed, since Wampanoag people under their chief, Massasoit, were friendly to the new colonists, helping them plant corn and hunt. The cold and scarcity of resources took a harsh toll on the colonists, however, causing more than half to die in the first year. By the time Bradford called for celebration of the first Thanksgiving in the fall of 1621, he was thanking God not only for the bountiful harvest, but also for the colony's very survival.

The real settlement of New England didn't begin until the arrival a decade later of another band of religious seekers, the Puritans. Unlike the Pilgrims, the Puritans did not advocate a complete break from the Church of England. Rather, they believed the church could be reformed from within by returning to a stricter interpretation of the Bible and dispensing with many of the trappings and rituals that the Church of England had picked up from Catholicism. An increasingly dictatorial King Charles I, however, abolished parliament and began cracking down on any religion that didn't subscribe to the official tenets of the Church of England. In 1629, settlers under minister and orator John Winthrop decided to leave England altogether to found a new "shining city on a hill" that would serve as a paragon of morality to the rest of the world.

The following year, 1630, a full complement of eleven ships carrying more than 1,000 passengers landed on the tip of Cape Cod near Provincetown. Finding scarce resources, they moved on to land on another small peninsula that the Native Americans called Shawmut, or "Land of Living Waters," due to the teeming schools of fish in its harbor. There they resolved to found their city, which they named Boston, after the city in East Anglia where many of them had originated.

Boston wasn't exactly uninhabited—the first English settler of the peninsula was Rev. William Blackstone, a hermit who came there alone around 1623 and built a house by a freshwater spring beneath three hills he called the "trimountain." But he was happy to sell the land to the new arrivals, and Winthrop and his crew declared Boston the new capital of the Massachusetts Bay Colony in 1632. Immediately, they proceeded to enforce a strict moral code that imposed death as punishment for crimes ranging from taking the Lord's name in vain to talking back to your parents. From that center, colonists quickly spread out north and west to form dozens of new cities and towns, fueled by waves of thousands of new immigrants over the next decade. The settlement of New England had officially begun.

More Settlers Arrive

At the same time that the Pilgrims and Puritans were settling Massachusetts, a hardier band of hunters and woodsmen finally established beachheads in northern New England. English aristocrat Sir Ferdinando Gorges established the Council of New England in 1621 and began making land grants and sending groups to hunt and fish the area. An early grant called the Laconia Company spanned the Merrimack and Kennebec Rivers north of Massachusetts Bay. While the company was disbanded a few years later, many of the settlers remained, forming a loose confederation of parishes in what would later become New Hampshire and Maine. In 1624, they sent the first shipment of white pine to England, starting what would later become a rich trade in lumber for ships' masts.

Meanwhile, as the persecuted Puritans became themselves persecutors, religious "heretics" left Massachusetts Bay in search of new colonies where they could themselves worship in peace. A Salem minister named Roger Williams, an early proponent of the separation of church and state, was found guilty of heresy and banished in 1636. Traveling southwest, Williams and a few followers settled on Narragansett Bay and founded the city of Providence. A few years later, the English crown dispensed an official charter for the Colony of Rhode Island. From the beginning, this colony proved infinitely more tolerant than others in New England, recognizing freedom of religion, freedom of speech, and other rights we recognize today. Williams also enjoyed friendly relations with the Narragansett people, who were proving more hostile to the Puritans.

Soon after Williams founded Providence, another group led by Anne Hutchinson, a teacher who believed that inspiration came directly from God without need of a church, came to Rhode Island to found the city of Portsmouth in 1638. Some of these settlers later moved farther south to found the city of Newport. At the same time, Hutchinson's fellow iconoclast, Rev. John Wheelwright, took his congregation north to settle in what would later become New Hampshire. Originally founding the town of Strawbery Banke (which would later become Portsmouth), Wheelwright was kept moving by the expanding boundaries of Massachusetts Bay Colony, founding the towns of Exeter, New Hampshire, and eventually Wells, Maine.

Finally, several factions within the Puritan sect split off to form their own colonies. Discouraged with the strictures on government participation in Boston, Rev. Thomas Hooker set out to found Hartford along the Connecticut River in 1636, and set up a more inclusive form of government in which every male member of the church could vote. Farther south, a pair of English merchants formed the colony of New Haven in 1638. The two colonies merged to form the colony of Connecticut in 1662.

King Philip's War

Unlike in Rhode Island, however, the new inhabitants of Connecticut didn't enjoy friendly relations with the native inhabitants. Soon after Europeans made incursions into the area, a pair of British merchants were found killed by Pequots on the Connecticut River. That incident set off an escalation that led to raids and reprisals on both sides and eventually a plan by the settlers to wipe out their native enemies. The Pequot War of 1637 was in reality a quick business, in which 130 settlers together with Narragansett and Monhegan allies wiped out the entire Pequot tribe.

That war was only a skirmish in the upcoming Indian Wars that would completely alter the colonies in the next few decades. After the deaths of Plymouth Colony's Governor Bradford and his Native American ally Massasoit, tensions between settlers and the Wampanoag people along the Massachusetts-Rhode Island border began to simmer. They eventually boiled over in 1675 in what would become known as King Philip's

War. The conflict began when colonists arrested Massasoit's son Alexander on spurious charges. During the march he was forced to make to Plymouth, he sickened and died. Seeing the writing on the wall, Massasoit's younger son Metacomet (whom the colonists called Philip) launched a preemptive raid on the Massachusetts town of Swansea. The colonists counterattacked by invading the Wampanoag camp at Mount Hope in Bristol, forcing 1,500 of the Wampanoag to escape by floating rafts across the river.

The war that followed drew together many of the Native American tribes in New England in a last-gasp attempt to push back English expansion. Despite burning Providence and many other towns in the yearlong campaign, the Native Americans were defeated by their lack of supplies and treachery among warring tribes as much by the English force of arms. By the time peace was signed in 1676, Philip and more than 5,000 Native Americans had been killed, with many more sold into slavery; on the English side, 500 colonists had been killed. After the war, many area tribes were permanently relocated to Rhode Island's South County, near the town of Charlestown, effectively spelling an end to autonomous Native American presence in southern New England in all but the far western frontier of Massachusetts.

The Colonial Period

Following King Philip's War, the residents of New England continued to expand and prosper. At the same time, England's Puritan-friendly regent, Oliver Cromwell, was replaced by the restoration of the monarchy under James II, who saw an opportunity to bring greater control over the bustling colonies. The ill-fated Dominion of New England, as the new government was called, only lasted two years—in some sense, however, it began the conflict between England and its colonies that would end in war a century later. In 1685, James named Sir Edmund Andros as viceroy over Massachusetts, Plymouth, Rhode Island, Connecticut, New Hampshire, and New York. After he levied taxes on the colonists, however, there were widespread protests against the arrangement. When William and Mary overthrew James in England's "Glorious Revolution," New Englanders also overthrew Andros, returning the colonies to direct rule by governors (including a united Massachusetts colony when Massachusetts Bay and Plymouth merged in 1691).

For the next century, New England's seemingly limitless supply of natural resources ensured that the region soon became a major player in the world's economy. In Massachusetts, religious zealotry gave way to a new dominion—not of God, but of cod. The "almighty codfish" was full of meat, could be salted and dried for long voyages by sea, and filled the waters around Massachusetts Bay by the schoolful. Based on the rich trade in the fish, along with lumber, furs, and rum, Boston became the third-busiest port in the entire British Empire by the early 1700s (after London and Bristol). By mid-century, Boston and other New England ports, including Portsmouth, Salem, Newport, and New Haven bustled with ships bringing in coffee, tea, textiles, and luxury goods imported from England.

Along with the benefits of being a colony, however, New Englanders had to shoulder the responsibilities. In 1754, when the mother country became embroiled in a dispute with France over trading rights in the Ohio Valley, they were drawn into the fray. The resulting conflict, known as the French and Indian Wars, was fought in New York, Pennsylvania, and Quebec and eventually spelled the end of French claims to North America when it was resolved by the Treaty of Paris in 1763. However, many New Englanders fought in the conflict, and its aftermath was strongly felt in the region. The war directly benefited traders in Maine, New Hampshire, and the burgeoning territory of Vermont by eliminating competition from the French in the fur and lumber trade. Because the Native Americans allied with the French, the war also caused the defeat of the Algonquain and Mohawk tribes who badgered inhabitants in western and northern New England with periodic raids. The most important effect of the war, however, was economic. Saddled with debt from its mammoth military undertakings, England decided to levy taxes on the colonies to pay for the war. After all, the Crown reasoned, hadn't the colonies been the ones who benefited the most from the defeat of the French and Native American tribes? Unfortunately for England, the colonists saw things differently.

WAR AND REVOLUTION

Early Rumblings

A decade before the outbreak of the Revolutionary War, few American colonists even considered independence from the Crown. Relations with England, while sometimes tense, were mutually beneficial for both parties, giving the colonies protection and a ready market for their goods, and giving England a source of raw materials and income. Millions of words have been spilled over what caused the quick snowball to war, but it essentially comes down to one: taxes. Even before the French and Indian Wars, the colonies had been curtailed by the Navigation Acts, which prohibited the colonies from trading directly with countries other than England (smugglers carrying molasses from the West Indies, of course, had no trouble circumventing these laws). Another provision that reserved any tree over 24 inches in diameter for use of the Royal Navy rankled northern woodsmen. But it wasn't until after the war that the British crown levied a tax directly on the colonies in the form of a stamp required for licenses and legal services. The protests against the Stamp Act of 1765 were surprising to the Crown in their vehemence—throughout the colonies, citizens fumed about taxation without representation in parliament and took to the streets to show their displeasure. The furor was so great that the law was repealed a year later.

In its place, however, Parliament enacted a series of laws that were even more damaging to the maritime trade of New England—the Townshend Acts of 1767. Named for the British Chancellor of the Exchequer, these acts levied a series of taxes on imports, including paint, lead, paper, and, most outrageous to the colonists, tea. Merchants in Boston immediately responded with boycotts of British products, convincing their colleagues in New York and Philadelphia to follow suit. In 1770, Bostonians even sent thousands of pounds of British goods back to England on a ship owned by rich merchant John Hancock. Eventually Parliament capitulated and repealed all of the taxes except one—the tax on tea.

In this atmosphere of heightened animosity, a simple argument about the payment of a barber's bill by a British soldier led to a confrontation with an angry mob that left five colonists dead. An early instance of the use of propaganda, the act was dubbed the Boston Massacre by Whig politician Samuel Adams and used to stir up resentment against British troops quartered in the city. Adams was a member of the Sons of Liberty, a radical underground group of activists who sought greater autonomy from the British Empire. After the incident, he scored a victory when British troops were removed from Boston. However, the incident did little to advance the cause of independence. The troops were defended by Adams's cousin, John Adams, and acquitted of murder at trial.

Elsewhere in New England, incidents displayed the growing sentiment of the colonists against the British. In Connecticut, the local branch of the Sons of Liberty succeeded in deposing the colonial governor and installing one of their own members, Jonathan Trumbull, in his place. In 1772, a group of patriots in Providence, Rhode Island, raided and set fire to the Royal Navy ship *Gaspee*. But the road to revolution was by no means sure until the night of December 16, 1773. That year, Parliament passed an even more stringent law on the importation of tea. Colonists fought back by dressing up as Native Americans and stealing aboard three British ships at night. There they dumped 90,000 pounds of tea into the harbor in an act provocatively dubbed the Boston Tea Party.

British retribution was swift. Upon receiving word of the act, Parliament passed the so-called Intolerable Acts, which set up a blockade of Boston Harbor and consolidated more power over the colonies in the hands of the Crown. Sympathetic governments in Rhode Island and Connecticut delivered aid to the residents of Boston during the blockade. The following September, delegates from all of the 13 colonies met in Philadelphia in the first Continental Congress and escalated the tension, declaring their opposition to *any* British law enacted without representation from the colonies. The stage was set for war.

From Lexington to Bunker Hill

After the Boston Tea Party, Sam Adams, John Hancock, and the rest of the Sons of Liberty moved quickly to prepare for the eventuality of armed conflict. With Hancock's money and Adams's fiery rhetoric, they were able to prepare colonists around the region both physically and emotionally for battle. They also began caching arms and ammunition in various storehouses close to Boston, and helped to organize militia companies that could join battle at a moment's notice—calling them "minutemen." For their part, the British army commanders knew that they were severely outnumbered by the colonists if war should break out, and realized that their best hope lay in seizing the caches of arms before the general populace could be whipped up to a war frenzy.

When British troops finally marched out from Boston to capture the ammunition stores in Concord in April 1775, setting alight the Revolutionary War, it wasn't the first time they had tried. A few months earlier, British general Thomas Gage had ordered a scouting party north of Boston in Marblehead to search for munitions stored in Salem. Despite a tense standoff with local minutemen, that day ended without bloodshed. In response, the Sons of Liberty set up an elaborate warning system to alert the populace should the troops try again. Two months later, on April 16, riders including Paul Revere had already raised the alarm ahead of the 700 soldiers that marched out of the city en route to Concord. At the time, Adams and Hancock were staying with a friend in the nearby town of Lexington. They hastily organized a show of resistance before themselves escaping back to Boston. By the time an advance party of 300 men under Major John Pitcairn marched into town, they found several-dozen minutemen and veterans of the French and Indian Wars ranged on the town common warily clutching their muskets. Someone fired a shot, and by the time the smoke cleared eight colonists were dead. The first battle of the American Revolution took only a few moments, but it was only the beginning of a day of increasing bloodshed.

The Battle of Lexington was followed by another battle a few hours later in Concord. There several hundred minutemen had assembled from neighboring towns on the hill overlooking the North Bridge. Seeing smoke rising in the distance, some feared that the British had set fire to the town, and began to march toward the bridge. A British platoon opened fire, killing two of the colonists. As word spread of the casualties to their comrades, minutemen by the thousands began taking up positions behind houses, trees, and stone walls between Concord and Boston. After destroying what they could of the colonial munitions (most had been hidden before British arrival), the tired British began marching back to Boston through a deathtrap. In the long march back, 73 British soldiers were killed, with another 200 wounded or missing. On the rebels' side, only 49 were dead, with 44 wounded or missing. The implications of the battles, however, went far beyond the actual results. By proving that they could stand up to the most fearsome army in the world and win, the patriots recruited many other colonists to their cause.

Their next test occurred two months later at the Battle of Bunker Hill. The battles at Concord and Lexington were mere skirmishes compared to the bloody confrontation that occurred in Charlestown on June 17, 1775. A few days before, the newly formed Continental

Army took up a position in Charlestown, just across the harbor from the British forces in Boston. For General Gage that was too close, and he decided it was time to knock out the colonials once and for all. Due to a last-minute change in plans, the so-called Battle of Bunker Hill actually occurred on Breed's Hill. Before the battle began, the colonists' commanding officer, Colonel William Prescott, noting that his troops were low on powder, supposedly made the famous statement: "Don't fire until you see the whites of their eyes." The ensuing battle succeeded in dislodging the colonists, forcing them to retreat back to Cambridge. But like Concord and Lexington, the battle showed the force of the inexperienced Americans over the superior fighting power of the British. In three assaults up the hill, the British lost more than 1,000 men, while the colonists only lost half that. Perhaps wishing to even the score, the British commander Howe later said that the death of popular American general Joseph Warren was equal to the death of 500 patriots. Nevertheless, the Battle of Bunker Hill showed the world that the American Revolution was definitely *on*.

The Siege of Boston

After Lexington, Concord, and Bunker Hill, the British Army found itself in a precarious position, holed up in Boston surrounded on all sides by countryside teeming with hostile colonists. Schooled by the French and Indian War, many of the colonists were skilled fighters and military strategists. One of them, George Washington, now assumed command of the Continental Army in Cambridge, Massachusetts, in June 1775, and began a tense standoff with British general William Howe, who had replaced Gage as commander. Not eager to risk another bloody battle like the one at Breed's Hill, Washington commissioned Boston bookseller Henry Knox to drag 59 cannons to Boston from Fort Ticonderoga in upstate New York, which had been captured the previous month by a force of Massachusetts and Connecticut soldiers under the command of Benedict Arnold, and Ethan Allen's Green Mountain Boys of Vermont. Knox arrived at the fort in December 1775, and took more than two months to complete the journey across more than 200 miles of snow and ice. On the night of March 14, 1776, Washington's forces quietly dragged the cannons to the top of Dorchester Heights, where they commanded a deadly vantage over the city. A few days later, on March 17, 1776, Gage evacuated the city by ship to Nova Scotia without firing a shot—leaving much of New England free from British forces on land.

Battles Across New England

After the early successes in Massachusetts, the most important engagements of the war continued in the southern and mid-Atlantic states. However, over the next seven years of fighting, each of the New England states except New Hampshire would see blood spilled on its soil. Before he famously turned traitor, Benedict Arnold took his troops through the woods of northern Maine in an ill-fated attempt to attack Quebec City on December 31, 1776. Undone by hunger and smallpox, Arnold was defeated in his attacks on the city. Most of the fighting that did occur in Maine itself happened off its coast. Even before Dorchester Heights, ships of the fledgling Maine navy captured the loyalist sloop *Margaretta* off the coast of Machias in what is regarded as the first naval battle of the war. In response, the British sent a fleet of six ships to bombard Falmouth, Maine (outside Portland), nearly burning the entire town to the ground. Later in the war, in 1779, Maine saw one of the conflict's largest naval battles, when more than 20 colonial ships attacked a fleet of British warships stationed in Castine in Penobscot Bay. The campaign ended in disaster, however, in part due to the foolhardy actions of one Paul Revere, who was captaining a ship at the end of the Continental line and broke ranks, foiling the fighting formation. In one of the ironies of history, the commanding officer of the British fleet was General Peleg Wadsworth, the grandfather of Henry Wadsworth Longfellow, who years later would immortalize Revere in his poem "The Midnight Ride of Paul Revere."

Amazingly, even after the Battle of Bunker Hill, colonists were still split on the virtues of declaring full independence from Great Britain. First among the colonies, Rhode Island bit the bullet to declare itself a sovereign nation on May 4, 1776, two months before the Declaration of Independence. The state did not fare well in the ensuing war, however. In December 1776, after a sea battle off the coast of Point Judith, the British fleet blockaded Narragansett Bay, trapping much of the Continental Navy in Providence. For the next few years, they occupied Newport, terrorizing the populace and bringing shipping to a standstill. In 1778, Washington attempted to liberate the port by sending Massachusetts general John Sullivan and 8,000 men to attack. However, a fierce storm prevented allied French ships from landing with reinforcements, and Sullivan was unable to take the city. The British remained in Newport until 1779, when they voluntarily withdrew to aid fighting farther south.

Of all the New England states, the hardest hit during the war was Connecticut, which was an enticing target due to its rich industrial base and its proximity to British strongholds in New York. In April 1777, 2,000 British troops sacked Danbury, defeating 200 militiamen (again led by Arnold) and destroying vast amounts of tents, food, and other stores that would have come in handy for Washington when he was freezing in Valley Forge that winter. To help the troops survive, Connecticut governor Jonathan Trumbull helped round up cattle and drive them down to Pennsylvania for Washington's troops. Over the next few years, Connecticut was pillaged several more times, at Greenwich, New Haven, Fairfield, and Norwalk. The most devastating attack took place in September 1781, toward the end of the war, in Groton and New London. There Benedict Arnold—now fighting on the British side—took 2,000 troops and decimated the forts in both cities, burning much of New London to the ground.

The Battle of Bennington

When the war broke out, Vermont wasn't even yet an independent colony. Much of what would become Vermont was occupied by settlers in land grants from the governor of New Hampshire, who fought competing claims against encroachers from New York. In January 1777, an assembly declared Vermont an independent republic, initially called New Connecticut. (Even so, neither Vermont nor Maine were among the original 13 states. Vermont wasn't admitted into the union until 1791. Maine remained part of Massachusetts until 1820.) The fledgling republic gained new legitimacy a few months later during the Battle of Bennington, which proved to be the first battle in which the colonials beat the British in combat. The crucial victory led to the turning point of the war a few months later at Saratoga, and helped convince France and Spain to intervene on the side of the Americans.

The battle took place in two parts in August 1777, when, fresh from victory at Fort Ticonderoga, British general John "Gentleman Johnnie" Burgoyne was marching down the Hudson River Valley to meet up with British troops from New York. The plan was to cut off New England from receiving supplies and reinforcements from the rest of the colonies, thereby setting it up for easy capture. Feeling the pinch of lack of supplies himself, however, the general made a fatal mistake when he decided along the way to capture a large storehouse of food and munitions in the small town of Bennington, Vermont.

Under command of German colonel Friedrich Baum, Burgoyne sent some 500 troops—including several hundred of the dread Hessian mercenaries—to raid the town. Unbeknownst to him, however, American colonel John Stark had previously set off from New Hampshire with 1,500 troops of his own. On August 16, Stark took the battle to the enemy, swarming up a ridge along the Wolloomsac River to attack Baum's position. In a short but bloody battle, his militiamen killed Baum and captured many of his men.

Certain of victory, the excited Americans began pursuing the enemy, when they were surprised by a relief column of another 600 Hessian soldiers under Lieutenant Colonel Heinrich von Breymann. Stark was pushed to retreat back toward Bennington. The tide of the battle turned once more, however, with the arrival of Colonel Seth Warner and 300 of his Green Mountain Boys, who had marched from Manchester, Vermont. In the second engagement, the Germans were routed and fled to the Hudson, while the Americans claimed victory.

The battle was an embarrassing defeat for Burgoyne, whose army suffered some 900 casualties to Stark's 70. At a time in the war when American morale was low, the battle also proved once again that backcountry farmers and militiamen could defeat the most disciplined troops of Europe. Just two months later, with his forces depleted and short on provisions, Gentleman Johnnie was forced to surrender at Saratoga.

War's Aftermath

As any history book will tell you, the Revolutionary War was won not by the Americans, but by the French and Spanish, who entered the war after the victory at Saratoga and blockaded American ports against the British, swinging the tide of battle in favor of the newly independent republic. In 1783, a full decade after the Boston Tea Party, British general Charles Cornwallis surrendered at Yorktown, leaving 13 newly independent states. Like most of the rest of the country, New England was in rough shape by war's end, hamstrung by debt from the massive amounts of money needed for the war effort. Because of its unique position, however, it was able to bounce back more quickly than other areas. Since most of the fighting had occurred farther south, New England ended up with its infrastructure intact—in fact, once its blockades were lifted, it even benefited from the lack of competition from New York and Philadelphia, which were still embroiled in fighting. Initially the region felt the loss of the Tory upper class, which fled once fighting started. In their place, however, rose a new American merchant class who had made fortunes in previous decades smuggling molasses and financing privateers against the British. They quickly assumed control of New England and set about doing what Yankees did best—making money.

19TH CENTURY

The Federal Period

No longer hampered by British strictures on trade, this new class of bourgeoisie was soon sending ships to the far ports of the world in search of trading goods. For a time, the city of Salem was the richest in the world from its cornering of the trade in pepper with the East Indies. Whaling ships from Nantucket and New Bedford sailed the South Seas in search of whales, growing rich themselves off the trade in spermaceti oil and whalebone corsets, which were all the rage on the Continent. Boston, meanwhile, remained the largest port in the United States, vying for supremacy with Philadelphia and New York in the years after the Revolution. All over the region, signs of the new wealth appeared in the form of stunning brick mansions and elm-lined streets.

Politically, New England also vied with the other colonial powerhouses—Pennsylvania, New York, and Virginia—to determine the path of the new country. Many prominent Bostonians, including John Hancock, Samuel Adams, and John Adams, were part of the founding fathers at the Constitutional Convention in 1789, where they pushed for a stronger federal government to raise armies, tax the populace, and set trade policies. The Federalists, as they came to be known, had their strongholds in New England and New York, and reached their apogee when John Adams was elected president in 1796. A national backlash, however, soon found the southern agrarians in power under Virginian Thomas Jefferson, and the influence of the Federalists waned. Many New England states opposed the War of 1812 with Britain and abstained from sending troops (thankfully, a push to secede and form the New England Confederacy around this time failed). Over the ensuing decades, the Federalists competed with the more agrarian southern states to push policies that would benefit the manufacturers that became the underpinning of the northern economy.

Industrialization

The "dark satanic mills" (as English Romantic poet William Blake called them) sprouted throughout England in the 18th century, transforming Europe into an industrialized economy. North America was slow to follow suit until after the war. In 1790, a British engineer named Samuel Slater was called in to rebuild the machinery at Moses Brown's textile mill in Pawtucket, Rhode Island. The innovations he put in place transformed the factory and began a trend that would blanket New England with mills at a record pace over the next few decades. In many ways the region was ideally suited for manufacturing, with many fast-running rivers to generate power, a steady supply of raw materials thanks to the shipping trade, and poor soil for the competing industry of farming. In short order, cities were transformed into mill towns with sturdy brick factories and blocks of rowhouses for low-wage workers who toiled endlessly spinning and weaving textiles. Along with the textile mills, other cities in the region won fame for production of consumer goods, including shoes, paper, and clocks. A Scottish visitor to New England in the 1830s declared Niagara Falls and the mill town of Lowell, Massachusetts, the two greatest wonders of America.

As the New England factories churned out the goods, a new class of aristocrats emerged on Beacon Hill and in the seaport and manufacturing towns. Called Brahmins, they were known as much for their wealth as for their enlightened sense of noblesse oblige. Many were educated at universities such as Harvard, Yale, and Brown, which became national centers of learning and spawned scholars and researchers in natural science. Espousing Yankee values of thrift and modesty, many of the Brahmins eschewed more garish forms of wealth for the prestige of philanthropy and the arts. After all, many of their fortunes were one generation removed from rum running and opium trading. Many Brahmins never forgot how they came by their wealth and took measures to redeem themselves, founding the first public library in Boston and museums such as the Museum of Fine Arts.

Abolitionists and Transcendentalists

When Oliver Wendell Holmes Jr. declared in 1858 that Boston was the "hub of the solar system," he was referring not only to its wealth and financial influence, but also its intellectual influence. Over the two centuries since the Puritans arrived, Bostonians had gradually shed their strict morals and small-minded prejudices to develop a new, more all-embracing religious philosophy. The austerity of Puritanism—which taught that people were either elected to be saved or they were destined to be damned—may have commanded fear and respect in the days of the colonies, but post-Revolutionary New England was a prosperous, urbane culture, proud of its status as a national center of ideas.

Called Unitarianism, the new religion taught that God's salvation was available to anyone, not just those chosen few who were predestined for heaven. One by one, the New England Congregational churches "went Unitarian" and embraced this new philosophy, which emphasized an intellectual approach to the divine. And along with it came a new national conscience. Although early Unitarians were socially conservative, on political issues they were emphatically liberal. Congregants such as suffragist Susan B. Anthony were instrumental in organizing the women's movement. And prodded by ministers like William Ellery Channing and firebrand Theodore Parker, Boston stood at the forefront of the abolitionist movement—despite a long tradition of slavery in New England, which was a prominent part of the "triangle trade" linking the United States, Britain, and the Caribbean Islands in a brutal trading cycle of human lives, molasses, and rum.

At the same time that Unitarianism was spreading across the country, it spawned a rebellion against itself in the form of a new philosophy, transcendentalism. In many ways, transcendentalism took the fundamental tenet of Unitarianism, that anyone could be saved, and took it a step further, declaring that churches themselves were unnecessary since people could experience a direct connection to the divine. Transcendentalists found this in a mystical communion with the natural world. Buoyed by a mystical communion with nature, its adherents called for a radical individualism that would break free from the tired conventions of Europe. From their home base in Concord, its two chief adherents, Ralph Waldo Emerson and Henry David Thoreau, laid down its philosophy and formed a nucleus of writers, including Bronson Alcott (and his daughter Louisa May) and Nathaniel Hawthorne, who would begin the flowering in American literature.

New England in the Civil War

No amount of philosophizing, however, could prevent the inevitable political clash of the Civil War. While none of the actual fighting of the war took place in New England, it could be argued that it was a New Englander who fired the first shot. Outraged by the passage of the Fugitive Slave Act, which demanded that captured slaves be returned to southern masters, Brunswick, Maine, resident Harriet Beecher Stowe wrote the novel *Uncle Tom's Cabin*, which galvanized public support in favor of the war. Tens of thousands of New Englanders enlisted in the fight, forming regiments from all six New England states. Among the most acclaimed was the Massachusetts 54th, the nation's first all-black regiment, which was led by Bostonian Colonel Robert Gould Shaw, and suffered tremendous casualties in the heroic but tragic assault on Fort Wagner in July 1863. That same month, another New Englander, Joshua Chamberlain, won renown for his role in the Battle of Gettysburg. A professor at Bowdoin College, also in Brunswick, Maine, Chamberlain led the heroic defense of Little Round Top, saving the Union line through a dramatic flanking maneuver that caught the enemy by surprise. Two years later, in 1865, he received the flag of truce from the Confederate Army. Thus it's said in Maine that Brunswick both started and ended the war.

MODERN TIMES

The Immigrants Arrive

After the Civil War, the Golden Age of Sail gave way to the Age of Steam, as the railroad emerged to transport goods long distances. Increasingly isolated in the corner of a vast and growing country, New England gradually gave up its advantages in trade and manufacturing. New York surpassed Boston as the nation's largest port, and the opening up of the West and California decreased New England's dominance in the China trade. Even so, New England's Brahmin class continued to preside over vast amounts of wealth from their factories, and they began to show it in more and more elaborate ways. In addition to travel to other parts of the country, the railroad opened up many parts of New England to tourism, and grand Victorian "summer cottages" (read: mansions) and hotels were built along the coasts of Rhode Island and Maine, in the mountains of New Hampshire, and in the valleys of the Berkshires.

By the turn of the century, however, changes were occurring in the population. The first waves of immigrants from Ireland began in the early 1800s, but they intensified during the Great Hunger of 1850, during which two million people emigrated from the country. Many of them found their way to Boston, the closest major American city, and from there dispersed throughout the region. Poor but hardworking, many of them were welcomed in the mills. As their numbers swelled, however, a violent anti-Irish backlash began to coalesce among traditional Yankees anxious to hold on to their power and influence. In the mid-1850s, political groups called Know-Nothings burned Catholic churches and terrorized Irish communities.

The Irish won out by sheer numbers. By 1850, they comprised one-third of the city of Boston, with other cities boasting similar percentages. The new immigrants also organized themselves politically, forming a network of patronage politics in urban wards. Within just a few generations, they completely changed the political makeup of the region, as represented in Boston by the colorful politician James Michael Curley. Curley spent almost as much time in prison as in political office in his early years—but eventually worked his way up to get elected to the U.S. House of Representatives in 1911. After failing to get reelected, he returned to Boston, where he presided over the city as mayor or governor for 30 years. A hugely popular and hugely corrupt politician, he was eventually convicted of mail fraud and pardoned by President Harry Truman in 1947.

Waves of other immigrants followed the Irish, including Italians and French Canadians, who also found work in the factories of the region. Not as complacent as the mill girls of a century earlier, the new immigrants helped push for improvements in working conditions. A 21-year-old Irish woman led her fellow female immigrants of more than two dozen different nationalities in walking out of a mill in Lawrence, Massachusetts, to perpetrate the Bread and Roses strike, one of the most significant watersheds in the labor movement. On the darker side, two Italian anarchists, Nicola Sacco and Bartolomeo Vanzetti, were unfairly accused of robbery and murder in 1920. Their case became a national cause célèbre, stirring up strong sentiments and prejudices about communists, immigrants, the labor movement, and the death penalty. Despite shoddy evidence and the intervention of prominent intellectuals such as Upton Sinclair and H. L. Mencken, however, they were found guilty and executed in 1927. Exactly 50 years later, Massachusetts governor Michael Dukakis issued a proclamation exonerating them.

Decline and Rebirth

By the time of World War II, New England was in a period of slow decline. Many of the mills and factories that generated New England's wealth had become obsolete, and companies left the region in search of cheaper labor in other states and countries. At the same time, the urban centers that thrived in the previous century were abandoned by the middle class, who settled in streetcar suburbs on their outskirts. Despite various schemes to resurrect their cores, "urban renewal" was mostly a disaster, further hollowing out cities by bulldozing neighborhoods and erecting lifeless skyscrapers in their wakes. The sole bright spot in the postwar era was the election of one of New England's native sons, the charismatic war hero John Fitzgerald Kennedy, as president in 1960. Even that hope was dimmed, however, when Kennedy was killed by an assassin's bullet three years later. After struggling with the rest of the nation through the 1960s and 1970s, however, the region rebounded in the 1980s by playing to one of its strengths: knowledge.

New England was one of the first regions of the country to realize the potential of the computer to transform American society. Led by a wealth of well-educated engineers from Massachusetts Institute of Technology (MIT) and other area colleges, small technology firms grew into huge computer companies within a decade. The so-called Massachusetts Miracle revitalized the region and began a reversal of fortunes that injected wealth and self-confidence back into the cities. Since then, New England has been at the forefront of other technological revolutions, including the Internet and biotechnology, which has further bolstered its population and industrial base and left it well poised for the 21st century.

Government and Economy

GOVERNMENT AND POLITICS

It's been said that democracy was founded in Greece and perfected in New England, though it was likely a self-congratulating local that said it. But for many living in small towns, there's the opportunity to participate in "town hall meetings" that are far more participatory than in other regions of the country, and there's a deep focus on the local. In cities, meanwhile, Democratic politics hold enormous sway. There is more political diversity to the region than immediately meets the eye, however, from the liberal values of Vermont to the more libertarian voters in New Hampshire.

ECONOMY

Four industries dominate the modern New England economy: technology, academia, medicine, and finance—with tourism a close fifth. The area is second only to Silicon Valley in its concentration of technology firms, which tends to make booms bigger and recessions deeper than in other parts of the country. The great number of colleges and universities in the area has spawned a cottage industry of professors and researchers, who have also contributed to the region's status as a hub of medical innovation.

In addition to these urban pursuits, the area still has substantial concentrations of farming (particularly dairy), fruit cultivation (cranberries, apples, and blueberries), and fishing (whitefish and lobster). All these industries, however, struggle to compete with cheaper imports from other countries or overfishing of fragile stocks. Where there is hope for local farms, it lies in the burgeoning sectors of organic foods and community-supported agriculture, which has strong local support.

People and Culture

Imagine a New Englander—are you thinking of a flinty, white, English-speaking Yankee? There are certainly plenty of those, but the region's always been far more diverse than the stereotype implies. Dozens of tribal groups came first, and early immigration added English, French, and African people to the mix—the first enslaved African arrived in 1619, and many more followed.

Which isn't to say that there's no such thing as a "New England" character. Locals see themselves as hardily self-sufficient, shaped by the cold winters and history of independent thought. It's not quite as gregarious as the openly friendly South and West, but wind someone up about the weather, fishing, politics, weather, beer, or weather, and you'll get an earful.

New England is home to some 14.4 million people, with the majority of New England's population centered in the southern part of the region. Maine and New Hampshire each has 1.3 million each—staggering considering the vast size difference between the two. Meanwhile, Vermont tops out with just 600,000 people.

ETHNICITY AND CULTURE

The most recent census figures reveal that New England averages slightly higher than the rest of the country in its numbers of white and Hispanic residents: just above 83 percent, compared to the nation's 77 percent. The second-largest group of inhabitants are black, at roughly 7 percent, followed by 1 percent Chinese Americans.

Two major strands of culture typify the region: the thriving rural culture that keeps alive farming, fishing, and livestock traditions, and the educated, intellectual culture that flows from the colleges and universities. The most typical New England towns contain evidence of both: county fairs that still generate excitement in the populace, and cultural institutions such as museums, theaters, and art galleries that can be found in even the most remote corners of the region.

RELIGION

The region's earliest settlers may have been strict English Protestants, but due to waves of immigrants from French Canada, Italy, Ireland—and most recently, from Latin and South America—Catholics are now far and away New England's largest religious group.

The most popular branches of Protestantism (members of which make up roughly one-third of the area's population) are Episcopalian, Congregational, Baptist, Methodist, and Pentecostal. Meanwhile, one of the world's most sizable concentrations of practicing Jews calls Massachusetts home, and groups of the liberal-minded Unitarian Universalist church can also be spotted throughout New England. Sizable Muslim and Hindu populations can be found in many of the region's cities.

LANGUAGE

English is by far the most widely spoken tongue in each of New England's states, with pockets of other languages, which include both the Native American languages that pre-date European arrival, and many languages spoken by more recent immigrants.

Should outsiders give their best shot at a New England accent, odds are good that they'd imitate something from Boston, or perhaps Maine. The classic characteristics, including dropping word-final r's, and what linguists call the "cot-caught merger"—while some English speakers pronounce the words "cot" and "caught" (or "nod" and "gnawed") as distinct, New Englanders often produce them as identical sounds.

In many places, the most distinctive accents are harder and harder to come by, much to the chagrin of residents with an ear for appreciating quirky dialect. Language and accent change is complex, but it's worth noting that there's not an inexorable shift toward standardization, as many observers assume. In fact, New England was the site of a famous linguistic experiment that showed just the opposite. In the decades following World War II, when there was greatly increased mobility and tourism, the linguist William Labov found that some characteristics of the Martha's Vineyard accent were getting even stronger, theorizing that the shift was a reaction against some of the social changes that were then transforming island life.

THE ARTS

A love of music and the arts has dominated New England's cultural scene for centuries, and thanks to the legacy of the Boston Brahmins (those blue-blooded families who ruled the city's society and industry in the 19th century) there are plenty of places to appreciate all of them—from the Portland Museum of Art in Maine, to the small theaters of North Conway, New Hampshire, and the independent art galleries of Burlington, Vermont.

Literature is also a big part of New England's abundant arts community—historically and in the present day. Writers Nathaniel Hawthorne, Edith Wharton, and Henry David Thoreau helped define the American character as they saw it from New England, and scribes such as Arthur Miller and John Updike have continued the tradition.

But much of the culture found in this area of the country is just as easily found in its streets, pubs, and parks. In and around Portland, a thriving rock and folk music scene dominates the nightclubs and bars. Farther afield, in rural areas, you'll find plenty of folk-inspired performances—perhaps most notably distinct are the Acadian and Quebecois dance and folk music in northern areas of Maine.

Essentials

Getting There

New England is easily accessible by road, rail, and air (and even sea if you are coming by ferry from New York or Canada). While Logan Airport, in Boston, is the most obvious entrance, several of the region's smaller airports may offer cheaper flights from some cities. Amtrak's rail network isn't very extensive, but it does connect to most major New England cities, a good car-free option for exploring. If you want to get beyond urban areas, however, having your own transportation is essential.

AIR

With up to 1.5 million passengers passing through its gates each month, **Boston-Logan International Airport** (One Harborside Dr., East Boston, 617/428-2800, www.massport.com/logan-airport/) is the largest and busiest transportation hub in the region. The airport serves nearly 50 airlines, of which 13 are international, including Aer Lingus, Air Canada, Air France, Alitalia, British Airways, Iberia, Icelandair, Lufthansa, SATA (Azores Express), Swiss, and Virgin Atlantic Airways. International flights arrive in Terminal E. From the airport, a variety of options take passengers to downtown Boston, which is only a mile away.

Several of the area's smaller regional airports are a good option for travelers looking to save a few bucks or get to other New England states without having to pass through Boston first.

Another option for southern New England is **Bradley International Airport** (Schoephoester Rd., Windsor Locks, CT, 860/292-2000, www.bradleyairport.com), located halfway between Springfield, Massachusetts, and Hartford, Connecticut; it's about a 45-minute drive from either city. In New Hampshire, **Manchester Airport** (1 Airport Rd., Manchester, 603/624-6556, www.flymanchester.com) has competed aggressively with Logan in the areas of price and convenience. It's located about a 1.5 hour drive from the White Mountains, and a 30-minute drive from Portsmouth, New Hampshire, and carries a half-dozen domestic airlines as well as Air Canada.

While not usually cheaper, several other regional airports offer easy access to northern New England. **Burlington International Airport** (1200 Airport Dr., S. Burlington, VT, 802/863-1889, www.btv.aero) is located right in downtown Burlington, and offers limited flights from cities including Atlanta, Cleveland, Detroit, New York, and Washington DC. **Portland International Jetport** (207/774-7301, www.portlandjetport.com) also offers several domestic routes from cities in the eastern United States to those looking for easy access to south and Mid-Coast Maine. Both Burlington and Portland are served by discount flights from New York on JetBlue airlines. Lastly, far northern Maine is home to **Bangor International Airport** (207/992-4600, www.flybangor.com), which offers flights from a handful of cities including Atlanta, New York, Philadelphia, Cincinnati, Detroit, and Minneapolis. The airport is also served by shuttles from Boston via American and Delta. Despite their names, none of the three northern New England airports offers commercial international flights.

TRAIN

Amtrak (800/872-7245, www.amtrak.com) runs frequent trains along the Northeast corridor to Boston, including the **Acela Express,** the first U.S. high-speed service, from New York (3.5 hours) and Washington DC (6 hours).

Previous: a tractor on a farm road in Vermont; surfing in New Hampshire.

But unless you are in a rush, it can often make more sense to save $50 and take the **Regional** service, which also runs to Boston from New York (4.5 hours) and Washington (7 hours), stopping along the way in New Haven, New London, Providence, and several smaller cities on the Connecticut and Rhode Island coasts.

For travelers heading to northern New England, Amtrak offers the aptly named **Vermonter** route, which runs to St. Albans from New York (10 hours) and Washington DC (14 hours). Along the way, it passes through a number of cities in the Connecticut River Valley, including New Haven, Hartford, Amherst, Brattleboro, Waterbury, and Burlington—though the "Burlington" station is in Essex Junction, eight miles from downtown. Also, Amtrak's **Ethan Allen** route offers once-a-day service to Rutland, Vermont, from New York City (10 hours) by way of Albany.

From the west, Amtrak's **Lake Shore Limited** route offers service to Boston from Buffalo (12 hours), and Cleveland (15 hours), stopping along the way in Springfield and Worcester. Connecting to that route, Amtrak's **Adirondack** route offers service to Boston from Montreal, Quebec (12 hours), with a change of train in Albany.

BUS

New England is accessible from many domestic and Canadian locations via **Greyhound Bus Lines** (800/231-2222, www.greyhound.com). Nearby major cities offering service to Boston include New York (4.5 hours), Philadelphia (7.5 hours), Montreal (7.5 hours), Washington (10.5 hours), Buffalo (10.5 hours), Toronto (14 hours), and Cleveland (16 hours).

In recent years, the budget carrier **Megabus** (www.us.megabus.com) has expanded service in New England, linking Boston with Burlington (4 hours), Hartford (2 hours), New Haven (3 hours), Portland (2 hours), and New York (2 hours), often at lower prices.

CAR

The major auto route into New England is I-95, which enters the southeast corner of Connecticut and snakes up the coast to Boston. The drive takes about three hours from the New York border without stops—four hours from New York or eight hours from Washington DC. This direct route, however, can often get clogged with truck traffic, especially through areas of eastern Connecticut and Rhode Island, where it drops to two lanes each way. Many travelers prefer to take a detour at New Haven north on I-91, then west on I-84 and I-90 to Boston; while slightly longer, this route is often quicker.

From the west, the main route into New England is I-90, also known as the Massachusetts Turnpike (or Mass Pike for short). I-90 is a toll road, and it takes a little over two hours to drive its length, from the border of western Massachusetts to Boston. From Canada, there are two border crossings into Vermont; one is at I-89, which offers quick access to Burlington and central Massachusetts and Connecticut by way of connection to I-91. The other crossing, at the far northern end of I-91, offers quicker access to New Hampshire and Boston via connection to I-93. Several smaller highways offer border crossings into the wilderness of northern Maine. Some of New England's highways have tolls, and it's worth traveling with cash and small change to be prepared.

SEA

Travelers coming from Atlantic Canada can take the express route from Yarmouth, Nova Scotia, to Portland, Maine (6.5 hours) aboard **The CAT** (877/359-3760, www.catferry.com), a high-speed car ferry that makes round-trips on each route daily. Two year-round car ferries also make the trip to Connecticut from New York's Long Island. **Cross Sound Ferry Services** (860/443-5281, www.longislandferry.com) offers several daily trips from Orient Point to New London (1.5 hours). The **Bridgeport & Port Jefferson Steamboat Company** (631/473-0286, www.bpjferry.com) offers trips between those two cities (1.25 hours) every hour.

Getting Around

While it's possible to explore New England using public transportation, that means planning your trip around the most convenient networks—opting to see just the towns on bus and train lines would make a great vacation, but good luck getting to a small Maine or Vermont town without a car.

Once you're there, however, many places are wonderfully pleasant to see on foot or by bicycle, without the hassle of paying for parking or negotiating urban traffic.

AIR

Puddle-jumpers between Boston and many of the area's regional airports offer a quick and easy way to shoot around the region. Be forewarned, however, that relying on air travel for inter-city travel isn't cheap. In most cases, you'll save money by flying direct from your home to a regional airport, rather than stopping in Boston first. Better yet, it's often more economical to rent a car or travel by bus between cities.

TRAIN

In addition to the routes coming in from outside New England, **Amtrak** (800/872-7245, www.amtrak.com) offers the regional **Downeaster** service from Boston to Portland (2.5 hours). The train stops in several smaller towns along the way, including Dover, New Hampshire; and Wells and Old Orchard Beach, Maine. Note, however, that it's not possible to buy a one-ticket ride from New York to Portland, since the southern train runs to South Station, and the Downeaster embarks from North Station. Travelers from the South Shore to Maine must take a short subway trip between the two Boston stations to continue their trip. The other main rail line is the **Vermonter** service, which links Washington DC and New York with the Connecticut coast, central Massachusetts, and a series of stops in Vermont.

BUS

It may not be the fastest way to tour New England, but **Greyhound** (800/231-2222, www.greyhound.com) maintains a comprehensive web of routes that touches most cities, colleges, and tourist attractions in the region. Until recently, the Springfield-based **Peter Pan Bus Lines** (800/343-9999, www.peterpanbus.com) was an independent company that competed with the national behemoth. Now the two companies share routes and schedules, however, making travel on either interchangeable. Other smaller, regional carriers serve out-of-the-way parts of northern New England—the largest being **Concord Coach Lines** (603/228-3300 or 800/639-3317, www.concordcoachlines.com). Other carriers have slowly been disappearing in recent years, snatched up by Greyhound—often at a loss of regional routes with low ridership. (See the appropriate destination chapters for more details.)

CAR

Highways are efficient and in general well maintained, and traffic moves briskly aside from rush hour around major cities. The region is bisected north-south by I-91, which runs along the Connecticut River Valley along the border of New Hampshire and Vermont and down through central Massachusetts and Connecticut. In Vermont it connects with I-89 and in New Hampshire with I-93, which runs all the way to Boston. An alternative to I-93 is U.S. 3, which parallels the interstate in New Hampshire and then runs through Boston along the South Shore to Cape Cod. Skirting around the city, I-95 is the main coastal thoroughfare from the Connecticut-New York border all the way to northeast Maine. For inland Maine, travelers are relegated to slower undivided highways, including U.S. 201 to the Moosehead Lake region, and Route 11 to the Allagash.

Car Rental Companies

The following companies have branches at major cities and airports:

- **Alamo:** 800/462-5266, www.alamo.com
- **Avis:** 800/331-1212, www.avis.com
- **Budget:** 800/527-0700, www.budget.com
- **Dollar:** 800/800-4000, www.dollar.com
- **Enterprise:** 800/261-7331, www.enterprise.com
- **Hertz:** 800/654-3131, www.hertz.com
- **National:** 800/227-7368, www.nationalcar.com
- **Thrifty:** 800/367-2277, www.thrifty.com

East to west, the region is bisected by I-90, otherwise known as the Massachusetts Turnpike or Mass Pike, which runs the length of Massachusetts. To the south, the Pike connects near Worcester to I-84, which then runs east-west through Connecticut. North of the Pike, the highway is paralleled by Route 2, which is slower but can be a more efficient way to get to the northern Berkshires and southern Vermont. Traveling east or west in northern New England, meanwhile, can be a frustrating exercise, since all major roads lead north-south to Boston. Several federal highways, including U.S. 2 and U.S. 4, aid to accomplish the task, but if you use them, be sure to leave more time for small-town stoplights and mountain switchbacks.

BICYCLE

The rural parts of New England—especially Vermont—are justifiably popular with bike tourists. Because the landscape is relatively gentle compared with the western United States, small roads wander throughout the countryside. Traffic can be an issue in some places, as those small roads serve as daily commutes for rural residents, but drivers are generally aware of and friendly to cyclists.

Some of the cities are quite bike friendly, as well. Burlington tops the list, but Portland is easy to navigate on two wheels. The ultimate New England bike vacation might be Acadia National Park, where a network of carriage roads winds all over the island.

Sports and Recreation

The abundance of mountains, lakes, beaches, parks, and ocean all over New England means lots of outdoor fun. In winter, skiers flock to snowy peaks in New Hampshire, Maine, and Vermont. Summer brings mountain biking and hiking, and waterways fill with craft of all kinds.

Serious sea lovers head to the coasts and islands of Maine, with a longstanding and venerable history of fishing and boating, and plenty of resources to show for it. Meanwhile, the widely varied parks and preservation lands throughout New England are excellent grounds for bird-watching of all kinds, year-round.

HIKING AND CAMPING

New Englanders love camping, and prove it year after year by filling their region's campsites in droves—on holiday weekends, finding one with available sites can be a challenge. On such popular dates, it pays to make a reservation. Also, not all campgrounds offer sites for both RVs and tents; call ahead to be sure.

ROCK CLIMBING

Northern New England is a veritable playground for mountaineers, who flock in all seasons to the area's challenging rock-climbing faces. Popular climbing areas are found in Acadia National Park and in New Hampshire's White Mountains, including Franconia Notch, Cathedral Ledge, Ragged Mountain, and Cannon Cliff.

KAYAKING AND CANOEING

Wherever there's a coast in New England, there are usually plenty of places to put in a kayak and head out to sea for a salty run. The most pristine rivers in the region are in northern Maine, where the St. John and Allagash Rivers offer more than 100 miles of interconnected lakes and rivers, most of which are a gentle Class I or II in difficulty. The same can't be said of the Penobscot and Kennebec Rivers slightly farther south, near Baxter State Park. This is where *serious* kayakers and rafters go to get wet, with rapids rising to Class IV, and one stretch of Class V on the Penobscot that will test even the most experienced paddlers. The longest canoe trail in the Northeast, the **Northern Forest Canoe Trail** (www.northernforestcanoetrail.org) spans 740 miles for rivers and waterways on the way from Old Forge, New York, to Port Kent, Maine.

SAILING

Coastal New England is quite literally awash in sailing culture—from preppy spectators to lifelong, bona fide seadogs. With New England winters as harsh as they are, sailing communities tend to come alive in the late spring, summer, and fall. For the largest concentrations of charters and docks (public and private), sailing schools and outfitters, head in the direction of those towns with a long tradition of seafaring.

HUNTING, FISHING, AND BIRD-WATCHING

Every season, without fail, droves of dedicated sportsmen and sportswomen descend upon the backwoods and seas of New England, seeking to watch, catch, or take home some of its bounty. Local regulations and licensing requirements can be strict; certain animals (marine mammals, for example) are protected in certain districts, and specific rules apply to most species for trapping, baiting, shooting, and catching. So be certain to check with the local fish and game offices of your area of interest before planning your trip.

Hunting areas are well regulated and plentiful, particularly in northern New England, where animals from woodcock and deer to turkey and moose roam.

Deep-sea fishing is one fruitful option in the summer and fall. Fish such as cod, striped bass, tuna, and lobster are popular catches—though many forms of fishing (particularly lobstering) are largely chartered activities. Moving-water fishing, meanwhile, takes place mostly in summer and early fall. Serious trout and bass anglers gravitate toward the Rapid and Kennebec Rivers in Maine; the Androscoggin, Saco, and Mohawk Rivers in New Hampshire; and the Missisquoi, Batten Kill, and Connecticut Rivers in Vermont. In winter, ice fishing is popular in many small, northern towns—particularly in the area around Lake Champlain, Vermont. The sport requires hardy enthusiasts to cut holes in the ice above ponds and lakes, and catch fish as they cruise beneath the hole.

Any time of year, bird-watchers can feast their eyes in any number of wildlife refuges. Some of the best include Maine's Moosehorn and Petit Manan refuges and Vermont's Missisquoi and Silvio O Conte refuges.

SKIING AND WINTER SPORTS

Skiing and snowboarding in New England keep entire small-town economies revved up December-March (and for true addicts, April), and every year pulls many an urbanite out from their city bubble and into face-to-face, downhill encounters with nature.

New England slopes vary greatly in difficulty and the crowds they draw. As would be expected, the more southern resorts and better-known, big-name spots tend to get packed with day-trippers from Boston, whereas the out-of-the way and independently owned and operated resorts often have small, dedicated followings of skiers. Favorites in Maine include Sugarloaf, Sunday River, Big Squaw, and Saddleback. New Hampshire's mountains are plentiful, offering a wealth of downhill options. The best are Bretton Woods, Attitash, Loon Mountain, Waterville Valley, and Wildcat. Vermont, meanwhile, draws some of the region's most serious skiers—to top mountains like Stowe, Stratton, Okemo, Killington, Jay Peak, and Mad River Glen.

Ice-skating, too, is a popular winter activity—done in town and city parks, and at recreation rinks. Most are open to the public, usually charge a small fee, and are listed with local town halls. Local parks are also full of sledding opportunities.

Food and Accommodations

Throughout the text, food listings include the range of prices for dinner entrées, including sandwiches but not salads. Lunch is often significantly cheaper. Accommodations listings include the range of rates for a standard double room in high season (roughly May-October). Depending on location, prices can be much higher during peak times (e.g., foliage or ski season) and steeply discounted in winter and spring.

NEW ENGLAND CUISINE

Traditional New England fare revolves around the seafood of the area's coast, but pays homage to the cooking methods of its British origins—the likes of boiled lobsters, baked stuffed shrimp, fried cod, and steamed clams. Other foodstuffs native to the region also play a big part in the regional cuisine—cranberry sauce, maple syrup, corn bread, and baked beans, for starters.

These days, the culinary options in New England are as diverse as the population; you're as apt to find Thai-inspired bouillabaisse and tapas-style Punjabi specialties as you are classic clam chowder. But if you're up for trying the region's specialties at their source, don't miss these traditional New England dishes:

The clambake: A great pile of seafood that includes steamed lobster, mussels, and clams is served with traditional sides, usually corn on the cob and potatoes. Traditionally these are steamed together in a hole dug on a beach, but restaurant versions are certainly available.

Lobster: Steamed or broiled, this native crustacean is a messy but glorious affair. The meat lies inside a tough shell, which is cracked by the diner using metal crackers and a small fork, and dipped in melted butter before eating.

Clams: Generally divided into types—hard shell or soft shell—clams are a true New England delicacy. Soft shells, or steamers, are usually eaten either steamed or fried. (If steamed, diners pull them from the shell, remove and discard the neck casing, and dip them in broth and drawn butter before eating.)

Hard shell clams are served differently: The smallest ones, known as littlenecks and cherrystones, are most frequently served raw with horseradish and cocktail sauce, while the largest hard shells are chopped up and used in chowders and stuffings.

Clam chowder: Dating back to the 18th century, New England clam chowder is by far the most popular of the region's creamy fish stews. Most restaurants have their own recipes, using a bit more potatoes here, a different ratio of bacon to cream there (but not tomatoes—that is what distinguishes Manhattan clam chowder and is therefore heresy in New England). Sampling and finding your favorite is the real fun.

How to Eat a Lobster

For some, it's an intimidating and off-putting exercise in utter messiness. For others, it's a deliciously visceral process with a delightful end: some of the sweetest crustacean meat on the planet. However you view the process of eating a lobster, experts agree that the best way to tackle the creature is from the outside in, and working from small to big. Note that while plenty of creative preparations of the delicacy do exist, purists swear by a simple boiled specimen—its precious meat dressed only in a squeeze of lemon and dipped in drawn butter.

- Start by breaking off the legs, holding the lobster by its back and pulling/twisting off the legs individually. Snap each in half at its joint and chew out the meat.
- Next, take off the claws, tearing them at the joint closest to the body (twisting if necessary), then again at the joint closest to the claw itself. Use your fork to push out all the meat (many say the knuckle meat is the most delicious). Next use your crackers to crush the large claw, extracting all the meat, ideally in one large piece.
- Grasp the tail with one hand and the back with the other hand, then twist and gently pull to separate the two sections. Some people also choose to eat the green tomalley (the digestive gland) and, in a female lobster, the roe (the unfertilized eggs). Whether you follow suit depends on your personal palate.
- Hold the tail with both hands, your thumbs placed just on the inside, on the white cartilage, your index fingers wrapped around the red shell on the tail's back. Pressing in with your index fingers and out with your thumbs, split the tail down the middle, revealing the whole of the tail. Pull out with a fork or your fingers and devour.

ACCOMMODATIONS

Many tourist destinations celebrate their peak seasons in the summer, when the weather is the nicest; not so in New England. Peak travel here is in the fall, particularly in late September and October when the foliage is at its most dramatic and students are pouring into area colleges. Many hotels jack up their prices by a factor of two or even three during this brief crowded season. The same can be said, on a smaller scale, for ski season, especially around February vacation, when rates in some locations in northern New England can reach a peak higher than their nearby ski mountains.

If leaf-peeping and skiing aren't your thing, you can save a lot of money by traveling in late August or early September when the summer humidity has dissipated, but hotel prices haven't yet skyrocketed. Of course, the opposite holds true for beach destinations. New Englanders make the most of their brief period of heat between Memorial Day and Labor Day. Do yourself a favor and schedule your beach vacation on either side of these magical dates, when you'll beat both the crowds and high prices—and the weather is often just as nice (of course, you are gambling that New England's mercurial climate will cooperate).

Along with the rest of the country, New England has seen a steady rise in the price of accommodations at all levels, making it difficult to find any bargains among the major-name hotels. Bed-and-breakfasts, especially in more rural areas, can be an attractive alternative; often run by couples or families, they can offer dirt-cheap prices without sacrificing amenities or hominess. Those who prefer the anonymity of a motel will find more bargains (though less consistency) in independent operations.

Travel Tips

HEALTH AND SAFETY

People travel to New England from all over the globe simply to receive care from the area's doctors and hospitals, which are widely regarded as among the best there is. So rest assured, should you need any medical attention while here, you'll be in good hands. That said, certain precautions will help you stay as safe as possible.

Compared with the rest of the nation, New England is relatively low in crime. Even in capitals like Boston, Portland, Providence, and Hartford, if you follow the basic rules of common sense (take precautions in watching your belongings, avoid walking alone late at night, and be aware of your surroundings), odds are safety won't be a problem.

In the New England countryside, one of the biggest threats to visitors' safety can be the natural world they seek. When hiking the White Mountains or canoeing the endless rivers, it is essential to know about the dangers of exposure to the elements. Visit the local tourism offices for specific tips on preparing for an outing, and if you are at all unsure of your outdoors skills, consider hiring a guide to take you on your excursion.

ACCESS FOR TRAVELERS WITH DISABILITIES

Public transportation in the vast majority of New England is wheelchair-accessible, as are most major hotels, museums, and public buildings. Even many beaches and campgrounds in Massachusetts are accessible, though the remoter the destination, the greater the possibility that it will not be.

The greatest challenge for travelers in wheelchairs in New England may be accessing historic neighborhoods and inns that have not been retrofitted with wider doorways and elevators. Some inns have converted one or more rooms with roll-in showers, while others are completely inaccessible.

Those with permanent disabilities,

Ticks and Lyme Disease

Forget snakes, bears, and moose—ask a New Englander what wildlife they're scared of, and they'll say **ticks.** The eight-legged creatures are tiny—from the size of a poppyseed to just under three millimeters—and easy to miss. Some are carriers of **Lyme disease,** a dangerous bacterial infection. Not all ticks can carry Lyme disease, but the deer tick sometimes does, and it's the most common species in the Northeast. Taking the following precautions will help protect against Lyme:

- Wear long pants tucked into your socks when walking through high grass and bushy areas.
- Use insect repellent that contains DEET, which is effective against ticks.
- Shower within a few hours of coming inside, and check carefully for ticks. If you find a tick, use tweezers to grasp it near to your skin, and firmly remove without twisting. Don't worry if the mouthparts remain in the skin; once the tick is separated from the body, it can no longer transmit the bacteria that cause Lyme.

Carefully checking for ticks once a day is a good practice. Don't panic if you find a tick, as it takes around 36 hours for the bacteria to spread. The first symptoms of Lyme disease are often flu-like, and occur 3-30 days after infection. They're often accompanied by a rash or bull's-eye redness around the bite. If you experience these symptoms, it's smart to visit a doctor. Prompt treatment of Lyme disease is generally effective, but the disease can be fatal if untreated.

including the visually impaired, should inquire about a free **Access Pass** (888/275-8747, ext. 3) from the National Park Service. It is offered as part of the America the Beautiful—National Park and Federal Recreational Lands Pass Series. You can obtain an Access Pass in person at any federal recreation site or by submitting a completed application (www.nps.gov/findapark/passes.htm, $10 processing fee may apply) by mail. The pass does not provide benefits for special recreation permits or concessionaire fees.

TRAVELING WITH CHILDREN

Travel all over New England is extremely family friendly. Most hotels offer cribs in the room upon request, and public transportation and attractions offer discounted fares for children. The majority of restaurants are happy to offer high chairs, and many have kids' menus.

Some inns and bed-and-breakfasts, however, are not open to children—generally drawing the line at 12 or so.

INFORMATION AND SERVICES

Internet and Cellular Access

Wireless Internet is available in most cafés, as well as many other businesses. Local libraries are a good place to find computers with Internet access free of charge, as most make these services available to visitors. Most hotels and bed-and-breakfasts offer free wireless Internet, though some smaller, rural inns may not.

While all New England cities have full cell coverage, many rural areas do not, so it's worth having access to a paper map when traveling through the countryside.

Business Hours

Business hours vary widely between cities and towns, but most stores and offices in state capital cities follow a schedule of 9am-5pm -6pm Monday-Friday, 10am-6pm Saturday, and noon-5pm Sunday. In smaller cities and towns, particularly those in rural areas, expect more erratic weekend hours—or the possibility that they may simply stay closed until Monday.

Tipping

A 15-20 percent tip is expected in New England restaurants, and 15 percent is customary in bars, hair salons, and spas if you are satisfied with the level of your service. At hotels, $1 per bag for porters is the norm, doormen usually receive $1 for hailing a taxi, maids usually receive $1-2 per night, and concierges are given anywhere from a few dollars to $20, depending on the services they have provided. In taxis, 10-15 percent is customary.

Magazines

Several regional magazines provide useful information for travelers, including *New England Travel*, an annual but comprehensive magazine exploring all of the region's attractions, and *Yankee Magazine*, for events, festivals, landmarks, restaurants, and tours all over New England. Several states and cities and even subregions produce their own magazines as well, including *Vermont Life* and *Down East*, the monthly periodical dedicated to all things Maine.

Visas and Officialdom

PASSPORTS AND VISAS

Visitors from other countries must have a **valid passport** and **visa.** Visitors with current passports from one of the following countries qualify for **visa waivers:** Andorra, Australia, Austria, Belgium, Brunei, Chile, Czech Republic, Denmark, Estonia, Finland, France, Germany, Greece, Hungary, Iceland, Ireland, Italy, Japan, Latvia, Liechtenstein, Lithuania, Luxembourg, Malta, Monaco, the Netherlands, New Zealand, Norway, Portugal, San Marino, Singapore, Slovakia, Slovenia, South Korea, Spain, Sweden, Switzerland, Taiwan, and the United Kingdom. They must apply online with the Electronic System for Travel Authorization at www.cbp.gov and hold a **return plane ticket** to their home countries less than 90 days from their time of entry. Holders of **Canadian passports** don't need visas or waivers. In most countries, the local U.S. embassy can provide a **tourist visa.** Plan for at least two weeks for visa processing, longer during the busy summer season (June-Aug.). More information is available online at http://travel.state.gov.

EMBASSIES AND CONSULATES

New York City and Boston are home to consulates from around the world. Travelers in legal trouble or those who have lost their passports should contact the consulate of their home country immediately. The **U.S. State Department** (www.state.gov) has contact info for all foreign embassies and consulates. The **British Consulate** (www.gov.uk) has offices in the **Boston** area (1 Broadway, Cambridge, 617/245-4500) and **New York City** (845 3rd Ave., 212/745-0200). The **Australian Consulate** has an office in **New York City** (150 E. 42nd St., 34th Fl., 212/351-6600), and the **Canadian Consulate-General** is in **Boston** (3 Copley Pl. #400, 617/247-5100) and **New York City** (1251 Avenue of the Americas, 212/596-1628).

CUSTOMS

Foreigners and U.S. citizens age 21 or older may import (free of duty) the following: one liter of alcohol, 200 cigarettes (one carton), 50 cigars (non-Cuban), and $100 worth of gifts. International travelers must declare amounts that exceed $10,000 in cash (U.S. or foreign), traveler's checks, or money orders. Meat products, fruits, and vegetables are prohibited due to health and safety regulations.

Resources

Suggested Reading

REFERENCE

Feintuch, Bert, ed. *The Encyclopedia of New England.* New Haven, CT: Yale University Press, 2005. A good book to read *before* you go, this 1,600-page, eight-pound tome will tell you everything you want to know about New England and then some, including entries on Walden Pond, fried clams, Ben & Jerry's, and the Red Sox. Instead of a disjointed alphabetical arrangement, the book cogently organizes contents by subject matter.

HISTORY

Cronon, William. *Changes in the Land: Indians, Colonists, and the Ecology of New England.* New York: Hill and Wang, 1983. The classic study of early New England history debunks myths and shatters preconceptions about Pilgrims and Native Americans and how each interacted with the landscape.

Fairbrother, Trevor. *Painting Summer in New England.* New Haven, CT: Yale University Press, 2006. From a recent exhibition of the same name at the Peabody Essex Museum, this beautiful art book includes dozens of paintings by American impressionists, along with stories about the artists.

McCullough, David. *1776.* New York: Simon & Schuster, 2005. Rather than writing a start-to-finish account of the Revolution, McCullough drills down to the pivotal year in which the fortunes of George Washington turned, from the tense standoff of the siege of Boston to the ultimate victories at Trenton and Princeton.

Paine, Lincoln P. *Down East: A Maritime History of Maine.* Gardiner, ME: Tilbury House Publishers, 2000. A look back at more than four centuries of pirates, privateers, lobstermen, and windjammers from a maritime historian and native Downeaster.

Vowell, Sarah. *The Wordy Shipmates.* New York: Riverhead, 2007. The popular essayist and National Public Radio contributor not only writes one of the most irreverent and entertaining histories of the early days of Puritan and Pilgrim New England, but makes those ancient times surprisingly relevant to our own United States.

Woodard, Colin. *The Lobster Coast: Rebels, Rusticators, and the Struggle for a Forgotten Frontier.* New York: Viking, 2004. From early Scotch-Irish woodchoppers to 20th-century oil painters, this clearly written account populates the map of Maine with colorful historical characters.

NATURAL HISTORY AND ECOLOGY

Albers, Jan. *Hands on the Land: A Natural History of the Vermont Landscape.* Boston: MIT Press, 2002. In a gorgeous oversized book, Albers details the various factors—geological, ecological, and economic—that have transformed the Green Mountain State.

Kessler, Brad. *Goat Song: A Seasonal Life, A Short History of Herding, and the Art of Making Cheese.* New York: Scribner, 2009. In this lovely and earnest little book, longtime writer Brad Kessler sets out to live the dream that tugs at many of us: leaving the city to live a simpler life on the farm. What he finds in two years of raising goats is nothing short of connection to our most mythic religious archetypes.

Kurlansky, Mark. *Cod: A Biography of the Fish That Changed the World.* New York: Penguin, 1998. The settlement and economic rise of New England is inseparable from the plentiful groundfish that once populated its waters in astounding numbers.

National Audubon Society. *National Audubon Society Regional Guide to New England.* New York: Knopf, 1998. The amateur naturalist would do well to pick up this guide, which details many local species of trees, wildflowers, reptiles, and mammals, with 1,500 full-color illustrations.

Wessels, Tom. *Reading the Forested Landscape: A Natural History of New England.* Woodstock, VT: Countryman Press, 2005. A good read before heading off into the hills, this book helps put features of the landscape into their proper context.

LITERATURE

Frost, Robert. *The Poetry of Robert Frost: The Collected Poems, Complete and Unabridged.* Henry Holt and Co., 1979. The New England landscape infuses Frost's poetry, much of which was written in Vermont and New Hampshire.

Jewett, Sarah Orne. *The Country of the Pointed Firs.* 1896, Dover, 2011. Maine's customs, dialect, and traditions come to life in this often-overlooked masterpiece.

Stegner, Wallace. *Crossing to Safety.* 1987, Random House, 2002. A quintessential Western author tells a finely woven story of love and loss against the backdrop of northern Vermont.

CONTEMPORARY FICTION AND MEMOIR

Bergman, Megan Mayhew. *Birds of a Lesser Paradise.* Simon & Schuster, 2012. Writing from a farm in Vermont, Bergman draws New England's cows, chickens, and exotic birds into her intimate short stories.

Elder, John. *Reading the Mountains of Home.* Cambridge, MA: Harvard University Press, 1999. With the company of Robert Frost's poetry, a Vermont writer watches a year unfold in the Green Mountains.

Greenlaw, Linda. *The Lobster Chronicles: Life on a Very Small Island.* New York: Hyperion, 2003. The sword boat captain featured in Sebastian Junger's nonfiction book *The Perfect Storm* returns with a fascinating memoir of her return to her family's home on Isle Au Haut in Maine to try her hand at the lobstering business.

Irving, John. Many of the most popular books of this cult American novelist are set in New England. For example, *The Cider House Rules* (New York: William Morrow, 1995) is centered around an orphanage in Maine, *The World According to Garp* (New York: Ballantine, 1990) takes place in part at a New England boarding school, and *A Prayer for Owen Meany* (New York: William Morrow, 1989) concerns several generations of a troubled New England family.

GUIDEBOOKS

Appalachian Mountain Club Books (www.outdoors.org/publications) publishes dozens of guides considered gospel by outdoors enthusiasts in the region. They are jam-packed with no-nonsense directions for hiking and canoeing every inch of the New England wilderness. Among them are the *White Mountain Guide* and *Maine Mountain Guide*, as well as several guides for canoeing and kayaking.

Corbett, William. *Literary New England: A History and Guide*. New York: Faber and Faber, 1993. An excellent guide to sights associated with poets and writers who called New England home, it includes detailed directions to hard-to-find graves, historic sites, and houses.

Hartnett, Robert. *Maine Lighthouses Map & Guide*. Howes Cave, NY: Hartnett House Map Publishing, 2000. A foldout map that provides detailed directions to every lighthouse along the rocky fingers of the Maine coast. Hartnett also publishes a map to lighthouses in Massachusetts and New Hampshire (yes, there are two).

Kershner, Bruce, and Robert Leverett. *The Sierra Club Guide to the Ancient Forests of the Northeast*. San Francisco: Sierra Club Books, 2004. Despite centuries of human habitation and exploitation, a surprising number of old-growth stands still exist in New England. This guide takes you inside their mossy interiors, and explains what makes old-growth forests so unique.

PODCASTS

Rumble Strip (www.rumblestripvermont.com). Host Erica Heilman shares fresh and unexpected stories from Vermont's farmers, criminals, waitresses, and musicians.

Internet Resources

The websites maintained by state tourism agencies can be surprisingly useful, with tips on finding scenic byways, events, and on-call staff.

NEW ENGLAND

Discover New England
www.discovernewengland.org
This site highlights seasonal events and current happenings in every corner of New England, and suggests driving tours and weather information, plus gives a brief primer on each state.

NewEngland.com
www.newengland.com
Run by *Yankee* magazine, this site is packed with local landmarks, recommended itineraries, foliage reports, event listings, and vacation planners.

FALL FOLIAGE REPORTS

Get in-depth and up-to-date foliage reports on each state, starting in early September and throughout autumn, from the following websites: **Vermont** (www.vermont.com/foliage.cfm), **New Hampshire** (www.visitnh.gov/foliage-tracker), and **Maine** (www.mainefoliage.com).

DESTINATION WEBSITES

Expect to find basic background information about the destination, plus essentials such as hours, locations, entrance fees, driving directions, and special deals or packages currently offered.

Maine

Maine Tourism
www.visitmaine.com
This site offers information on everything to see and do in Maine, including fall foliage, outdoor recreation, family-friendly outings, restaurants, shopping, events, and accommodations.

Portland, ME
www.visitportland.com
With coverage that stretches across southern Maine, this site is an excellent resource for trip planning.

Acadia National Park, ME

www.nps.gov/acad

Maps, campground information and booking services, and online passes are available on this site.

New Hampshire

New Hampshire Tourism

www.visitnh.gov

Find all kinds of visitors' information on the state, including local foliage reports, travel itineraries, online photo galleries, deals on seasonal travel packages, and lodging and restaurant listings.

Mt. Washington Valley, NH

www.mtwashingtonvalley.org

Just about anything happening in the valley shows up on this site: local events throughout the year, dogsledding and cross-country skiing—plus how to find the best local crafters and artists, as well as shopping, restaurant, and hotel listings.

Vermont

Vermont Tourism

www.vermontvacation.com

Here you'll find information on nightlife and dining, shopping, accommodations, ski resorts, local churches, and businesses, plus help on getting around the area by public transportation and finding local festivals.

Index

A

B

C

D

E

F

G

H

IJ

K

L

M

N

O

P

QR

S

T

UV

WXYZ

List of Maps

Photo Credits

Title page photo: © Jen Rose Smith; page 4 © Jiawangkun | Dreamstime.com; page 5 © Jen Rose Smith; page 6 (top left) © The Chamber Collaborative of Greater Portsmouth/Nicki Noble, (top right) © Jen Rose Smith, (bottom) © Nick Cote/Maine Office of Tourism; page 7 (top) © Jen Rose Smith, (bottom left) © Jo Ann Snover | Dreamstime.com, (bottom right) © Jen Rose Smith; page 8 © Michael Ver Sprill | Dreamstime; page 10 (top) © Snehitdesign | Dreamstime, (bottom) © Brett Pelletier | Dreamstime; page 11 (top) © F11photo | Dreamstime, (middle) © Donland | Dreamstime, (bottom) © Deana Freeman | Dreamstime.com; page 12 © Donland | Dreamstime.com; page 15 © Schooner Lewis R. French; page 17 (top left) © Jen Rose Smith, (top right) © Cllhnstev | Dreamstime.com; page 18 © Jen Rose Smith; page 20 (top) © Jeb Wallace-Brodeur/Mad River Glen, (bottom) © Sierra Machado; page 21 © Peanutroaster | Dreamstime.com; page 24 © Jen Rose Smith; page 35 © Reinhardt | Dreamstime.com; page 43 © Chandler Burgess/Killington Resort; page 52 © Jeb Wallace-Brodeur/Mad River Glen; page 57 © Anikasalsera | Dreamstime.com; page 60 © Howardliuphoto | Dreamstime.com; page 66 © Ronibenish | Dreamstime.com; page 72 © Alwoodphoto | Dreamstime.com; page 76 © Vera Chang; page 80 (top) © George Disario/NH Division of Travel & Tourism, (bottom) © George Disario/NH Division of Travel & Tourism; page 81 © The Chamber Collaborative of Greater Portsmouth/Rick Dumont Images; page 84 © The Chamber Collaborative of Greater Portsmouth/Rick Dumont Images; page 92 © David J Murray/Portsmouth Chamber of Commerce; page 103 © Squam Lakes Natural Science Center; page 106 (top) © Sierra Machado, (bottom) © Sierra Machado; page 107 © Rob Karosis/NH Division of Travel & Tourism; page 116 © NH Division of Travel & Tourism; page 118 © Jen Rose Smith; page 120 © NH Division of Travel & Tourism; page 128 © Rob Karosis/NH Division of Travel & Tourism; page 133 (top) © Appalachianviews | Dreamstime.com, (bottom) © Nick Cote/Maine Office of Tourism; page 135 © Pinkcandy | Dreamstime.com; page 141 © Nick Cote/Maine Office of Tourism; page 146 © Iainhamer | Dreamstime.com; page 171 © Jen Rose Smith; page 188 © Jen Rose Smith; page 189 © Alwoodphoto | Dreamstime; page 198 © Maine Office of Tourism; page 201 (top) © R51coffey | Dreamstime.com, (bottom) © Phil Savignano Photography/Maine Office of Tourism; page 203 © Kittycat | Dreamstime.com; page 207 © Ryan Flynn | Dreamstime; page 208 © Karenfoleyphotography | Dreamstime.com; page 217 © Jen Rose Smith; page 221 © Maine Office of Tourism; page 224 © Jen Rose Smith; page 226 (top) © Luckydoor | Dreamstime.com, (bottom) © Sierra Machado; page 249 (top) © Americanspirit | Dreamstime.com, (bottom) © NH Division of Travel & Tourism

MOON ROAD TRIP GUIDES

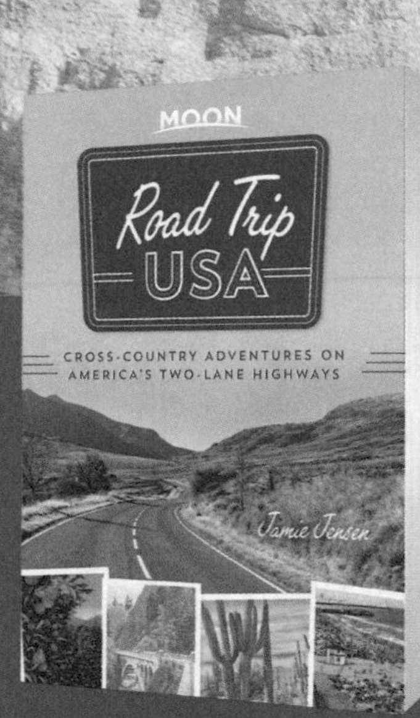

Road Trip USA

Criss-cross the country on America's classic two-lane highways with the newest edition of *Road Trip USA!*

Packed with over 125 detailed driving maps (covering more than 35,000 miles), colorful photos and illustrations of America both then and now, and mile-by-mile highlights

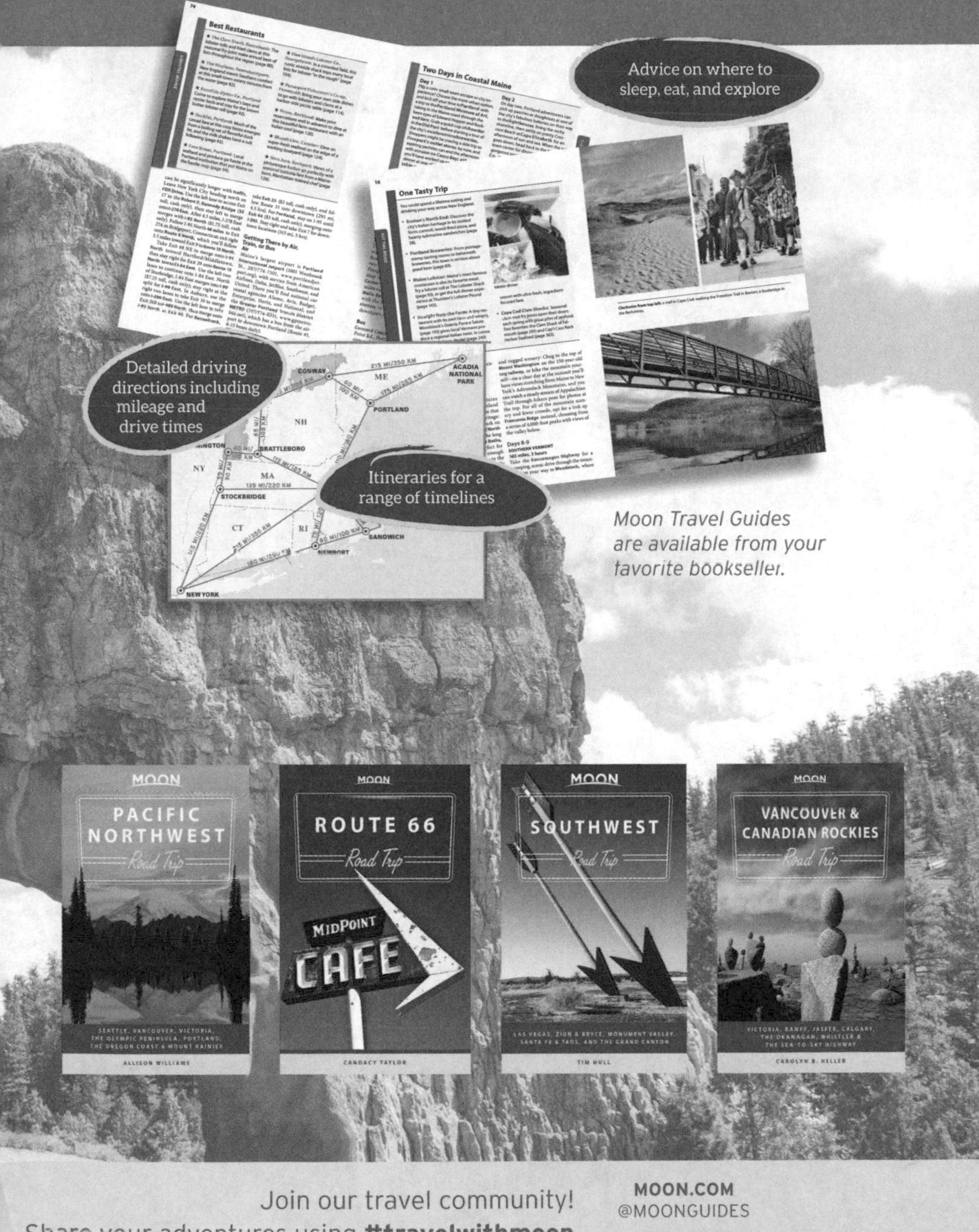
Advice on where to sleep, eat, and explore
Detailed driving directions including mileage and drive times
Itineraries for a range of timelines
Moon Travel Guides are available from your favorite bookseller.
MOON
PACIFIC NORTHWEST
Road Trip
SEATTLE, VANCOUVER, VICTORIA, THE OLYMPIC PENINSULA, PORTLAND, THE OREGON COAST & MOUNT RAINIER
ALLISON WILLIAMS
MOON
ROUTE 66
Road Trip
MIDPOINT CAFE
CANDACY TAYLOR
MOON
SOUTHWEST
Road Trip
LAS VEGAS, ZION & BRYCE, MONUMENT VALLEY, SANTA FE & TAOS, AND THE GRAND CANYON
TIM HULL
MOON
VANCOUVER & CANADIAN ROCKIES
Road Trip
VICTORIA, BANFF, JASPER, CALGARY, THE OKANAGAN, WHISTLER & THE SEA-TO-SKY HIGHWAY
CAROLYN B. HELLER